Archery and Crossbow
Medieval Flanders

1300–1500

Archery and Crossbow Guilds in Medieval Flanders
1300–1500

Laura Crombie

THE BOYDELL PRESS

© Laura Crombie 2016

All Rights Reserved. Except as permitted under current legislation no part of this work may be photocopied, stored in a retrieval system, published, performed in public, adapted, broadcast, transmitted, recorded or reproduced in any form or by any means, without the prior permission of the copyright owner

The right of Laura Crombie to be identified as the author of this work has been asserted in accordance with sections 77 and 78 of the Copyright, Designs and Patents Act 1988

First published 2016
The Boydell Press, Woodbridge
Paperback edition 2018

ISBN 978 1 78327 104 7 hardback
ISBN 978 1 78327 305 8 paperback

The Boydell Press is an imprint of Boydell & Brewer Ltd
PO Box 9, Woodbridge, Suffolk IP12 3DF, UK
and of Boydell & Brewer Inc.
668 Mt Hope Avenue, Rochester, NY 14620–2731, USA
website: www.boydellandbrewer.com

The publisher has no responsibility for the continued existence or accuracy of URLs for external or third-party internet websites referred to in this book, and does not guarantee that any content on such websites is, or will remain, accurate or appropriate

A CIP catalogue record for this book is available from the British Library

Contents

List of Illustrations vi
Acknowledgements vii
List of Abbreviations viii

Introduction: Archery and Crossbow Guilds in Flemish Civic Society 1
  1 'For security, guard and defence' of this town: Guilds' Origins and Military Service 21
  2 'Guild-brothers': Guild Organisation and the Membership of the Archery and Crossbow Guilds of Bruges, 1437–81 51
  3 'For drinking in recreational assemblies': The Archery and Crossbow Guilds as Social and Devotional Communities 89
  4 'For the honour of the duke and of the town': Guilds and Authority 126
  5 'For friendship, community and brotherhood': Archery and Crossbow Competitions as Part of Civic Honour and Identity 159
  6 Archery and Crossbow Guilds and their Competitions in Regional Networks and as Tools of Social Peace 190
Conclusion: Guilds in Civic Society 221

Bibliography 224
Index 255

Illustrations

Map of medieval Flanders — x

1. Reproduction of the *Leugemeete* wall painting, Ghent STAM inv. 9555 2/6 and inv. 9555 3/6, photograph by Michel Burez. Reproduced by permission of STAM © www.lukasweb.be – Art in Flanders vzw — 40
2. Seal of the Crossbowmen of Sluis, 1497, SAG, SJ, 155, 1. Reproduced by permission of Gent Stadsarchief — 110
3. Seal of the Crossbowmen of Veurne 1440, SAG, SJ, 155, 2. Reproduced by permission of Gent Stadsarchief — 110
4. Seal of the Crossbowmen of Condé, 1462, OSAOA, gilden, 507/ II/ 14 A. Reproduced by permission of Oudenaarde Stadsarchief — 111
5. Seal of the Crossbowmen of Tournai, 1462, OSAOA, gilden, 507/ II/ 14 A. Reproduced by permission of Oudenaarde Stadsarchief — 111
6. Pendant of Sharpshooters' Guild with St Sebastian, mother and child, and crucifixion, c.1500, Germany, Augsburg, silver gilt, the Fine Arts Museums of San Francisco, gift of Julius Landauer, 60.2.6. Reproduced by kind permission of Fine Arts Museums of San Francisco — 113

The author and publishers are grateful to all the institutions and individuals listed for permission to reproduce the materials in which they hold copyright. Every effort has been made to trace the copyright holders; apologies are offered for any omission, and the publishers will be pleased to add any necessary acknowledgement in subsequent editions.

Acknowledgements

This work could not have been completed without the help and support of colleagues in Glasgow, York and in Belgium and the funding of the Carnegie Trust for the Universities of Scotland. Firstly, I thank my professors, Graeme Small and Matthew Strickland, for introducing me to the history of the Low Countries and archery and for being unfailingly supportive. I would like to acknowledge the huge amount of support from the Medieval History Department at Ghent University, especially Professor Jan Dumolyn, who pushed me to work with challenging sources and bring in depth I could not otherwise have done. Other members of the department have also been extremely kind in sharing work, knowledge and understanding, especially Dr Frederik Buylaert (now at the Vrij Universiteit in Brussels), Dr Jonas Braekevelt, Dr Hannes Lowagie and Mr Andy Ramandt. Dr Andrew Brown was kind enough to provide me with parts of his excellent monograph on Bruges before publication, which saved me from many errors, as well as providing advice and support. This work was finished during my time at the University of York and I thank my new colleagues, especially Dr Victoria Blud, for listening to, and even reading, parts of it and for much advice and support. All remaining mistakes and simplifications are my own. I have been extremely fortunate in working with rich and detailed archives, managed by kind and helpful experts. I am indebted to staff at Bruges Stadsarchief, Ghent Stadsarchief, Oudenaarde Stadsarchief, Aalst Stadsarchief, Archives Générales du Royaume, Archives Municipales de Lille, Archives Municipales de Douai and the Archives Départementales du Nord. The Bruges archery guild of Saint Sebastian has been particularly supportive and I am extremely grateful to Marc Lemahieu and Andre Vande Walle for allowing me access to this rich archive.

Abbreviations

AAM	Armentières, Archive Municipal
ABVH	*Annalen van de Belgische Vereniging voor hospitaalgeschiedenis*
ACAM	*Annales du Cercle Archéologique de Mons*
ADN	Archives Départementales du Nord
ADN, LRD	ADN, Lettres reçues et dépêche
AGR	Archives Générales du Royaume
AGN	*Algemene Geschiedenis der Nederlanden*
AML	Lille, Archives Municipales
AML, CV	Lille, Archives Municipales, Comptes de la Ville
AML, OM	Lille, Archives Municipales, Ordonnances des Magistrates
AML, PT	Lille, Archives Municipales, Pièces aux Titres
AML, RM	Lille, Archives Municipales, Registre aux Mandates
AML, RT	Lille, Archives Municipales, Registre aux Titres
AMR	Roubaix, Archives Municipales
ASAOA	Aalst Stadsarchief, Oude Archief
ASEB	*Annales de la Société d'Émulation de Bruges / Handelingen van het Genootschap voor Geschiedenis te Brugge*
BASS	Brugge, Archief Sint-Sebastiaan
BCRH	*Bulletin de la commission royale d'histoire*
BMBGN	*Bijdragen en mededelingen betreffende de geschiedenis der Nederlanden*
BO	*Brugs Ommeland*
CC	Chambre des Comptes
CV	Comptes de la Ville
DAM	Douai, Archives Municipales
EHR	*English Historical Review*
HMGOG	*Handelingen der maatschappij voor geschiedenis en oudheidkunde te Gent*
JIH	*Journal of Interdisciplinary History*
JMH	*Journal of Medieval History*
JMMH	*Journal of Medieval Military History*
JMG	*Jaarboek voor Middeleeuwse Geschiedenis*

MTMS	*Millennium: Tijdschrift voor middeleeuwse studies*
ORF	M. de Laurière (et al.), *Ordonnances des roys de France de la troisième race recueillies par ordre chronologique*, vols 1–21 (Farnborough, 1967–68)
OSAOA	Oudenaarde Stadsarchief, Oude Archief
PCEEB	*Publications du centre Européen d'études Bourguignonnes*
PP	*Past and Present*
RAB	Brugge, Rijksarchief
RAG	Gent, Rijksarchief
RAG, RVV	Gent, Rijksarchief, Raad van Vlaanderen
RBPH	*Revue belge de Philologie et d'Histoire/Belgie tijdschrift voor philogie en geschiedenis*
RH	*Revue Historique*
RN	*Revue du Nord*
SAB	Brugge Stadsarchief
SAG	Gent Stadsarchief
SAG, SJ	SAG, Fonds Sint Joris
SAG, SJ, NGR	SAG, Sint Jorisgilde, Niet Genummerded Reeks
SH	*Spiegel historiael*
STAM	STAM museum Ghent (formerly the Bijlokemuseum)
TVG	*Tijdschrift voor geschiedenis*
TVSG	*Tijdschrift voor sociale geschiedenis*
UBG	Universiteitsbibliotheek Gent
UH	*Urban History*

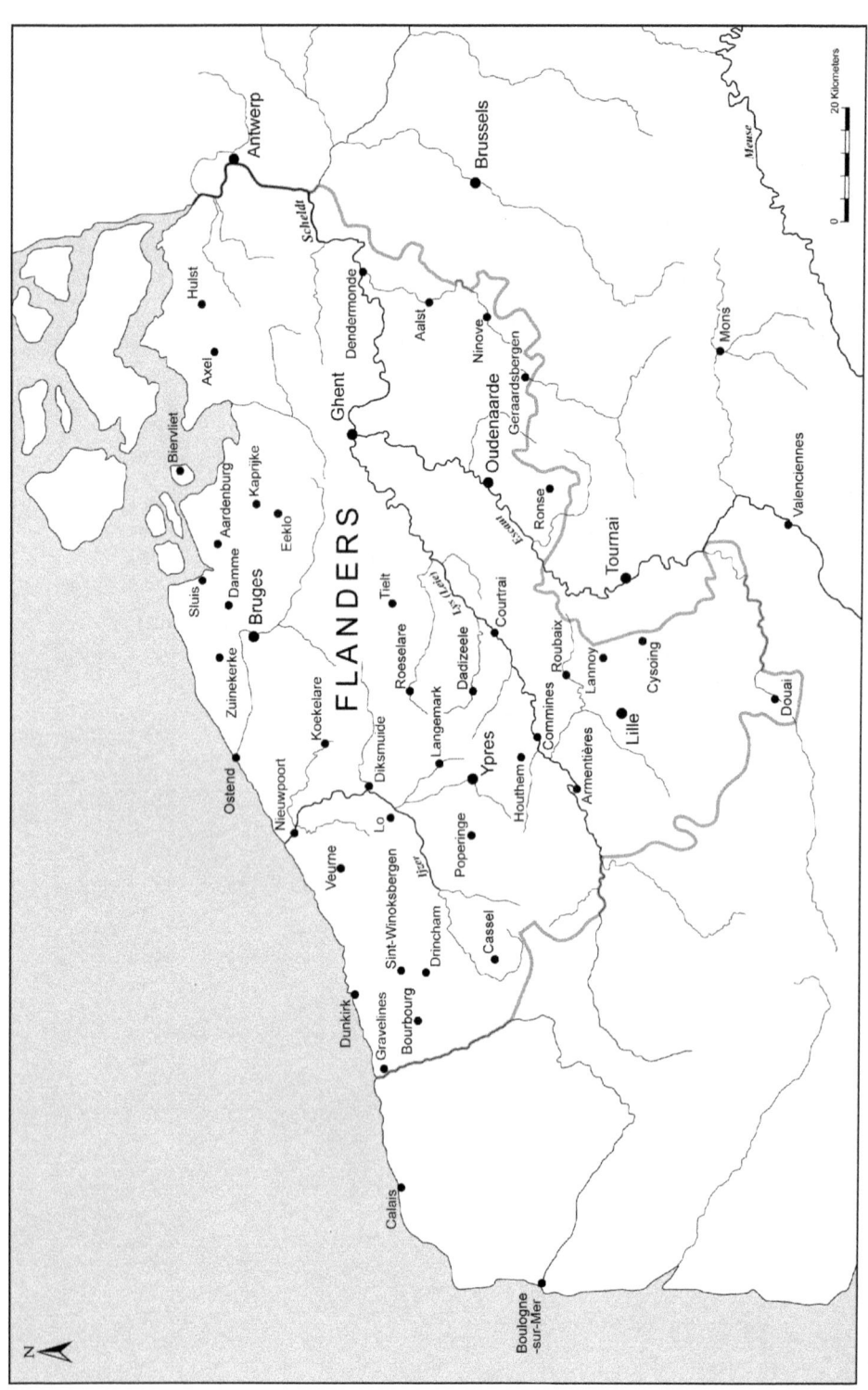

The County of Flanders, 1369–1500

Introduction

Archery and Crossbow Guilds in Flemish Civic Society

In 'the noble city' of Tournai in 1394, 'In Honour of God and the King of France/ There was made in very fine ordinance'. In July and August fifty teams from across the Low Countries came together for a 'feast and noble affair/ the handsome game of the crossbow'. They competed to 'hit two targets', the two large targets being set up at each end of the market place in the town centre. As the crossbowmen entered Tournai they passed through streets bedecked with cloth. 'Everything was decorated very well/ by skilled workers/ and hung with cloths/ to show castles argent on a field of gules [i.e. the arms of Tournai].' Other buildings were draped in the French royal colours – green and white – demonstrating Tournai's loyalty to the king and sense of civic pride. The crossbowmen processing past these buildings were no less elaborate. Those of Bruges carried gold and silver and all had been given funds by their town officials to pay for their journey to Tournai. Many other civic authorities had likewise given their guild-brothers money 'for the honour of the town'. A near-contemporary poem describing the events lists each of the fifty towns that had sent teams. They included great Flemish centres such as Ypres and Lille and small towns like Dixmuide and Sluis; guilds came from Brabant, Hainaut and Holland, from nearby places like Condé and from more distant French towns, including Laon and Paris. Numerous prizes of 'silver, gold and finery' were given for the best individual and group shooters, for those who had travelled the greatest distance and for the guild that performed the best play.[1] The event was not a one off; rather, it was part of an elaborate series of archery and crossbow competitions staged in the Low Countries throughout the fourteenth and fifteenth centuries.

Where had these skilled crossbowmen competing for prizes learnt their skills? Who were they? Were they rich civic elites, or craftsmen from the middling

---

[1] UBG, HS 434, ff. 87v–90r; the poem is discussed in L. Crombie 'Target Languages; Multilingual Communication in Poetic Descriptions of Crossbow Competitions', in A. Armstrong and E. Strietman (eds), *The Multilingual Muse: Transcultural Poetics in the Burgundian Netherlands* (forthcoming).

ranks of urban society? Why did Tournai host such an elaborate event and allow such a potentially dangerous activity to take over civic space during much of the summer? What did the fifty towns that sent their crossbow guilds to Tournai in 1394 hope to gain from the event? In answering these seemingly simple questions, the present study seeks to investigate the formation and activities of the archery and crossbow guilds and to enquire what roles the guilds played within and beyond their civic societies. In addition, the guilds will be used to consider overlapping identities and the ways in which civic values, even urban pride, could be represented in spectacular shooting competitions like that in Tournai in 1394.

These questions will be addressed with reference to Flanders, which was the most urbanised and best-documented region of the Low Countries. This book will bring in as many sources as possible from the guilds themselves, from civic authorities, from princely records and from literary sources, like the poem cited above. Case studies using sources from large and small towns will add depth to particular arguments and a regional pattern will be brought in wherever possible. The six following chapters will analyse the guilds so as to emphasise the part they played in civic society and their ability to represent their societies' values.

Chapter one will set out the guilds' origins and their military service. It will consider where the shooters in Tournai in 1394 learnt their skills and why the guilds were so well funded by their civic authorities. The archery and crossbow guilds began to receive civic recognition at times of civic confidence and demonstrated civic status and values, just as structures such as belfries and town halls did. Although warfare is not the only explanation for the guilds' development, their military roles both for civic defence and in princely armies must be considered, as they provided an ability for common action when the Common Good of Flanders was at stake. The role of war in civic identity will also be considered.

Chapter two begins with an explanation of the guilds' organisation and a discussion of what sorts of men became guild-brothers, unpicking existing assumptions about 'elite' or 'bourgeois' membership. In the analysis of guilds' organisation, their relationship to other forms of community will be considered, as will be the meaning of the 'jonghe' guilds. It will be argued that the latter were not, as has been assumed, youth groups. A prosopographical study of the membership of Bruges guilds between 1437 and 1481 will provide an understanding of who the guild-brothers were and the patterns of guild membership.

Chapter three moves from looking at the brothers as individuals to an analysis of the guilds as communities and examines the social and devotional activities of the guild-brothers and sisters. In demonstrating that guilds were not all-male organisations this chapter will emphasise the array of activities and support systems within the guilds and demonstrate their links to other forms of urban culture and other groups. The guilds' patron saints, their creation and strengthening of a corporate identity and their care for the spiritual well-being of members will be examined across Flanders. It will be argued that the guilds were unified communities, with chapels and with roles for men, women, children and priests. For a deeper analysis of charity, devotional space and attachment to chapels, Ghent is used as a case study, emphasising the support and piety found within cultural groups.

Chapter four looks at other forms of relationships. The relationship between the guilds and princely and/or civic authorities will be considered in an examination of the guilds as civic groups and as an important part of urban–aristocratic networks. The dukes of Burgundy gave the guilds numerous charters, some for a military purpose and others, like the use of livery, to encourage the guilds to demonstrate their loyalty. Relations with the nobility were never as simple as the lords imprinting their influence upon guild-brothers, and in many cases nobles were guild-brothers, taking part in guild competitions and wearing guild liveries. In other words, they were a part of guild communities. Noble members helped guilds to achieve rights, acquire lands and be recognised; but guilds could help nobles, especially in the crisis years of the 1480s. Guilds built bonds with nobles, but guild-brothers received their most important support from the civic powers that they could represent, receiving civic wine, wearing civic livery, spending civic funds and shooting on civic land. Much of this support was given 'for the honour of the town', linking the guilds to wider civic ideologies and urban standing.

Finally, chapters five and six will turn to the guilds' great competitions, the *landjuwellen*. Competitions began to attract municipal funding during the same period as the guilds themselves did, and grew during the fourteenth and fifteenth centuries to become some of the largest and most elaborate events in Flanders. Taking over civic space for weeks, even months at a time, archery and crossbow contests presented numerous opportunities for winning civic honour and demonstrating the prowess of the guilds – and, by extension, the towns that funded them – and prizes were given for shooting as well as for display and drama. Such events needed civic and ducal permission in order to take place. All documents associated with the competitions emphasise brotherhood, the opportunities to augment civic honour and the consent of the prince. These spectacular events brought together hundreds of shooters and thousands of followers, granted the shooters wine and offered immunity from prosecution for accidental deaths. Yet, as chapter six will argue, these events did not dissolve into violence, as some jousts did, nor cause ill will; rather, in the language of their invitations, their setting and use of existing river and trade networks, they promoted regional unity and strengthened commercial networks. Of course, some disputes did occur and the competitions were no utopias of peace and brotherhood, but the competitions, like the guilds themselves, strove for unity and to enhance the Common Good of Flanders. Together, these six perspectives on the guilds will permit an appreciation of their significance in civic society; through an analysis of the guilds the multifaceted nature of urban society and its hopes for unity can be better understood.

Before the guilds themselves can be analysed, an introduction is needed to the guilds and other studies, to the region and to the sources used in the present study. Throughout this book the groups of archers and crossbowmen are referred to as 'shooting guilds'. The word 'guild' in English has many connotations and can be overused. As Reynolds demonstrated in 1977, 'words like guild, fraternity and society' were very widely used in medieval Europe to describe many different kinds of associations, while modern historians have 'their odd convention of using the word "guild" in preference to all the others, and then assuming that guilds were basically trade associations'.[2] Since Reynolds wrote, works on guilds – craft guilds and others – have expanded greatly, making the word more ubiquitous, and yet it is still associated with trade or craft groups. For the shooting guilds, French sources refer to the archers and crossbowmen as *confréries*, occasionally *compaignes*, best translated as confraternities and companies. Although 'archery confraternities' would be a literal translation, the English term has connotations of devotional practice. The Flemish sources, which are the most numerous, refer to *schutersgilden* or simply *gilden* – less often, *schutters*; the term 'gild' is very common in Flemish sources and is how the groups are best known. The Flemish 'gild' can be applied to devotional and social groups as well as craft guilds; indeed, medieval Flemish craft organisations could refer to themselves as 'gild' or *ambachten* or *broderschappen*. In looking at the groups in Germany, Tlusty renders *schützengesellschaften* as 'shooting societies', although 'schützengilden' is also used regularly in medieval and early modern sources.[3] Here the groups will be referred to as 'guilds', primarily as this is the most literal translation of the most commonly used term, but also because 'guild' is taken to denote a brotherhood or association and its Germanic root implies payment of tribute;[4] it is therefore a fitting term here for *schutersgilden*.

The shooting guilds analysed here have much in common with craft guilds, as will be demonstrated in chapters two and three. It would be simplistic to imagine that the shooters existed in a vacuum, and a major aim of the present study is to consider the shooting guilds as an integral part of their civic societies and to place them firmly within urban historiography. Members of shooting guilds were also members, as chapter two will emphasise, in craft guilds, in chambers of rhetoric, in devotional confraternities and in parish communities. Yet the shooting guilds were something separate and are groups deserving of analysis in their own right. Like craft guilds, the shooters were dedicated to

---

[2] S. Reynolds, *An Introduction to the History of the English Medieval Town* (Oxford: Oxford University Press, 1977), 166.

[3] A. B. Tlusty, *The Martial Ethic in Early Modern Germany, Civic Duty and the Right of Arms* (Basingstoke: Palgrave Macmillan, 2011), 189–210.

[4] D. Keene, 'English Urban Guilds, c.900–1300: The Purposes and Politics of Association', in A. A. Gadd and P. Wallis (eds), *Guilds and Associations in Europe, 900–1900* (London: University of London Institute of Historical Research, 2006), 3–4.

patron saints – the archers usually to Saint Sebastian and the crossbowmen usually to Saint George – maintaining chapels to their patrons and meeting on feast days.

The present analysis of the guilds' place within their urban world begins with their first appearance in civic records, in the early fourteenth century. Foundation myths and possible older traditions will be considered, as will be the possibility that the guilds were older than the first surviving written reference to their activities. The start date for this study is therefore relatively clear, but the end date is more of a challenge. Several studies of individual guilds, such as those by Moulin-Coppins or Autenboer, extend into the nineteenth century.[5] There is a case for attempting to provide a complete history of the Flemish guilds, but the purpose here is to use the guilds to better understand the late medieval urban world and to place them firmly within existing studies. To do so, a more in-depth analysis is needed and this necessitates a 'late medieval' end date. Although several dates are possible, the transition from 'late medieval' to 'early modern' is not always clear and so the pragmatic end date of 'c.1500' will be applied. A few sixteenth-century examples will be brought in, but the intention is to use the guilds to analyse fourteenth- and fifteenth-century urban society and civic representations.

The guilds have been studied before – although often in isolation – in one form or another. They fascinated many nineteenth-century scholars of Northern France and the Low Countries; many such studies are extremely useful, especially those that transcribe now lost documents. Yet many antiquarian studies are also weakened by an over-reliance on prescriptive documents: that is, they believed that what *should*, according to the charters, have been done *was* done.[6] Local

---

[5] J. Moulin-Coppens, *De Geschiedenis van het oude Sint-Jorisgilde te Gent* (Gent: Hoste Staelens, 1982); E. Van Autenboer, *De Kaarten van de schuttersgilden van het Hertogdom Brabant (1300–1800)* vols. 1–2 (Tilburg: Stichting Zuidelijk historisch contact, 1993).

[6] L-A. Delaunay, *Étude sur les anciennes compagnies d'archers, d'arbalétriers et d'arquebusiers* (Paris: Champion, 1879); A. Janvier, 'Notice sur les anciennes corporations d'archers, d'arbalétriers, de coulveriniers et d'arquebusiers des villes de Picardie', *Mémoires de la société des antiquaires de la Picardie* 14 (1855), 5–380; E. de Barthélemy, *Histoire des archers, arbalétriers et arquebusiers de la ville de Reims* (Reims: P. Giret, 1873); E. vanden Berghe-Loontjens, *Het aloude gilde van de handboogschutters st Sebastiaan te Roosselare* (Rousselare: Ackerman, 1904); F. le Bon, *L'ancien Serment des arbalétriers de Nivelles et ses statuts* (Nivelles: Ch. Guignarde, 1886); E. Van Cauwenberghe, 'Notice historique sur les confréries de Saint Georges', *Messager des sciences historique des arts et de la bibliographie de Belgique* (1853), 269–300; A. Wauters, *Notice historique sur les anciens serments ou gildes d'arbalétriers, d'archers, d'arquebusiers et d'escrimeurs de Bruxelles* (Bruxelles: Briard 1848),1–36; A-G. Chotin, *Histoire de Tournai et du Tournésis, depuis les temps les plus reculés jusqu'à nos jours*, 2vols (Tournai: Massart et Janssens, 1840), vol. 1, 348–64; T. de Sagher, 'Origine de la guilde des archers de Saint Sébastien à Ypres (1383–1398)', *Annales de la société d'histoire et d'archéologie de Gand* 5 (1903), 116–30; E. Matthieu, 'Sceaux des serments ou guildes de la ville d'Enghien', *ACAM* 25 (1878) 9–18; C. Bamps et E. Geraet, 'Les Anciennes gildes et compagne militaire de

studies of one guild or the guilds of one town were not, of course, limited to the nineteenth century and here the Ghent guilds have received particular attention.[7]

The purpose here is not to criticise such studies. Local descriptive works on individual guilds have a valuable place within local history, particularly those of the shooting guilds that still exist or have been refounded. The purpose here is different: to present the guilds to a wider audience, to place them firmly within their urban and historiographical context and to analyse them as an integral part of, even representatives of, their civic societies.

The Region

Shooting guilds are not unique to Flanders; they existed in towns, even villages, across the Low Countries and beyond, in France, Germany and Eastern Europe, including in Poland.[8] The present study focuses on the county of Flanders so

---

Hasselet', *Annales de l'académie royale d'archéologique de Belgique*, 4ᵉ série 10 (1897), 21–46; Anon, 'Le Sceau des archers de serment de Douai (1460)', *Souvenirs de Flandre Wallon*, 2ᵉ série 1 (1881), 103–7.

[7] B. Baillieul, *De Vier Gentse Hoofdgilden* (Gent: Stadsbestuur, 1994); P. de Burgraere, *Notice historique sur les chefs confréries Gantois de Saint Sébastien et de Saint Antoine* (Gand: Vander Haeghen, 1913); J. Cieters (ed.), *Tentoonstelling, 550 jaar schietspelen van de Sint-Jorisgilde* (Gent: Kredietbank, 1990); P. Voitron, *Notice sur le local de la confrérie de Saint Georges à Gand (1381 à 1796)* (Ghent: Messager des sciences historiques de Belgique, 1889–90); F. De Potter, *Jaarboeken der Sint-Jorisgilde van Gent* (Gent: Hage, 1868); Moulin-Coppens, *Sint-Jorisgilde te Gent*; H. Baillien, 'De Tongerse schutterijen van de 14ᵈᵉ tot de 16ᵈᵉ eeuw', *Het oude land van Loon* 34 (1979), 5–34; P. Bruyère, *Les compagnies sermentées de la cite de Liège aux temps modernes, l'exemple des jeunes arbalétriers (1523–1684)* (Liège: Société des Bibliophiles Liégeois 2004); P. de Cock, *Geschiedenis van het Koninklijk Handbooggild St. Sebastiaan* (Ninove: Anneessens, 1972); W. Iven, et al., *Schutters gilden in Noord-Brabant: tentoonstelling, Noordbrabants Museum, 's-Hertogenbosch, 21 mei–7 augustus 1983: catalogue* (Helmond: Uitgeverij Helmond, 1983); P. Knevel, *Wakkere burgers de Alkmaarse schutterij; 1400–1795* (Alkmaar: Stedelijk Museum, 1994); K. Papin, 'De handboogschuttersgilde van Sint-Winnoksbergen in 1469', *Westhoek* 17 (2001), 3–40. In addition to these published works, there is unpublished scholarship on different shooting guilds. See C. Ducastelle et J.-M, Cardot, 'Les confréries ou serments d'archers et d'arbalétriers au Moyen Age dans le nord de la France, études apuyée sur les exemples du Douai et de Lille', Mémoire de Maîtrise, Université Du Lille III, 1992, 2vols; S. Van Steen, '"Den ouden ende souverainen gilde van den edelen ridder Sinte Jooris": het Sint-Jorisgilde te Gent in de 15e eeuw, met prosopografie (1468–1497)', Diss. lic. Geschiedenis, Universiteit Gent, 2006; G. De Zutter, 'Kunst en Kunstambacht in het Leven van een schuttergild het Sint-sebastiansgilde te Gent', Diss. lic. Geschiedenis, Universiteit Gent, 1975.

[8] T. Soens, E. van Onacker and K. Dombrecht, 'Metropolis and Hinterland? A Comment on the Role of Rural Economy and Society in the Urban Heart of the Medieval Low Countries', *Low Countries Historical Review* 127 (2012), 82–8; the on-going thesis of Kristof Dombrech, at Ghent University, on villages around Bruges and their social

as to allow for depth of analysis and, as the county has an impressive range of records, so as to use different approaches, make comparisons and offer wider conclusions. The Flemish shooters are, as Reintges (the author of the only general study on shooting guilds) noted in 1963, the earliest documented guilds,[9] meaning that studies of the Flemish guilds are useful to studies of guilds elsewhere. Indeed, the study of guilds outside of Flanders holds great possibility for future study, as many such guilds attended the competitions organised by Flemish guilds. Some French examples will be brought in here to emphasise the significance of regional networks. In particular, Tournai will be used, as it was in the interesting position of being a French city surrounded by lands ruled by the dukes of Burgundy. Focusing on a relatively small, well-documented region allows for better engagement with a wealth of studies of other urban groups. By drawing on the excellent scholarship on Flanders, the guilds can be studied within the context of other medieval groups and other interpretations of urban society. Using this focus, the place of guilds within urban societies and their part in overlapping identities can be appreciated, as can the modes and challenges of civic representation.

Late medieval Flanders was the most urbanised area north of the Alps, with powerful towns full of social and cultural groups and run by aldermen and councillors who took pride in their civic values. The 'Three Towns' of Ghent, Ypres and Bruges, joined by the Franc of Bruges to make the 'Four Members', wielded a great deal of authority and influence.[10] The towns' relationship with their rulers was – as will be explored – not always harmonious, as traditions of civic autonomy clashed with princely centralisation. Despite such tensions, court

---

groups, including the archery guild of Dudzele, will broaden the understanding of rural shooting guilds; M. Carasso-Kok and J. L.-Van Halm (eds), *Schutters in Holland – Kracht en zenuwen van stad* (Zwolle: Waanders, 1988); Autenboer, *De Kaarten van de schuttersgilden van het Hertogdom Brabant*; P.-Y. Beaurepaire, *Nobles jeux de l'arc et loges maçonniques dans la France des lumières* (Cahors: Editions Ivoire-Clair, 2002); B. Brassât, *La belle histoire du noble jeu de l'arc en pays de Brie* (Lésée-sur-Seiné: Editions Amatteis, 1991); T. Reintges, *Ursprung und Wesen der spätmittelalterlichen Schützengilden* (Bonn: L. Röhrscheid, 1963); Tlusty, *The Martial Ethic in Early Modern Germany*, 189–208; W. Hillebrand, 'Die Ordnungen und Rechnungen der Schützenbruderschaft St. Sebastian zu Goslar, 1432–529', in *Festschrift für Gerhard Cordes, Band 1: Literaturwissenschaft und Textedition* (Neumünster: Tyska, 1973), 74–90; The shooting guilds and their competitions in the Holy Roman Empire are the subject of a PhD in progress in Paris by Jean-Dominique Delle Luche, with the working title 'Sociétés et concours de tir dans les villes de l'Empire, XVe–XVIe siècles'.

9   Reintges, *Ursprung und Wesen*, 15–26.
10 F. Buylaert and A. Ramandt, 'The Transformation of Rural Elites in Late Medieval Flanders: Oligarchy, State Formation and Social Change in the Liberty of Bruges', *Continuity and Change* 30 (2015), 39–69; L. Gilliodts-van Severen, *Coutume du Franc de Bruges* (Bruxelles, 1879); E. Warlop, *Bijdragen tot de geschiedenis der vorming van het Brugse Vrije: bronnen, gebied, instellingen* (Gent, 1959).

and civic societies were strongly linked,[11] the shooting guilds being an important part of these links, as will be explored in chapter four. Across the county, each town saw itself as a civic community. A complex interaction of different groups (like the craft guilds) that had their own communities brought them together into a more or less cohesive whole. The archery and crossbow guilds were part of these urban communities and part of civic society as well as being potential urban defenders, and their competitions allowed for the performance of ideals of unity.

The borders of Flanders were not static between 1300 and 1500. The county was in the unusual position of being divided between France and the Holy Roman Empire, with the Scheldt river forming the boundary between the two. The boundary had allowed the counts to develop a good degree of autonomy during the twelfth century, but by the end of the thirteenth century the growing power of the Capetian state allowed the French King Philip IV, 'the Fair' (d.1314), to attempt to gain control of the county. The rich towns supported their ruler, Count Guy of Dampierre (r.1251–1305), against the French. Famously, this led to the victory of the Flemish militia over the French cavalry at the battle of Courtrai, the battle of the Golden Spurs, 11 July 1302.[12] The battle was a great and heroic victory for the Flemings, but its lasting significance has often been over-stated.

Just two years later, on 18 August 1304, the French army crushed the Flemings at Mons-en-Pevel.[13] The defeat led to the signing of the Treaty of Athis-sur-Orge, by which Walloon Flanders (the castellanies of Lille, Douai and Orchies) became part of France, not Flanders.[14] The southern towns were returned to Flanders on

---

[11] A. Brown and G. Small, *Court and Civic Society in the Burgundian Low Countries c. 1420–1530* (Manchester: Manchester University Press, 2007), 1–34. W. Blockmans and E. Donckers, 'Self-Representation of Court and City', in W. Blockmans and A. Jansese (eds), *Showing Status: Representation of Social Positions in the Late Middle Ages* (Turnhout: Brepols, 1999), 81–111; M. Damen, 'Princely Entries and Gift Exchange in the Burgundian Low Countries: A Crucial Link in Late Medieval Political Culture', *JMH* 33 (2007) 233–49; N. Murphy, 'Between Court and Town: Ceremonial Entries in the Chroniques of Jean Molinet', in J. Devaux, E. Doudet and É. Lecuppre-Desjardin (eds), *Jean Molinet et son temps* (Turnhout: Brepols, 2013), 155–61.

[12] J. F. Verbruggen (trans. K. DeVries and R. Ferguson), *The Battle of the Golden Spurs, Courtrai, 11 July 1302* (Woodbridge: Boydell, 2002); idem, 'De naam Guldensporenslag voor de slag bij Kortrijk (11 juli 1302)', *Revue Belge d'histoire militaire* 24 (1982) 701–6; E. M. Hallam, *Capetian France, 987–1328* (London: Longman, 1980), 280–3.

[13] V. Lambert, 'Guldensporenslag van fait-divers tot ankerpunt van de vlaamse identiteit (1302) de natievormende functionaliteit van historiografische mythen', *BMBGN* 115 (2000), 365–91; J. Bovesse, 'La régence comtale Namuroise en Flandre (juillet 1302–mai 1303)', in *Recht en instellingen in de oude Nederlanden tijdens de middeleeuwen en de nieuwe tijden. Liber amicorum Jan Buntinx* (Louvain: Universitaire pers, 1981), 139–65.

[14] H. Van Werveke, 'Les charges financières issues du traité d'Athis (1305)', in his *Miscellanea Mediaevalia verspriede opstellen over economische en sociale geschiedenis van de Middeleeuwen* (Gent, 1968) 227–42; B. Delmaire, 'Guerre en Artois après la bataille de Courtrai (1302)', in *Actes du 101e congrès national des sociétés savantes, Lille, 1976. Section*

the marriage of Philip the Bold, duke of Burgundy, the youngest son of King John II and Margaret of Male, heiress to Louis, count of Flanders, in 1369 – probably with the expectation that they would be returned to France at a later date.[15] The guilds of Walloon Flanders will be analysed throughout the present study; indeed, the part played by the guilds in the reintegration of Walloon Flanders to the county is an interesting question, as will be discussed in chapter five.

Although defeated, Flanders was still a rich county and continued to trade and prosper. As will be seen, the town of Bruges was a great trading port, gathering together merchants from across Europe. Other towns – especially Ghent – maintained their textile industry, using English wool. Trade with England and political allegiance to France – in theory at least – placed the counts of Flanders in a delicate position between two powerful and often warring monarchs. Guy was succeeded in 1305 by his son Robert III, who, as we shall see, faced the challenging task of strengthening and restoring his war-weary county. Robert was succeeded by his son, Louis of Never, in 1322.[16] Louis had been brought up at the French court; his close bonds with the new Valois dynasty divided him from his county, especially the 'Three Towns', for whom the English wool trade was essential. When Louis died supporting the French at the battle Crécy his only son and successor, Louis of Male, favoured a more ambitious policy and, on the death of his father-in-law, John III duke of Brabant, without a male heir in 1355, he launched an attack on the duchy (the campaign, and the shooting guilds' part in it, will be discussed in chapter one). The war led to the conquest of Mechelen, which was partially integrated into his domains. The town was not, however, part of Flanders, nor part of Brabant: it was a small, independent lordship ruled directly by the count and his Burgundian successor.[17] A few examples from Mechelen will be brought into the present study where relevant.[18]

Louis of Male's ambitions continued: he seems to have hoped to build an English alliance so as to gain independence from France. In 1364 Louis and King Edward III agreed to a marriage between Louis' daughter Margaret and

---

de philologie et d'histoire: La guerre et la paix, frontières et violences au Moyen Âge (Paris, 1978), 131–41, 227–42; G. Small, *Late Medieval France* (Basingstoke: Palgrave Macmillan, 2009), 47–8.

[15] R. Vaughan, *Philip the Bold, The Formation of the Burgundian State* (London: Longmans, 1962; Woodbridge: Boydell, 2002), 16–38; Small, *Late Medieval France*, 138–41.

[16] D. Nicholas, *Medieval Flanders* (London: Longman, 1992), 164–9, 180–346, 273–304.

[17] P. Avons, 'Mechelen en de Brabantse steden (1312–1355). Een bijdrage tot de parlementaire geschiedenis van de Derde Stad', *BTG* 53 (1970), 17–80; A. Kempeneer, 'Les aliénations de Malines au XIVe siècle. Étude sur la situation politique de la seigneurie (1300–1357)', *Bulletin du cercle archéologique littéraire et artistique de Malines* 15 (1905), 17 (1907), 19 (1909).

[18] See L. Crombie, 'The Archery and Crossbow Guilds of Late Medieval and Early Modern Mechelen', in P. Stabel (ed.), *Shifting Civic Identities in the Late Medieval and Early Modern Town; The Case of Mechelen* (forthcoming) for more details.

Edward's fifth son, Edmund Earl of Cambridge. The betrothed couple were, as was common, related and so required papal dispensation to marry – a dispensation that the pope, Urban V, refused to grant.[19] With an English alliance lost, a French alliance became more likely and, although Louis was not initially keen on the match, a marriage alliance was made between Margaret and Philip the Bold, to whom she was also related but for which the pope had no hesitation in granting a dispensation. Philip was the youngest son of the French King Jean II and had already been granted the duchy of Burgundy. The couple were married in Ghent in June 1369. On Louis' death in 1384 Philip the Bold became count of Flanders. Over the next century he and his successors would, through alliances, marriages, purchase and no small amount of luck, come to rule most of the Low Countries. As the richest part of their domain, Flanders always remained important to the Burgundian dukes, with John the Fearless (d.1419), Philip the Good (d.1467) and Charles the Bold (d.1477) all spending significant amounts of time in Flanders and staging many of the most elaborate events – such as the Feast of the Pheasant – in Flanders. The lands ruled by the dukes are difficult to define, but they grew to become a great power, causing tensions with their theoretical overlord, the king of France. Within Flanders, all four Valois dukes of Burgundy joined crossbow guilds as part of their efforts to build links with the Flemish towns, as will be discussed in chapter four. The Burgundian dukes are well known, for their wealth and spectacular festivities, as the 'Dukes that outdid Kings'.[20]

With the death of Charles the Bold in 1477 a change was inevitable. Mary, Charles's only child and heiress, faced opposition from the towns for the repressive policies of her father and was obliged to issue the Great Privilege on 10 February, restoring numerous lost rights to the towns. She faced a danger not just from her own towns, but from Louis XI, whose armies quickly attacked Burgundian lands, so that by February, when he entered Péronne, Picardy and most of the lands bordering the Channel had accepted French rule.[21] Flanders resisted Louis, as we will see in chapter one, and even supported Mary's new husband, Maximilian Habsburg, in the field. Maximilian was the son of the Holy Roman Emperor and his marriage to Mary set the stage for the growth of the

---

[19] Nicholas, *Medieval Flanders*, 227–8; L. Crombie, 'The Low Countries', in Anne Curry (ed.), *The Hundred Years War. A Geographical Approach* (Basingstoke: Palgrave Macmillan, forthcoming).

[20] L. Crombie, 'Burgundy', and 'The Low Countries', both in A. Curry (ed.), *The Hundred Years' War, A Geographical Perspective* (Basingstoke: Palgrave Macmillan, forthcoming); the quote comes from the title of C. A. J. Armstrong, 'The Golden age of Burgundy: Dukes that Outdid Kings', in A. G. Dickens (ed.), *The Courts of Europe* (London: McGraw-Hill, 1977), 55–75.

[21] P. M. Kendall, *Louis XI* (London: Cardinal, 1974), 390–1; P. Stabel, 'Militaire organisatie, bewapening en wapenbezit in het laatmiddeleeuwse Brugge', *Revue belge de philologie et d'histoire* 89 (2011), 1049–71; J. Haemers, *For the Common Good, State Power and Urban Revolts in the Reign of Mary of Burgundy* (Turnhout: Brepols, 2009), 22–3.

Habsburg empire under their grandson Charles V. Mary's early death in 1482 left her four-year-old son, Philip the Fair, as count of Flanders. As will be discussed in chapter five, the regency for the young count was far from stable, although hopes for peace and stability reappeared as Philip reached his majority.

The tensions in 1477 and 1482 between town and prince were not new; as is well known, the region had a tradition of big and small revolts. The most famous of these is probably the rebellion led by Jacob van Artevelde in the 1340s that saw Flanders forming an alliance with England and Edward III being proclaimed king of France in Ghent in 1340.[22] Jacob's son, Philip, led another rebellion from 1379 to 1382 and tension continued into the fifteenth century with the famous Bruges rebellion of 1436 and the 'Ghent war' of 1449–53, to name just the largest rebellions. What, if any, role the guilds played in rebellion is unfortunately unclear; as will be shown in chapter two, it is likely that they deliberately covered up any link to rebellion. The guilds' roles in making peace after the wars and rebellion are clearer, as chapter six will show, and are important for understanding the urban idealisation of peace. Ideals of the 'Common Good' are frequent across the region and, despite, or perhaps because of, violence and rebellion, towns idealised harmony, working for a stable community. The archery and crossbow guilds were part of civic desires, receiving charters and grants for 'the good of the town' and civic honour.[23]

The Flanders analysed here does not claim to be the perfect definition of Flanders; debates could be brought in over Imperial Flanders and French Flanders, as well as the status of different towns. Yet, in looking at the county as a whole the present study, particularly the final chapters, hopes to offer some thoughts on how fifteenth-century townsmen perceived their own county and who *they* thought of as Flemish.

Records of competitions imply that every town, and even village, in Flanders had at least one shooting guild. Yet not all have surviving records that allow for a full analysis, as will be discussed below. The two largest towns, Ghent and Bruges,

---

[22] Crombie, 'The Low Countries'; J. Sumption, *The Hundred Years War*, vol. 2 (London: Faber and Faber), 426–35; Nicholas, *Medieval Flanders*, 226–7.

[23] 'Introduction', to E. Lecuppre-Desjardin and A.-L. Van Bruaene, *De Bono Communi, the Discourse and Practise of the Common Good in the European City, 13th–16th Centuries* (Turnhout: Brepols, 2010), 1–9; Haemers, *Common Good*, 2–9; J. Dumolyn, 'Urban Ideology in Later Medieval Flanders. Towards an Analytical Framework', in A. Gamberini, J.-P. Genet and A. Zorzi (eds), *The Languages of Political Society, Western Europe 14th–17th Centuries* (Roma: Viella, 2011), 85–7; idem, 'Justice, Equity and the Common Good; the State Ideology of the Councillors of the Burgundian Dukes', in D'Arcy J. D. Boulton and J. R. Veenstra (eds), *The Ideology of Burgundy* (Leiden: Brill, 2006), 151–94'; idem, and P. Stabel, 'Stedelijkheid in harmonie en conflict: gemeenschap, spanningsvelden en sociale controlemechanismen in de stad', in E. Taverne et al. (eds), *Nederland stedenland: continuïteit en vernieuwing* (Rotterdam: naio10 uitgevers, 2012), 56–71; idem, J. Haemers et al., 'Medieval Voices and Popular Politics', *Studies in European Urban History (1100–1800)* 33 (2014), 1–12.

will of necessity take up more of the following, and as much information as possible has been gleaned for Ypres, the third of the 'Three Towns'. Other towns have been studied but particular attention will be paid to Lille, Douai, Oudenaarde and Aalst. That guilds existed in towns of vastly different sizes is important, and that towns of vastly different sizes maintained guilds in the same way, enacting the same sorts of spectacles and rituals, is revealing. Examination of smaller towns will be brought in wherever possible, although the evidence for them is far more limited. It is clear from records of competitions that all towns had guilds, and competition records from Hulst, town accounts for Caprijk and Ninove and charters from Croix and Armentières will be analysed, among others. These smaller towns will be introduced as they appear, but it is worth pausing here to provide a few words of introduction to the larger and better-documented towns.

Ghent was the largest town of medieval Flanders, with a population of some 50,000 by the mid-fifteenth century.[24] The town was a textile centre and about a third of the workers in the town earned their money from the textile industry. Because of the power of the cloth industry, the town had strong connections to England and imported huge amounts of wool, which, as noted, could lead to internal tension and violence as well as the rebellions mentioned above.[25] Yet studies of Ghent, particularly Arnade's analysis of its rituals and Boone's studies of its place within Burgundian state formation show that urban groups and rulers used rituals and celebrations to emphasise unity, and to promote civic status.[26] As chapter one will discuss, the guilds in Ghent are possibly the oldest; indeed in 2014 a celebration was held in Ghent to mark the seven hundredth anniversary of the foundation of the crossbow guild.[27]

Bruges was the second-largest town in Flanders in terms of population, with around 36,700 residents in the mid-fifteenth century.[28] The town was far richer

---

[24] P. Stabel, 'Composition et recomposition des réseaux urbains des Pays-Bas au Moyen âge', *UH* 12 (2008), 58.

[25] D. Nicholas, *The Metamorphosis of a Medieval City, Ghent in the Age of the Arteveldes, 1302–1390* (Lincoln: University of Nebraska Press, 1987), 6–11, 17–21, 154–61.

[26] P. Arnade, *Realms of Ritual, Burgundian Ceremony and Civic Life in Late Medieval Ghent* (Ithaca, NY: Cornell University Press, 1996); idem, 'Crowds, Banners and the Market Place; Symbols of Defiance and Defeat During the Ghent War of 1452–3', *Journal of Medieval and Renaissance Studies* 24 (1994), 471–97; M. Boone, *Gent en de Bourgondische hertogen ca. 1384–ca. 1453, een sociaal-politieke studie van een staatsvormingsproces* (Brussel: Koninklijke academie voor wetenschappen, letteren en schone kunsten van België, 1990); idem, *Geld en macht: de Gentse stdsfinanciën en de Bourgondische staatsvorming (1384–1453)* (Gent: Maatschappij voor geschiedenis en oudheidkunde, 1990); idem, 'Dons et pots-de-vin, aspects de la sociabilité urbaine au bas Moyen Âge. Le cas gantois pendant la période bourguignonne', *RN* 70 (1988), 478–81; idem and Prevenier, 'The "City-State", Dream', in J. Decavele (ed.), *Ghent, in Defence of a Rebellious City* (Antwerp: Fonds Mercator, 1989), 81.

[27] P. Verlende et al., *1314–2014, Gedenkboek, 700 jaar Sint-Jorisgilde Gent* (Gent: Academia Press, 2014).

[28] Stabel, 'Composition et recomposition', 58.

than its neighbours, and remained the trade gateway of Flanders for most of the period under consideration. Bruges can be considered as a 'cradle of capitalism' and was home to some of the first international trading companies, as merchants from across Europe gathered in the town.[29] Brown's studies of civic culture in Bruges, as well as Dumolyn's studies of Bruges's socio-political make-up and values, emphasise the complexities of Bruges society and the political forces that could pull the civic community apart, although most urban groups strove for unity, peace and prestige.[30] The Ghent and Bruges guilds are particularly well documented, as we shall see, and so these guilds take up a prominent part of this study. The suggestion is not, however, that the Ghent and Bruges guilds were exceptional; rather, that there were common forms of guild community, even guild language, across and beyond Flanders.

Ypres, the last of the Three Towns, is of necessity less well represented in this study, as the archives were destroyed, along with most of the town, in the First World War. Ypres was an extremely wealthy trade and textile centre in the twelfth and thirteenth centuries, but was in economic decline by the fourteenth century. Despite this, the town retained its economic power and influence during the period under consideration here and had a population of perhaps 8,800 in the mid-fifteenth century.[31] Ypres was close to the linguistic border in Flanders, it was predominantly Flemish speaking, but was more influenced by

---

[29] J. Murray, *Bruges, Cradle of Capitalism, 1280–1390* (Cambridge: Cambridge University Press, 2005).

[30] A. Brown, *Civic Ceremony and Religion in Bruges c.1300–1520* (Cambridge: Cambridge University Press, 2011); idem, 'Civic Ritual: Bruges and the Count of Flanders in the Later Middle Ages', *EHR* 112 (1997); idem, 'Bruges and the "Burgundian Theatre-State": Charles the Bold and Our Lady of the Snow', *History* 84 (1999); idem, 'Ritual and State Building; Ceremonies in Late Medieval Bruges', in J. Van Leewen (ed.), *Symbolic Communication in Late Medieval Towns* (Leuven: Leuven University Press, 2006); idem, 'Devotion and Emotion: Creating the Devout Body in Late Medieval Bruges', *Digital Philology: A Journal of Medieval Cultures* 1 (2012), 210–34; J. Dumolyn, *De Brugse opstand, van 1436–1438* (Heule: UGA, 1997); idem, 'Population et structures professionnelles à Bruges aux XIVe et XVe siècles', *RN* 81 (1999), 43–64; idem, 'Dominante klassen en elites in verandering in het laatmiddeleeuwse Vlaanderen', *JMG* 5 (2002); idem, 'Economic Development, Social Space and Political Power in Bruges, c.1127–1302', in H. Skoda, P. Lantschner and R. L. J. Shaw (eds), *Contact and Exchange in Later Medieval Europe, Essays in Honour of Malcolm Vale* (Woodbridge: Boydell, 2012), 53–5; idem, '"Our Land is Founded on Trade and Industry." Economic Discourse in Fifteenth-Century Bruges', *JMH* 36 (2010).

[31] Stabel, 'Composition et recomposition', 58; P. Boussemaere, 'De Ieperse lakenproductie in de veertiende eeuw opnieuw berekend aan de hand van de lakenloodjes', *JMG* 3 (2000), 131–61; M. Boone, 'Social Conflicts in the Cloth Industry of Ypres (late 13th–early 14th centuries): The Cockerulle Reconsidered', in M. Dewilde et al. (eds), *Ypres and the Medieval Cloth Industry in Flanders: Archaeological and Historical Contributions / Ieper en de middeleeuwse lakennijverheid in Vlaanderen: Archeologische en historische bijdragen* (Asse-Zellik: Instituut voor het archeologisch Patrimonium, 1998), 147–53.

French culture than its northern neighbours, and it was central to trade within the county. It would be fascinating to know more about the Ypres guilds, as the archers there seem to have been particularly active in competitions, as we shall see in chapter five. Much can still be learnt from the copies of the town accounts kept in Brussels and from other fragmentary evidence and published chronicles.

Lille and Douai were part of Walloon Flanders, briefly ruled directly by the French king and French speaking. Lille was the larger of the two, with a population of some 12,000 in the mid-fifteenth century as compared to Douai's 8,000.[32] Lille grew in importance during the period, indeed it can be said that the Burgundian dukes saved Lille. They made it an administrative centre through the creation of a *chambre des comptes* in 1386 and Philip the Good constructed a palace in the town.[33] Lille was not just a centre of administration; Chastelain called it 'une ville de plaisirs' and famous noble events like the Feast of the Pheasant were held there.[34] Lille was also an important trade town and part of many commercial and festive networks, as chapter five will demonstrate. Both Lille and Douai were generous to their guilds, sending them to numerous competitions and granting them annual sums of money. The town accounts of Lille are particularly detailed, allowing for a detailed analysis of the competitions hosted and attended, while the Douai guild has left an invaluable guild-book, containing the earliest known oath of a shooting guild.

Attention must also be paid to medium-sized towns, and the two with the richest archives for the shooting guilds are Oudenaarde and Aalst. Oudenaarde was a medium-sized town in central Flanders with a population of some 6,500 in the mid-fifteenth century, while Aalst was smaller, with just 3,500 residents.[35] As will be discussed in depth in chapter five, Oudenaarde was very well situated for trade, being on the river Scheldt between Ghent and Tournai. Unlike its northern neighbour, Oudenaarde emphasised luxury over quantity in the textile trade and was a noted centre of tapestry production. It seems to have used its guilds to show off its status as a producer of luxury textiles, as the Oudenaarde crossbow guild was among the best-funded shooting guilds, as will be discussed in chapters five and six. Oudenaarde was also home to an impressive procession with large play wagons and a vibrant dramatic tradition, which may well be linked to the shooting guilds and their ability to use cloth and displays. Aalst had an important mint and produced many of the surviving medieval Flemish coins. Much of its textile trade relied on local wool, keeping production small,

---

[32] Stabel, 'Composition et recomposition', 58.
[33] L. Trenard, *Histoire de Lille, tome 1* (Lille: Faculté des lettres et sciences humaines de Lille, 1970), 197–204, 219–34; J.-B. Santamaria, *La Chambre des comptes de Lille de 1386 à 1419. Essor, organisation et fonctionnement d'une institution princière* (Turnhout: Brepols, 2012).
[34] D. Clauzel, *Finances et politique à Lille pendant la période bourguignonne* (Dunkerque: Les Editions des Beffrois, 1982), 13; Trenard, *Histoire de Lille*, 224–5.
[35] Stabel, 'Composition et recomposition', 58.

although the flax and linen industry began to develop at the end of the fourteenth century. Despite its size, the town had some legal autonomy and the power of its hinterland – the land of Aalst – was impressive; the town also had strong links to the Hanse merchants.[36]

Other, smaller towns have also been brought in as far as possible. The above choices are driven by surviving sources, but urban values and economic and festive connections were as important for the smaller centres as for the trade gateway of Bruges.[37] Throughout, the guilds will be linked to other studies that have shown the strength and variety of urban traditions as well as the significance of interaction with the ducal court and the diversity of cultures within towns. It is important to remember that the urban community of Flanders was not just about individual towns. The cultural connections between towns have been analysed in the works of Stein and Boone, showing that the Low Countries' 'excellent water networks and roads' were vital in 'encouraging a very intense inter-urban traffic' of material goods and cultural products, points that we will return to in chapters five and six.[38]

The Sources

Town financial accounts form an essential starting point for our study. The town accounts of Ghent and Bruges begin in the 1280s, but record more about income and taxes than the precise details of spending. The growth in account keeping in the county, indeed across Europe, in the fourteenth century may well be

---

[36] Nicholas, *Medieval Flanders*, 111–12, 151, 174, 264–7, 331–7.

[37] P. Stabel, *De kleine stad in Vlaanderen: bevolkingsdynamiek en economische functies van de kleine en secundaire stedelijke centra in het Gentse kwartier (14de–16de eeuw)* (Brussel: Paleis der Academiën, 1995); idem, 'Demography and Hierarchy; The Small Towns and the Urban Networks in Sixteenth-Century Flanders', in P. Clark (ed.), *Small Towns in Early Modern Europe* (Cambridge: Cambridge University Press, 1995); idem, *Dwarfs Among Giants, the Flemish Urban Network in the Late Middle Ages* (Leuven: Garant, 1997); idem, 'Composition et recomposition', 29–58.

[38] R. Stein, 'An Urban Network in the Low Countries. A Cultural Approach', in R. Stein and J. Pollman, *Networks, Regions and Nations, Shaping Identities in the Low Countries* (Leiden: Brill, 2010); G. Marnet, 'Chambers of Rhetoric and the Transmission of Religious Ideas in the Low Countries', in H. Schilling and I. G. Tóth (eds), *Cultural Exchange in Early Modern Europe, 1400–1700 vol. 1, Religion and Cultural Exchange* (Cambridge: Cambridge University Press, 2006), 274–96; W. Blockmans, 'Stedelijke netwerken in de Nederlanden voor de industrialisatie', *Leidschrift; historisch tijdschrift* 7 (1990–91), 59–68; H. Lowagie, 'Stedelijke communicatie in de late middeleeuwen. Aard, motivaties en implicaties politieke', *RBPH* 87 (2009), 273–95; M. Boone and H. Porfyriou, 'Markets, Squares, Streets: Urban Space, a Tool for Cultural Exchange', in D. Calabi and S. T. Christensen (eds), *Cities and Cultural Exchange in Europe 1400–1700, Cultural Exchange in Early Modern Europe, 2* (Cambridge: Cambridge University Press, 2007), 227–53.

connected to the circulation of paper.[39] The financial accounts of Lille begin in 1301. For all the Three Towns civic officials must have had an understanding of income and outgoings from an earlier date, but it was not until the very end of the thirteenth century that civic administrators began to organise finances on a scale requiring detailed records.[40] In some smaller towns, such as Douai, accounts are scattered and fragmentary until the 1380s, or even the fifteenth century as in Oudenaarde.[41] Accounts are more plentiful for the late fourteenth and fifteenth centuries, as contemporary copies of virtually all Flemish towns' accounts were sent to the ducal *chambre des comptes*. Town accounts are often difficult to read, both palaeographically and analytically, but are extremely rewarding: they list all monies given to the towns every year, and all payments. Guilds were given money for military service or for attending competitions, and they were granted wine or even lands for the honour they brought to the town. Accounts were written continuously and contemporarily, although the possibility of fraud or mistakes should not be forgotten.[42] They provide many details on where the guilds went, when and why, and how much they received in return, allowing the guilds' inter-urban competitions to be analysed and their place within their own urban hierarchy to be considered.

As we shall see, guilds obtained many rights and privileges through charters. Such rights were granted by the rulers of Flanders, by local noblemen, even by ecclesiastical lords, and all charters set out what was expected of the guilds and the rights they should receive. Many charters from the rulers of Flanders have been published, especially the Burgundian charters, but the privileges given by towns and local lords are also accessible in print, and still more are available in archives.[43] Charters could be granted to large or small towns,

---

[39] J. Vuylsteke, *Gentsche stads – en baljuwsrekeningen 1280–1336*, 3vols (Gent: Meyer-van Loo, 1900–1908); G. Small, 'Municipal Registers of Deliberations in the Fourteenth and Fifteenth Centuries: Cross-Channel Observations', in G.-P. Genet and F.-J. Ruggiu (eds), *Les Idées passent-elles la Manche? Savoirs, Représentations, pratiques (France-Angleterre, Xe–XXe siècles)* (Paris: Presse-Sorbonne, 2007), 37–66.

[40] M. A. Richebé, *Compte de recettes et dépenses de la ville de Lille, 1301–1302* (Lille: Leleu, 1894); J. Gilssen, 'Les Villes en Belgique, histoire des institutions administratives et judiciaries des villes belges', *Recueils de la société Jan Bodin* (1954), 531–600.

[41] DAM, CC 200 onwards, organised accounts from 1383; earlier fragments CC 201 ter; OSAOA, stadsrekening, 684, 1406 onwards; AML, CV, 16012–16274; AGR,CC, 31419–31495; AGR, CC, Microfilm 684.1–6; SAG, 400;SAB, 216.

[42] For example a town clerk of Tournai wrote in a margin of the accounts 'the crossbowmen were paid twice for going to Jeumont where they won the sovereign prize', A. de la Grange, 'Extraits analytiques des registres des consaulx de la ville de Tournai, 1431–1476', *Mémoires de la Société historique et littéraire de Tournai* 23 (1893), 305.

[43] P. Bonenfant (ed.), *Ordonnances de Philippe le Hardi, de Marguerite de Male, 1381–1405*, vols 1–2. (Bruxelles: Ministère de la justice, 1965–74); J. M. Cauchies (ed.), *Ordonnances de Jean Sans Peur, 1405–1419* (Bruxelles: Ministère de la Justice, 2001). Charters issued by Philip the Good to the county of Flanders have been drawn together and analysed in the 2012 thesis of J. Braekevelt, 'Charters of Philip the Good for the County of Flanders

sometimes in nearly identical language, others with interesting variations, as will be discussed in chapter four. Charters and civic ordinances set out what was expected of guilds, from how many men could enter the guild, to what weapons they should carry, and even where and when the guild-brothers should attend mass. The prescriptive documents make clear the values placed upon guilds by princely or civic powers and hint at strong relationship between the guilds and these authorities. Many such ordinances, though not all, were issued at the request of the guilds in question, and so they standardised existing norms. Others refer to 'ancient customs' and 'ancient service', again emphasising that the regulations they record were not innovations. Rather, the charters can be seen as standardising what already existed. The charters are well preserved and often very detailed, but how far the rules were followed is not always clear. Charters have been used here to show the privileges that the guilds received and the expectations placed on them, with some analysis of the language used by princely officials to consider how guilds were viewed by those in power.

The records kept by the guilds themselves are some of the more rewarding for a study of the shooters. Guild financial records are not as complete as town accounts and can be difficult to use, but they are nevertheless extremely valuable. The cost of food and drink from Bruges, records of bequests from Ghent and the cost of liveries from Oudenaarde all give glimpses into the internal, private workings of guild social and devotional choices.[44] Guild records also include invitations to and descriptions of competitions, the locations and sizes of the guilds' secular properties, even their military service.[45] It is probable that every guild kept records, but their survival is far from uniform. For example, chapel accounts from Aalst survive only for one year,[46] while from Bruges they are complete, although less detailed from 1454 to 1481, and again from 1486 to 1492. Guild records are no more taken at face value than ducal charters, and the choice either to record or not to record will be discussed in the context of rebellion in chapter two, as will the absence of records of disorder in chapter six. In creating their guild-books, guild-brothers constructed a narrative of their guild for their guild, providing detailed if highly subjective images of life in a medieval shooting guild.

Records of ecclesiastical authorities, groups, even buildings, have not survived in as great numbers as for secular ones. The violence of the sixteenth century, the French Revolution, the World Wars, as well as accidental fires

---

and Lordship of Malines' (PhD thesis, Universiteit Gent, 2012). I am extremely grateful to the author for transcriptions and references to charters. G. Espinas, *Les origines du droit d'association dans les villes de l'Artois et de la Flandre française jusqu'au début du XVIe siècle*, vol. 2, *Documents* (Lille: Raoust, 1941).

[44] SAG, SJ, NGR; SAG, SJ, 155; SAG, Sint Sebastian, 155/1; SAG, LXVII, Sint Jorishospitaal; SAB, 385, Sint Joris; BASS rekeningen; BASS rekeningen; OSAOA, gilden 507/II/10A.

[45] SAG, SJ, NG; OSAOA, gilden 507/II/3B.

[46] ASAOA, 156, Rekening van de gezworenen van het Sint Joris gild, 1461–2.

like the one that destroyed the Franciscan monastery in Bruges which housed the chapel of Saint Sebastian, have all taken their toll. Yet much of value has survived and, with careful analysis, can yield valuable insight into guild piety as well as guild membership and wealth. Papal bulls granted rights and privileges to guilds in many towns, not just the great centres of Ghent and Bruges but also the secondary town of Oudenaarde.[47] I know of no surviving Flemish shooting guild chapel, yet inventories and descriptions have survived, providing hints of the splendours that once existed.[48] These records, and particularly the Ghent accounts of bequests and their limitations, will be discussed in more depth in chapter three.

Narrative sources including chronicles have also been used as far as possible, although often those written for lords focused on court rather than civic events. Among the most useful narrative sources is one from a guild-brother. The manuscript in the Ghent University Library called *Bouc van Pieter Polet* was written (presumably by Pieter, as it ends with his signature) sometime before 1506.[49] Pieter was a crossbowman and alderman of Ghent and his book describes two of the great events of that guild, the crossbow competitions of 1440 and 1498. As his own work and the town accounts show, Pieter was one of the men who organised the 1498 shoot. It is likely that he found out all he could about the 1440 shoot before 1498 and recorded the latter shoot a few years after it had taken place; the *bouc* is therefore useful for the planning and remembering of crossbow competitions. It is possible that another civic chronicle was written by a crossbowman: the Ypres chronicle usually called *'wondrous happenings'* and attributed to Olivier van Dixmuide.[50] The original is now lost and the chronicle may not be the work of one man.[51] However, it is likely that the Olivier van Dixmuide who wrote at least part of the chronicle and was alderman in 1423 and 1425[52] was the same Olivier van Dixmuide who, as headman of the great crossbow guild, was given a uniform and generous expenses in 1428.[53] Several Oudenaarde chronicles, and that of the nearby abbey of Enaeme, describe crossbow competitions or the guilds themselves.[54] An eighteenth-century

---

[47] SAG, 155, 2; BASS, charter 4; OSAOA, gilden 507/II/2A.
[48] STAM, Sint Sebastiaangilde; privilegieboek, inv 1059, ff. 10–12; SAG, SJ, NGR, 7.
[49] UBG, Hs. 6112, *Dit es den bouc van ... Pieter Polet*.
[50] Olivier van Dixmuide (ed. J.-J. Lambin), *Merkwaerdige Gebeurtenissen, Vooral in Vlaendern en Brabant en ook in de aengrenzende landstreken van 1377 tot 1443* (Ypres, 1835).
[51] P. Trio 'The Chronicle Attributed to "Oliver van Diksmuide"; a Misunderstood Town Chronicle of Ypres from Late Medieval Flanders', in E. Kooper (ed.), *The Medieval Chronicle V* (Amsterdam: Rodopi, 2008), 211–25.
[52] Lambin's introdcuction to *Merkwaerdige Gebeurtenissen*, iii– xii.
[53] Given to 'Olivier van Dixmuide, headman of the great shooters', AGR, CC, 38653, f. 35.
[54] Chronicle of Ename quoted in Cauwenberghe, 'Notice historique sur les confréries de Saint Georges', 279–91; several anonymous, unpublished and in poor condition town chronicles in OSAOA, 241.

compilation of Oudenaarde chronicles by the archivist Bartholemeeus de Rantere is also useful, particularly as parts of the early chronicles are no longer legible or are too delicate to be consulted directly.[55]

Many other chronicles set out not to describe the history of one town, but all of Flanders, or larger areas, and many of these mention shooting guilds. The *Excellent Chronicle of Flanders*, printed in 1531, sets out the history of Flanders from its mythical, giant-slaying founder, Liederic, to Charles V, and is concerned with dynastic events and wars. Yet this huge chronicle provides a wealth of detail on the Ghent crossbow competition of 1498, as will be discussed in chapters five and six.[56] The *Chroniques de Brabant et de Flandre* and the works of Nicholas Despars[57] set out to give grand narratives of their age, but take the time and space to describe guilds or their shoots, again showing that contemporaries saw the guilds as a significant group, worthy of being recorded. In Liège the canon Jean Stavelot, writing a continuation of the chronicles of Jean d'Outremeuse, is most concerned with matters of local or even European importance, with a focus on ecclesiastical matters. He described a crossbow competition in Liège in 1441 and proudly recorded that the crossbowmen of Liège travelled to Flemish competitions.[58] Even the blind abbot of Tournai, Gilles de Muisit, writing in the mid-fourteenth century, described and praised the Tournai crossbow competition of 1350 and the splendour of the Flemish teams.[59] The guilds and their competitions became civic powers that could not be ignored, leaders of civic culture as well as some of the most spectacular groups in their towns.

The archery and crossbow guilds of Flanders were part of their region, part of their towns and part of the connections between court and civic cultures. They were not all the same, but in considering guilds in towns large and small and in drawing on a range of civic, ducal and ecclesiastic sources the following study hopes to offer an explanation of who the crossbowmen gathered in Tournai in 1394 were, and to unpick the many reasons why civic authorities gave the guilds money for land, for drink and to attend spectacular

---

[55] Original is OSAOA, Bartholomeeus de Rantere, microfilm 1484–6; Bartholomeus de Rantere, *Geschiedenis van Oudenaarde, van 621–1397*, ed. E. Dhoop and M. De Smet (Oudenaarde, 1986), and *1397–1468* (Oudenaarde, 1986).

[56] W. Vosterman, *Dits die excellente cronike van Vlaanderen, beghinnende van Liederik Buc tot keyser Carolus (Antwerp, 1531)* [Konilijke Bilbiotheek, Brussels VH 27.525], ff. 285v–291v.

[57] J. J. de Smet, *Recueil des chroniques de Flandres/ Corpus chronicorum Flandriae*, 4vols (Brussels: Hayez, 1837–65), vol. 3, 37–93; N. Despars, *Cronijke van den lande ende graefscepe van Vlaenderen van de Jaeren 405 tot 1492* (Amsterdam, 1562: Bruge: Messchert, 1839–42); F. Buylaert, 'Memory, Social Mobility and Historiography. Shaping Noble Identity in the Bruges Chronicle of Nicholas Despars (+ 1597)', *Belgisch Tijdschrift voor Filologie en Geschiedenis* 87 (2011).

[58] Jean de Stavelot (ed. A. Borghet), *Chronique* (Bruxelles, 1861).

[59] Gilles le Muisit (ed. H. Lemaitre), *Chronique et Annales* (Paris: Renouard, H. Laurens, 1906).

competitions. Although negatives are harder to analyse, the choice not to fund guilds will also be considered, as Ghent was conspicuously absent from the festivities of Tournai in 1394.

Monies and Measures

Unless otherwise stated, in the following all monies are given in pounds of Flanders, with twelve pennies (*d*) making one shilling and twenty shillings (*s*) making £1.[60] Some accounts and grants were given in groats, or occasionally French royal money, *livres Paris*. The value of all currencies across the fourteenth and fifteenth centuries was subject to change and inflation, but Flemish money was slightly more stable than that of France or England. Wine was a common gift or payment for many guilds, given in several different measurements: one *los* or *lot* or *kane* was approximately 2.09 litres while one *stoop* equated to 1.2 litres.[61]

---

[60] P. Spufford, *Monetary Problems and Policies in the Burgundian Netherlands (1433–96)* (Leiden: Brill, 1977).

[61] M. Somme, 'Étude comparative des mesures à vin dans les états bourguignons au XVe siècle', *RN* 58 (1976), 171–83; M. Damen, 'Giving by pouring; the functions of gifts of wine in the city of Leiden, 14th–16th centuries', in *Symbolic Communication in Late Medieval Towns*, 83–100.

1

'For security, guard and defence' of this town

Guilds' Origins and Military Service

On 5 June 1461 Philip the Good granted a charter of rights to the archers and crossbowmen of Gravelines. He allowed the guild-brothers of the archery guild of Saint Sebastian and the crossbow guild of Saint George to carry their 'bastons et armures loisibles' throughout his lands. Philip did so, his preamble states, with the advice of the men of the Council of Flanders and the Great Council and the privilege was granted for the 'bien, garde et deffence' (well-being, guard and defence) of Gravelines. Twenty years earlier a slightly longer charter had been issued to the lord of Drincham allowing him to re-establish an archery guild. The guild had been granted a charter by John the Fearless, but these letters had been burnt, and so Philip was persuaded to grant new privileges to Jehan, lord of Drincham. Philip recognised the good service of Jehan of Drincham and allowed him to (re-)establish an archery guild of 150 men, wearing his own livery, dedicated to Saint Sebastian and free to bear arms across Flanders. The 1441 charter was granted for the 'seurte, garde et deffense' (security, guard and defence) of the lordship of Drincham and rights were granted 'comme font les archiers des autres confraires de notre dit pais de Flandre' (as made for the other archery guilds in our land of Flanders).[1]

Numerous other examples could be added of charters and rights being granted to guilds for the guard and defence of their towns. In both of the above cases charters are almost the only details known about the guilds. Gravelines was a relatively new town, founded in the 1160s as an outpost of Saint-Omer, but as a coastal port it was often caught up in conflict. John the Fearless had to defend it in 1405 and it was subjected to English pillage in 1412–13.[2] Drincham was even smaller, meaning that a guild of 150 men was likely to be a personal retinue of some sort, as we shall see below, and yet the language here is very close to earlier charters granted to far larger towns. In 1405 the archers of Lille

---

[1] Espinas, *Les origins*, vol. 2, 536–539.
[2] Nicholas, *Medieval Flanders*, 110–12, 323–5; A. Derville, 'Les origines de Gravelines et de Calais', *RdN* 66 (1984), 1051–69; S. Curveiller, 'Territorialités, institutions et sources fiscales en Flandre maritime au Moyen Age', *RdN* 79 (1998), 897–919.

were granted permission by John the Fearless to bear their arms across Flanders 'for the defence' of Lille and in 1430 those of Mechelen had been granted land and an annual income 'for the defence of the town'.[3]

The language of defence and protection is ubiquitous in charters from the fourteenth and fifteenth centuries. It could be assumed from these charters that guilds were simply an extension of the militia and grew out of a simple necessity for civic self-defence. Indeed many older studies have assumed that the guilds did have military origins and, in doing so, have misunderstood the place of guilds within the broader civic society. In studying guilds' first appearance and the language used to describe them, it becomes clear that guilds did not develop in a straightforward military context but were socio-cultural groups from the time of their earliest appearance. There may be some link between guilds and paramilitary groups, the so-called Hoods, but shooting guilds were separate entities. Although guilds did not emerge simply through warfare, they were militarily important groups and an invaluable part of civic defence and peace keeping. In addition they were active within larger princely hosts across the fourteenth and fifteenth centuries, as will be shown through analysis of their part in five campaigns. In examining the guilds' origins, their links to paramilitary groups, their part in civic defence and their role within larger hosts the present chapter will address the question of where archers and crossbowmen learnt their skill and start to consider the purpose of the guilds within their towns.

Guilds' Origins

The armies of Europe had made use of archers and crossbowmen long before 1300. As Strickland has shown, French towns had provided soldiers to royal armies since the time of Philip Augustus, among them archers and crossbowmen.[4] In Flanders the power of the urban contingents was demonstrated famously and forcefully at the battle of Courtrai in 1302, in the 'miracle of the fourteenth century' whereby the townsmen defeated a great French chivalric host.[5] It is tempting to see the guilds as emerging from these victories, or older military service, and several studies have made this case. From Vereecke's 1858 study claiming that the Ypres crossbow guild was founded by veterans returning from the battlefield, to Renson's 1976 suggestion that guilds were founded in the new 'confident spirit' following the battle, the link between war and guild foundation is venerable.[6] Neither study provides evidence for its claim, nor does it reconcile

---

[3] AML, RT, 15879, f. 215; Mechelen Stadsarchief, cartularia, A I, 1, ff. 11v-13.
[4] M. Strickland and R. Hardy, *The Great Warbow* (Stroud: Sutton, 2005), 254.
[5] Oman, *A History of the Art of War in the Middle Ages*, 113–21; J. F. Verburggen, *De krijgskunst in West-Europa in de Middeleeuwen (IXe tot begin XIVe eeuw)* (Brussel: Paleis der Academiën, 1954), 196–7.
[6] J. J. J. Vereecke, *Histoire militaire de la ville d'Ypres, jadis place-forte de la Flandre occidentale* (Gand: Van Doosselaere, 1858); M. Mus, *Geschiedenis van de Ieperse boogschutters vanaf*

the new, confident guilds with the minimal role played by crossbowmen in the battle of Courtrai.[7]

More broadly, the idea that guilds were in fact 'founded' or 'created' at a set moment in time permeates a good deal of the literature. The above-quoted charters do not claim to 'create' the guilds in question, rather, they refer to ancient customs and bestow new rights and recognition on established groups. Yet for more than a century authors have looked for princely creators and Delbrück's 1929 statement that French guilds had been 'encouraged' by the kings since 1368, but that soon noble 'suspicions' and, more importantly, a lack of bows and arrows meant that 'the inclination to train oneself in the art of archery was probably very limited'[8] has found surprisingly few detractors. On the contrary, numerous local studies argue that the guilds were 'founded' by figures of local importance, from Duke Henry III of Brabant's 'founding' of the Brussels guild in 1213 to the famous chivalric hero Simon de Lalaing's 'registering' of the Quiévrain archers in 1415.[9]

Rights and privileges received from lords were, of course, important. In particular they can be used to trace patterns of guild size and this can be linked to, among other factors, defensive priorities. Table 1 sets out how many members selected guilds should have had, based on princely charters. The table makes clear that the size of a guild was not directly related to the size of the urban population.[10] The years of the charters shown in the table should not be seen as the dates of creation of the guilds but, rather, as the points at which the guilds obtained princely recognition.

---

hun opkomst tot aan de eerst wereldoorlog (Leuven: Vlaamse Volkssport Centrale, 1988), 5–9; R. Renson, 'The Flemish Archery Gilds, from Defence Mechanisms to Sports Institutions', in *The History, Evolution and Diffusion of Sports and Games in Different Cultures* R. Renson and D. Nager (eds) (Brussels: HISPA, 1976),135–159.

[7] Verbruggen, *The Battle of the Golden Spurs*, 152–62.

[8] H. Delbrück (trans. W. J. Renfroe), *History of the Art of War within the framework of Political History*, vol. 3 (London: Greenwood Press, 1982 first published 1929) 446–7, 512–15.

[9] De Potter, *Jaarboeken*, 12; Wauters, *Notice historique*, 3–5; O. Petit-Jean, *Historique de l'ancien grand serment royal et noble des arbalétriers de Notre-Dame de la Sablon* (Bruxelles: Du Marais, 1963), 13–18; T. Dernier, *Notice sur le serment des archers de saint Sébastien de Quiévrain* (Quiévrain: Lecocq, 1873), 5–7; Matthieu, 'Sceaux des serments ou guildes', 15–23; M. Millon, *Les archers Dunkerquois, histoire de la société des archers réunis de Saint Sébastien (1322 à 1965)* (Dunkerque: Impr. L'Indépendant, 1965), 18; P. Delsalle, 'La Confrérie des archers de Cysoing, fondée en 1430 par la Baronne de Cysoing et le Duc de Bourgogne', *Bulletin de la société historique et archéologique de Cysoing et de la Révèle* (1975), 14–19.

[10] Populations drawn from Stabel, 'Composition et recomposition', 58–62.

Town	Estimated population c. 1450	Archers	Year	Crossbowmen	Year of charter
Ghent	50,000	c. 300		c. 300	
Bruges	36,736	c. 300		c. 300	
Mechelen	20,000	As many as needed	1430	60	1432
Lille	12,000	40		60	1443
Douai	8,000			120	1480
Ypres	8,780	80	1400		
Sluis	8,640			60	1455
Courtrai	8,460	60	1423		
Oudenaarde	6,480			60	1408
Nieuwpoort	5,040	80	1522		
Dendermonde	4,500			60	1398
Aalst	3,520	80	1431	60	1430
Sint-Winnoksbergen	3,460	100	1447		
Menin	1,520	60	1521		
Axele	1,372			60	1465
Tielt	1,252	100	1430	100	1430
la Bassée	1,200	60	1522		
Commines	800	150	1455	150	1455
Lannoy	240	50	1459		
Koekelare	not given, very small	60	1469		
Annappe	not given, very small	80	1518		
Pecquencourt	not given, very small			50	1511
Ingelmunster	not given, very small	30		30	1462
Cysoing	not given, very small	80	1431		
Wattignies and Estrées	not given, very small	40		80	1405
Zuienkerke	not given, very small	60	1449		
Houthem	not given, very small	60	1440		
Elverdinge and Vlamertinge	not given, very small	600 archers and crossbowmen	1447		
Dadizeele	not given, very small	40	1463		
Croix	not given, very small			30	1410
Boezinghe	not given, very small			80	1409
Lo	not given, very small			80	1410
Drincham	not given, very small	150	1441		

Table 1 Charters and Populations

The numbers of guild-brothers set out in charters varies greatly across Flanders, as do the possible motivations for guild sizes. In many, a military influence can be presumed; Sint-Winnoksbergen had less than half the population of Courtrai, yet required 100 archers to Courtrai's sixty. The high number of guild-brothers required for Sint-Winnoksbergen must be explained by the needs of defence, with Sint-Winnoksbergen (modern Bergues) lying close to English-held Calais. Coastal towns also have far larger guilds than inland ones of similar size. As noted above, Gravelines was granted rights for security, and possibly needed this force for protection, as it was the southernmost port of Flanders. Equally, Nieuwpoort has a disproportionately large guild, with eighty crossbowmen in a town of just over 5,000 people. Like Gravelines, Nieuwpoort was a coastal city, just south of Oostende, and so would need more protection than inland and relatively peaceful Lille.

Of course not all variations can be linked to defensive considerations. Both Lille and the nearby small town of Croix were required to have thirty crossbowmen; it is possible that the Croix guild was deliberately copying its larger and more prosperous neighbour (this relationship will be discussed in more depth in chapter six). Equally, the numbers in guilds could change: in 1431 Philip the Good granted rights to the eighty archers of Aalst, yet a decade earlier he had granted a similar charter, stating that there should be fifty archers.[11] The reason for change is not explained, but it may be that Aalst had increased in ducal favour and was therefore able to persuade Philip to augment its number, presumably because the guilds were valued by the civic officials. Civic officials would not, presumably, have made such a request if they did not see a pressing need for more archers to defend their town and to be 'always ready to serve', but also for 'the honour of the town', as the 1431 charter makes clear.

For lords issuing such charters, deciding how many men to require a guild to have would have been a balancing act. As Cauchies has demonstrated, local requirements would have had to be taken into account because, as we shall see, officials needed enough shooters to aid local justice and to protect the town. Yet they would not want too many guild-brothers because many armed men, especially those with immunity from prosecution for accidental deaths, could cause a danger of disorder and accidents.[12] Such ducal charters, then, make clear the ways that the lords perceived the guild and the town, as the larger numbers set out in charters are likely to indicate that the town was seen to be at risk of invasion or other threats. Guilds were defenders, and so in granting charters princes took care to ensure there were enough guild-brothers to defend the town and provide for it security. Yet the charters did not create guilds. Almost every

---

[11] RAG, RVV 7351, ff. 209–210; ASAOA, 3, peysboek, ff. 115v–116.
[12] J.-M, Cauchies, '"service" du prince "sûreté" des villes. À propos de privileges délivrés aux confréries ou serments d'archers et d'arbalétriers dans les Pays-Bas au XVe Siècle', *RN* 94 (2012), 242–5.

one of the charters listed above either mentions a specified forebear or refers to 'ancient' customs or traditions.

There are two guilds that are far too large to be explained by civic military factors. The 150 men in the Drincham guild are likely to be a personal retinue linked directly to the lord; the charter emphasises that they wear his livery and device. The 1447 charter to the archers and crossbowmen of Elverdinge and Vlamertinge is even more disproportionate, not least as Elverdinge and Vlamertinge were both small villages close to Ypres – indeed both are part of the modern municipality. The 1447 ordinance is no ordinary charter. It was granted to Corneille, 'Bastard of Burgundy', Philip the Good's eldest natural child and the first to hold the title 'Grand Bâtard'. Corneille was killed fighting the Ghent rebels at the battle of Bazel in 1452 and all of his titles, including 'Grand Bâtard', passed to his younger brother Anthony, who will be examined in more depth in chapter four. Corneille's claim to the lordship of Elverdinge was far from straightforward as he was not married to Margareta, the lady of Elverdinge but did have at least two children with her (Jérôme and Jean, the latter of whom died at the battle of Guinegate).[13] The 600 shooters of these two guilds were free to bear arms across Flanders and were granted tax exemptions and permitted to wear robes, hood and cloaks of a device to be ordered by Corneille. It is likely that this 'confraire', like that of Drincham, was in fact an armed retinue granted by Philip to his eldest son, along with the governorship of the duchy of Luxembourg, in an effort to grant him power and wealth.

The Drincham and Elverdinge and Vlamertinge charters aside, the above charters are useful for connecting guild size and defensive capabilities to civic size and situation. That guilds' sizes were not proportional to urban population is interesting and demonstrates that they remained linked to their local area. In France, in contrast, the *Francs-Archers* were instituted in 1448. French royal ordinances required one fully armed archer or crossbowman from a set number of hearths to be sent to the royal army. The *Francs-Archers* were connected to royal policy, particularly the final victories of the Hundred Years' War, rather than to their local area, and were often resented by their towns.[14] Shooting guilds could, as we shall see, serve beyond their town, but their responsibility was first and foremost to their own town. The shooting guilds were seen as assets, as representations of honour, not burdens.

Guilds were an asset to towns for defence and peace-keeping as well as for spectacle. As civic groups, they must be understood in a civic context; equally,

---

[13] R. Vaughan, *Philip the Good, The Apogee of Burgundy* (London: Longman, 1970: Woodbridge: Boydell, 2002) 134–5, 196, 222, 279–282, 321–2; H. Cools, 'In het spoor van "de grote bastaard" II', *Het land van Beveren* 33 (1990), 42–55.

[14] P. Laurent, *Les Francs-archers de Mézières (1448–1534)* (Mézières: René & Aubry, 1888); Baron de Bonnault d'Houët, *Les Franc -archers de Compiègne, 1448–1524* (Paris: Picard, 1897) A. Huyon, 'Les Francs-Archers; un exemple de réserve active', *Revue historique des armées* 1 (1989); Strickland and Hardy, *Warbow*, 354–6.

ducal charters setting out what *should* happen cannot be taken as representative of what *did* happen. The numbers of guild-brothers set out above were clearly important to princes and, in most cases, linked to defensive concerns. Yet guilds and their civic communities did not always follow the rules; guilds were allowed to grow and evolve. The Saint Sebastian archery guild of Lille should have numbered forty guild-brothers. Yet two membership lists, one from 1415 and a second from 1419, contain respectively 76 and 117 names. The archers had received immunity from prosecution for accidental deaths in 1417 and were evidently becoming more prestigious during these years, making the guild more appealing.[15] Only forty archers per year received civic livery, so there may be layers of membership that are not accessible via simple membership lists, or it may simply be that civic rulers were unwilling to give the archers an unlimited clothing budget. In allowing the membership to expand, it is clear that Lille did not perceive more archers to pose a significant risk of disorder or shooting accidents; rather, these were respected and honourable men. As we shall see, the archers of Lille were active in defending the town, so it may be that the town realised that it needed more defenders and so allowed the guild to grow.

In allowing a guild to grow far beyond the prescribed number, Lille is far from unique. As we have seen, Aalst received ducal permission to increase the number of archers in the town in 1431, but the crossbow guild was growing too. A membership list from the crossbow guild of Saint George written in 1462 has 138 names. From 1408, the Oudenaarde guild should have numbered sixty crossbowmen, yet a 1497 list includes an incredible 708 names.[16] In both Aalst and Oudenaarde these lists are likely to be copies of older ones and may include deceased members. It is unlikely that all of the 708 Oudenaarde members were active in one year, yet these lists make clear that numbers were not being capped.

Nothing could be found in Flemish sources to explain this. In Tournai the archers and crossbowmen were inspected, their numbers set at 140 and 100 respectively, and any brother found to be over sixty years of age or otherwise 'deficient' would be removed.[17] No charter clauses like this survive for any Flemish town and, as we shall see, many men were in the Bruges guilds for decades. It is possible that in 1415 Lille had forty able-bodied, skilled archers; the other thirty-six names in the list might represent aged members no longer able to serve on the battlefield, or even boys too young to do so. While it is possible, it seems unlikely that around half the guild-brothers were incapable of shooting or serving militarily. It is more likely that towns acted independently in allowing

---

[15] AML, PT, 15879, f. 215; AML, RM, 16973, 48, 90; ADN B1601, f. 157; all three guilds received funds for livery each year, e.g. 1520, AML, CV, 16255, f. 151.

[16] ASAOA,156, Rekeningen van de gezworenen van het Sint Joris gild, 1461–2, ff. 3v–5v; OSAOA, gilden, 707/II/8A; 507/II/17A.

[17] H. Vandenbroeck, *Extraits analytiques des anciennes registres des Consaux de la ville de Tournai, 1385–1422*) (Tournai: Mémoires de la Société historique et littéraire de Tournai, 7, 1861), 52.

the guilds to grow and in deciding for themselves how many guild-brothers specific guilds should have. That each town kept track of guild membership is interesting in itself, and shows that the guilds' growth was not unchecked, but that the size of a guild was related to local priorities.

Civic powers could overrule ducal ones in deciding how large the guilds should be in order to serve their own defence and festive and cultural needs. If towns could influence guild formation after they had been given rights, it seems only natural to assume that they could also influence guild formation and organisation before the guilds received charters or any princely recognition. Indeed, in placing guild origins firmly in the hands of local lords the above-mentioned studies give little credit to the towns themselves or to urban desires and agency.[18] Most studies link guild foundations to lords – but what did guilds write about their own foundation?

The guild-book of the Ghent crossbow guild of Saint George was begun around 1497. A death-list (which will be discussed in chapter three), beginning in 1468 and continuing to the end of the eighteenth century, takes up the vast majority of the book. Before they listed their members, the guild-brothers of Ghent included some history, using their ideas about their own past to create a narrative about themselves so as to explain the guild to fifteenth-century members. The book was kept, and used, in the guild hall until the very end of the eighteenth century,[19] and so writing some history is significant, as the story would likely be seen, perhaps even read out, on many occasions. The writing is very neat, especially when compared to some of the later lists of names. It fills just over one folio, again implying that the story was meant to be read and/or heard. The guild did not link its foundation to a Burgundian duke, nor even to their immediate predecessors as counts; rather, the anonymous guild clerk wrote that the guild had been created by Count Baldwin IV in 1016. The text adds that guild-brothers served in the crusades, following Godfrey of Bouillon to Jerusalem.[20] Several later guilds also claimed to have taken part in the crusades, but the Ghent guild seems to have been the only one to write down its crusader claims in the fifteenth century.

---

[18] Fitting with wider studies that under-estimate civic role in warfare, see for instance Philippe Contamine's works treating towns as almost passive observers of war, choosing only to open or close gates in the face of threats; P. Contamine, 'Les fortifications urbaines en France à la fin du Moyen Âge: aspects financiers et économiques', *RH* 260 (1978), 23–47; 'La noblesse et les villes dans la France de la fin du Moyen Âge', *Bullettino dell'Istituto Italiano per il Medio Evo e Archivio Muratoriano*, 91 (1985), 467–89; 'The soldiery in Late Medieval Urban Society', *French History* 8 (1994), 1–13; idem, *Guerre, état et société à la fin du Moyen Âge* (Paris: Mouton, 1972), 45–6.

[19] For Ghent and the crossbow guild under Napoleon and the guild's re-establishment in the early nineteenth century see B. Baillieul, 'De Sint-Jorisgilde in het Manchester van het Vasteland', in *Gedenkboek*, 71–8.

[20] STAM, G 3018/3, f. 1r–v.

The Ghent guild-brothers pushed their foundation back by some three centuries, setting out a prestigious creation myth associated with a powerful ancient figure. Town foundation myths are well known and attested across late medieval Europe.[21] Brabant tales, for instance, recounted the establishment of towns by Brabon, emphasising their antiquity and status. Further, in giving copies of these texts to their new Burgundian rulers, local powers helped to legitimise the duchy, with its separate identity within a growing Burgundian state.[22] Like their towns, archery and crossbow guilds wished to be seen as ancient and powerful, and therefore adapted foundation myths to construct a history with a view to augmenting their prestige and affirming group identity. Ghent's choice of Baldwin IV, and the very precise date, is interesting. Nicholas has called Baldwin IV 'one of the most important' medieval counts, as he extended Flanders and its influence over the Scheldt, being granted the Hainaut town of Valenciennes in 1015,[23] which perhaps explained why the guild believed that he would have granted it a charter in 1016. The Ghent guild-brothers' narrative may, of course, be older, but that it was written down at the end of the fifteenth century is interesting. The 1490s were also years of hope, as Philip the Fair came of age and the influence of Maximilian (temporarily, as it would turn out) came to an end in Flanders. The establishment of an ancient foundation and of a tradition that was older than both Habsburg and Burgundian power at that time added prestige and so legitimacy to the crossbowmen. Other groups and particular the civic authorities in Ghent were very attached to 'ancient' customs, and the Ghent crossbowmen set themselves up to have impressively ancient customs. By making clear their antiquity, the crossbowmen reinforced their identity as a prestigious and heroic group that had existed before, and would exist after, the power of the current dynasty.

The importance of being older than a current dynasty is clear in some French ordinances. For instance, in the 1350s many guilds claimed to have charters that gave them exemptions from taxation claimed by the Capetian monarchs. As

---

[21] K. Tilmans, 'De humanistische stedenmythe: Cultuurkritiek avant-la-lettre', in R. Aerts and K. van Berkel (eds), *De Pijn van Prometheus: Essays over cultuurkritiek en cultuurpessimisme* (Groningen: Historische uitgeveri, 1996), 68–82; R. Van Uytven, 'Stadsgeschiedenis in het Noorden en Zuiden', *AGN* 2 (1983), 188–253; G. Small 'Les origines de la ville de Tournai dans les chroniques légendaires du bas moyen âge', in A. Chatelet, J. Dumoulin and J.-C. Ghislain et al. (eds), *Les grands siècles de Tournai (12e–15e siècles): recueil d'études publié à l'occasion du 20e anniversaire des Guides de Tournai* (Tournai: Fabrique de l'Eglise Cathédrale de Tournai, 1993), 104–12; E. Lecuppre-Desjardin, *La Ville des cérémonies, essai sur la communication politique dans les anciens Pays-Bas Bourguignons* (Turnhout: Brepols, 2004), 68–71.

[22] S. Bijker 'The Function of the Late Medieval Brabantine Legend of Brabon', in *Networks, Regions and Nations*, 91–109.

[23] Nicholas, *Medieval Flanders*, 45–8.

regent for his imprisoned father following the battle of Poitiers,[24] the Dauphin Charles (future Charles V) acknowledged the ancient status of the Caen crossbowmen, and in 1358 his ordinance 'recognised' that the crossbowmen had an impressive range of tax exemptions. The year before, he had confirmed that the Rouen crossbowmen had held tax exemptions and other rights since 1322 that made the fifty guild-brothers 'free and quit of all tailles made for the debts of the said town' and of the obligations to watch the walls and of any 'taxes, tailles, subsidies and aids' and the Arrière-ban[25] and all other charges except the ransom of the king, should he ever be captured.[26] It is easy to see a simple financial motivation here; and indeed, the hopes of the guilds to avoid the new, heavy taxes brought in to fund the Hundred Years' War must be a factor in these confirmation charters. Yet the urge here for the French guilds to depict themselves as ancient, and specifically as having rights that predated the Valois dynasty, is also important and indicates the guilds' sense of identity as prestigious and well-established, even in the fourteenth century.

One French guild took this sense of identity and ancient foundation even further. The Tournai crossbowmen placed their origin even further back and associated themselves with a seventh-century king. In May 1448 the crossbowmen asked magistrates for a copy of their foundation charter, which, they claimed, gave them exemption from the watch and had been granted by King Dagobert.[27] The myth almost certainly refers to Dagobert I (d. 639), described by Fouracre and Gerberding as 'a hero among the later Merovingians' and by James as 'the last great Frankish king of the Merovingian Dynasty'.[28] Dagobert I worked to unify his kingdom, defeating foes in war and strengthening his kingdom; he was seen as a great, even ideal king. He was generous to the shrine of Saint Denis, even granting tax exemptions, and sent out missionaries across his kingdom, including sending Saint Amandus to Tournai. This mission resulted in the

---

[24] King Jean II had been captured by the Black Prince, eldest son of Edward III, at the battle of Poitiers in September 1356. Jean remained a prisoner, in extremely luxurious settings, in England until 1360, and would return to captivity voluntarily after his son broke the terms of his release in 1363 to die in the Savoy in April 1364. For the battle, Jean's captivity and the resultant instability in France see Sumption, *The Hundred Years' War*, vol. 2, 195–293; J. N. Palmer, 'The War Aims of the Protagonists and the Negotiations for Peace', in K. A. Fowler (ed.), *The Hundred Years War* (London: Longman, 1971), 51–74; F. Autrand, 'The Peacemakers and the State: Pontifical Diplomacy and the Anglo-French Conflict in the Fourteenth Century', in P. Contamine (ed.), *War and Competition between State Powers* (Oxford: Oxford University Press, 2000), 249–77.

[25] The feudal levy; for its use see C. Allmand, *The Hundred Years War* (Cambridge: Cambridge University Press, 1988), 93–5.

[26] *ORF*, vol. 3, 297–8; vol. 6, 538–41.

[27] de la Grange, 'Extraits analytiques des registres des consaulx de la ville de Tournai', 135.

[28] P. Fouracre and R. A. Gerberding (eds), *Late Merovingian France: History and Hagiography, 640–720* (Manchester: Manchester University Press, 2006); E. James, *The Franks* (Oxford: B. Blackwell, 1988), 230.

foundation of the monastery that became St-Amand's, which the late fifteenth-century Tournaisian writer Jehan de Nicolay described as being founded by Dagobert, meaning that Dagobert had connections to Tournai and so could be considered as something of a local hero.[29]

The note could, conceivably, refer to Dagobert II (d. 679). This later Dagobert was a less militaristic king, exiled to Ireland for twenty years and murdered shortly after his return; his violent death saw him become venerated as a saint in the monastery he had founded in Stenay-sur-Meuse, in the Ardennes.[30] Whether the crossbowmen meant Dagobert I or II, or indeed even if they were deliberately being ambiguous and simply wished to claim ancient status, the claim linked the guild to an ancient tradition of loyalty to the monarchy, just as the town prided itself on its loyalty.

The Tournai guild, like the Ghent guild, used its own version of its past to present itself as a prestigious and privileged group. Shooting guilds are not unique in making such claims: the Jousters of the White Bear of Bruges were named for Count Baldwin 'Iron Arm' (d. 879), who is said to have driven the 'White Bears' from Flanders. The winner of the annual contest was a 'Forester', in honour of the early counts.[31] Both jousters and shooters in Flanders were aware of the history of their counts and linked their foundations to great Flemish heroes, identifying themselves as separate and special groups, so as to create an internal identity dependent on the distant *Flemish* past, not on the princes or lords of their day.

Much historiography has placed guilds' origins in princely hands, while guilds themselves looked to a distant past for an honourable identity. The guilds' own myths can never be entirely disproved, however unlikely they seem. Equally, the influence of princely charters should not be ignored; but for a stronger sense of when guilds became recognised groups, and what sorts or organisation did occur, we must turn to town accounts and fourteenth-century urban sources. Archery and crossbow guilds were civic groups, so it seems logical to look to civic sources for their origins and development.

The earliest town accounts, whether from Ghent and Bruges before 1300 or Lille in 1301, all refer to shooters: 'schutters', 'zelscutters' or 'les arbaletriers'.[32] It is important to note that the shooters of c.1300 were not described as belonging

---

[29] I. Wood, *The Merovingian kingdoms, 450–751* (London: Longman, 1994), 154–5; J. M. Wallace-Hadrill, *The Long-Haired Kings: And Other Studies in Frankish History* (London: Methuen, 1962), 90–100, 182, 230; E. James, *The Origins of France: From Clovis to the Capetians, 500–1000* (London: Macmillan, 1982), 140–3; Jehan Nicolay (ed. F. Hennebert), *Kalendrier des Guerres de Tournay (1477–1479)* (Bruxelles: Aug. Decq, 1853), 105.

[30] Wood, *Merovingian kingdoms*, 231–4; Wallace-Hadrill, *Long-Haired Kings*, 238–9; James, *Origins of France*, 151

[31] J. Dumolyn, 'Une Idéologie urbain "Bricolée" en Flandre médiévale: les *Sept Portes de Bruges* dans le manuscrit Gruuthuse (debut du XVe siècle)', *RBPH* 88 (2010), 1052–3; A. Van den Abeele, *Ridderlijk Gezelschap van de witte beer* (Brugge: Walleyn, 2000), 85–91.

[32] Vuylsteke, *Gentsche stads – en baljuwsrekeningen 1280–1336*, vol. 1. 41, 46, 52, 62, 67, 69 ; E. Gailliard and L. Gilliodts-Van Severen, *Inventaire des archives de la Ville de Bruges*

to guilds, but they may well have been the seeds from which the guilds would grow and develop. In looking at the craft guilds of Bruges, Dumolyn has shown that the groups originated as organisations of mutual aid. As civic governors realised that the proto-guilds could not be suppressed, they took control and supervised them, issuing ordinances and regulations in the 1250s and 1260s. By the 1280s, craft guilds emerged as legally incorporated groups, and a generation later they began to push for civic power and representation.[33] It is likely that the shooting guilds developed in a similar manner, with archers and crossbowmen forming groups to help each other financially, if injured in war, as well as spiritually, to say prayers for the dead. Later civic governors began to supervise and patronise them, bringing them into the urban body politic. It is likely that groups of archers and crossbowmen existed in the very early fourteenth century, if not earlier, supporting one another and practising their skills. In considering the origins of the Ghent crossbow guild, Boone has linked civic military prowess to the political situation in thirteenth century Flanders and emphasised clearly the difficulties of pinning down specific 'foundation' dates for any guild.[34]

The shooting guilds appear in civic sources only a generation or so after the craft guilds were recognised as legally incorporated groups in most towns. These early references are one-line statements in town accounts; they show that guilds existed, but reveal very little about what form their organisation took. Guild ordinances and regulations appear in the second half of the fourteenth century – these will be analysed in more depth in the next two chapters.

The sources used here are civic financial accounts that set out, year by year, the total incomes and expenditures of the urban treasurer(s). Flemish town accounts are organised and formulaic, and within a few years of their first appearance become remarkably similar across the region. First the large receipts are set out, particularly taxes on wine, and then smaller incomes, including taxes on property and goods brought into the city. After all the incomings has been set out and totalled the accounts then list all of the outgoings. The level of detail in outgoings varies but, in general, patterns emerge, with civic costs coming first, then the costs of gifts and other civic expenses.[35] Towns had paid taxes to their lords and organised some of their own finances before the fourteenth century. The decision to begin to write down a record of their incomes and outgoings,

---

9*volumes* (Bruges: Gailliard, 1871–85), vol. 2, 376, 389, 411. Richebé, *Compte de recettes et dépenses de la ville de Lille*, 56, 65–7, 72.

[33] Dumolyn, 'Economic Development, Social Space and Political Power in Bruges', 53–5.
[34] Boone, 'De Sint-Jorisgilde van Kruisboogshutters', in *Gedenkboek*, 9–18.
[35] Introduction to Vuylsteke, *Gentsche Stads – En Baljuwsrekeningen, 1280–1336*, vol. 1; A. Vandewalle, 'De oudste stadsrekeningen van Brugge. Bij een nieuwe editie', *ASEB* 133 (1996), 139–43; M. van der Heijden, 'Stadsrekeningen, stedelijke financiën en historisch onderzoek', *NEHA-Bulletin: Tijdschrift voor de economische geschiedenis in Nederland* 13 (1999), 129–66; R. W. M. Van Schaïk, 'Oorsprong en croege ontwikkeling van stadsrekeningen in de Nederlanden', *ASEB* 133 (1996), 144–62.

and to check them year on year, is linked a civic sense of pride, which will be discussed in more depth shortly.

There may, beyond Flanders, be hints of the transitional stage when shooters started to act as guilds. In the small town of Floreffe in the province of Namur, in 1698 new registers were copied out containing the statutes and ordinances of different urban groups. The rights of the crossbowmen included a charter from Count Guy of Flanders, also marquis of Namur, issued in 1295 and setting up a 'compagnions d'arbaletries' of twenty men who received tax exemptions in return for being ready to serve.[36] No medieval version of the charter survives, and a copy made four centuries after the fact must be treated with great care; it is entirely possible that this is the same sort of foundation myth as is present in Tournai and Ghent, as discussed above. It is also possible that the Floreffe charter hints at what was happening informally elsewhere, and that groups of shooters were starting to be organised at the very end of the thirteenth century, although they were yet to develop into sophisticated shooting guilds.

Archers and crossbowmen began to receive civic funds, implying civic recognition, in the 1310s and 1320s. The earliest solid reference to a shooting guild from Flanders that I have found is from Ghent, in the expenses of the 'present-master'. The 'master' was a civic official responsible for giving gifts, usually wine, to groups and individuals seen as important to civic society. Gifts were regularly given to visitors, messengers, lords and respected individuals or groups within urban society. In studying the present-master lists for the Burgundian period, Boone has shown that a third of recipients of civic wine (256 out of 792 individuals) were 'membres de l'élite politique'[37] from within the town, and the remaining gifts of wine went to visitors. It may be an obvious point, but it seems one worth emphasising, that the urban official responsible for demonstrating urban largesse distributed wine to residents as well as to visitors. It is in this list, in the context of the political elite and prestigious visitors, that the first firm reference to a Flemish shooting guild appears. In 1314 the present-master gave the crossbow guild of Saint George wine worth £12 8s 4d for its annual shoot. The archers of Saint Sebastian began to receive wine for their annual shoot in 1320;[38] the guild may have received funding earlier, but accounts for 1317–20 have not been preserved. A gift of wine emphasised that the archery and crossbow guilds were valued by the administrators of Ghent, and given wine when few other social or cultural groups were. It is also important to note that the grant of wine predates guild ordinances and privileges, which survive in Ghent from the 1360s.[39]

---

[36] P.-D. Browers, 'Les compagnies d'arbalétriers dans l'ancienne comte de Namur', *Annales de la société d'archéologie de Namur* 37 (1925), 142–6.
[37] Boone, 'Dons et pots-de-vin', 478–81.
[38] Vuylsteke, *Gentsche Stads – En Baljuwsrekeningen, 1280–1336*, vol. 1, 86, 158; Boone, "De Sint-Jorisgilde van Kruisboogshutters', in *Gedenkboek*, 7–15.
[39] SAG, 310, 2.2, f. 37r.

The Ghent records are the earliest and most detailed references to shooting guilds, but they are not unique. In Bruges the crossbowmen were receiving money annually for their *papegay* shoot by 1336–37, decades before they had received any rights or charters.[40] In Lille, the first reference to shooting guilds is to be found in the accounts of the annual procession of Notre Dame de la Trielle, with the *Confreres* of the crossbow guild being paid to attend the procession in 1323. By 1330 the Lille crossbowmen were receiving annual gifts of wine for their papegay shoot, the event at which the best shooter from within the town would be selected. The Lille records are complete for this period, but have been badly damaged by damp, so an earlier reference to the guilds may have been lost.[41] Generally, then, Flemish towns began to sponsor their guilds between 1314 and 1330, giving them wine for cultural and devotional events, but not for military service. As organised groups, as recognised guilds, the shooters gained recognition in the second and third decades of the fourteenth century; but this is not to say they were *founded* in these years – such a term is not appropriate for the development of guilds.

It is no coincidence that the first half of the fourteenth century, the period in which guilds began to receive civic support, was an important period for the expression of civic identities. By 1300, the great Flemish towns had been growing in size for two centuries, although they were passing their economic peak. The towns were investing in monuments to pride and their autonomy. As Coomans has observed, the towns and their mercantile 'elites' had 'a strong sense of their own economic and political power', embodied in new building projects, new representations of status, even of urban pride.[42] In Ghent new ramparts were begun around 1300, plans for a 'proud Belfry with corresponding Cloth Hall' were drawn up and craft guilds entered civic politics, although of course the 'old patriciate' was never fully removed.[43] Around 1300 Bruges was one of the most prosperous towns in northern Europe.[44] A new hall (Waterhalle) was built between 1284 and 1295; in addition the town took 'civic responsibility' for

---

[40] SAB, 216, rekeningen 1336–7, f. 100.
[41] AML, CV, 16016, f. 21v; AML, CV, 16020, ff. 29–31.
[42] T. Coomans, 'Belfries, Cloth Halls, Hospitals, and Mendicant Churches: A New Urban Architecture in the Low Countries around 1300', in A. Gajewski and Z. Opačić (eds), *The Year 1300 and the Creation of a New European Architecture* (Turnhout: Brepols, 2007), 185–7.
[43] Prevenier and Boone, 'The "City-State" Dream', 81–3.
[44] R. Van Uytven, 'Stages of Economic Decline; Late Medieval Bruges', in J-M. Duvosquel and E. Thoen (eds), *Peasants and Townsmen in Medieval Europe* (Gent, 1995), 259–69; J. Marechal, 'Le Départ de Bruges des marchands étrangers aux XVe et XVIe siècles', *ASEB* 88 (1951), 1–41; W. Brulez, 'Brugge en Antwerpen in de 15e en 16e eeuw; een tegenstelling?', *TVG* 83 (1973), 15–37; P. Stabel, 'From Market to Shop, Retail and Urban Space in Late Medieval Bruges', *UH* 9 (2006), 79–101; ibid 'Composition et recomposition'; W. Blockmans, 'Brugge als Europeen handelscentrum', in E. Aert, W. Blockmans et al. (eds), *Brugge en Europa* (Brugge, 1992), 41–56.

religious buildings and was investing in municipal ones. In the 1330s, around 12% of Bruges's annual budget was being spent on 'public works' and the civic rulers of Bruges, who included many craftsmen by the 1330s, invested in municipal buildings, demonstrating their invigorated sense of self. It was this atmosphere of civic pride and civic investment that gave rise to civic support for guilds and allowed the archery and crossbow guilds to flourish in Flanders earlier than elsewhere.

It was not just Ghent and Bruges that witnessed investment in civic space, civic pride and civic shooting guilds. The Ypres cloth hall and belfry were completed in 1304 and the belfry of Courtrai around 1307, as were other municipal buildings and walls across Flanders. Many such belfries feature on thirteenth- and fourteenth-century civic seals, highlighting a growing civic pride and sense of self. The cloth halls similarly demonstrated the power of the towns; though not adorned, they made their power clear through size and functionality.[45] It is against this backdrop of urban pride and urban control that shooting guilds first appear that invested in urban identity and urban protection.

In providing urban protection and enhancing urban pride, one might even compare the shooting guilds to town walls. Town walls had clear defensive purposes, but they also represented urban ideals and autonomy. Walls made the town into a closed space, even to some extent idealised space, politically, socially and economically separating urban space from the outside world. Within their walls, towns had their own rights, legislating more and more in the fourteenth century, governing the behaviour and actions of their citizens. Like the guilds, walls were integral to civic defence, and Flemish towns invested heavily in defence, not just in building walls but also in inspecting, maintaining and guarding them.[46] Walls protected towns; but more than this, they represented towns, just as the guilds did and just as civic buildings did. Such civic investments and growing sense of civic identity were important in shaping – literally and metaphorically – civic identity, while demonstrating municipal liberties and a corporate identity. To give just one example of this, in Bruges the procession of the Holy Blood, which will be discussed in more depth below, circumambulated

---

[45] G. Blieck, 'Le Château dit de Courtrai à Lille de 1289 à 1339: Une Citadelle avant l'heure', *Bulletin monumeltal* 3 (1997), 185–90; M. Boone and E. Lecupre-Desjardin, 'Espace vécu, espace idéalisé dans les villes des anciens Pays-Bas bourguignons', *RBPH* 89 (2011), 111–28; H. Pirenne, *Histoire de Belgique des origines a nos jours, tom. 1–4*, tom. 1 (5e edition, Bruxelles: La Renaissance du Livre, 1928) 179–88, 282–5, 197, 314–15, 437; P. Stabel, 'Markets in the Cities of the Late Medieval Low Countries: Retail, Commercial Exchange and Socio-Cultural Display', in S. Cavaciocchi, *Fiere e mercati nella integrazione delle economie europee, secc. XIII–XVII: atti della 'Trentaduesima settimana di studi', 8–12 maggio 200.* (Firenze: Le Monnier, 2001), 802–5.

[46] Contamine, 'Les fortifications urbaines au France à la fin du moyen âge', 23–47; G. Bliek and L. Vanderstraeten, 'Recherches sur les Fortifications de Lille au Moyen Âge', *RN* 70 (1988), 107–22; A. Salamagne, 'Les garnisons des villes et châteaux dans le Nord de la France aux XIVe et XVe siècles', *RN* 83, 707–29.

the walls, marking out the civic space.[47] Although facing political and economic crises in the first half of the fourteenth century, Flemish towns were investing in symbols of their own identity and emphasising their civic standing and power. The guilds embodied this desire to demonstrate civic strength and protect civic interests. As Cauchies has noted, the guilds appeared 'comme l'expression d'un enjeu de droit', representing the rights and values of their towns in numerous important ways.[48]

The archery and crossbow guilds were by no means the only festive groups to be recognised by their towns. Flemish towns were also home to urban jousters, the White Bear of Bruges and the Epinette of Lille being the most famous. As with the shooting guilds, it is hard to place a firm foundation date on the jousters. Several towns had funded urban jousts since the end of the thirteenth century, and Brown's analysis of the Bruges records shows that the jousters there 'constituted a specialised group' by the 1320s. The jousters continued their activities until the end of the fifteenth century, with great jousting events being held in civic market places that included the richest townsmen and many members of the nobility in regular spectacles.[49] As Brown and Buylaert have emphasised, the jousts were 'never mere flights of fancy'; rather, they were stages on which urban and noble relationships could be played out or redefined, and certain townsmen could demonstrate or enhance their standing and reputation – both of these roles that shooting guilds could also fulfil.[50] The shooting guilds may have influenced the development of the third group of civic performers, the chambers of rhetoric. These groups of urban dramatists, who competed in regional events and maintained social and religious activities, may have developed out of drama events within shooting competitions, or from dramatic parts of processions, and, like the shooters, they thrived on their regional competitions. Van Bruaene's studies of the groups have made clear their ability to work for harmony and for honour in competitions that could win pride as well as prizes and could promote peace as well as position.[51] As chapter three will show, many archers

---

[47] Brown, *Civic Ceremony*, 37–9.
[48] Cauchies, '"Service" du prince, "sûreté" des villes', 419.
[49] E. Van den Neste, *Tournois, joutes, pas d'armes dans les villes de Flandre à la fin du Moyen Âge (1300–1486)* (Paris: Ecole des chartes, 1996); C. Fouret, 'La violence en fête: la course de l'Epinette a Lille a la fin du moyen âge', *RN* 63 (1981), 377–90; Van den Abeele, *Ridderlijk Gezelschap van de witte beer*; Brown and Small, *Court and Civic Society*, 210–11, 225–30; Brown, *Civic Ceremony and Religion*, 137–50; 170–82; 254–9.
[50] A. Brown 'Urban Jousts in the Later Middle Ages: the White Bear of Bruges', *RBPH* 78 (2000) 315–30; Buylaert, 'Memory, Social Mobility and Historiography', 377–408.
[51] H. Liebrecht, *Les Chambres de Rhétorique* (Bruxelles: La Renaissance du Livre, 1948); A-L. Van Bruaene, 'The Chambers of Rhetoric in the (Southern) Low Countries; A Flemish-Dutch Project on Literary Confraternities', *Confraternitas* 16 (2005), 3–14; eadem, 'In Principio Erat Verbum. Drama, Devotion, Reformation and Urban Associations in the Low Countries', in C. Black and P. Gravestock (eds), *Early Modern Confraternities in Europe and the Americas* (Aldershot: Ashgate, 2006), 64–80; eadem,

and crossbowmen were parts of these other groups, and it is important to note that shooting guilds developed as *a* representation of the rights and values of their town, not *the only* representation of those rights and values.

Militias and Paramilitary Groups

The archery and crossbow guilds developed as an expression of urban rights in the early fourteenth century, but they did not develop in isolation. With their walls and their tradition of autonomy, the Flemish towns were military powers in their own right. As Stabel has shown, late medieval Flemish towns considered their military power essential to maintaining their political position, with well-organised and adaptable militias and a strong ideal of civic solidarity.[52] As will be shown, the archery and crossbow guilds were a leading part of civic military forces and important embodiments of civic solidarity. Yet shooting guilds were not the only martial groups in Flemish towns and the position of the paramilitary forces known as *Kaproenen*, as well as the militias, must also be considered before the military significance of the shooting guilds can be analysed.

In Ghent, Bruges and Ypres, the *Witte, Roed* and *Blauwe Kaproenen* (White, Red and Blue Hoods) were a form of police force or paramilitary organisation. In Bruges the Red Hoods were made up of forty to one hundred well-disciplined men, organised by quarters. They had to be *Poorters* (citizens) of good reputation chosen from among the craft guilds under the nine head-deans of the guilds and the six headmen of the *zestendelen* (six administrative areas of Bruges).[53] In Ghent the White Hoods could protect the town, providing escorts and acting for the good of their community. The *Kaproenen* were regulated and organised to protect civic interests and to arrest trouble makers; their ordinances promoted discipline and good reputation – and from first impressions it would seem they had much in common with the shooting guilds. Yet the *Kaproenen* were seen in rather different lights by contemporaries and by historians, emerging as violent and disreputable groups, in contrast to the honourable and disciplined archery and crossbow guilds.

Boone describes the *Kaproenen* as 'exporting terror and violence' in order to maintain urban privileges.[54] The *Witte Kaproenen* seem to have been particularly

---

Om Beters Wille. Rederijkerskamers en de Stedelijke cultuur in de Zuidelijke Nederlanden (1400–1650) (Amsterdam: Amsterdam University Press, 2008); eadem, 'Harmonie et honour en jeu; les competitions dramtiques et symboliques entre villes de Flamades et Brabaconnes aux quinziemes et sieziemes siecles', in M. Boone, E. Lecuppre-Desjardin and J.-P. Sossons (eds), *Le verbe, l'image et les représentations de la société urbaine au moyen âge* (Anvers: Garant, 2002), 227–78.

[52] Stabel, 'Militaire organisatie', 1049–71
[53] Stabel, 'Militaire organisatie', 1051–61.
[54] M. Boone, 'Gouverner les villes flamandes au Moyen Âge: aspects politiques, idélogiques et financiers', in J. A. Solórzano Telechea et al. (eds), *La gobernanza de la ciudad europea en la Edad Media* (Nájera: Instituto de Estudios Riojanos, 2011), 284–5.

violent: they attacked and killed Bruges workers on the Leie Canal before and during the Ghent War of 1379–85. In the same period their leader, Jan Yoens, ordered his men to kill the bailiffs sent to arrest him. Such violent actions against fellow Flemish workers and civic officials must be seen as dishonourable, and as going against the values that the towns so often tried to promote. As a result, the White Hoods were disbanded by Philip the Good in 1453, although they were briefly re-formed after the death of Charles the Bold and are recorded as attacking the town of Anthoing in 1478.[55] Such volatile groups had their uses for the towns, especially in periods of rebellion, but their brutality meant that they could not represent civic values. Far from building regional communities, the *Kaproenen* disrupted networks. The shooting guilds and the *Kaproenen* had no official relationship. It must be stressed that no overlap in membership can be found, although it must also be admitted that membership lists are scant for the fourteenth century. It is not impossible that some shooters were, as individuals, part of the *Kaproenen*, but the paramilitary, violent world of the *Kaproenen* was very different from the cultural and communal world of the shooting guilds, and the identities and purposes of the two organisations were very different.

The Hoods had their uses, but they were not reliable and did not represent the towns in defence or on the battlefield, as the shooting guilds did. With a membership drawn from the entire working population, the civic militias can be assumed to have been more representative of their towns. All craft guilds were obliged to send a certain number of men to the militias, as were members of the 'patrician' classes. Militia men, with their diverse mix of carpenters, butchers, weavers and all other craft guilds, tended to be less well trained or disciplined than the shooting guilds or the *Kaproenen*. Though less well trained, militias could quickly become skilled in the use of the pike; their fearsome *goedendags*[56] helped to secure victory at Courtrai in 1302. At the other end of our period, militia men were providing valuable service in 1477 as months of violence ensured that they became experienced fighters.[57] Late fifteenth-century militias included men trained in the use of gunpowder weapons, and the militias were used and supplied for defensive purposes, and may even have included naval units in coastal towns.[58] Civic militias could, then, be sophisticated and were certainly

---

[55] M. Vandermaesen, M. Ryckaert and M. Coornaert, *De Witte Kaproenen: de Gentse opstand (1379–1385) en de geschiedenis van de Brugse Leie* (Gent: Provinciebestuur Oost-Vlaanderen, 1979), 12–22, 42–3; Nicholas, *Metamorphosis*, 10; Arnade, *Realms of Ritual*, 107; Jehan Nicolay *Kalendrier des Guerres de Tournay*, 214–15.

[56] A goedendag was more like a very long club than a pike, roughly five feet long with a brutal spike on the end; it was extremely effective against a cavalry charge.

[57] Allmand, *Hundred Years War*, 58; Nicholas, *Medieval Flanders*, 192–202; Stabel, 'Militaire organisatie', 1049–71.

[58] K. DeVries, 'Provisions for the Ostend Militia on the Defense, August 1436', *JMMH* 3 (2005), 176–83; J. Huyttens, 'Recherches sur l'organisation militaire de la ville de Gand au Moyen Age', *Messanger des Sciences Historiques de Belgique* (1858), 413–52; J. F. Verbruggen, 'De orginasatie van de milite te Brugge in de XIVe eeuw', *ASEB* 87

important for urban defence and towns' sense of their own military significance. The militias were far larger than either the shooting guilds or the *Kaproenen*. The composition records of the Bruges militias have been used to better understand the make-up of the town, and a few older studies of militias exist, but both the militias and the *Kaproenen* would benefit from greater study.

The towns of Flanders were, then, investing in symbols of their own autonomy and were home to several paramilitary organisations. How the three military groups – guilds, Hoods and militia – worked together in practice is best illustrated by a Ghent wall-painting known as the *Leugemeete* (Figure 1). The image, showing the militia under their guild banners, armed and in armour, was discovered in the chapel of Saint John and Saint Paul in 1846. Although the chapel, along with the painting, was destroyed in 1911, copies were made and are now preserved in the Ghent STAM museum. Part of the image shows the Saint George guild at the front of the militia. The crossbow guild are under their banner and bear their weapons prominently, followed by contingents from each craft guild under their respective banners, bearing what look like pikes but may be *goedendags*.[59] The crossbowmen are in the front, as they should be, given that civic regulations stated that 'no one will stand before the banners of Ghent and Saint George' or of the count on military expeditions.[60] Both visual and written sources make clear that the guilds were a small part of the militias, but a leading part, and a part that attracted more than its fair share of funding (and therefore documentation) and so deserve analysis in their own right.

Guilds and Civic Defence

References to guilds defending their town, or being required to do so, are numerous. The role of guilds within civic defence is best understood through a case study. Lille has been used here partly for pragmatic reasons because – along with Ghent and Bruges – it has some of the oldest and most complete town accounts. But, just as importantly, Lille did not rebel during the period under consideration, and so all defences would be recorded and rewarded, meaning that we have more chance of finding a complete picture of guild activities across

---

(1950), 163–7; *Het Gemeenteleger van Brugge van 1338 tot 1340 en de namen van de Weerbare Mannen* (Bruxelles: Palais des Académies, 1962); 'De Getalsterkte van de ambachten in het Brugse gemeenteleger (1297–1340)', *Belgisch Tijdschrift voor Militaire Geschiedenis* 25:6 (1983, 1984) 461–80; and those translated by K. DeVries, 'Arms and the Art of War: The Ghentenaar and Brugeois Militia in 1477–79', *JMMH* 7 (2009) 135–46.

[59] The image is discussed in Prevenier and Boone, 'The "City-State" Dream', 84; reproduction in Gent, STAM, inv. 9555; H. Koechlin, *Chapelle de la Leugemeete a Gand. Peintures murales. Restitution* (Ghent: Vanmelle, 1936), 12–20; Pirenne, *Histoire de Belgique*, tom. 1, 297–8; M. Boone, 'De Sint-Jorisgilde van Kruisboogshutters', in *Gedenkboek*, 13–14; J. Baldewijns, 'Oudste voorstelling van de Gentse stadsmilities', in *Gedenkboek*, 33–8.

[60] SAG, 97, 2ter, zwarten boek f. 165v.

Figure 1. Reproduction of the Leugemeete wall painting, Ghent STAM inv. 9555 2/6 and inv. 9555 3/6, photograph by Michel Burez. Reproduced by permission of STAM © www.lukasweb.be – Art in Flanders vzw

the fourteenth and fifteenth centuries. As will be discussed in the next chapter, guilds could obscure their own records of any part played in rebellion.

In 1347 Lille, fearing the approach and pillage of English armies in the wake of the fall of Calais, ordered watches to be made of the walls. All able-bodied men were required either to watch or to pay money. Additional ordinances made clear that all members of the archery and crossbow guilds had to be present and would, unlike the rest, be paid for their service.[61] The guilds were not the sole defenders of their town, but they were a prominent part of the force Lille called up when invasion was feared, although in fact the town was not besieged by the English. Lille was in danger again in 1382; now a Flemish town, it felt itself to be threatened by the rebellious Ghent forces in the wake of the battle of Beverhoutsveld in which Ghent had defeated the Bruges forces.[62] Ghent was defeated a few months later at Roosebeke, but the months in between were ones of instability.[63] During those months the shooting guilds again demonstrated their military purpose and strong position within the civic forces. The Lille magistrates passed ordinances that guild-brothers should protect walls and must not leave the town. In addition, the town officials paid named guild-brothers to watch strategically important parts of the walls in this time of crisis.[64]

When threatened by attack in 1347, and again in 1382, Lille needed all of its citizens to step up, but placed particular importance on the archery and crossbow guilds. The role of the guilds in civic defence and as an integral part of Lille's strategy for self-protection continued into the fifteenth century. The guild-brothers were called on to watch the walls again as John the Fearless went to war in 1411, and after the death of Charles the Bold in 1477. Later still, from 1513 to 1515, the archery and crossbow guilds, and with them the culveriners' guilds, guarded the walls and protected the English artillery for the feast of the Emperor Charles V and the English King Henry VIII.[65] For eighteen months the guilds repeatedly protected the town, and the great lords and their goods within the town. From the mid-fourteenth century to the early sixteenth century, the guilds were Lille's first choice for civic defenders.

The archery and crossbow guilds, and later the culveriners' guilds, protected Lille from besieging armies, allowing for civic self-defence and so enhancing civic autonomy. Threats did not come simply from invading armies and warring forces; towns also worked to keep their hinterlands safe from criminals and roving bandits. In 1488 the aldermen of Lille sent their shooting guilds out to

---

[61] AML, CV, 16045, ff. 11–14v.
[62] For the battle K. DeVries, 'The Forgotten Battle of Bevershoutsveld, 3 May 1382: Technological Innovation and Military Significance', in M. Strickland (ed.), *Armies, Chivalry and Warfare in Medieval Britain and France: Proceedings of the 1995 Harlaxton Symposium* (Stamford: Harlaxton Medieval Studies, 1998), 289–303.
[63] J. Sumption, *The Hundred Years War volume 3* (London: Faber and Faber, 2009), 456–510.
[64] AML, OM, 373, f. 3v, f. 6v, f. 12v. f. 35.
[65] AML, CV, 16112, ff. 19v–22v; 16155, ff. 78–81v; 16216, ff. 65–80; 16249–51; 16251, ff. 197v–204.

a nearby stronghold in the forests, called Rorques, which had been seized by a military band, described as 'pillagers', who were attacking local labourers and destroying houses. Crossbowmen, archers and hand-gunners drove out the 'undesirables'.[66] As noted in the introduction, the long regency for Philip the Fair brought instability; it is not clear who the 'pillagers' were but they are likely to have been unpaid soldiers or mercenaries. In defending the hinterlands and roads in and out of Lille, the guilds were part of the defence for keeping the town safe and ensuring that Lille maintained a good reputation.

The Lille records make clear that the guilds were also expected to help the sergeants and other officers in keeping the peace and capturing violent offenders within civic society. Both the archers and the crossbowmen of Lille were expected to aid sergeants in arresting violent offenders, but in 1463 one archer, Colin Carlier, refused to fulfil these obligations. Carlier had, 'in great irreverence of justice', refused to help the sergeant of Lille to apprehend a violent young man and had rudely told the sergeant to 'tie the boy up so he could not bite'.[67] Carlier was punished for failing to live up to the civic ideals embodied by the guilds and was sent on pilgrimage to Saint Lamberts in Liège. Such a punishment is telling; by temporarily removing Carlier from the town, the pilgrimage would allow peace to return, as well as keep Carlier from his business and his community. The seriousness with which Carlier's refusal to help with civic justice was treated shows that the guilds' assistance to peace keeping was not simply an empty gesture. We have seen that rules on numbers of members could be broken, but it is clear that shooting guilds did have to follow other rules and that their responsibility to aid justice and peace keeping was an integral part of their prominent place in civic society and that their duties to the town had to be upheld.

The Lille sources are the fullest, but scattered references make clear that across the county guilds were a part of civic security. In numerous settings, guilds helped to ensure that great civic events were carried out securely and honourably, and they were often called upon to form guards of honour for princes and civic officials. During Philip the Bold's entrance into Bruges in 1369, during Margaret of York's entrance into Lille in 1471 and in countless other entrances, the archery and crossbow guilds were part of the 'dialogue' made in entrance ceremonies.[68] In 1484 the shooting guilds escorted the young Philip the Fair into Bruges, meeting him beyond the town. Guarding visiting princes had, of course, a military significance, but far more important was the symbolic role

---

[66] AML, CV, 16227, f. 109.
[67] AML, RM, 15917, f. 114.
[68] Brown and Small, *Court and Civic Society*, 165–7; W. Blockmans, 'Le dialogue imaginaire entre princes et sujets: Les Joyeuses Entrées en Brabant en 1494 et 1496', *PCEEB* 34 (1994), 35–53; N. Murphy, 'Between England, France and Burgundy: Amiens under the Lancastrian Dual Monarchy, 1420–35', *French History* 26 (2012), 143–63; Lecuppre-Desjardin, *La Ville des Cérémonies*, 136–58.

at work. The guilds would have been among the first urban representatives to greet the prince, and so would be seen by him and his retinue as representatives of the town; they would then enter the town with the prince and so be seen as close to him by other townsmen.[69] In addition to positioning themselves close to the prince, the guilds also accompanied civic authorities in and out of civic space. For instance, in August 1456 the Courtrai shooting guilds escorted their aldermen all the way to Oudenaarde and back again, providing the town representatives with security and an honourable guard, thus advertising loyalty and corporate aspirations.[70] Guarding civic officials again made clear the guilds' prominence and prestige, linking them to civic power and even to civic pride.

Service within Princely Armies

Archery and crossbow guilds developed, with civic support, into groups that helped to maintain civic defence forces and keep towns and their hinterlands safe. In addition, the guild-brothers were also called on numerous occasions to go beyond their walls, to serve their count and their county. Rather than attempting to construct a long narrative of all guild service to all princely armies, here the significance of the guilds within larger armies will be demonstrated through five short case studies. By analysing the princely campaigns of 1356, 1411, 1436, 1474 and 1479, the participation of guilds within larger civic hosts serving their princes can be better appreciated. In each example some background of the campaign will be provided before the significance of guilds within a far larger host is set out. Just as importantly, attention will also be paid to how the campaigns were remembered by contemporary civic observers. Together, these case studies will show that guilds represented their towns in war.

The five campaigns are not taken to be representative of all princely military efforts across the fourteenth and fifteenth centuries; rather, these examples have been selected to demonstrate continuity in the military responsibilities of the guilds. It will be shown that guilds served their lords in arms before, during and after the Burgundian period. The durability of guild service is important. It is likely that guilds served in a meaningful way before 1356, although only scattered references survive, and it is just as likely that they continued to serve – as they continued to guard their towns – after 1479. These five campaigns show guilds as loyal and valued soldiers of the Dampierre counts, the Valois dukes and their Habsburg successors.

Louis of Male became count of Flanders on the death of his father in 1346. Louis of Nevers had been extremely Francophile, and at times naïve; ruling as a

---

[69] Gilliodts-van Severen, *Archives de la ville de Bruges*, vol. 4, 239–40.
[70] H. Godar, *Histoire de la gilde des archers de Saint Sébastien de la ville de Bruges* (Bruges: Stainforth, 1947), 87–8; AML, CV, 16210, f. 161r–v; OSAOA, microfilm 687, rekeningen 1455–6, f. 216; Brown and Small, *Court and Civic Society*, 166.

French prince, he inspired little support or loyalty in his county.[71] Louis of Male, by contrast, moved away from his father's policies. He resided in Flanders and looked to Flemish interests, although he also worked to limit the powers of the Three Towns. He was the first count to issue charters in Flemish, and he refused to perform homage to the king of France for his French lands until the towns of Walloon Flanders were returned. Flanders, under Louis, was strong and looking to expand. The Scheldt town of Dendermonde had been incorporated in 1355, and in 1356, when a dispute over his wife's dowry led to Louis's claiming the town of Mechelen, the Flemish towns supported their count in the so-called war of Brabant succession.[72] An analysis of this short and successful campaign highlights not only the strength of Louis and his county as a whole, but also the displays of civic strength and civic support for Louis, represented by the guilds.

The war began with a contest for control of the River Scheldt, the great Flemish trade artery. Flemish control of the river would have boosted civic incomes as well as princely power, and the civic support for this campaign can be seen in the naval force that besieged Antwerp in August 1356.[73] This force included urban contingents, among whom particular attention was paid by contemporaries to the shooting guilds. The besieging army included the Bruges archery guild, led by its headman Jan van Varssenare.[74] In the same month a powerful Flemish land force moved through Brabant, burning property and threatening the towns, arriving before Brussels on 12 August. Louis and his army won a resounding victory at the battle of Asse on 17 August, where the host included noblemen and the urban militias as well as the shooting guild-brothers.[75] In the wake of the battle it was guilds, rather than the militias more generally, that were rewarded. The Oudenaarde Saint George guild, for instance, was awarded an annual grant of wine for its part in the battle.[76] Equally, in memorialising the event, civic writers praised their guilds, rather than the militias. The *Breve Chronicon Flandriae* eulogises the heroism of the Dendermonde crossbowmen and their

---

[71] Nicholas, *Metamorphosis*, 2–10; idem, *Medieval Flanders*, 209–24; M. Vandermaesen, 'Kortrijk in vuur en bloed. De gevangenneming van graaf Lodewijk II van Nevers omstreeks 17 juni 1325', *De Leiegouw* 32 (1990) 149–58; idem, 'Toverij en politiek rond de troon van Lodewijk II van Nevers graaf van Vlaanderen. Een merkwaardige aanklacht (1327–1331)', *HMGOG* 44 (1990) 87–98.

[72] Nicholas, *Medieval Flanders*, 225–6; S. Boffa, *Warfare in Medieval Brabant 1356–1406* (Woodbridge: Boydell Press, 2004), 3–9; F. Blockmans, 'De erfstrijd tussen Vlaanderen en Brabant in 1356', *Bijdragen en mededelingen van het historisch genootschap Utrecht* 69 (1955).

[73] M. A. Goovaerts, 'La flotte de Louis de Male devant Anvers en 1356', *BCRH* 13 (1886), 33–58.

[74] Godar, *Histoire des archers*, 59–71; Gilliodts-Van Severen *Inventaire des chartres, table analytique*, 18–19.

[75] Boffa, *Warfare in Medieval Brabant*, 6–7; E. de Dynter, *Chroniques des Ducs de Brabant*, 4 vols (Bruxelles: Hayez, 1854–1860), vol. 3, 548–9; Nicholas, *Medieval Flanders*, 266–7.

[76] OSAOA, gilden 507/II/1A.

commander 'Jean dit Longus', with barely a mention given to the militias.[77] The guilds were the only parts of the army that contemporaries focused on; they were not the only force present, but they were representatives of their towns.

Further evidence of the significance of guild support to Flemish rulers can be seen in the events of the reign of John the Fearless. John did not visit Flanders until 1398, but on his entries in 1405, after the deaths of his parents, he agreed to reside in Flanders and to answer requests in Flemish.[78] As opposition to John grew in France, he needed Flanders more and more, and so, as will be discussed in chapter four, he took part in urban events, including crossbow competitions. When the League of Gien formed against him in France in 1410, with the aim of 'rescuing' the mad King Charles VI from his influence,[79] John had to rely on his domains in Burgundy and the Low Countries. That the towns supported John in his wars, despite refusing subsidies in previous years, is shown by the force that he gathered around Douai in August 1411, which included the urban militias as well as nobles from all of his lands. The militias were, as in 1356, led by the shooting guilds, including ten crossbowmen from Lille, eleven from Ninove, 120 archers and an unspecified number of crossbowmen from Bruges.[80] The army moved quickly through Vermandois, capturing the town of Ham on 14 September. Again, civic pride in such success is clear, with the Ghent *Memorieboek* proudly noting that Ham had been 'conquered by the citizens of Ghent'.[81] The campaign attracted some enthusiastic support, but John's army could not stay in the field indefinitely.[82] The momentum of 1411 could not be maintained, but the guilds had, in the short term, proved an important part of a larger ducal force.

The guilds were again called into ducal service for the siege of Calais in 1436, although under rather different circumstances than the previous campaigns we have discussed. Philip the Good was not successful in his siege of the English-held port and he had far less Flemish support in the attack; indeed many writers have assumed that his plan was doomed to fail.[83] Flanders, as we have seen, had always been in a precarious balance between France and England. When Philip changed his allegiance, recognising Charles VII, rather than Henry

---

[77] *Breve chronicon Flandriae* in Smet, *Recueil des chroniques*, vol. 3, 548–51.
[78] Nicholas, *Medieval Flanders*, 323–6.
[79] Small, *Late Medieval France*, 132–5; R. Vaughan, *John the Fearless; The Growth of Burgundian Power* (London: Longman, 1966: Woodbridge: Boydell, 2002), 67–85.
[80] Vaughan, *John the Fearless*, 87–96; B. Schnerb, *Jean sans Peur, le Prince Meurtrier* (Paris: Payot, 2005), 513–548; idem, *Les Armagnacs et les Bourguignons: la maudite guerre* (Paris: Perrin, 1988), 101–25; AML, CV, 16155, f. 80; AGR, CC, 37085, ff. 10v–11; L. A. Vanhoutryve, *De Brugse Kruisbooggilde van Sint-Joris* (Handzame: Familia et patria, 1968), 54–6; SAB, 210, accounts 1411, ff. 104–118v; SAB, 385, Sint Jorisgilde, register met ledenlijst enz. 1321–1531, f. 68; Godar, *Histoire des archers*, 89–93.
[81] P. J. van der Meersch (ed.), *Memorieboek der stad Ghent: van 't Jaar 1301 tot 1793*, 4vols (Gent: Annoot-Braeckman, 1852–1861), vol. 1, 154.
[82] Vaughan, *John the Fearless*, 145–8; Schnerb, *Jean sans Peur*, 513–48.
[83] J. Doig, 'New Source for the Siege of Calais in 1436', *EHR* 110 (1995), 404–7.

VI of England, as king of France at Arras in 1435, Flanders had to change its allegiance too, risking the all-important wool trade. Recognising the challenges of encouraging Flanders to support him, Philip made valuable concessions, agreeing not to change the coinage, prohibiting the sale of English cloth in all his domains and pledging to use only Flemings as Flemish officials.[84] Despite his best efforts, the advance to Calais did not go smoothly. The siege began on 9 July but, by the time the fleet arrived on the 27th, the militias of Ghent and Bruges had been defeated, and both left the next day. It is not, however, the failure of the siege of Calais that concerns us here but, rather, the role that the archery and crossbow guilds played in the host, and Philip's confidence in calling them out.

The Burgundian host was an impressive one, including great lords, artillery and urban contingents from the two Burgundies and the Low Countries, as well as the fleet under the command of Simon de Lalaing.[85] Among the Flemish militias the guilds were just one part of the force, but they were a significant and leading part, as is shown by the civic expenses. Douai had provided £2,400 as well as the service of its militia and guildsmen. The Bruges contingent included thirty archers among the militia of 450 men.[86] As the militia and archers were both present it is extremely likely that the Bruges crossbowmen were present at the siege too, but their new guild book, begun in 1437, does not to mention the siege or subsequent rebellion.[87] Ghent sent its militia, and members of shooting guilds were paid separately in the town accounts.[88] The Ypres chronicle *Wondrous Happenings* described the Ypres crossbowmen as an 'outstanding group' among the civic militia as they left for the siege.[89] As noted, the Olivier van Dixmuide who wrote at least part of the chronicle was headman of the great crossbow guild, and so he may have been exaggerating so as to praise himself and his guild-brothers. Yet other accounts are similar; the town of Oudenaarde sent its militia in 1436, but included special expenses for a new banner for the Saint George guild and paid its headman £12 'for good advice' to the town before leaving for Calais. Even the small town of Ninove sent its shooting guilds as well as its militia, and here again a new guild banner marked them out as a leading part of the host.[90] Across Flanders, towns sent out a number of men and a good

---

[84] Nicholas, *Medieval Flanders*, 327–8.
[85] K. DeVries and R. D. Smith, *The Artillery of the Dukes of Burgundy, 1363–1477* (Woodbridge: Boydell Press, 2005), 230–6, 221–4; M. Somme, 'L'armée bourguignonne au siège de Calais', in P. Contamine and M. Keen (eds), *Guerre et société en France, en Angleterre et en Bourgogne XIV–XV siècle* (Villeneuve-d'Ascq: Université Charles de Gaulle. Centre d'histoire de la région du Nord et de l'Europe du Nord-Ouest, 1991), 196–213; Vaughan, *Philip the Good*, 74–84.
[86] DAM, EE4; Godar, *Histoire des archers*, 95–101.
[87] SAB, 385, Sint Jorisgilde, register met ledenlijst enz. 1321–1531.
[88] De Potter, *Jaarboeken*; SAG, 400, rekeningen, 15, ff. 43–49v.
[89] Olivier van Dixmude, *Merkwaerdige gebeurtenissen*, 148.
[90] Rantere, *Geschiedenis van Oudenaarde*, vol. 2, 39–57; OSAOA, CV, 1436–1448, microfilm 686; AGR, CC, 37103, ff. 5–7v.

deal of money and equipment to the siege of Calais and, across Flanders, the shooting guilds were given special attention in the fitting out of the militias. In 1436 the guilds were a small but privileged part of a larger host.

Despite the failure of the siege of Calais, 1436 was not the last time the towns and their guilds provided military service to Philip the Good. In 1453, the towns of Southern Flanders supported Philip against Ghent. His victorious host at the battle of Gavere included crossbowmen from Lille, archers from Douai and Aalst, hand-gunners from Mechelen and bowmen from Hainaut.[91] Although the militias were bigger, it was again the guilds that represented their towns and the guilds that attracted praise and privileges, even after the action had ended. In 1455, ten guild-brothers from the Douai archery guild found themselves banished from the town for unspecified crimes, but Philip pardoned them in recognition of the guilds' 'good and loyal service' in the wars with Ghent. The ducal pardon demonstrates that the service provided by the men of Douai was valued and was remembered by ducal and civic audiences. The reputation of the Douai archers extended to France too; in 1449 Charles VII requested that they should come to serve him at the siege of Beauvais.[92]

The continuation of service and the strength of interactions can further be seen in the campaigns of Charles the Bold. The relationship between Charles and the Flemish towns, especially Ghent, was famously volatile. Nicholas describes Charles's interactions with the towns as 'tactless' and 'petty or capricious', resulting in the towns becoming 'serious enemies' of the regime, while Vaughan points out a 'catalogue of urban suspicions and hostility' toward Charles.[93] Certainly civic authorities disliked their count, but towns and their military forces, as represented by the guilds, were still willing to serve in his armies, as analysis of his 1474 campaign to capture the imperial town of Neuss makes clear.

The siege of Neuss failed in its ambition to conquer the Rhine, or even to take control of Cologne in support of Charles's eastern allies.[94] With the conquest of Guelders in 1471–73, expansion towards Cologne did not seem as ridiculous as some have implied. Further direct access to the Rhine would, like control of the Scheldt in 1356, have been of benefit to the Flemish towns, allowing easier trade routes and free access to water routes within the Empire. Motivations remain debatable, but the Flemish towns provided a small but meaningful aid to Charles

---

[91] DAM, BB1; Olivier de la Marche (ed. M. Petitot), *Collection complète des mémoires relatifs à l'histoire de France, Olivier de la Marche*, 2vols (Paris: [s.n]: 1825) vol. 2, 68–9; P.-J. van Doren, *Inventaire des archives de la ville de Malines* (8vols, Malines: vol. 1–6: Van Velsen, vol. 6–8: Hermands, vol. 7–8: A. Olbrechts-De Maeyer, 1859–1886),vol. 3, 110–11; Cauchies, '"Service" du prince, "sûreté" des villes', 428–9.
[92] DAM EE14, 5.
[93] Nicholas, *Medieval Flanders*, 392–3; R. Vaughan, *Charles the Bold: The Last Valois Duke of Burgundy* (London: Longman, 1973; Woodbridge, Boydell, 2002), 39–40.
[94] J.-M. Cauchies, 'Charles le Hardi à Neuss (1474/5); folie militaire ou contrainte politique?', PCEEB 36 (1996), 105–16; Vaughan, *Charles the Bold*, 327–8; J.-P. Soisson, *Charles le Téméraire* (Paris: B. Grasset, 1997), 235–44.

in his siege at Neuss, and again it was the guilds as the leading contingents of the militias that attracted the praise and that were granted privileges.

The army that advanced to Neuss in July 1474 contained noblemen, English and Italian mercenaries and artillery as well as the urban contingents.[95] Within Charles's host were twenty archers from Lille, twenty archers, six crossbowmen, six hand-gunners and two varlets from Douai, thirty archers and sixty crossbowmen from Bruges and ninety crossbowmen from Mechelen.[96] The guilds were, once again singled out for praise from the towns and the prince. The Mechelen crossbow guild obtained a new and generous charter in 1475 in recognition of its notable service at Neuss. According to the charter, thirty-six out of the ninety crossbowmen sent to the siege had died, so the surviving guild-brothers received tax exemptions and greater freedom of movement.[97] The guild-brothers at Neuss were small in number, but when writers in Mechelen reflected on the value of their civic contribution to the siege, it was the crossbowmen whom they identified as representing the town in arms, and it was they who received ducal privileges.

A final example of the guilds in war demonstrates that the obligation, even willingness, to serve their prince and to represent their towns in war continued beyond the reigns of the Valois dukes. Mary of Burgundy's short reign (1477–82) was a period of division and rebellion, with the towns rapidly turning against her husband, Maximilian King of the Romans.[98] Yet the crisis that Flanders faced from French invasion meant that the towns were willing to provide men and money for ducal armies, whether by sending the militias to Spiers to defend the border against the French garrison at Tournai in 1477, or in providing manpower for Maximilian's armies.[99]

The Burgundian host at Guinegate was united and was representative of the new powers in the Low Countries. Maximilian marched towards Thérouanne with a modernised army; it may have been the first non-Swiss force to use the Swiss pike formation that had proved so effective against Maximilian's father-in-law two and a half years earlier. The events of 1479 also indicate a certain amount of disorder among the French, or at least an unwillingness to obey the king. Louis XI had ordered the garrison and his commanders not to leave Thérouanne

---

[95] M. Ballard, 'An Expedition of English Archers to Liège in 1467 and the Anglo-Burgundian Marriage Alliance', *Nottingham Medieval Studies* 34 (1990), 152–74; Strickland and Hardy, *Warbow*, 361–8; la Marche, *Mémoires*, vol. 2, 290–7; DeVries and Smith, *The Artillery of the Dukes of Burgundy*, 174–8.

[96] AML, CV, 16212, f. 130v; DAM, BB1, f. 41; Vanhoutryve, *De Brugse Kruisbooggilde*, 56–61; Godar, *Histoire des archers*, 80–137; SAB, 210, rekeningen 1475–6, f. 137.

[97] Doren, *Inventaire des archives de la ville de Malines*, vol. 1, 158; W. van den Steene, 'De deelneming van de Mechelse schutters aan het beleg van Neuss (1474–1475). Een erelijst van teruggekeerde gildebroeders van St. Sebastiaan', *Taxandria* 57 (1985) 185–97.

[98] Haemers, *Common Good*, 18–21, 59–67, 131–5, 216–26.

[99] Stabel, 'Militaire organisatie', 1058–61.

and not to give battle to the 'Flemings' and 'rebels', and yet they did, causing the king to react angrily in letters sent in early September.[100]

The army was composed of two flanks, one led by Engelbert, count of Nassau. Engelbert was not just an experienced military leader and knight of the Golden Fleece, but was also a member of the Bruges crossbow guild.[101] It is likely that Engelbert's position between court and civic cultures helped to unify the host in 1479 (the significance of aristocratic guild-brothers like Engelbert will be analysed in more depth in chapter four). As noted, Jean de Burgundy, illegitimate grandson of Philip the Good, died at the battle and many other nobles associated with the court of Charles the Bold were present, as were imperial cavalrymen. Also among the host were archery and crossbow guild-brothers from Lille and Bruges, again as smaller parts of larger militia but once again demonstrating loyalty and civic pride.[102] The battle, and indeed the complicated interactions between Maximilian and Louis XI in the North before the Treaty of Arras (1482), deserve further analysis, but it is important to note that guilds were part of a larger urban force willing to serve their lords in 1479, as they had been a century earlier for the good of Flanders.[103] The archery and crossbow guilds of Flanders were important parts of princely armies, able to defend their cities and to represent their towns on the battlefield during the fourteenth and fifteenth centuries.

Archery and crossbow guilds came into being in the second and third decades of the fourteenth century. It is very likely that archers and crossbowmen met and practised together earlier, as informal communities, but such informal, unwritten organisations cannot be analysed. Guilds were not 'founded' in a certain year by a certain lord; rather, they were funded by their civic authorities as cultural and social groups (these activities will be examined in more depth in the next two chapters) and as civic defenders. The first reference to guilds obtaining civic sums of money must be linked to civic expenditure on buildings and to decisions to record expenditure, for it was in the early fourteenth century that the towns of Flanders worked to present themselves as cultural and political powers. The rulers of Flanders gave rights to the guilds, recognising their role in civic defence, with considerations of security and protection influencing the desired (if not actual) size of many guilds. The shooting guilds, like their towns,

---

[100] J. Vaesen (ed.), *Lettres de Louis XI, roi de France*, 11vols (Paris: Renouard, 1883–1909), vol. 8, 50–72.

[101] G. Small, *Georges Chastelain and the Shaping of Valois Burgundy. Political and Historical Culture and Court in the Fifteenth Century* (Woodbridge: Boydell, 1997), 206–8; SAB, 385, Sint Jorisgilde, register met ledenlijst enz. 1321–1531, f. 3v.

[102] AML, CV, 16218, f. 106v; E. Richert, *Die Schlacht bei Guinegate, 7 August 1479* (Berlin: G. Nauck, 1907); J. F. Verbruggen, *De slag bij Guinegate 7 augustus 1479: de verdediging van het graafschap Vlaanderen tegen de koning van Frankrijk, 1477–1480* (Brussel: Koninklijk Legermuseum, 1993), 81–122; Delbrück, *History of the Art of War*, vol. 4, 4–9.

[103] Jean de Dadizeele (ed. A. Voisin), *Mémoires inédits de seigneur Jean de Dadizeele* (Bruges: Vandecasteele-Werbrouck, 1850), 93–104; Haemers, *Common Good*, 22–7.

created foundation myths for themselves as an important component of their group identity and purpose, which will be analysed in more depth in chapter three. Guilds emerged in towns with other paramilitary groups and were an integral part of civic defence and the protection of civic autonomy. Military matters and the guilds' military roles were important and durable; the guilds brought security to their towns and assisted in peace keeping. Their service on their town walls and in driving out criminals and their participation in larger princely hosts underlines their significance to the civic authorities and emphasises their central place within civic society, and how this fitted in with princely campaigns.

2

'Guild-brothers'

Guild Organisation and the Membership of the Archery and Crossbow Guilds of Bruges, 1437–81

In 1383 the bailey and aldermen of Douai set out the rights and privileges of their crossbow guild. The guild should elect a constable on Trinity Sunday who should be 'the most notable member of the *serment*' and who should have been 'sufficient', and the constable should then be presented to the aldermen to take his oath for the year 'as is the custom'. He was responsible for the guild's finances, and would be given money and wine by the aldermen to support the guild-brothers 'being together in community' on specified days for weekly shooting and for their annual papegay competition, for mass and for an annual meal. The detailed ordinance goes on to make clear that new members had to have a powerful bow, as well as suitable arms, and be skilled in shooting, as well as pay 36s to enter the guild. When the charter was confirmed by Philip the Bold in May 1400 a few additions were made, including the requirement that 'the said crossbowmen will be companions of honest life and good renown' and be bourgeois and residents of the town.[1]

The Douai charter provides a huge amount of detail on what was expected of crossbowmen in the town, but it also raises a number of questions. How were guilds organised and run? How did one enter the archery and crossbow guilds? And, perhaps most crucially, who were the shooters? The first two questions will be answered with reference to sources from across Flanders and an effort made to consider geographical differences as well as commonalities across the region. In considering organisation and officials, the significance of unity and the strength of bonds formed within the shooting guilds can be appreciated. Such unity will be examined in more depth in the next chapter in considering the devotional and social internal workings of guilds. The focus here will be on the regulation and structure of guilds. In order to uncover what sorts of backgrounds the archers and crossbowmen came from, and in unpicking existing

---

[1]   ADN, B1147–12.681; part of the charter has been translated and discussed in L. Crombie 'The First Ordnances of the Crossbow Confraternity of Douai, 1383–1393', *Journal of Archer Antiquarians* 54 (2011), 92–6.

assumptions of elite or middle-class status, a case study is necessary. The second half of this chapter will briefly set out some regional patterns before turning to an in-depth prosopographical analysis of the archery and crossbow guilds of Bruges. Overall, the chapter will explain the construction and constitution of the archery and crossbow guilds and demonstrate their place within civic society.

Organisation and community

As we have seen, guild-brothers of the archery and crossbow guilds served in wars throughout the fourteenth and fifteenth centuries. The military influence of such service can be seen in some of the language and structures within the guilds, but military factors are not the only influence at work in guild organisation. Guilds began to achieve civic recognition in towns that were replete with other social and cultural organisations and that were investing in their sense of self and civic pride. It should come as no surprise, then, that shooting guilds drew on different models, influenced by craft guilds and devotional confraternities, to establish their own communities and sense of unity. In thinking about urban groups, the word *community* is almost ubiquitous. It is often used without consideration: a surprising number of works use the word in their title without unpacking the ideas behind it.[2] Burke has commented that *community* is 'at once an indispensable term and a dangerous one', and many others have commented that the term is overused.[3] It is overused, but if properly defined and explained it is a very useful term, and one that fits the shooting guilds and their organisation.

Looking at English urban groups, Dyers has noted the 'dilemmas' in discussing *communities* and proposed defining the term as groups of individuals with shared values and a 'collective sense of purpose'. This is a useful definition here, as guild-brothers certainly came together with a shared sense of purpose. Looking at an earlier period, Reynolds again emphasised communities as having collective activities and being controlled less by formal relations and more by 'shared values and norms'.[4] As we shall see, the shooting guilds certainly had formal relations, as well as shared values and a strong sense of honour. Perhaps

---

[2] Many are excellent, but have used *community* without analysing its meaning, e.g. M. Booney, *Lordship and the Urban Community, Durham and its Overlords, 1250–1540* (Cambridge: Cambridge University Press, 1990) refers to the 'urban community' and 'religious communities' without explaining the term; P. Oldfield, *City and Community on Norman Italy* (Cambridge: Cambridge University Press, 2009), 6–9 takes care to define 'Norman' and 'city', and 'communal' as 'an adjective meaning "that which relates to or benefits the community"', but not 'community' itself, though he does discuss other categories within the urban community, 184–225.

[3] P. Burke, *Languages and Communities in Early Modern Europe* (Cambridge: Cambridge University Press, 2004), 5; K. Farnhill, *Guilds and the Parish Community in Late Medieval East Anglia c. 1470–1550* (Woodbridge: York Medieval Press, 2001), 11–12.

[4] C. Dyer, 'Taxation and Communities in Late Medieval England', in R. Britnell and J. Hatcher (eds), *Progress and Problems in Medieval England* (Cambridge: Cambridge

the most detailed discussion of *community* comes from Kümin's 2013 study, *The Communal Age*. He also notes the issues of indiscriminate use of the term, before defining local communities as small-scale topographical units, with a more or less extensive membership using shared resources and institutions to exercise rights and duties on behalf of their fellow inhabitants, with collective responsibilities. He emphasises that local communities overlapped, and that such communities would be linked to corporations, guilds and parishes which might have shared socio-economic interests as well as devotional ones.[5] Shooting guilds certainly had shared resources and institutions, and utilised these to exercise their rights and duties with a collective sense of responsibility and a wish to keep order within the guild. As we shall see, their membership overlapped with other communities, but it will be demonstrated that archery and crossbow guild members came together with a 'collective sense of purpose', exercised their rights and were communities.

The archery and crossbow guilds were communities; this should not be taken to mean that all guild-brothers were equal in status. Rather, hierarchy was a central part of guild structure and organisation. The highest guild official, elected usually for life, was the headman (*hooftman*), an important local figure who could help to raise or maintain the guild's standing within urban society. In Bruges the archers often chose headmen from powerful patrician[6] families – for example, Jacob Adornes, who was co-founder of the Jerusalemkerk, alderman, civic-treasurer and courtier of Philip the Good and was elected headman by 1454.[7] The crossbowmen also selected men of standing, including the patrician Symoen van Aertricke and Knight of the Golden Fleece Lodewijk van Gruuthuse, who will be discussed in more depth in chapter four. Headmen were not just prestigious individuals, but were active guild-brothers, seen as leaders but also as brothers.

The practical organisation of guilds, and efforts to maintain their shared sense of purpose, were undertaken by annually elected officials. As noted for Douai, this man was a constable, while for most Flemish-speaking towns the same official was known as a dean. He undertook many of the guild's collective responsibilities, in particular managing the annual money it received from members and civic funds. In having an annually elected official who should not have held office in consecutive years, the archery and crossbow guilds were being governed in the same sort of way as craft guilds. Craft guilds elected deans, who should not have held office in consecutive years, as well as other officials, usually

---

University Press, 1996), 168–9; S. Reynolds, *Kingdoms and Communities in Western Europe 900–1300* (Oxford: Oxford University Press, 1997), 2–3.

[5] B. Kümin, *The Communal Age in Western Europe, c.1100–1800, Towns Villages and Parishes in Pre-Modern Society* (Houndmills: Palgrave Macmillan, 2013), 2–4; *The Shaping of a Community, The Rise and Reformation of the English Parish, c.1400–1560* (Aldershot: Ashgate, 1996), 1–3.

[6] This term will be explained below, pp. 72–3.

[7] BASS, rekeningboeken 1454–6, vol. 2, f. 10.

called 'finders', to ensure that regulations were followed and to maintain their own collective sense of purpose.[8] The election process, or indeed which guild-brothers could hold office, is unfortunately not documented for the shooting guilds. Elections themselves were held on significant days: in Lille the archers elected their dean on the same day as they shot the *papegay*,[9] while in Aalst the crossbowmen did so on Saint George's day, 23 April.[10] There are some hints that being a constable was not entirely desirable: a charter from Nivelles adds that, if elected to office, crossbowmen could not refuse, and if they did so they would be fined 10s.[11] Similarly in Dendermonde, once chosen to be a constable a member could not refuse, on pain of being removed from the confraternity and being required to pay double what his death-fee would have been, while the Douai register notes simply that guild-brothers could not refuse to serve as constable.[12] To try to understand how shooting guild constables were elected, we can look to other groups, as it is clear that shooting guilds used the urban models around them to form their own communities.

For much of our period, civic aldermen in the great Flemish towns were appointed by committal officials. Yet their election process took great care to emphasise that the best and most honest men had been chosen, and that gifts and feasts were not linked to corruption. The presentations of the newly elected 'good men' to their urban society became a means of expressing the power of the newly elected individual, as well as the power of their office, to the town at large.[13] The shooting guilds, which included aldermen, employed the same means of communication and used the same techniques to legitimise both the power of the individual dean and the dean as representative of the guild. In Douai, as well as being respectable, the constable had to be 'free from dishonesty', and 'sufficient',[14] and so serve guild values. The Lille crossbowmen, from 1443, had two constables 'for the good honour and conduct' of the guilds, of whom the senior constable would 'control' all cases of 'disruption or questions' between the *confreres* and punish 'ruffians' within the guilds.[15] In Aalst the constable was

---

[8] J. De Groot, J. D'Hondt and P. Vandermeersch, *Brugse ambachten in documenten, de schoenmakers, timmerlieden en schrijnwerkers (14de–18de eeuw) door Andre Vandewalle* (Brugge: Gemeentebestuur, 1985), especially 13–18; Nicholas, *Medieval Flanders*, 202–3; for the dean's ability to 'articulate his opinons' and role in meetings see J. Dumolyn and J. Haemers, '"A Bad Chicken was Brooding", Subversive Speech in Late Medieval Flanders', *PP* 214 (2012), 45–78.

[9] AML, PT, 5883, ff. 28–31.

[10] ASAOA, 4, boek met den haire, ff. 71v–73.

[11] Le Bon, *L'Ancien serment des arbalétriers*, 5–9.

[12] *Ordonnances de Philippe le Hardi*, vol. 2, 297; DAM, Arbalestiers de Douay, 24II 232, f. 5–5v.

[13] J. van Leeuwen, 'Un rituel de transmission du pouvoir: le renouvellement de la Loi à Gand, Bruges et Ypres (1379–1493)', *RN* 362 (2005), 763–89.

[14] DAM, Arbalestiers de Douay, 24II232, f. 1v.

[15] AML, PT, 5883, ff. 28–31.

to stop any 'animosity or troubles' between brothers.[16] The constables organised their guilds, they kept accounts and they kept order and, in doing so, promoted shared values and maintained a shared sense of honour.

Below the constables or deans were officials responsible for ten men. Such officials may be linked with military training and service, but could just as easily be linked to competitions, which included teams of around ten shooters. French sources simply called these men '*dixeniers*'; Flemish sources occasionally call them *dixeniers* or *proviseurs*. In regulations, their number is specified, so Aalst should have had sixty crossbowmen with six *dixeniers*, keeping order and ensuring that the guild-brothers practised their shooting as required.[17] Guilds were expected to practise every week in their gardens, and many towns paid them to do so. In Lille ten men shot each Sunday, led by their *dixenier*, and were then rewarded with 12s for wine to be drunk in 'recreational assembly'.[18]

Some, but by no means all, shooting guilds had a varlet. Among the crossbowmen of Douai, the varlet called the men to shoot, notified brothers of the annual meal and informed them of deaths so that they could attend the funeral. By 1444 the varlet was being provided with a livery at civic expense, showing that his role in bringing together the crossbowmen was valued by civic authorities as well as by the guild. A Lille membership list of 1415 includes 'Denys le Baiduyn varlet of the archers', but no surviving charter sets out his responsibilities. In Aalst, as in Douai, the varlet was responsible for calling the guild-brothers to the annual shoot. If a member missed a shoot, he had to pay a fine of 5s, but if the varlet had not told a member about it, he had to pay the fine. Varlets could also carry messages; in 1394 Lille gave 'Pierre Biuyen, varlet of the crossbowmen of Tournai 4 lots of wine' for telling them about a competition.[19] Although they are not as well attested as deans, varlets brought the guild-brothers together within one town, even across a region, helping to uphold their values and sense of purpose.

To help reinforce and propagate their prestigious self-image, as well as for practical purposes, guilds used clerks. While not prestigious figures, these men were perhaps the most important officials from a historian's point of view. Some clerks are identifiable, recording and signing their own names in the guild books they created as well as being active shooters.[20] They wrote the accounts on which this study is based, although whether they simply noted down the words of the constable or were more intimately involved with the accounts cannot be ascertained. That shooting guild clerks kept such detailed annual accounts is again important. Craft guilds kept accounts, but usually of rents and members

---

[16] ASAOA, 7, *den boek met den haire*, ff. 71v–72.
[17] RAG, RVV, 7351, ff. 212v–213.
[18] AML, RM 16973, 215; SAG, 301/27, f. 82v; AML, CV, 16208, f. 120v.
[19] DAM, AA 94, f. 71; CC 217, 107v; AML, RM 16973, 91; ASAOA, 3, peysboek f. 152v–153; AML, CV, 16125, f. 34v.
[20] SAB, 385, st Jorisgilde, Rekeningen 1445–1480, f. 92v.

– they rarely recorded the details of attendance and outgoings that the shooters did.[21] That the guilds invested in recording their events and in preserving these records demonstrates that they believed themselves to be powerful groups. Clerks also recorded in these account books the ancient foundation ideals and older deeds discussed above, demonstrating a desire to link themselves to continuing traditions.

The rest of the members should have been united and should have supported each other. The next chapter will look at social and religious activities within the guilds, and demonstrate ways of strengthening unity as well as examples of disunity. Here, in analysing guild structure, it is important to consider the language guilds used for themselves and their members. In French sources the most common name by which members refer to one another is *'confrere'*. This term is in part religious, and was used to describe members of lay associations formed with the aims of piety and charity, implying the closeness of the group.[22] The term was in use for centuries. In 1382, oaths were taken from the *confreres* of the crossbow of Douai, and as late as 1560 lands were granted to the *'diseniers* and *confreres* of the archers of Saint Sebastian' of Douai.[23] In Lille, numerous items in the town accounts are granted to 'king constable and *confreres* of the *serment* of the crossbowmen' or archers.[24] Flemish sources are less consistent; the town accounts of Oudenaarde often refer to the community, *gheselle* of the guilds, a term used in some Ghent sources, although more often members are called brothers, *broeren*.[25] The Bruges lists refer to the named individuals as *gildebroeders*, and even letters of invitation, such as that from Hulst in 1483, refer to *broeren*. The regular use of 'brothers' for members is not unique to shooting guilds: numerous craft guilds refer to members as *ghildebroeders*. Yet the term is used carefully and meaningfully by shooting guild-brothers to emphasise their community and their bonds to one another.

As noted in the introduction, larger towns had multiple guilds, with two guilds of crossbowmen, two guilds of archers and a later guild of gunners not uncommon. Guild-brothers were usually not permitted to be in more than one guild at any one time. As we shall see, nobles were able to be in multiple guilds, but for non-nobles membership in more than one guild was unusual – although,

---

[21] In Bruges, the Goldsmith guild has detailed rents, but few details of spending, RAB, ambachten, 191. Others, like the bow-makers, record a lot of detail about new members and their fees, but again few detailed outgoings, RAB, ambachten, 116–126; some guilds, like the Bruges skinners, do have full accounts, RAB, ambachten, 255; H. Lamerti, 'Les Comptes d'une corporation de Bruges', BCRH 77 (1908), 269–300.

[22] P. Robert, *Dictionnaire Alphabétique et Analogique de la Langue Française* (Paris, 1969), 893; C. Vincent, *Des charités bien ordonnées: les confréries normandes de la fin du XIIIe siècle au début du XVIe siècle* (Paris: École normale supérieure de jeunes filles, 1988), 27–30.

[23] DAM, AA94, f. 70v; DAM, 2 II 2/ 12.

[24] AML, CV, the terms used in annual gifts of wine to both archers and crossbowmen, and later gunners, e.g. f. 16185, accounts of 1444, f. 40v.

[25] OSAOA, Microfilm 684, is 1406–1422 20v; SAG, SJ, NGR, 2.

in Bruges at least, it was possible. A Lille case from 1493 shows that other towns and other guilds were less flexible in allowing individuals to maintain multiple memberships. Olivier de le Barre and a second, unnamed man were brought before the aldermen of Lille for having left the archery guild and joined the crossbow guild. The archers were angry not because the men had left the guild but because they had done so without paying the necessary fees. The aldermen did not ask them to leave the crossbow guild, and indeed the crossbowmen guild showed no concern at having these two new members. The men were required to pay the death-fee required by the archery guild – 24s – and the joining fee of the crossbow guild – 36s – but were otherwise not punished. Clearly, Olivier and his companions were wealthy, able to pay 60s in or around June 1493.[26] What motivated the men to change guilds is unclear, and this is the only reference I have found to members leaving one shooting guild for another. It is likely that such moves went on, as nothing in the case implies there was any novelty in what the two men had done – rather, the issue was that they had done so without paying the required fees. Perhaps the two men felt the crossbow guild to be more prestigious, or perhaps they simply wanted a new challenge.

In several Flemish-speaking towns the smaller guilds are referred to as *jonghe* – leading modern writers to call them youth groups. Arnade is typical in discussing the Ghent 'youth groups' and the important task of the older men in 'instructing young men in lessons about civic power', although, as Arnade himself admits, no Ghent document refers to age restrictions.[27] The Ghent *jonghe* crossbowmen had their own chapel, with mass books and even an instructional manual for women. They elected most of their own officials, although their dean was always a 'notable' of the *oude* guild.[28] They were also responsible for defending part of Ghent's walls from 1438 – and action that does not sound appropriate for groups composed exclusively of under-18s. In Ypres the *jonghe* archers and crossbowmen organised regional competitions, attracting *oude* teams as well as *jonghe* ones.[29] That *jonghe* and *oude* guilds competed together, for the same prizes, once again implies that they were men of equal physical stature and ability. It is, of course, impossible to prove a negative from the silence of documents, but further evidence can be drawn from Bruges and francophone sources to add weight to the idea that *jonghe* guilds were new guilds of lesser status, not comprised of youths.

In Bruges the *jongehof* is first mentioned in a charter of 1435.[30] The new guild is 'established and dedicated to Saint George for the *jonghe* shooters, and the brotherhood are to be governed by the *oude* guild, which have been established for a long time and are the leading guild in Flanders'. The language here might

---

[26] AML, RM, 15920, f. 91.
[27] Arnade, *Realms of Ritual*, 72–4.
[28] SAG, SJ, NGR, 6, 7.
[29] SAG, 301, 4, f. 81r; AGR, CC, 38647, ff. 39v–40.
[30] SAB, 385, Sint Joris / Jongehof, 1.

imply a youth group, supervised by adults, just as the Ghent reference to a member of the *oude* guild acting as dean for the *jonghe* guild does. Yet such requirements could just as easily demonstrate those of great status allowing others to take up their exalted and privileged sport. Within the new *jonghe* guild of Bruges, each guild-brother had to own a bow, or get one within twelve days of his entrance, and keep it in his house. The *jonghe* guild-brothers bought their own livery, marched in procession and chose some of their officials, although under the supervision of the *oude* brothers. If they did not have the correct equipment they would be fined 20s. If a member missed the *papegay* shoot, or the mass that preceded it, he would be fined 5s. The detailed charter makes no allusion to age, nor to a point at which members must leave the *jonghe* guild and join the *oude*. In a mid-sixteenth-century membership list a Bruges archer is identified as 'Guyot de Rinere, clerc vand (en) jonghe boghe', presumably meaning he was both an archer and the clerk of the *jonghe* guild, and therefore a member of two different shooting guilds, *jonghe* and *oude*, at the same time.

Language is again important in understanding who the *jonghe* guilds were. Documents written in French consistently call the secondary guilds *petit*, not *jeun*, even in Flemish-speaking areas. In 1516, in a charter written in Flemish, the Bruges officials granted new rights to the lesser crossbow guilds, calling them *jonghe*. When the charter was confirmed by Charles V, in French, the guild was referred to as *petit*.[31] The confirmation, granted in 1557, stated that the guild had been in existence for over a hundred years, had its own garden and, like the greater guild, had the right to bear arms anywhere in Flanders and to go to win prizes at any competition. In Lille and other French-speaking towns the lesser guilds are called *petit*, in contrast to the *grand* guilds, and again no reference survives that makes any allusion to age. The guilds also served together in Bruges: in 1488–89 '16 shooters of the *oude* crossbow guild 12 shooters of the *jonghe* crossbow guild and 14 shooters of the hand bow' were paid the same sums for watching the town walls.[32]

It is not possible to prove that the members of *jonghe* and *petit* guilds were all adults, as no membership lists survive, and in any case lists rarely give the ages of new members. It is, however, important to note that every study that has mentioned the *jonghe* guilds has referred to them as youth groups. Many writers, including Moulin-Coppens, have even stated that members had to be under eighteen, but they have provided no proof.[33] Children were present in *oude* guilds: the Bruges Saint Sebastian guild records a separate subsection of women and children in the guild each year. Larger shooting guilds could 'instruct young men in lessons about civic power' internally – they did not need to set up separate guilds for this purpose. Where other youth groups existed

---

[31] SAB, 385, Sint Joris / Jongehof, 2 and 3.
[32] SAB, 17, oorlog, 1481–89, f. 91v.
[33] Moulin-Coppens, *Sint Jorisgilde te Gent*, 59; Boone, *Gent en de Bourgondische hertogen*, 114–15.

in the Low Countries, such as devotional confraternities for young men, clear reference was made to who was in the group.[34]

No document could be found in any Flemish archive that mentions any age restrictions for any shooting guilds or an obligation for a guild-brother to leave a *jonghe* guild for an *oude* one at a certain point in his life. Yet the assumption, ubiquitous in writings on the guilds, is that the *jonghe* guilds were youth groups. This is one of many reasons why historians need to return to archives and not rely on nineteenth-century accounts of urban groups. Beyond Flanders, some examples of genuine youth groups did exist; in particular, the case for under-18s in the *jeunes arbalétriers* of early modern Liège has been argued convincingly, and in Switzerland youths had their own separate gun shooting contests.[35] It is very likely that the *jonghe* and *petit* Flemish guilds were new groups, less ancient and prestigious than the *oude* or *grand* guilds, and not youth and senior groups, just as towns saw multiple adult chambers of rhetoric in the sixteenth century and a diversification of crafts guilds over time.

Entrance

Shooting guilds were, then, organised communities and their constables, deans, *dixeniers* and varlets all helped to keep order and to strengthen the community. So, how did one enter this community, and how were new members integrated into the guild?

Money is perhaps the most obvious answer to this question, although it is not the only one, as status and skill were also important. For many guilds their entrance fees were relatively high, especially as men also had to own weapons on their entry into guilds. To enter the Lille crossbow guild of Saint George in 1443 cost 36s, while the entrance fee for the Lille archers was slightly lower at 24s.[36] From 1431 a new archer in Aalst had to pay 20s as well as buy a pot of wine, and charters from across and beyond Flanders require relatively large sums of money from new members.[37] To put these figures into context, Howell has estimated the average daily wage for a master mason in the second half of the fifteenth century to be 11d.[38] It is likely that these high fees were linked to high status, as van Kan has argued was the case for shooting guilds in Holland, where membership was limited to the rich.[39] There is some evidence that high entrance

---

[34] R. Muchembled, 'Die Jugend und die Volkskultur im 15. Jahrhundert. Flandern und Artois', in P. Dinzelbacher and H.-D. Mück (eds), *Volkskultur des Europäischen Spätmittelalters* (Stuttgart: Kröner, 1986), 35–58.

[35] Reintges, *Ursprung und Wesen*, 293–7; Tlusty, *The Martial Ethic*, 198.

[36] AML, RT, 15883, f. 28; AML, RM, 15920, f. 91.

[37] RAG, RVV, 7351, ff. 209–10.

[38] M. Howell, *Commerce before Capitalism in Europe, 1300–1600* (Cambridge; New York: Cambridge University Press, 2010), 306.

[39] F. J. W. van Kan, 'Around Saint George: Integration and Precedence during the Meetings of the Civic Militia of The Hague', in Blockmans and Jansese (eds), *Showing*

fees caused problems for some Flemish guilds. In 1465 the crossbowmen of Axelle complained to Philip the Good that the guild was 'greatly diminished' and was now 'small in number' because the entrance fee was too high. In light of this, Philip wrote that those 'wishing to enter in the said guild of Saint George in the said place of Axelle will be received without having to pay any charge'.[40]

Enforcing high membership fees could, then, cause a decline in membership numbers. We saw in the previous chapter that some guilds had considerably more members than they should have had, so it should come as no surprise that rules on paying entrance fees were also relaxed. In Bruges, only 51 out of 902 crossbowmen are recorded as paying an entrance fee. A few instances of non-payment can be explained by a four-year gap in accounts, but over 90% of guild-brothers entered without being recorded as paying any fee. There is no explanation for this in the guild books, just as there is no explanation for why more members were in guilds than were technically permitted. Bruges is unusually detailed, but fragments from elsewhere provide a similar picture. In Aalst in 1499, eleven men entered the crossbow guild. One 'Henric van Belle, knight, lord of Zoetstrad' paid £12, two others paid £6 and the rest paid nothing.[41]

Although nothing can be proved from the silence of documents, it is likely that Flemish guilds allowed in more members and often allowed guild-brothers in without fees because they were otherwise well funded. As chapter four will explain, guilds received generous funding from their towns, including annual subsidies, land, wine and extra grants, should they attend or host competitions. Guilds were often land-owners by the fifteenth century, either through bequests left by members on their deaths or through wise investments, and, over time, entrances fees may have been less important for guild finances. The Axelle charter may also hint that guilds feared that they would not be able to recruit if they enforced their high fees – indeed it is possible that different factors influenced the non-paying of fees in different towns. Wealthy guilds like those in Ghent and Bruges did not need membership fees, while smaller guilds like that of Axelle feared high fees would deter members.

It is worth emphasising that the shooting guilds are unusual in allowing members in without paying fees, whatever their motivation. Many craft guilds in Flanders were meticulous in recording entrance fees, and whether or not new members were masters' sons; thus the shooting guilds are rather different from groups around them. In studying English guilds Amos has noted that guilds often limited their numbers and set high entrance fees so as to enhance their prestige.[42] It seems that the Flemish shooting guilds were doing quite the

---

Status: Representation of Social Positions in the Late Middle Ages (Turnhout: Brepols, 1999), 177–95.

[40] SAG, 'Vreemde Steden', doos 7, I am grateful to Dr Jonas Braekevelt for this reference.
[41] ASAOA, 155, Register Sint Joris guild, f. 10v.
[42] M. A. Amos, '"Somme Lordes and Somme others of Lowe Estates", London's Urban Elite and the Symbolic Battle for Status', in D. Biggs, S. D. Michalove and A. Compton

reverse, allowing in large numbers with few or no fees. The guilds, it seems, were not concerned that their large communities would lose prestige. They may also have been influenced by the other benefits of larger communities. As Trio demonstrated in studying devotional confraternities, more members meant more spiritual benefits – in particular, more prayers and higher attendance at funerals.[43]

Entrance to a guild was not dependent on paying a fee, nor was size limited by charters, yet it is by no means the case that membership was open to all. In Aalst from 1421 a new archer would be accepted only with the consent of the guild community, just as in Lille from 1443 new members entered only with the consent of the constable and guild-brothers.[44] How such consent was obtained or recorded is unclear, but such regulations emphasise again that guilds were communities and should behave with unity and promote their shared values and act for the benefit of all. As will be discussed in the next chapter, disorder did happen, but guilds worked to avoid it. For similar reasons they would not want to admit a new guild-brother who was already in a dispute with existing members, as such a situation could only have provoked conflict.

In some towns there seems to have been a sort of municipal control on membership. Indeed the above requirements to be good and worthy may cover some informal modes of control. In Béthune control was made clearer, as from 1459 a new crossbowman would only be received with 'the advice and deliberation' of the bailey and aldermen.[45] The aldermen of Ghent also took care to oversee their guild: a 1366 membership list shows that most of the officials of the guild were aldermen. It has been suggested that this shows municipal control over the guild, but it could, as in the Bruges case discussed below, simply reflect guild-brothers being drawn from among the most powerful in urban society.[46] In 1413 Ghent municipal policy was formalised and the Saint George guild was to be governed by two deans, chosen by the political leaders of Ghent.[47] Control was extended in 1423, when all guild officials and all new members had to be approved by a civic official and the first alderman of Ghent was automatically appointed as headman of the crossbowmen, with the second alderman, representing the craft guilds, as the sub-dean.[48] Such municipal

---

Reeves (eds), *Traditions and Transformation in Late Medieval England* (Leiden: Brill, 2002), 173.

[43] P. Trio, 'The Social Positioning of Late Medieval Confraternities in Urbanized Flanders; From Integration to Segregation', in M. Escher-Apsner (ed.), *Mittelalterliche Bruderschaften in europäischen Städten/ Medieval Confraternities in Towns* (Frankfurt-am-Main, 2009), 99–110.

[44] ASAOA, 3, peysboek, ff. 152v–153; AML, RT, 15884, f. 134r–v.

[45] Espinas, *Les origins*, vol. 2, 214–16.

[46] Arnade, *Realms of Ritual*, 70–1; Nicholas, *Metamorphosis*, 44.

[47] SAG, 310, 10, 1 f. 28 r–v; 310, 2, 2, f. 37; 310/22, f. 101r.

[48] SAG, 300/27, f. 82v, f. 17; Boone, *Gent en de Bourgondische Hertogen*, 118–19; A. L. Van Bruaene, 'A Breakdown of Civic Community?', in N. A. Eckstein and N. Terpstra

control is not surprising, given the privileged status of the guilds and the value of their military service.

Control was enforced not just over who could become a member, but over the movement of members. In 1383 the magistrates of Lille passed regulations that the 'brave crossbowmen' were forbidden to leave the town for more than three days without a grant from the aldermen. This restriction was not repeated when the crossbowmen's charter was reissued in 1458, but by 1483 had been imposed on the gunners. A similar restriction was imposed on the highest officials in Lille, *les conseillers pensionnaires*, in 1384.[49] Even if they were enforced only in crisis years, as the silence of 1458 implies, such restrictions are significant, showing that in times of military necessity the guilds had to stay and defend their town. The shooting guilds of Lille were seen to be as important as municipal officials, and so had the same restrictions, emphasising that honour and obligation were linked.

Potential guild-brothers may have had to pay money, and they certainly had to be acceptable to at least the community, if not to civic officials. The importance of honour and reputation are also clear in numerous guild charters. As early as 1348 the crossbowmen of Oudenaarde had to be 'good men' and 'pleasing', as well as skilled shooters, and from 1398 a new crossbowman in Dendermonde had to be 'dignified.' In 1447 the archers of Sint-Winnoksbergen had to be 'men of good fame and renown'. The crossbowmen of Douai had to be 'of suitable life and of good renown in their ways and habits' and those of Roubaix 'of honest life fame, renown and dignity'.[50] In the small town of Pecquencourt, crossbowmen had to be 'good men of pleasing manners and be without dishonesty' and would consequently be fined for using 'enflamed words' – presumably insults.[51] Indeed the emphasis on being 'worthy' is ubiquitous across Flanders, underlining the importance of good reputation and of being seen as worthy. Such an emphasis is again to be expected, as many charters make numerous references to guilds being privileged 'for the honour of the town' as we shall see in chapter four. Social standing and reputation were central facets of medieval life, yet they are difficult to quantify. In the medieval town, one's ability to trade, even one's place in society, could be determined by reputation, and it has even been argued that the 'pursuit of reputation' was at the heart of all activities within a social framework.[52] Reputation could be augmented: in analysing English craft guilds,

---

(eds), *Sociability and its Discontents, Civil Society, Social Capital, and Their Alternatives in Late Medieval and Early Modern Europe* (Turnhout: Brepols, 2009), 280.

[49] AML, OM, 379, f. 33; AML, RM, 15884, f. 137; 15920, f. 12; C. Pétillon, 'Le Personnel Urbain de Lille (1384–1419)', *RN*, 65 1983, 411–12.

[50] OSAOA, gilden, 507/II/1A; *Ordonnances de Philippe le Hardi* vol. 2, 296–300; RAG, RVV, 7351, ff. 220–221; DAM, Arbalestiers de Douay, 24I1232, f. 2; AMR, EE1.

[51] ADN 1H 369.

[52] P. Marsh, 'Identity; An Ethnogenetic Perspective', in R. Trexler (ed.), *Persons in Groups: Social Behaviour as Identity Formation in Medieval and Renaissance Europe* (Binghamton, NY: Medieval & Renaissance Texts & Studies, 1985), 19.

Rosser has suggested the idea of 'moral credit', which could be gained through membership of prestigious groups whose self-identity and self-worth was predicated on their members being honourable.[53] The Flemish guild-brothers likewise needed sufficient moral credit to represent the guild, to represent the town and to be trusted with their status and their privileges.

To maintain a high standing and a good community, guilds strove to control behaviour. An early civic ordinance for the crossbowmen of Ghent, from 1360, emphasised 'moral behaviour' and that no members should 'risk shame'. In Lille crossbowmen could be removed if found to be 'unworthy of the noble guild'.[54] More specifically, civic powers sought to control behaviours and to uphold values through oaths. Aldermen and other municipal officials took oaths upon entering office (usually in their town halls) that were given importance not just through their words, but through ritual and symbolic settings. The new aldermen were bound to uphold the honour of the town, and municipal oaths could change to reflect changing civic priorities.[55] Like the towns they represented, the guilds used oaths to uphold behaviour and standing.

Promises made on entrance into a shooting guild, like those made by new aldermen, made clear what was expected of members, setting a high moral standard. In Douai, by 1383, new crossbowmen were required to promise to 'guard and defend ... the *diseniers* and *confreres*, the body and the honour of our very redoubtable lord monsieur the Duke of Burgundy ... the body of the law and the aldermen of the town and of the provost and lieutenant'.[56] Regulations on how and where oaths should be taken do not survive, although the guilds may have followed other groups in swearing on relics within their chapels.[57] At least one Lille guild-brother took his oath in the guild's garden, its practice ground. Jehan Landas, on entering the Lille archery guild in April 1415, took his oath in its garden before the Porte de Courtrai, in the presence of Hue de Lannoy, governor of Lille.[58] The words of the Douai oaths, entered into the guild-register and spoken by each new guild-brother, helped to bring a new member into the guild community, making clear the values he should abide by and the moral credit he should work towards. New guild-brothers swore to 'guard and

---

[53] G. Rosser, 'Workers' Associations in English Medieval Towns', in P. Lambrechts and J.-P. Sosson (eds), *Les métiers au Moyen Age: aspects économiques et sociaux* (Louvain-la-Neuve: Fédération internationale des instituts d'études médiévales, 1994), 284–7.

[54] Moulin-Coppens, *Sint Jorisgilde te Gent*, 28–30; AML, PT 5883, ff. 21–83.

[55] J. Van Leeuwen, 'Municipal Oaths, Political Virtues and the Centralised State; The Adaptation of Oaths of Office in Fifteenth Century Flanders', *JMH* 31 (2005), 185–7; eadem 'Beloftes van een baljuw: de evoluties van een ambtseed te Brugge (14de–15de eeuw)', *MTMS* 13 (1999) 123–35.

[56] DAM, AA94, f. 70v.

[57] J. Koldeweij, 'Gezworen op het kruis of op relieken', in J-C. Klamt and K. Veelenturf (eds), *Representatie: Kunsthistorische bijdragen over vorst, staatsmacht en beeldende kunst, opgedragen aan Robert W. Scheller* (Nijmegen: Valkhof pers, 2004) 158–79.

[58] AML, RM, 16973, f. 79.

defend ... the body and the honour of our very redoubtable lord ... the body of the law and the aldermen of the Douai and of the provost and lieutenant'.[59] The process of entrance into a shooting guild was a key ritual in building bonds of brotherhood, with the taking of oaths integrating new members into a corporate unit that should have been concerned for communal honour and shared values.

Requirements to be honourable and acceptable are interesting, but they are not the only requirements for new guild-brothers. Potential new members had also to own arms and to be skilled in their use. How potential members acquired the requisite skills in towns that banned the use of bows and crossbows to anyone who was not in a guild is not recorded. In England all men were required, from 1363, to practise archery at the local butts each week. In contrast, Flemish towns passed laws *against* anyone using bows or crossbows, and later guns, within their walls, meaning that potential guild-brothers had two options.[60] First, one could enter the shooting guild as a child and learn within the guild – certainly there were children in the guilds, but only small number. Second, a potential bowman could simply go outside the town to practise, as civic ordinances covered only civic space, that is, the space within the walls. The numerous bans from Lille ordering 'commons' not to shoot crossbows directly at the walls shows that many were indeed shooting outside of the walls; moreover, they also suggest that the aldermen did not want to ban them from practising there, merely from shooting *at* the walls.[61]

However they acquired their skills, new members were expected to be militarily capable. Like the above requirement, the need to be skilled is omnipresent in charters from large and small towns across the period. New guild-brothers in Wattignies and Estrées, from 1405, would not be received unless they were 'good and sufficient' archers. Likewise, in 1440, to join the archery guild of Cysoing, new members had to be 'good and skilled and able for the shooting of the bow'.[62] A new archer would not be received into Sint-Winnoksbergen guild in 1447 unless he was 'skilled in the playing' of the bow, and the same requirement appears in the 1430 charter to both the archers and crossbowmen of Tielt.[63] Such requirements are to be expected for shooting guilds, which, as we have seen, continued to serve in civic defence and in princely armies across the period. Although there were, as we shall see, some women and children in the guild, there was an expectation for all guild-brothers to be skilled and capable, or at least that they had been on entrance. There were no requirements for elderly or injured guild-brothers to leave their guilds.

---

[59] DAM, Arbalestiers de Douay, 24II232, f. 2v.
[60] S. Gunn, 'Archery Practice in Early Tudor England', *PP* 209 (2010), 53–81; Strickland and Hardy, *Warbow*, 198–201; AML, OM, 373, f. 3v, f. 41; 376, f. 20v; 378, ff. 98v–99v, 136–137v; 379, ff. 13–15v, f. 133.
[61] AML, OM, 378, f. 131, 21 May 1471.
[62] ADN, B1600, ff. 25v–26; AML, CV, 16973, 231.
[63] RAG, RVV, 7351, ff. 220–221; 221v–222.

As well as being skilled, guild-brothers also had to be armed; again, this is not particularly surprising. To enter the Lille crossbow guild a man had to have a crossbow worth 60s, along with 'other arms needed for the exercise of the bow', within six weeks of joining. From 1453 the Lille archers had to have 'good bow and sufficient armour'.[64] In 1383 the crossbowmen of Douai simply had to own a 'suitable bow'; by 1499 it was specified that they had the choice of having one of wood or metal. The archers of Aalst, in 1421, had to have a 'bow and two dozen good shots' in the town, but when serving the duke they were to bring 'two good bows and four dozen arrows'.[65] A requirement to be armed might seem obvious for a guild required to serve in war and, indeed, to practise and to take part in competitions.

The ownership of weapons was not unusual in large towns. As Stabel has shown, numerous Bruges men owned an impressive range of offensive and defensive weapons by the fifteenth century.[66] Larger towns had craft guilds dedicated to making weapons; indeed as we shall see, there were bowyers and other armourers in shooting guilds with weapons available to purchase. The cost of weapons varied depending on their composition and quality. In 1437 in Bruges a crossbowman was expected to have a bow worth £3 (60s) and a Lille crossbowman should have left a crossbow of the same value to the guild on his death from 1443.[67] In contrast, in 1396 in Arras crossbowmen required only a bow worth 16s.[68] Indeed cheaper crossbows could be purchased: a crossbow of yew worth 12s was purchased as a gift for an unspecified official by the aldermen of Compiègne in 1452.[69] However much they cost, weapons were about protection and military readiness, but they were also a demonstration of status and of identity. In only allowing in armed, skilled men, the guilds ensured that their members were worthy of membership, able to enact the values of guild life. Further, weapons were often expensive and this might offer another explanation as to why so many guild-brothers were allowed to enter without paying.

As noted, some guilds required a purchase of wine as well as money and arms in order to enter a guild. It is impossible to know if these drinks were purchased or not, but the intention to have drinks and the importance placed on drinking together as part of a new member's integration into the guild is significant in itself. When entering the crossbow guild of Lille, new members were required to pay 24s 'for the profit of the guild' and 12s 'for drinking in a recreational assembly on the day of their entry'. On his first day in the guild a

---

[64] AML, PT, 5883, ff. 28–31; AML, OM, 377, f. 141.
[65] DAM, Arbalestiers de Douay, 24II232, f. 2, ff. 10v–11; ASAOA, 3, peysboek, ff. 152v–153.
[66] Stabel, 'Militaire organisatie', 1049–1074.
[67] SAB, 385, Sint Jorisgilde, register met ledenlijst, 1321–1531, ff. 50–59v; AML, PT, 5883, ff. 28–31.
[68] Espinas, Les origins, vol. 2, 54.
[69] d'Hoeuet, Les Francs-archers de Compiègne, 143.

new crossbowman bought drinks for his brothers, designating his new place in the community and ensuring that bonds would be strengthened through drinking together. The same 1442 regulation required a crossbowman to leave 12s 'which will cover drinking for the *confreres* who carry the body' as part of his death-fee, meaning that time in the guild was bookended by drinking together.[70] Small towns also recognised the importance of drinking together in order to build bonds, and in Aalst, from 1421, a new archer was required to pay 20s to the guild and, further, to buy one 'pott' of wine, while in Dendermonde new crossbowmen bought one or two lots of wine for their brothers, depending on their status.[71] Guilds were communities with values and with an emphasis on unity and honour; membership fees were set high but do not seem to have been enforced, while other rules emphasised life and reputation in the entrance requirement. How far the requirement to buy drinks was followed cannot be known, but the repeated writing of rules requiring the purchase of drinks demonstrates the unity within guilds and the power of wine and beer to enhance it.

Membership

The unity of membership should have been enhanced through drinking and should have been regulated by officials with a shared sense of purpose. Many of the regulations discussed above imply that guilds were all-male groups, with concern for war and for martial skills resulting in masculine identities and masculine groups. A few guild regulations mention guild-sisters. For instance, in 1494 new regulations emphasised that all guild-brothers and guild-sisters of Aalst had to be obedient to the dean.[72] In 1473 Charles the Bold and Margaret of York gave a large donation to the brothers and sisters of the Saint George guild of Ghent.[73] Yet, in the main, the ordinances of archery and crossbow guilds are silent on clerical members and on female members. Regulations do not make clear what, if any, formal relationships existed between the priests paid to say mass and the guild-brothers, nor do they set entrance costs for women and children. Indeed the ordinances quoted above give little insight into who the guild-brothers were, beyond being of good life and good reputation. In the following a number of membership lists will be used to look as closely as possible at the members of the archery and crossbow guilds, first noting general patterns across Flanders and then turning to a case study of Bruges.

Membership lists reveal the perhaps surprising presence of churchmen, women and children. On the one hand, the appearance of churchmen on such lists seems incongruous with the reputation of the crossbow as 'diabolical', stemming

---

[70] AML, PT, 5883, ff. 28–31; AML, CV, 16188, f. 71–71v.
[71] ASAOA, 3, peysboek ff. 152v–153; *Ordonnances de Philippe le Hardi*, vol. 2, 296–300.
[72] ASAOA, 7 *den boek met den haire*, f. 72.
[73] SAG, SJ, NGR, 25.

from the Second Lateran Council's banning its use against Christians.[74] Yet, on the other hand, the weapon's reputation had improved between the twelfth and fourteenth centuries. Equally, all ranks of ecclesiastics are to be found in many other urban socio-cultural groups; indeed, clerical membership of urban confraternities in the Low Countries is well known, with many studies, especially those of Trio, emphasising that priests and regular brothers entered fraternities so as to help build links between churchmen and their local communities.[75]

The shooting guilds may also have permitted clerical membership so as to build links with other civic communities. In Aalst, the crossbow guild's 1488 membership lists includes eight priests, a small but significant 3% of the 228 members. A further two 'religious' and seven priests joined the guild in 1489, along with civic officials from other Flemish and Brabant towns, including Antwerp. All of these men joined as non-residents, and it may be that they played little active role in the guild and that their entrances were, rather, part of an effort to build regional networks.[76] Although the numbers of priests here are small, their presence reveals the strength of the guild community and the ability of that community to intersect social boundaries.

Social boundaries regarding clerical orders might be intersected, but gender boundaries were rather more fixed. Female participation in archery and crossbow guilds, as in craft guilds and other urban groups, is poorly documented. As Decraene has shown for early modern confraternities, documents were drawn up by men for men; even where women dominated in a quantitative way, they did not enjoy the same rights and privileges as brothers. In craft guilds, women were rarely members in their own right, but they could become members, even masters, through their husbands or fathers. This is especially true of widows. Flanders in general and Ghent, in particular, had inheritance laws that were more favourable to wives than elsewhere in Europe, allowing for widows to continue their husbands' professions and businesses.[77] Single women who were

---

[74] P. Norman and S. J. Tanner (eds), *Decrees of the Ecumenical Councils*, vol. 1 (London: Georgetown University Press, 1990), 203. I am grateful to Dr Daniel Gerrard for this reference.

[75] P. Trio, 'Lay Persons in Power: The Crumbling of the Clerical Monopoly on Urban Devotion in Flanders as a Result of the Rise of Lay Confraternities in Late Medieval Flanders', in Black and Gravestock, *Early Modern Confraternities*, 53–63; C. Black, *Italian Confraternities in the Sixteenth Century* (Cambridge: Cambridge University Press, 1989), 32–57; A.-J. Bijstervelde, 'Looking for Common Ground: From Monastic Fraternitas to Lay Confraternity in the Southern Low Countries in the Tenth to Twelfth Centuries', V. Hoven Genderen and P. Trio 'Old Stories and New Themes; An Overview of the Historiography of Confraternities in the Low Countries from the Thirteenth to the Sixteenth Centuries', both in E. Jamroziak and J. Burton (eds) (*Religious and Laity in Western Europe, 1000–1400* (Turnhout: Brepols, 2006), 287–314; 357–84.

[76] ASAOA, 155, Register Sint Joris guild, 1335–1583, ff. 4–7v.

[77] E. Decraene, 'Sisters of Early Modern Confraternities in a Small Town in the Southern Low Countries (Aalst)', *UH* 40 (2013), 247–70; M. E. Weisner, 'Guilds, Male Bonding and Women's Work in Early Modern Germany', *Gender History* 1 (1989), 125–37; M.

not related to guild-brothers may have joined the shooting guilds (as single women in London did) to gain 'the benefit of respectability' that came from guild membership – or even to find husbands.[78]

In looking at female participation in chambers of rhetoric, Van Bruaene has found that women could be members. Female *rederijkers* (rhetoricians) could be very talented writers, but were not active in the public sphere of guild activities, just as women could not perform male activities like military service or holding municipal office. Van Bruaene's observations for chambers of rhetoric, that around 10% of members were female, even though the groups emphasised a 'strong male groups identity' into which the female members 'never fully integrated', with statutes 'keeping women on the margins',[79] fit neatly with the patterns for female members of shooting guilds. Late-medieval women could not be shooters and they did not take part in processions, shoots or meals, meaning that female activity in guilds is hard to trace, but guild-sisters are present.

In Aalst, the crossbowmen's records between 1488 and 1500 include the names of 776 members, of which ninety were women (11.5% of the guild).[80] The vast majority are identified in relation to a guild-brother, like 'Margriette, wife of Jan Weytins' or 'the daughter of Anthonus Breyls', but at least five women are named in their own right and do not seem to be related to any of the guild-brothers. The records of the Bruges archery guild feature a separate list of women and children, each paying 2*d* a year in fees rather than the 6*d* a year paid by guild-brothers. Every year the records include 'payments from the women and the children'; in 1454 this list has twenty-eight members paying 2*d*, compared to the 265 guild-brothers who pay 6*d* (almost 10%), but, as the gender of children is not always given, the true figure for female membership may be lower. As we shall see, the Ghent records are far more detailed and have been analysed by Sarah van Steene. Among the 1396 members within the Saint George guild between 1468 and 1498 there appear 114 women (8.2% of the guild). As in other towns, the majority are the wives, sisters, widows or occasionally mothers of guild-brothers, but around one third of the women were not, as far as van Steen could tell, related to any of the guild-brothers.[81]

Danneel, *Weduwen en Wezen in het laat-middeleeuwse Gent* (Leuven: Garant, 1995); S. Hutton, *Women and Economic Activities in Late Medieval Ghent* (London; New York: Palgrave Macmillan, 2011); L. Guzzetti, 'Women's Inheritance and Testamentary Practices in Late Fourteenth and Early Fifteenth-Century Venice and Ghent', in E. E. Kittell and M. A. Suydam (eds), *The Texture of Society, Medieval Women in the Southern Low Countries* (Basingstoke: Palgrave Macmillan, 2004), 79–108.

[78] A. Prescott, 'Men and Women in the Guild Returns', in M. Fedelma Cross (ed.), *Gender and Fraternal Orders in Europe, 1300–2000* (Basingstoke: Palgrave Macmillan, 2010), 31–51.

[79] A.-L. Van Bruaene, 'Brotherhood and Sisterhood in the Chambers of Rhetoric in the Souther Low Countries', *Sixteenth Century Journal* 36 (2005), 11–35.

[80] ASAOA 155, Register Sint Joris guild, ff. 6v–9r.

[81] Steen, *Den ouden ende souverainen gilde van den edelen ridder Sente Jooris*, STAM, Sint-Jorisgilde, G 3018/3.

Percentages of women among crossbow guilds in Bruges, Ghent and Aalst are close to the 10% noted by Van Bruaene for the chambers of rhetoric. As in chambers, the guild-sisters had no public role in guild culture: they did not represent guild honour, just as they could not be part of civic honour. The only woman recorded as taking any part in a medieval shooting competition was Margaret of Bavaria, wife of John the Fearless, in Oudenaarde in 1408, and even she is simply a well-dressed part of the spectacle.[82] In tournaments women could give favours, even judge events – part of the 'quasi-theatrical space of tournaments' which could offer 'a space for maidens ... to play with heterosexual desire'.[83] In archery and crossbow competitions no role is assigned to women, beyond that of a 'beautiful young girl' in Tournai who, as we shall see, selected apples to determine the order in which guilds would shoot in 1455.[84] Guild-sisters did not enjoy the same rights and privileges as guild-brothers. As in chambers of rhetoric, they were hidden in public events, but that they are present at all is useful for understanding the communal nature of guilds and their different functions for different members.

Membership in Bruges, 1437–81

Guilds differed in size, but shared some basic concepts of organisation and, more importantly, an identity as moral and prestigious. Many fragments of evidence for guild membership across Flanders could be pulled together, and indeed many membership lists are mentioned, yet in order to understand who members were and the composition of shooting guilds relative to wider civic societies, a single case study is necessary. To accept that the guilds could, even that they did, represent their towns, it is essential to know how far they *were* representative of their towns. Indeed, to understand any group a study of its members is vital, and prosopography, which can be defined as 'an attempt to bring together all relevant biographical data of groups of persons in a systematic and stereotypical way', allows for an understanding of group identity.[85]

---

[82] See below, pp. 153–4.
[83] K. M. Philips, *Medieval Maidens. Young Women and Gender in England, 1270–1540* (Manchester: Manchester University Press, 2003), 164; see also N. F. Regalado, 'Performing Romance: Arthurian Interludes in Sarrasin's *Le Roman du Hem* (1278)', in E. Birge Vitz, N. F. Regalado and M. Lawrence, *Performing Medieval Narrative* (Woodbridge: Boydell, 2005), 103–21.
[84] Brown and Small, *Court and Civic Society*, 222–3.
[85] K. Verboven, M. Carlier and J. Dumolyn, 'A Short Manual to the Art of Prosopography', in K. S. B. Keats-Rohan (ed.), *Prosopography, Approaches and Applications, a Handbook* (Oxford: Unit for Prosopographical Research, Linacre College, University of Oxford, 2007), 37; H. de Ridder-Symoens, 'Prosopographical Research in the Low Countires Concerning the Middle Ages and the Sixteenth Century', *Medieval Prosopography* 14 (1993), 27–120; F. Lequin 'De prosopografie', *SH* (1985), 34–9; M. Boone, 'Biografie en prosopografie, een tegenstelling? Een stand van zaken in het biografisch onderzoek

In studying any group it seems obvious that studying the members themselves will reveal more about group standing, their functions and their interaction with powers than an analysis of charters can. Yet, for shooting guilds only three small studies have been undertaken on guild membership.[86] Many authors, even those whose works are otherwise excellent, have made generalisations about the status of guild-brothers, based on the rights and charters.[87] Arnade described the guilds as 'staffed by townsmen of means but patronised selectively by noblemen and Burgundian sovereigns'. In a similar way, Gunn, Grummit and Cools declared that the guilds were 'manned by master-craftsmen and officered by the town elite'.[88] Neither of these statements reflects the social flexibility and mobility that the guild offered and, moreover, neither is proved. As a result, the nature of guilds and how they fitted into the urban milieu has not been fully understood.

To provide such an understanding, one town must be analysed in depth. Bruges has been chosen here as a case study partly as it was probably the wealthiest town of Flanders, as well as a gateway trade city. Although it was in economic decline, Bruges was, in terms of fifteenth-century trade, still the trade 'Gateway of Flanders' and the second-largest town in terms of population. If 'poorer' guild-brothers were present in Bruges, then it seems likely that they would have been present in smaller towns too.[89] Bruges has also been chosen

---

over Pieter Lanchals (ca. 1430/40–1488): een Bruggeling in dienst van de Bourgondische staat', *MTMS* 7 (1993), 4–13.

[86] Papin, 'De handboogschuttersgilde van Sint-Winnoksbergen', 1–16; Van Steen, *'Den ouden ende souverainen gilde van den edelen ridder Sente Jooris'*; A. Janssens, 'Daar komen de Brugse kruisboogschutters van "oude", gilde van Sint Joris (tweede helft 15de eeuw)', *BO* 46 (2006) 81–136.

[87] Baillien, 'De Tongerse schutterijen van de 14de tot de 16de eeuw', 5–9; Delsalle, 'La Confrérie des archers de Cysoing', 14–19; Renson, 'The Flemish archery gilds, from defence mechanisms to sports institutions', 135–59; D. Snoep, 'Voorword', to Carasso-Kok and van Halm, *Schutters in Holland – Kracht en Zenuwen van stad*,13–15.

[88] P. Arnade, *Beggars, Iconoclasts, and Civic Patriots: The Political culture of the Dutch Revolt* (Ithaca, NY: Cornell University Press, 2008), 64–5; S. Gunn, D. Grummet and H. Cools, *War, State and Society in England and the Netherlands, 1477–1559* (Oxford: Oxford University Press, 2007), 46–7.

[89] Stabel, 'Composition et recomposition', 58; M. L. Gilliodts van Severen, *Histoire de la Magistrate Brugeoise* (Bruges: De Plancke, 1888); J. Gailliard, *Bruges et le Franc, ou leur magistrature et leur noblesse avec des données historiques et généalogique su chaque famille*, 6 vols (Bruges: Gailliard, 1857–1864); C. Vanden Haute *La Corporation des peintres de Bruges* (Bruges: Van Cappel-Missiaen, 1912); A. Vandewalle et al., *Brugse ambachten in documenten, de schoenmakers, timmerlieden en schrijnwerkers (14de– 18de eeuw)* (Brugge: Gemeentebestuur, 1985); J.-P. Sosson, *Les Travaux publics de la ville de Bruges. 14e–15e siècles, les matériaux, les hommes* (Bruxelles: Crédit communal de Belgique, 1977); J. M. Murray, 'Family, Marriage and Money Changing in Medieval Bruges', *JMH* 14 (1988), 115–25; Dumolyn, *De Brugse opstand*; idem. 'Population et structures professionnelles à Bruges', 43–64; Haemers, *Common Good*, 137–226; Van Uytven, 'Stages of Economic Decline', 259–69; Stabel, 'From Market to Shop', 79–101; idem, *De kleine stad in Vlaanderen*, 87–109.

as a case study for its extremely detailed records for both the archers of Saint Sebastian and the crossbowmen of Saint George.

The crossbowmen of Saint George have left a guild-book and account books. The guild-book, which includes a membership list from 1437 to the mid-sixteenth century, was a carefully thought-out and planned project, with the members, organised alphabetically by first name, entered in the book as they entered the guild. Accounts are not complete, but are very detailed between 1445 and 1465, and again from 1470 to 1481.[90] From these accounts 902 crossbowmen who were active in the guild between 1437 and 1480 have been identified. Of these, the names of fifteen are incomplete, having had parts or all of their surnames removed. All fifteen are in the earliest hand and must have been guild-brothers in 1437, when the list was begun. It is plausible that these fifteen men were in some way involved in the 1436–38 rebellion and that the honourable guild did not want to be associated with rebels.[91] The archers' records are far more detailed but cover a slightly shorter period, with no fifteenth-century membership list, but there are detailed account books covering 1454–56, 1460–65, 1465–72 and 1472–81. The accounts books list all members who attended each *papegay* shoot, each meal (often with seating plans), all members who bought uniform, as well as entrance and death-fees. From these records 755 archers have been identified, with the acknowledged possibility that homonyms may have been missed or, indeed, double counted.[92] The 902 crossbowmen and 755 archers, with a very small overlap of members in both guilds, as well as noble members listed separately in the Saint George guild, form the basis of the present study. Their names have been compared to the numerous other published and archival sources for Bruges.[93] The resulting information provides a window onto the

---

[90] SAB, 385, Sint Joris, register met ledenlijst, 1321–1531 and rekeningen, 1445–1480; Vanhoutryve, *De Brugse Kruisbooggilde*; Janssens, 'Daar komen de Brugse Kruisboogschutters'; N. Geiraert (ed.), *Militie en vermaak – 675 jaar Sint-Jorisgilde in Brugge: tentoonstelling, Brugge* (Brugge: Koninklijke en Prinselijke hoofdgilde Sint-Joris Stalen Boog, 1998).

[91] Dumolyn, *De Brugse Opstand*, 236, 324.

[92] Godar, *Histoire des archers*, 15–26; M. Lemahieu, *Het Wezen van de eerste Vlaamse schuttersgilden* (Brugge: Kon. Hoofdgilde Sint-Sebastiaan, 2008); idem, *De Koninklijke hoofdgilde Sint-Sebastiaan Brugge, 1379–2005* (Brugge: Kon Hoofdgilde Sint-Sebastiaan, 2005); BASS vol. 3: rekeningboeken, 1455–1472 and vol. 4 rekeningboeken, 1468–1513.

[93] SAB 114; SAB, 219; SAB, 130, poorterboeken, and the names in the town accounts, SAB, 219; SAB 336, kuipers, protocolboek, 1375–1777; SAB 345 peltiers, Gildeboeken; SAB, 324 droogsheerders, gildeboek; SAB 337 kulktstikkers, gildeboek, 1451–62; SAB, 299, makelaars, ledenregister; SAB 524, gilde Hulsterloo; SAB, 505, gilde Droogenboom. At the time of writing, a new inventory was in preparation for craft guilds in the RAB, but all numbers here refer to those in C. vanden Haute, *Inventaire sommaire des archives des corporations de la ville de Bruges conservées aux Archives de l'Etat* (Bruxelles: Archives générales du Royaume, 1909); RAB, ambachten, 116, boogmakers; 256–81, rekeningen van de huidenvetters; 470, vischkoopers, admissions, 1425–1795; wollewevers, registers, 487, 1407–26 and 488, 1451–1510; RAB, fonds OLV (91), n. 1531, accounts

composition of the guild-brothers. The following does not claim to be a complete picture but it offers evidence of the guild-brothers' place within civic society and argues for the guilds as representative of all but the very lowest levels of that society. Analysis of the guilds and their society has been grouped into six sections: nobility, *Poorters*, political powers, financial powers, professions and socio-devotional activities.[94] Such a study will reveal that the guilds were neither elite nor exclusive; rather, guild-brothers represented a cross-section of civic society with numerous ties to other groups, representing diverse sections of their urban world and an integrated community.

Nobles[95]

As noted, urban and court cultures were linked in the fifteenth century and Bruges was home to several groups that allowed aristocratic–urban interaction, so noble guild-brothers should be expected.[96] From the crossbow guild there are forty-eight noble members – twenty-eight on a separate list in the guild-book and twenty among the guild-brothers listed alphabetically. Five of these nobles were also in the archery guild and an additional six lords were archers and not crossbowmen, giving a total of fifty-four noble guild-brothers. Among the nobles are many of the great families of Bruges, either ennobled or seen as being noble. 'Patrician' is an imperfect term for these men, although they have been the focus of historical attention for generations. The issue of 'noble identity' continues to provoke much debate, often with the great Bruges families at the centre. As wealthy townsmen with the means to 'vivre noblement', the patricians could be seen as noble. There seems to have been no strict definition of nobility for the Low Countries, meaning that the lines between lower nobles and social climbers were permeable – indeed, the shooting guilds may have helped some rising

---

books (1467–1499); and a partial membership list, 1501; O. Mus, 'De Brugse compagnie Despars op het einde van de 15e eeuw', *ASEB* 101 (1964), 5–118; Vanden Haute, *La corporation des peintres*; Vandewalle, *Brugse ambachten in documenten*; J-A. Van Houtte, 'Makelaars en waarden te Brugge van 13ᵉ tot de 16ᵉ euwe', *BMBGN* 5 (1950), 1–30 and 335–53; R. A. Parmentier, *Indices op de Brugsche Poorterboeken*, vol. 1, 1418–1450, vol. 2, 1450–1794 (Brugge: Desclée De Brouwer, 1938); A. Jamees, *Brugse poortes, opgetekend uit de stadsrekeningen en ingeleid*, vol. 2, 1418–1478 (Handzame: Familia et Patria, 1980).

[94] For a more detailed version of this, with membership lists, see L. Crombie, 'The Archery and Crossbow Guilds of Late Medieval Bruges; A Prosopographical Study', *ASEB* 150 (2013), 245–336.

[95] This section has benefited enormously for the guidance of Frederik Buylaert and, in its later stages, his truly impressive work, *Repertorium van de Vlaamse adel (ca. 1350–ca. 1500)* (Gent: Academia Press, 2011).

[96] Brown 'Urban Jousts in the Later Middle Ages', 315–31; Brown and Small, *Court and Civic society*, 219–30; F. Buylaert, *Eeuwen van Ambitie, De Adel in Laatmiddeleeuws Vlaanderen* (Brussel: Verhandelingen van de Koninklijke Academie voor Wetenschappen, Letteren en Schone Kunsten van België, 2010), 249–97.

individuals to make connections.[97] Given the influence such families wielded in Bruges, a large number would be expected in 'elite' groups; as Brown has shown, three families (Adornes, Bonin and Aertricke) made up almost a third of the jousters of the White Bear between 1437 and 1447.[98]

Two of the three families identified by Brown as prominent in the White Bear are among the twenty-four patricians in the shooting guilds. Five guild-brothers came from the Aertricke family, including Jan van Aertricke (d.1458), a councillor of Philip the Good, and six from the Adornes. The fame of the latter family is notable: a Genoese mercantile family that arrived in Flanders in the fourteenth century, they established their reputation as the builders of the Jeruzalemkapel, modelled on the church of the Holy Sepulchre in Jerusalem, and held several civic offices.[99] One of the most prominent of the Adornes was Anselmus, a jouster with the White Bear, burg-master, a pilgrim to the Holy Land, a Burgundian courtier and ambassador to Scotland. Anselmus was also an archer: he attended the annual *papegay* shooting contest at least twenty times and attended at least seven guild-meals. Anselmus's father, Peter (d.1464), and his uncle Jacob (d.1465), the brothers who founded the Jeruzalemkapel, were also active members of the Saint Sebastian guild, as were three other Adorneses.

The Adorneses favoured the archery guild, with only Peter (d.1464) registered among the crossbowmen; other families were involved with both guilds. The Metteneyes achieved ennoblement through the hotelier network, having international connections, especially to Scotland, and collected many municipal taxes and held many civic offices.[100] Joris (d.1474) was a ducal councillor, alderman and active member in both the archery and the crossbow guilds, serving as dean of the former in 1464. Three of his family members were in the crossbow guild and five others in the archers, including Cornilis/Cornille, who was dean of the archers in 1472. Other families active with the guilds include the Van Themseke family, of whom five were members of the Saint George guild, and the Van

---

[97] P. de Win, 'The Lesser Nobility of the Burgundian Netherlands', in M. Jones (ed.), *Gentry and Lesser Nobility in Late Medieval Europe* (Stroud: Sutton, 1986), 95–118; F. Buylaert, W. de Clercq and J. Dumolyn, 'Sumptuary Legislation, Material Culture and the Semiotics of '*vivre noblement*', in the County of Flanders (14th–16th centuries)', *Social History* 36 (2011), 393–417; F. Buylaert and J. Dumolyn, 'Shaping and Reshaping the concepts of Nobility and Chivalry in Froissart and the Burgundian Chroniclers', *Fifteenth Century* IX (2010), 59–82; J. Dumolyn, 'Later Medieval and Early Modern Urban Elites: Social Categories and Social Dynamics', in M. Asenjo-González (ed.), *Urban Elites and Aristocratic Behaviour in the Spanish Kingdoms at the End of the Middle Ages* (Turnhout: Brepols, 2013), 3–18.

[98] Brown, 'Urban Jousts in the Later Middle Ages', 318.

[99] N. Geirnaert 'De Adornes en de Jeruzalemkapel, internationale contacten in het laatmiddeleeuwse Brugge', in N. Geirnaert and A. Vandewalle (eds), *Adornes en Jeruzalem: internationaal leven in het 15de – en 16de-eeuwse Brugge* (Brugge: Stad Brugge, 1983), 11–49; A. Macquarrie, 'Anselmus Adornes of Bruges, Traveller in the East and a Friend of James III', *Innes Review* 33 (1982), 15–22.

[100] Buylaert, *Eeuwen van Ambitie*, 233–244; ibid., *repertorium*, 481–83.

Clarout and de Baenst families, with three members each in the crossbowmen. High numbers of patricians are to be expected among the guilds – indeed, if anything is surprising here it is that there were not more nobles in the guilds or that there were great patrician families, such as the Bonins or Halewijn families, who seem to be absent from both guilds.

Also in the guilds were some of the greatest lords of the Low Countries, including Philip the Good and his eldest surviving illegitimate son, Anthony the Great Bastard. As will be discussed in more depth below, Philip the Good, like the rest of the Burgundian dukes, was a member of several Flemish shooting guilds. His name is the first on the crossbow guild's list, meaning that he joined the guild in or shortly after 1437, probably as a way to promote civic values and rebuild urban-aristocratic communities after the 1436–38 rebellion. Anthony was active with both the archers and the crossbowmen and it is likely that the 16th name on the list of nobles – Jan de Bourgogne – is that of another illegitimate member of the dynasty. Two other lords, Roeland of Uutkerke and Philip of Brabant, entered the crossbow guild at the same time as the duke. Both were great lords and notable ducal servants; the former was a veteran of the battle of Othée (1408) and had served as ambassador to England.[101] For many of these great lords, the level of activity in the guilds is difficult to ascertain, but for the fourth name of the Saint George list activity is clear. Lodewijk van Gruuthuse entered the guild around 1437, led the crossbowmen to a competition in Sluis in 1452, was given a uniform in 1455, and would be elected headman in 1479. We will return to Lodewijk in more depth in chapter four, for he was an important figure in and beyond Bruges – a jouster, a book collector, host for Edward IV while he was in Bruges and, as a reward, Earl of Winchester from 1472.[102] Within Bruges, Lodewijk was involved with several devotional confraternities as well as being a jouster with the White Bear. Between the two poles of patrician and prince, the remaining twenty-four nobles cover all noble ranks: minor nobility, like the Viscount of Veurne, and greater lords, including Jacob van St-Pol, lord of Fiennes, are present.

Poorters

Further evidence of the guilds' prestige and desirability comes from analysis of the numbers of members who can be traced in the *Poorters-list*. *Poorter* could

---

[101] W. Paravicini, *Guy de Brimeu. Der burgundische Staat und seine adlige Fürhungsschicht unter Karl dem Kühnen* (Bonn: Röhrscheid, 1975), 516.

[102] M. Vale 'An Anglo-Burgundian Nobleman and Artistic Patronage; Louis de Bruges, Lord of la Gruthuyse and Earl of Winchester', in C. Barron and N. Saul (eds), *England and the Low Countries in the Later Middle Ages* (Stroud: Sutton. 1995) 13–63; M.-P. Lafitte, 'Les manuscrits de Louis de Bruges chevalier de la Toison d'Or', in M.-T. Caron et D. Clauzel (eds), *Le Banquet du Faisan, 1454: L'Occident face au défi de l'Empire Ottoman* (Arras: Artois Presses University, 1997), 243–55; H. Cools, *Mannen met macht: edellieden en de moderne staat in de Bourgondisch-Habsburgse landen (1475–1530)* (Zutphen: Walburg pers, 2001), 77–85,120–29.

be translated as 'citizen' or bourgeois; they were associated with civic authority and taxation, being legally enfranchised, with rights and obligations. Only those who purchased citizenship are noted; men born *Poorters* would not be recorded. Despite such challenges, *Poorters* are worth analysing because they became, for many towns, a source of collective honour.[103] Analysing the *Poorters* in the two shooting guilds allows for an understanding of how open the guilds were to outsiders because, by virtue of our sources, the vast majority of men who can be identified as *Poorters* were either from outside of Bruges or from rising families. The presence of *Poorters* in the shooting guilds indicates that they never became closed elites as some craft guilds, particularly the butchers, did.[104] It is also possible that, as prestigious communities connected to other urban groups, the archery and crossbow guilds were attractive to newcomers seeking social interaction and professional and social contacts, as D'Andrea has shown prestigious Italian religious confraternities to have been.[105]

The pattern of new *Poorters* in fifteenth-century Bruges as a whole reveals a great deal about urban connections and how attractive Bruges was as an immigration centre. The 1440s were a decade of extremely high migration, as Philip the Good ordered the price for purchasing citizenship to be lowered to just £3 – in contrast to the 1446 price of £6 for a Fleming and £12 for a foreigner – to encourage people to move to Bruges, which was, he said, becoming depopulated.[106] The 1430s saw very low migration, as a result of instability and rebellion, while for the rest of the period under consideration here migration remained relatively high, until it began to decline in the 1470s.[107] Towns were always attractive to rural immigrants, as places of commerce, but purchasing citizenship was an investment. The streams of vagrants and beggars that towns feared, would not be able to pay; only newcomers who would contribute to the economy and to the town's income from taxes were welcomed.[108]

---

[103] M. Boone and P. Stabel, 'New Burghers in the Late Medieval Towns of Flanders and Brabant; Conditions of Entry, Rules and Reality', in R. C. Schwinger (ed.), *Neubürger im späten Mittelalter: Migration und Austausch in der Städtelandschaft des alten Reiches (1250–1550)* (Berlin: Duncker und Humblot, 2002), 317–332.

[104] P. Stabel, 'Guilds in Medieval Flanders: Myths and Realities of Guild Life in an Export-Oriented Environment', *JMH* 30 (2004)', 194–6; Werveke, 'Ambachten en erfelijkheid', 5–17.

[105] D. M. D'Andrea, *Civic Christianity in Renaissance Italy* (Woodbridge: Boydell Press, 2007), 40–2.

[106] M. Boone, 'The Desired Stranger: Attraction and Expulsion in the Medieval City', in L. Lucassen and W. Willems (eds), *Living in the City: Urban Institutions in the Low Countries,1200–2010* (New York: Routledge, 2012), 32–45; W. Blockmans, 'The Creative Environment; Incentives to and Function of Bruges Art Production', in his *Petrus Christus in Renaissance Bruges, an Interdisciplinary Approach* (Turnhout: Brepols, 1995), 13–15.

[107] Jamees, *Brugse poorters opgetekend*.

[108] Boone, 'The Desired Stranger', 32–45

The chronology of the *Poorters'* appearances in shooting guilds fits the above pattern, revealing that the guilds remained attractive, and open, between 1437 and 1481. It is an obvious point, but one worth emphasising, that guild-brothers who purchased citizenship did so *before* they entered the shooting guilds or a craft guild.[109] At least 118 crossbowmen had purchased their *Poorter* status, as had 148 archers; this represents respectively 13% and almost 20% of the guild-brothers. Like Bruges itself, the shooting guilds were not closed but were, rather, built on integration of new and old into a strong community. The pattern of shooters who purchased citizenship fits closely with that set out by James, despite a lack of information on the crossbowmen before 1437, and on the archers before 1454. The guilds welcomed few new *Poorters* after 1470, and almost as few in the 1430s, but large numbers – thirty-three crossbowmen and forty-eight archers – entered the guild in the 1440s While this pattern is not unexpected, it does demonstrate that shooting guilds did not wax or wane in attraction or openness but attracted *Poorters* in the same sorts of patterns as did the civic society.

It is also interesting to consider how far the *Poorters* had travelled, if indeed they had travelled at all. Geographical origins are imperfectly recorded, with ten archers and thirteen crossbowmen who purchased citizenship not providing a place of birth, but for the rest a picture emerges that fits with the *Poorters* in Bruges in general. Ten archers and eight crossbowmen, just under 7% of the 118 crossbowman and 148 archers who became *Poorters*, came from Bruges itself, with a further four in each guild coming from small settlements close to Bruges, including Damme and Slypen. Rather than immigrants, these guild-brothers were almost certainly individuals rising in status and wealth who wished to enter professional and political groups and who may have joined shooting guilds in order to help their social mobility. Separately from those listed above, eighty-one, over half, of new *Poorters* in the archery guild came from Flanders, with eight from Oudenaarde alone. The figure for the crossbowmen is slightly lower, with forty-nine, over 40%, coming from Flanders, findings that are in line with those of Bruges as a whole as Thoen has shown that most new *Poorters* to Bruges came from within Flanders.[110]

For the rest of the new *Poorters* who became shooters, as with new *Poorters* in general, most came from Brabant, Holland, Limburg, Hainaut or Namur, but a small number came from further afield. Seven new shooters came from France, two archers and three crossbowmen from Tournai, one archer from Normandy and one crossbowman from Paris. Despite changing relations between France, England and Flanders, no *Poorters* entered the guilds from English-held lands;

---

[109] SAB, 385, Sint Joris, register met ledenlijst, 1321–1531, ff. 50–59v.
[110] E. Thoen, 'Verhuizen naar Brugge in de late Middeleeuwen. De rol van de immigratie van de poorters in de aanpassing van de stad Brugge aan de wijzigende economische omstandigheden. (14e–16e eeuw)', in H. Soly and R. Vermeir (eds), *Beleid en bestuur in de oude Nederlande. Liber amicorum Prof. Dr. M. Baelde* (Gent: RUG. Vakgroep Nieuwe geschiedenis, 1993), 337–43.

perhaps bowmen were less free to leave Calais or Lancastrian-Normandy. Two guild-brothers had travelled even further to settle in Bruges: an archer had come from Chambéry in Savoy, and a crossbowman, Laser Lomelin, had come from Genoa. Guilds were clearly not closed elites, new families and new citizens could join and the pattern of new membership tallies with that observed in the entire city, with newly rich natives, Flemish migrants, immigrants from other parts of the Low Countries and a few more distant migrants among guild-brothers.

Political powers

Bruges was politically ruled and represented by two benches of twelve men, the *schepenen* (aldermen) and the *raad* (councillors), each with their own burgomasters. Officials were elected annually by ducal representatives and presented to the urban population in an important ritual that emphasised their legitimacy. Although individuals could not hold office for two consecutive years, many held office multiple times throughout their lives. Certain families, like the Metteneyes and Themsekes, provided considerable numbers of aldermen and councillors although, as Brown has noted, the government was 'neither a monolithic nor an unchanging body'.[111] As councillors and aldermen ruled Bruges and were ducally approved, archers and crossbowmen serving in these roles show the prestige of membership as well as the strong connections between guilds and civic values and culture.

The most powerful Bruges officials were the two annually elected burgomasters who oversaw the aldermen and councillors, respectively. In fifteenth-century Bruges, a total of sixteen crossbowmen and eleven archers acted as burgomasters (almost 2% of each guild). Among the aldermen, forty-seven were crossbowmen (5.3% of the guild) and thirty were archers (4% of the guild). That guild-brothers held the highest office in Bruges shows that some within the guilds were extremely powerful and that many more guild-brothers had access to the highest levels of civic power. Similar numbers of guild-brothers are present among the twelve annually elected councillors, with fifty-four crossbowmen (6.1%) and forty archers (5.3%) holding office at least once. These small but significant figures emphasise once again the prestige of the guilds and the worthiness of many of their members. Indeed, the figures may help to explain why the guilds were so well funded.

The aldermen and councillors were the most powerful officials, but they were not the only ones. Bruges was run by a complex set of urban officials who took care of every area of the town's well-being. Treasurers and other officials were responsible for managing civic funds, clerks and aides helped with drawing up documents and government bureaucracy, and a range of 'pensioners' received annual sums for services. Pensioners could be nobles or well-regarded residents who served their town in on-going capacities; in either case, Bruges's decision to

---

[111] Leeuwen, 'Rituel transmission', 767–8; Brown, *Civic Ceremony*, 29–31.

give annual on-going payments to individuals reflected their value to the urban community. Like all towns, Bruges also employed messengers, individuals who might carry important messages to the duke or simply travel to nearby cities to listen to 'gossip'.[112] Despite the challenges of the fifteenth-century, with rebellions and the much-debated economic decline of Bruges and the rise of Antwerp,[113] both the archery and crossbow guilds ensured that they were connected to every level of political powers.

The civic treasurers and their committee (*ghemittee*) kept the town accounts; this was a position demanding not just trust, but real skill. Fifteen crossbowmen and ten archers acted as treasurers, with a further crossbowman and three archers serving as clerks or aides, meaning that, in all, 1.8% of crossbowmen and 1.7% of archers served in the treasury. In addition, ten crossbowmen received pensions ranging from £10 to £300 annually, and nine archers received between £12 and £100 annually. Exactly what most of these men were doing for their town is not clear, although for one archer, Jan Tsolles, it can be assumed he was active as a scribe, since his pension rose steadily and his signature appears on numerous documents, including charters issued to craft guilds.[114] Finally, two crossbowmen and one archer acted as official civic messengers. It is possible that, in attending competitions, guilds acted as unofficial messengers, listening for news and reporting back to their town. As messengers would, by the nature of their job, be away from Bruges for extended periods, such men may have been less likely to join groups like the shooting guilds that demanded not just money, but hefty time commitments.

Guild-brothers were active in all levels of political administration in Bruges, and this included the protecting town. We have seen that the guilds remained active in defending their towns and in peace-keeping across the fifteenth century, so a sizable number might be expected to serve in other military roles. Bruges employed sergeants to aid the sheriff in keeping the peace, and garrisons to watch the walls and provide an armed police force where necessary. Eight crossbowmen were sergeants and just two were members of the garrison, while the archers included one sergeant and six members of the garrison. These low numbers could imply that the guilds were, as in Lille, expected to aid the peace-keepers, so having them serve in an official capacity was redundant. Guild-brothers were allowed to bear arms, and in this they were privileged and protected groups marked out from the rest of society. Civic or ducal powers might, then have considered it sensible to have others act as sergeants and

---

[112] Lowagie, 'Stedelijke communicatie in de late middeleeuwen', 273–95; idem, 'Omme messagier ende bode te zine van de vorseide stede. De Brugse stadsboden in de late middeleeuwen', *ASEB*, 149 (2012), 3–24.

[113] Van Uytven, 'Stages of Economic Decline; Late Medieval Bruges', 259–269; Marechal, 'Le Départ de Bruges des marchands étrangers', 1–41; Brulez, 'Brugge en Antwerpen in de 15e en 16e eeuw', 15–37; Stabel, 'From Market to Shop', 79–101.

[114] His signature is on a 1454 charter to the Candle-makers, RAB, ambachten, 635.

garrison members, keeping the guilds as a valued potential reserve for problems beyond the abilities of the sergeants.

Financial powers

As a great market place and wealthy city, Bruges had a well-developed and well-documented financial management system. The tax system was relatively complex: town accounts detail direct taxes as well as larger indirect ones.[115] Indirect taxes were the largest. For instance, wine taxes were collected by rich and powerful men who paid the town several thousand pounds and then collected the taxes themselves, presumably at considerable profit, although this was a risk. Many collectors were members of the patrician families, who augmented their wealth and standing through tax farming. Wouter Metteneye, for example, a crossbowman, was involved in collecting the wine taxes between 1416 and 1430, and along with four others who collectively paid large annual sums to the town (amounts varied between £15,000 and £20,000) for the right to collect the wine tax. Over the course of the fifteenth century twenty other crossbowmen (2.3% of the guild) and fourteen archers (1.9%) were involved in collecting the wine taxes.

Taxes on local (Brugsche) and imported (Delfsche) beer were collected in the same way, although for lower payments and lower profits. Twenty-seven crossbowmen (just over 3% of the guild),and ten archers (1.3%) were active in collecting beer taxes. Like those who collected wine taxes, these men were wealthy and had access to power networks within Bruges. Of course, numerous other taxes were collected, particularly on lands and on water rights. Some individuals involved in these collections paid Bruges just 40s a year, a few paid the town more than £20. In all, fifty-five archers (7.3%) and eighty-nine crossbowmen (just over 10%) collected some type of tax at least once. Many, though not all, of those involved in taxation were also from the patrician classes, but across the fifteenth century guild-brothers remained active in all levels of civic finance. Such figures may reveal why the guild accounts are themselves so well preserved and well organised but, more importantly, they reflect a link between those taking care of the financial well-being of Bruges and those representing its civic culture.

---

[115] Murray, 'Family, Marriage and Money Changing in Medieval Bruges', 115–125; J. H. A. Munro, 'Anglo-Flemish Competition in the International Cloth Trade, 1340–1520', *PCEEB* 35 (1995), 37–60; idem, 'The Usury Doctrine and Urban Public Finances in Late-Medieval Flanders (1220–1550): Rentes (Annuities), Excise Taxes, and Income Transfers from the Poor to the Rich', in S. Cavaciocchi (ed.), *La Fiscalità nell'economia europea secc. XIII-XVIII/ Fiscal Systems in the European Economy from the 13th to the 18th Centuries* (Firenze: Firenze university press, 2008) 973–1026.

Professions

Thus far, our figures have proved that the shooting guilds of Bruges were prestigious and well-connected communities. When considering who the majority of guild-brothers were, what sort of men were able to acquire the weapons and skills required for membership, and who in civic society was deemed morally worthy enough to be in a guild, it is important to analyse professions and socio-devotional activities. The next two sections provide an understanding of the composition and representativeness of guilds relative to the rest of civic society. Professional and socio-devotional memberships show the guild communities overlapping with others and offer details of the 'elite' or non-elite status of the Bruges shooting guilds. It is worth emphasising that nothing comparable has been attempted for any other shooting guild, nor for any other Flemish festive or cultural groups. The following sections emphasise that the shooters came from all but the very lowest levels of urban society and had the sorts of multiple identities discussed by Rosser in relation to English guilds.[116]

The study of professions begins with the information gleaned from the guild-registers and then draws information from as many craft guild sources as possible in Bruges. There are dangers here of homonyms – of mistakenly identifying two individuals with the same name as the same person – but, with careful checking of dates and any other available information (such as father's name), such issues have been minimised. The following does not claim to be either complete or infallible; rather, it offers sufficient information for an analysis of the guild members' professions and the range of their activities.

Not all craft guilds in Bruges have left records, and so the profession of some guild-brothers cannot be ascertained, but, drawing on those records that do survive, the professions of 324 crossbowmen and 413 archers can be analysed. Guild-brothers' professions need to be analysed in comparison to the rest of the town, otherwise the figures risk becoming meaningless. In Table 2 the percentage of archers and crossbowmen in each of Bruges's fifty-four craft guilds has been compared to the percentages of those guilds serving in the militia of 1436, using figures taken from Dumolyn's study of the Bruges 1436–38 rebellion.[117] The craft guilds are listed in the order of precedence in which they marched in procession and to war. Not all of the guild-brothers' professions fit into Table 2, as members can be traced in professions outside of the fifty-four crafts. These additional professions are listed alphabetically in Table 3. Table 2 is a little more precise

---

[116] G. Rosser, 'Finding Oneself in a Medieval Fraternity: Individual and Collective Identities in the English Guilds', in M. Escher-Apsner (ed.), *Mittelalterliche Bruderschaften in europäischen Städten: Funktionen, Formen, Akteure / Medieval confraternities in European towns: functions, forms, protagonists* (Frankfurt am Main; Oxford: Peter Lang, 2009), 29–46.

[117] Dumolyn, *De Brugse Opstand*, 353–7.

than Table 3, as it is not clear what percentage of men in Bruges belonged to the professions listed in Table 3. In both tables each man is assigned to just one profession – the profession he was first recorded in – although changes of profession were not unknown. Together, the tables provide a clear picture of the guilds' compositions.

ID	% of the 1436 militia	Craft	Translation	Number of archers	% archers	Number of cross-bowmen	% cross-bowmen
1	3.11	wevers	weavers[a]	16	2.12	11	1.46
2	3.11	volders	fullers	7	0.93	5	0.56
3	3.11	scheerders	shearers	9	1.19	3	0.34
4	1.11	ververs	dyers	4	0.53	8	0.90
5	2.89	vleeshouwers	butchers	1	0.13	3	0.34
6	1.11	viskopers	fishmongers	1	0.13	3	0.34
7	4.44	timmerlieden	carpenters	8	1.06	14	1.58
8	2.44	metselaars	masons	5	0.66	5	0.56
9	0.89	tegeldekkers	tilers	12	1.59	5	0.56
10	0.22	loodgieters	plumbers	2	0.26	1	0.11
11	0.22	plaasteraars	plasterers	2	0.26	3	0.34
12	0.22	strodekkers	thatchers	0	0	4	0.45
13	0.67	zagers	sawyers	3	0.40	2	0.23
14	0.89	wijnmeters	wine-measurers	1	0.13	1	0.11
15	0.44	wijnschroders	wine carriers	3	0.40	2	0.23
16	2.44	kuipers	coopers	5	0.66	1	0.11
17	0.44	wielwerkers	wheelwrights	0	0	6	0.68
18	0.89	draaiers	turners	3	0.40	8	0.90
19	1.33	schrijnwerkers	cabinet-makers	2	0.26	2	0.23
20	0.89	beeldenmakers en zadelaars	painters and saddlers	17	2.25	25	2.81
21	0.89	boogmakers	bowyers	11	1.45	7	0.79
22	0.22	lijnmakers	rope-makers	2	0.26	0	0
23	0.22	potters	potters	7	0.93	4	0.45
24	3.56	smeden	smiths[b]	8	1.06	3	0.34
25	1.33	zilversmeden	silversmith (and goldsmiths)	20	2.56	2	0.23
26	0.67	wapenmakers	armourers	6	0.79	1	0.11
27	0.67	tinnestoop-makers	tin-pot-makers	6	0.79	2	0.23

ID	% of the 1436 militia	Craft	Translation	Number of archers	% archers	Number of crossbowmen	% crossbowmen
28	3.11	cordewaniers	cobblers	8	1.06	14	1.58
29	0.67	zwarteleder touwers	curriers	4	0.53	3	0.34
30	1.56	huidevetters	tanners	4	0.53	0	0
31	0.67	dobberers	curriers[c]	0	0	1	0.11
32	0.89	beurzenmakers en witledertouwers	purse-makers and fine leather curriers	0	0	4	0.45
33	0.89	handschoenwerkers	glovers	7	0.93	0	0
34	0.22	kousemakers	hosiers	1	0.13	0	0
35	4.89	kleermakers	tailors	9	1.19	3	0.34
36	1.11	kulkstikkers	doublet-makers	1	0.13	4	0.45
37	0.67	lamwerkers	furriers[d]	3	0.40	1	0.11
38	1.56	oudeklederkopers	old-clothes-sellers	1	0.13	7	0.79
39	1.11	oudegrauwwerkers	second-hand furriers	0	0	0	0
40	1.11	wiltwerkers	furriers	0	0	0	0
41	2.67	bakkers	bakers	27	3.57	15	1.69
42	0.89	molenaars	millers	4	0.53	5	0.56
43	0.22	hoedemakers	milliners	0	0	0	0
44	0.22	tapijtwevers	tapestry-weavers	0	0	0	0
45	1.33	linnenwevers	linen-weavers	0	0	1	0.11
46	0.67	wolleslagers	carders	3	0.40	0	0
47	1.56	barbiers	Barbers/surgeons	9	1.19	2	0.23
48	0.67	rienmakers	girdlers	3	0.40	4	0.45
49	0.22	schedemakers	scabbard-makers	2	0.26	1	0.11
50	0.89	paternostermakers	rosary-makers	1	0.13	3	0.34
51	7.11	makelaars	brokers	4	0.53	10	1.13
52	0.67	fruitiers	fruit-merchants	2	0.26	3	0.34
53	3.33	shipper	shippers	14	1.85	3	0.34
54	1.56	grauwwerkers	furriers	3	0.40	5	0.56

Table 2 The Fifty-four Guilds Present in the 1436 Militia

'GUILD-BROTHERS' 83

^a Including not just wool-weavers but also fleece weavers (tijkwevers).
^b Includes other sorts of smiths, e.g. locksmiths.
^c The various leather guilds were connected and it is difficult to sum up the precision of the Flemish terms in English. The guilds of 'witledertouwers' 'zwatrledertouwers' and 'dobberers' have all been translated as 'curriers' or leather-workers, rather than the literal white, black and wet leather workers.
^d The three furrier guilds, lambwerkers, grauwerkers and wiltewerkers, worked different kinds of furs; they were linked but separate guilds. There was a hierarchy, with grauwerkers, the lowest, working with common animals that yielded cheap fur; lambwerkers mainly skinning sheep; and the wiltewerkers dealing in high-quality luxury furs, such as ermine. Moving between guilds was straightforward: crossbowman Jan Paye entered the grauwerkers in 1420, but later served as an inspector (vinder) for the wiltwerkers, as did fellow crossbowman Jacop de Groote, who became a grauwerker in 1430 and acted as 'vinder' of the wiltwekers in 1435 and as dean in 1441. Here, no wiltwerkers are recorded, as every archer or crossbowman who appears as a wiltwerker appeared as a grauwerker or lambwerker first.

Profession	Number of archers	% of archers	Number of crossbowmen	% of crossbowmen
basket-carriers	1	0.13	0	0
basket-weavers	1	0.13	0	0
beer-carrier	9	1.19	0	0
copyists (*boucscrivers*)	4	0.53	0	0
brewers	19	2.51	0	0
card-makers (*kaartenaar*)	3	0.40	0	0
chandlers	3	0.40	2	0.23
cheesemongers	0	0	1	0.11
clerks	4	0.53	1	0.11
comb-makers	1	0.13	0	0
cooks	3	0.40	1	0.11
corn-measurers	3	0.40	0	0
embroiderers	1	0.13	0	0
ferry-men	1	0.13	2	0.23
gardeners	1	0.13	0	0
bonnet-makers	11	1.46	5	0.56
labourers	6	0.79	0	0
loriners	3	0.40	0	0
merchants	4	0.53	4	0.45
mill-makers	2	0.26	0	0
money-changers	1	0.13	0	0
officials in cloth-hall	6	0.79	13	1.47
officials in grain market	2	0.26	4	0.45
officials in linen-hall	2	0.26	5	0.56

Profession	Number of archers	% of archers	Number of crossbowmen	% of crossbowmen
officials in *Vogelmarket*[a]	1	0.13	2	0.23
priests	0	0	1	0.11
ramen	4	0.53	1	0.11
scale-makers	3	0.40	0	0
ship-wrights	1	0.13	0	0
spicers	2	0.26	0	0
taveniers[b]	2	0.26	0	0
wardens in New Hall	1	0.13	1	0.11
wardens of mead	0	0	1	0.11
wardens of the herb market	0	0	1	0.11
wardens of the soap	4	0.53	4	0.45
wardens of wax	2	0.26	2	0.23
wardens of the *oude halle*	0	0	1	0.11
wardens of the selling of English wool	4	0.53	2	0.23

Table 3 Other Professions

[a] Bird market, i.e. for the sale of chickens, ducks etc.
[b] Two archers are recorded as being '*cabaretiers*'. This profession has been translated as inn-keeper, and these men would have run local taverns, rather than being the great hoteliers associated with *makelaars* and international trade.

The expected results for Table 2, as the sources are incomplete, would be for the percentages of guild-brothers involved in a specified craft to be consistently lower than the militia percentages – but a far more complex picture emerges. One of the most striking incongruities between the figures (but one that is to be expected) is the higher than average number of military-related professions in the shooting guilds. Bowyers made up only 0.89% of the militia, but 1.45% of the archers, while the armourers made up 0.67% of the militia and 0.79% of the archers; this figure would grow if the three lorniers (makers of spurs, harnesses and other horse equipment) were added. Both shooting guilds contained more military crafts than a cross-section of Bruges society as a whole, but this is largely to be expected, as guilds maintained a level of martial importance throughout the period and made extensive use of bowyers and fletchers. These figures might help to explain from where guild-brothers obtained their weapons.

For several other crafts, the numbers in the shooting guilds are largely in line with statistics for the militia. The bakers made up 2.67% of the force of 1436, and 3.57% of the archers and 1.69% of the crossbowmen. Lower figures should be expected for the crossbowmen, as many of them cannot be identified with a particular craft. Similarly, lambwekrers (mid-ranking furriers) made up 0.67% of the militia, and 0.4% of the archers and 0.11% of the crossbowmen.

For other, richer crafts, a different picture emerges. The number of painters in Bruges was small, making up only 0.89% of the militia. Although not as wealthy or prestigious as tapestry-weavers, these were, nevertheless, skilled and sought-after craftsmen. Not all would be artists; house painters are also present. Painters made up a very impressive 2.25% of the archers and 2.81% of the crossbowmen. Like the bowyers, painters could have been serving their guilds; both sets of account-books record payments for painting walls and shields. Gold or silversmiths were over-represented in the archery guild, although not in the crossbow guild, making up 1.33% of the militia, but an impressive 2.56% of the archery guild and just 0.23% of the crossbow guild. The great number of luxury craftsmen is significant, indicating that both guilds contained a marginally higher proportion of such men than Bruges as a whole, implying that the shooting guilds attracted the more prosperous citizens. Another indicator of the higher status and attractiveness of the shooting guilds is the lower numbers of those in less-prestigious occupations, such as second-hand clothes sellers, enlisted in the guilds. Such individuals made up 1.56% of the militia, but just 0.13% of the archers and only 0.79% of the crossbowmen. These figures indicate that men of lower status were less likely to be in the shooting guilds, but nevertheless guild-brothers are present from all professions and all levels.

Broadly speaking, our figures imply that the richer craft guilds are all well represented, and the humble ones under-represented, in turn implying a high status for the shooters. This is not a clear-cut distinction, as some high-status or rich professions are extremely under-represented. The wealthy brokers (*Makelaars*) made up 7.11% of the militia, and such wealthy and influential men were the kind that might have been expected to join shooting guilds. Yet they made up only 0.53% of the archers and 1.13% of the crossbowmen. Shippers would likewise have been wealthy, with connections far beyond Bruges; they made up 3.33% of the militia, but just 1.85% of the archers and 0.34% of the crossbowmen. It is possible that richer merchants and shippers had to be absent from Bruges for what could be lengthy periods, so they may have chosen not to join the time-consuming shooting guilds. Such figures highlight the dangers of labelling groups as 'elite' or, indeed, as 'bourgeois'.

Attention must also be paid to guild-brothers in Table 3. Members of both guilds were involved in the various markets of Bruges; such men may also have been linked to craft guilds, but would have been wealthy individuals and men of some influence. Officials from the grain, cloth, linen and bird markets make up 1.44% of the archers and an impressive 2.71% of the crossbowmen. The other wardens, of the soap, wax, drink and cloth halls, and the wardens of the English wool staple – men responsible for tax collection and quality inspection – made up 1.45% of the archers and 1.35% of the crossbowmen. Such figures imply that wealthier, powerful men were more likely to be crossbowmen, as do some of the figures in Table 2, but again, a diversity of guild-brothers emerges from some of the figures in Table 3.

Our figures further reveal that some guild-brothers were active in what can be considered as lower-status professions. Along with the nobles and artists were two inn-keepers. These were not the rich hostel owners involved in international trade, but rather humbler figures. Each guild also contained a ferry man and, perhaps most surprisingly, the archery guilds contained six labourers, the men responsible for loading and unloading boats in Bruges. These are very small percentages, but it should be remembered that the lower-status professions are less likely to be recovered than, say, the weavers. There are no membership lists for labourers, no lists of bequests made by ferrymen, so that any of the shooters can be shown to have been among these professions is noteworthy. At least one of the labourers, Heindric Raywaerts, held office in the archery guild, serving as a 'finder' (*zorgher*) in 1473, showing that high positions in the guilds were relatively open. The small number of lower-status professions indicates that guild membership was not closed to any professions: the guilds were representative of their towns politically, economically and professionally.

Socio-devotional activities

In considering guild-brothers' 'moral credit' and how individuals could be judged to be 'worthy' of guild membership, the non-professional activities of the guild-brothers become important. Further, their membership within socio-devotional groups gives further insight into the guilds' place within civic society and overlapping community with other groups. As the next chapter will demonstrate, archery and crossbow guilds were social and devotional groups in their own right, and so the multiple relationships discussed here should be not be seen as a negative comment on guild devotions. Rather, archers and crossbowmen who were jousters or in the brotherhood of Rosebeke provide further evidence of the place of guild-brothers within civic communities and underline the importance of not treating medieval individuals as one-dimensional figures.

Jousters had a good deal in common with the shooting guilds, including martial ideals and noble members, so an overlap in membership is to be expected. The jousters of the White Bear were a small and exclusive group. Usually between four and eight took part, although the largest event, in 1427, included twenty men. Brown has identified 252 men who participated in the White Bear between 1391 and 1487, and a further sixty-nine who took part in Lille events in the 1420s and 1430s.[118] As might be expected, many jousters were from the 'highest ranked citizens and families of Bruges', or those that owned lands outside the town, including several brokers. In addition, Brown has calculated

---

[118] Abeele, *Het Ridderlijk Gezelschap van de witte beer*; Despars, *Cronijke van den lande ende graefscepe*.

that 61% of the jousters entered civic governance.[119] Some men, particularly patrician families, including the Adornes and Metteneyes, were in both the shooting guilds and the jousters. In all, thirty-two crossbowmen (3.6% of the guild) and twenty archers (3.2% of the guild) jousted with the White Bear. Given the likely relationship between shooters and the development of the chambers of rhetoric, some overlap in membership is to be expected. Sadly, the two Bruges chambers of rhetoric – the Holy Ghost and the Three Samaritans – have left only fragmentary membership lists and accounts, and so just five crossbowmen and only one archer can be identified in the chambers.

Archers and crossbowmen were also among Bruges's many devotional confraternities and are important in understanding the place of guild-brothers within Bruges. One of the wealthiest confraternities was the *Drogenboom* (Dry Tree) confraternity, founded by 1396, with a relatively small membership of around sixty – or perhaps ninety – members annually, who included courtiers and international merchants.[120] The confraternity included nineteen crossbowmen (2%) and ten archers (1.3%) and several with their wives, indicating connections and interactions. The Rosebeke confraternity was founded to give thanks for the victory at Rosebeke in 1382, and undertook an annual pilgrimage, making it more active than *Drogenboom*. The Rosebeke guild had 'pretentions of social exclusivity', with court figures and numerous magistrates among its members; indeed, the confraternity seems to have helped confraternity members to gain access to civic power.[121] Although the membership lists do not begin until 1470, eighteen crossbowmen (2%) and ten archers (1.3%) are among the members, again indicating prestigious connections. Not all confraternities were so prestigious. The confraternity of Our Lady of the Snow had been founded by 1450 and become very popular after a miracle in 1464. It was huge, with over 900 members in the year ending August 1467 and over 1,300 by the mid-1470s. Members included Charles the Bold, Lodewijk van Gruuthuse, bishops of Tournai, but also poor widows, as the entrance fee was 4*d* and the annual subscription only 2*d*.[122] With so many members, a good number of archers and crossbowmen could to be expected in the confraternity, and in fact forty-seven crossbowmen (5%) and forty-four archers (almost 6%) were members of Our Lady of the Snow.

---

[119] Brown, *Civic Ceremony*, 141–5.
[120] A. De Schodt, 'La Confrérie de Notre-Dame de l'Arbre Sec', *ASEB* 28 (1876–7), 141–87; 60 paid members, but around 30 were later shown to be in arrears. I am grateful to Dr Andrew Brown for this reference; SAB, 505 gilde drogenboom, rekeningen; Brown, *Civic Ceremony*, 155–7; idem, 'Bruges and the "Burgundian Theatre State"', 578–9.
[121] Brown, *Civic Ceremony*, 1.
Brown, *Civic Ceremony*, 153–4; idem, 'Bruges and the "Burgundian Theatre State"', 577–8.
[122] RAB, OLV, 1531; Brown, *Civic Ceremony*, 160–1; idem, 'Bruges and the "Burgundian Theatre State"', 573–89.

Archery and crossbow guild-brothers, quite simply, came from all but the very poorest ranks of civic society and created a community with its own sense of purpose that overlapped with other urban communities. Within the guilds, councillors could drink with comb-makers and tax collectors might shoot with gardeners. Indeed, a mayor might find his skills being inspected by a labourer. It is simplistic to label either of the shooting guilds as 'elite' or 'exclusive'. The figures show that the crossbowmen included slightly more of the richest and most prominent Bruges citizens, but, unlike the jousters of the White Bear, both guilds drew members from all ranks of society and also allowed newcomers to enter. They were organised communities, with annually elected officials, that helped to promote a shared sense of purpose and did their best to promote unity for the benefit of all members. To enter a guild one should have paid money, although many did not, and one had to be armed, skilled and morally worthy. Guild-members did not just include men, as the membership lists reveal around 10% of members to be female, and the guild-brothers were certainly not elitist. The guilds were hierarchical, but they were communities that served together in war and in peace keeping, who elected officials and who practised together regularly, and whose members were drawn from a diverse range of socio-economic backgrounds to make them representative of their towns.

3

'For drinking in recreational assemblies'

The Archery and Crossbow Guilds as Social and Devotional Communities

Once a year the crossbowmen of Lille gathered together as a community to celebrate their prestigious identity, to hold their annual competition and to unite all of the members in bonds of brotherhood. The date varied a little from year to year, but was always in early summer. The day began with the crossbowmen gathering in their guild chapel dedicated to Saint George to hear mass and pray for any guild-brother who had died during the year. Next they went to their *jardin*, where all guild-brothers were expected to take part in the annual *papegay* competition, so-called because the guild-brothers shot at a small wooden parrot atop a large wooden pole. After the competition the guild-brothers, who were all expected to be in their guild livery and on their best behaviour, retired to the guild hall. There they sat down for their annual meal and spent the night eating and drinking together, possibly enjoying some entertainment related to the identity and narrative of their guild. Such a picture of festivities on a certain day is common in guilds across Flanders, although details and the level of available records vary substantially.

The Papegay

Crossbowmen in Lille were expected to attend the annual shooting competition, dressed in their livery, or risk being fined 5s.[1] Guild-brothers who failed to attend the feast risked fines – unless they were absent from the town – in large and small towns across the county. No evidence of fines being imposed has been recorded; but, as they were often specified to be used for drinks for those in attendance, it is possible that fines were paid, and drinks bought, without a written record being created.

The annual *papegay* shoot should have been attended by all, and the timing of the events is important. Many shooting competitions were held in late spring or early summer, presumably for the practical reason of a better chance of good

---

[1] AML, PT, 5883, ff. 28–31.

weather, and also on account of their cultural significance. In the small town of Pecquencourt, just east of Douai, the crossbowmen met for their *papegay* contest on 1 May, while those of Roubaix met on the Sunday after the Day of Saint Urban (25 May).[2] The crossbowmen of Douai held their competition, called *rossignol*, on the feast of *mi-carême* (mid-Lent), which is usually in mid–late March, and those of Dendermonde met on Ascension Sunday, which would usually have been in May.[3] As we shall see in chapters five and six, large regional competitions tended to be a little later, usually in June or July, and so holding civic shoots in May would allow constables to assess who their ten best shooters were, although whether civic shoots were held in May because the large competitions were in June or vice versa is an impossible question to answer.

The *papegay* shoots were held regularly across the fourteenth and fifteenth centuries, appearing annually in town accounts. In Douai in 1415–16 the archers were given twenty-four lots of wine (just over 50 litres) on Saint Sebastian's day and a further twelve lots (around 25 litres) for 'for drinking together as is the custom on the night of the shooting of the jay'. Douai continued to give wine and money to archers and crossbowmen for their feasts throughout the fifteenth century, for their shoot and for annual support.[4] In Lille the archers received twelve lots of wine for their *papegay* in the fourteenth century, although this was raised to sixteen lots in 1406. That year the crossbowmen received twenty-four lots for their *papegay* contest, an increase from sixteen lots. The lesser (*petit*) crossbowmen began to receive support for their *papegay* shoot in 1427, receiving sixteen lots of wine, while the lesser archers appear in 1437 and received nine lots of wine. The culveriners appear a little later, but from 1465 they were also given twelve lots of wine for their annual shooting competitions.[5] Every town for which town accounts have been analysed gave its guilds annual support, and usually refers at least once to an additional grant of wine or money being given to the guild on the day of its *papegay* shoot.

Financial records to *papegay* shoots are prolific across Flanders, yet descriptions of what the shoots actually consisted of are rather harder to trace, and a combination of sources must be pulled together to provide any description of the events. Shooters can be seen as small details in several early modern artworks, and two such works now in the Le Musée de l'Hospice Comtesse in Lille are particularly interesting. The first, a seventeenth-century oil on wood copy of a lost earlier image, shows the view toward Lille and the Château de Courtrai, and on the right archers shooting upwards at a bird on a small pole. A second image, made in 1729, depicts the celebrations following the birth of the Dauphin (Louis, son of Louis XV and father of Louis XVI, Louis XVII and Charles X) and shows the 'compagnie Bourgeoise de tireurs d'arc' gathered just outside of Lille

---

[2] ADN 1H 369; AMR, EE 1.
[3] DAM, AA 94; *Ordonnances de Philippe le Hardi*, vol. 1, p. 297.
[4] DAM, CC201–204.
[5] AML, CV, 16012–16263.

to shoot at a bird on a wooden pole.[6] Shooters can also be found on large early modern printed town maps, such as the 1618 *Flandria*, very large and very detailed illustration of Ghent. In the image, the crossbowmen of Saint George can be seen in their garden shooting at a small bird atop a tall pole.[7] The tradition continued into the seventeenth century, most famously in the monumental image of the Infanta Isabella Eugenia, joint sovereign of the Spanish Netherlands, shooting the *papegay* with the crossbowmen of Ghent. The image, now in the STAM in Ghent, shows Isabella with the crossbow, aiming up at the wooden bird atop a very large pole and surrounded by leading guild-brothers and civic dignitaries, her husband and co-sovereign seated behind her.[8] Although measurements cannot be recovered, there is no reason to doubt that these images depicting the same sorts of scenes that would have been witnessed at *papegay* contests in the fourteenth and fifteenth centuries.

The shoot itself can be only roughly reconstructed, but for guild-brothers across Flanders attendance at annual events was clearly desirable. Only in Bruges is it possible to trace how many guild-brothers did and did not attend the annual shoot, as only the Bruges archers have preserved lists of those who came to shoot at the small wooden bird each year.[9] In 1462 and again in 1454 there were 248 archers at the *papegay* shoot in Bruges, the highest recorded attendances. The lowest attendance was for the shoot in 1461, when there were just 169 archers, and the average attendance was 219.5. Some members attended many shoots, among them men like Anselmus Adornes, who attended at least twenty *papegay* shoots between 1454 and his death in 1483. He was not the most active guild-brother; a glover called Anthuenis van Rijsel attended at least twenty-three *papegay* shoots. There is no simple rich/active and poor/inactive divide here: a furrier called Adriaen vande Walle attended at least nineteen shoots while other Adorneses attended just one or two. It is not possibly to create a detailed analysis of attendance at these shoots, as only twenty-two attendance lists of have survived between 1454 and 1480. It is important to note that no brother, not even Anthuenis, attended every shoot and that many guild-brothers attended only a small number of shoots. The guilds wanted all members to attend and it is likely that all shoots attracted a good – though never complete – attendance.

All guilds held annual shooting competitions at which all members were required to attend and shoot at a wooden bird. The man who struck the bird with the best shot would be 'king' of the guild for the year. The same term was used across and beyond Flanders, implying guild interaction and a shared

---

[6] C. Monnet, *Lille, Portrait d'une ville* (Paris: Jacques Marseille 2003), 18–19, 150–1.
[7] A.-L. Van Bruaene and I. Coessens, 'Weerbare mannen? De Sint-Jorisgilde in tijden van opstand (1540–1620)', in *Gedenkboek*, 45.
[8] M. Twycross, 'The Archduchess and the Parrot', in *Gender and Fraternal Orders in Europe*, 63–90; Bruaene and Cossens, 'Weerbare mannen?', 51.
[9] BASS, vol. 3: rekeningboeken, 1455–1472 and vol. 4 rekeningboeken, 1468–1513.

community, and also the importance of the title itself.[10] Guild kings were prestigious, skilled men, but not necessarily the richest or most 'elite' guildbrothers. They were valued within the guilds, as we shall see below. An even higher guild honorific title existed: if a man shot the bird three years in a row, he would be called 'emperor'. In 1412 the crossbowmen of Oudenaarde received an extra grant of wine for their emperor, while the crossbowmen of Ypres had an emperor in 1473; even the smaller town of Ardenbourg had an emperor of its archers in 1463.[11] In large and small towns, shooting skill remained an important element of prestige within the guild community, and was perhaps even a way to advance socially within the guilds.

The kings were prestigious figures in the guilds, and indeed the guilds were not unique in having 'kings'. Certain jousters also had a king, and mock-kings were popular in much of medieval urban culture.[12] Although the title might be common, it is nonetheless meaningful, and in many guilds regalia came with the royal title. At least one guild, the crossbowmen of the small town of Ham in Picardy, won a small sum of money for becoming 'king', but no reference to a financial prize survives from the larger towns.[13] Guilds in Flemish towns probably did not give money to winners, so as not to appear to be gambling, which could have been seen as dishonourable.[14] Although they did not win money, in many places the kings did gain some sort of reward. The Bruges crossbowmen gave their king a uniform each year, while most other members had to pay for their own. In Douai, from at least 1440, the king had all of his expenses, including food and drink, paid by the guild, as did the king of the Roubaix crossbowmen.[15] Several sixteenth-century guild collars survive. These feature ornate birds and badges, some with ducal emblems like the cross of Saint Andrew, usually with names and dates.[16] The guild collars, unlike collars from noble orders like the Golden Fleece, would not be worn all the time, but only on

---

[10] RAG, RVV, 7351, f. 199v; G. Willame, *Notes sur les serments Nivellois* (Nivelles: Guignardé, 1901), 12; *ORF* vol. 9, 522–6.

[11] OSAOA, microfilm 684, accounts 1406–1422, register 2, f. 8; AGR, CC, 38697, f. 23; AGR, CC, 31760, f. 23.

[12] Dumolyn, 'Une Idéologie urbain "Bricolée" en Flandre medieval', 1054–5; A. van Gennep, *Le folklore de la Flandre et du Hainaut français*, 2vols (Paris: Maisonneuve, 1935–1936), vol.1, 255–70; W. L. Braekman, 'Driekoningenavond; koningsbrieden, liederen ed gedichten', *Volkskunde* 98 (1997), 1–8.

[13] Janvier, 'Notice sur les anciennes corporations', 278.

[14] Bans on gambling are numerous in town ordinances, for instance in 1516 Lille banned gambling with cards or board games, AML, OM, 379, 95v, 98; for the link between violence and gambling see J. M. Mehl, 'Jeux de hasard et violence à la fin du Moyen Age: une alliance éternelle?', *Ludica* 11 (2007), 89–95.

[15] AML, CV, payments every year, e.g. 1455, 16196, f. 73; SAB, 385, Sint Jorisgilde, Rekeningen 1445–1480, f. 3v; DAM, Arbalestiers de Douay 24II232, f. 3 bis v; AMR, EE1.

[16] R. van Hinte, 'A Silver Collar from the Wallace Collection, London', *Journal of the Society of Archer-Antiquaries* 14 (1971), 10–15; see Figure 6.

special occasions such as the procession. In Lille the king of the crossbowmen led the guild-brothers in the annual procession, with his 'symbol', presumably a staff or collar. Kingship allowed any member to rise to the top of guild society – even labourers could be kings – and guilds worked to be seen as honourable through titles and skill, not money.

Commensality

Just as they were expected to attend the annual shooting competition, all members were required to attend the meal that followed it and, for many guilds, another meal on the day of their patron saint. The guilds are far from unique in their emphasis on feasting together to build community. Indeed it is well known that working for unity through commensality was common in all guilds, confraternities or even noble organisations in and beyond Flanders, with all forms of guilds having some kind of meal. Such events might be connected to alms giving and feeding the poor, or might simply be a way to bring a confraternity or guild together as companions so as to maintain peace and brotherhood.[17]

Philip the Bold's 1398 ordinance to the crossbowmen of Dendermonde stated that on the 'day of the Ascension the guild-brothers will promise to eat dinner together' in their guild hall and each guild-brother was expected to pay equally for the meal 'whether present or not'. In Douai, the annual meal took place after the *papegay* shoot and all guild-brothers were to 'be in assembly (for) a dinner'. In the small town of Langhemark, the guild-brothers should have 'dinner all together' following their *papegay* shoot, according to a 1465 ducal charter. In larger towns there were two annual meals, and for the guilds of Bruges and Lille these were on the day of the *papegay* and on the day of their patron saint.[18]

Every shooting guild emphasised the need to eat together at least once a year. For most guilds these annual or bi-annual meals were partially funded by the civic authorities, demonstrating once more the pride and prestige the guilds brought to their towns. In Ghent, the greater crossbowmen received a total of 12

---

[17] G. Rosser, 'Guilds in Urban Politics in Late Medieval England', in A. A. Gadd and P. Wallis (eds), *Guilds and Associations in Europe, 900–1900* (London: University of London Institute of Historical Research, 2006), 28; idem, 'Going to the Fraternity Feast; Commensality and Social Relations in Late Medieval England', *Journal of British Studies* 33 (1994), 430–45; A. Douglas, 'Midsummer in Salisbury, the Tailors' Guild and Confraternity, 1444–1642', and M. Flynn, 'Rituals of Solidarity in Castilian Confraternities', both in *Renaissance and Reformation* 13 (1989), 35–51, 53–68; M. McRee, 'Unity or Division? The Social Meaning of Guild Ceremony in Urban Communities', in B. Hanawalt, and K. Reyerson (eds), *City and Spectacle in Medieval Europe* (Minneapolis: University of Minnesota Press, 1994), 189–197; J. R. Banker, *Death in The Community: Memorialization And Confraternities in an Italian Commune in the Late Middle Ages* (Athens, GA; London: University of Georgia Press, 1988), 75–83.

[18] *Ordonnances de Philippe le Hardi*, vol. 2, 296–300; RAG, RVV, 7351, f. 225v, f. 228–228v; DAM, Arbalestiers de Douay 24II232, f. 2; AML, PT 5883, ff. 28–31.

groats each year to pay for their annual meal. In Douai, the archers received £18 for costs associated with their annual shoot and the following meal.[19] In Lille the crossbowmen's statutes made clear that the town would give them additional funds to support the guild's cost in having fine meals and wines in the 'company of strangers and messengers', using meals to build communities that reached both across and beyond the town.[20]

Guilds used commensality to build and to emphasise their internal bonds. Such bonds did not have to be about equality in order to be meaningful. Medieval studies of feasting tend to emphasise the unifying strategies of such events and their potential to build bonds.[21] Of course, such values were present in guilds, but it is rare to be able to delve deeper into events and unpick the levels of hierarchy, as few medieval sources survive that allow the mechanics of commensality to be examined. However, Bruges, with its very detailed records, allows for an insight into the private and usually undocumented world of community and hierarchy. The archers of Saint Sebastian not only recorded accounts of spending for their meals but also listed which members sat at which of the five tables in the guild hall. Using these unusual and extremely valuable sources, it is apparent that the guilds of fifteenth-century Bruges, like the seventeenth-century militias analysed by Schama, balanced 'fraternity with station'.[22]

It should first be noted that although attendance at annual meals was desirable, few guilds record any kind of enforcement, beyond rules that all guild-brothers, whether present or not, should contribute to the cost of the event. As noted, in Bruges the average attendance at a *papegay* shoot was just under 220 guild-brothers, yet the meal that followed was attended, on average, by only around 81 guild-brothers, and attendance at the meal on the day of Saint Sebastian was lower still, at around seventy-one. As noted in the previous chapter, the names of 755 archers can be identified from Bruges in the second half of the fifteenth century and every one of them attended at least one *papegay* shoot. In contrast 368 guild-brothers are not recorded as attending the meal that followed the shoot. This figure is partially explained by gaps in our evidence, but it is clear that many guild-brothers did not attend the annual meal following their shoot. Moreover, of the 755 named guild-brothers in fifteenth-century Bruges, 256 are not recorded as attending any meal, either on the day of the *papegay* or on the day of Saint Sebastian. Such figures invite the question of why there should be such a drop-off in attendance at meals. Absences cannot be explained by absence from Bruges, as the meal followed the annual shoot.

---

[19] SAG, 301/25 f 75r, 7 Feb. 1419; DAM, CC205 onwards.
[20] AML, PT, 5883, ff. 28–31
[21] Rosser, 'Going to the Fraternity Feast', 430–45; Douglas, 'Midsummer in Salisbury', 35–51; McRee, 'Unity or Division?'189–97.
[22] S. Schama, *The Embarrassment of Riches, an Interpretation of Dutch Culture in the Golden Age* (London: Fontana Press, 1988), 177–82.

It might be tempting to conclude that many members were absentees and that only the wealthiest attended multiple feasts, but guild attendance, and participation in guild commensality, was far more complex. A significant number of members, 44%, attended between one and five meals, showing that the unifying potential of meals, as well as their social function, was understood – but members did not have to attend every year. Others were far more active, including Jan Tsolles, who attended at least nineteen meals and was dean of the guild four times and king in 1472. Yet Jan Tsolles would not be considered an 'elite' member: he was a scribe and civic clerk, educated and reasonably wealthy, but not in the highest ranks of civic society. Others played even smaller roles in guild activity, as guild-brothers were also part of various other communities within Bruges and may not have seen the archers as their most important networks. Although attendance was an ideal, it was not essential for every guild-brother every year.

The hierarchy at work within the guild can be analysed in detail through seating plans. Those of 1470 have been analysed elsewhere,[23] so here an overview of the two meals of 1468 will be given. This was a peaceful year, one that brought great prestige and glamour to Bruges through the wedding in June of Charles the Bold and Margaret of York in Sluis, followed by spectacular entrances into Bruges.[24] Unlike the later 1470s, when factions became an issue for many within Bruges society and may have kept guild-brothers from attending, 1468 saw few such impediments.[25] An analysis of both meals for this year therefore provides a window into the workings of a relatively peaceful urban community and the forms of interaction within guild commensality. Attendance at each meal saw a near-average numbers of attendees, with sixty-seven men at the meal of Saint Sebastian (20 January) and sixty-five at that of the *papegay* in mid-summer, twenty-five of the guild-brothers being present at both meals. At the meal of Saint Sebastian there were four tables which sat, eleven, twenty-three, twenty-two and eleven men, while at the *papegay* feast the same four tables sat eleven, twenty-two, seventeen and fourteen men.

On Saint Sebastian's day the eleven men at the top table included some powerful and prestigious men, two high-ranking guild-brothers, the guild-king (Jacob Pots) and the headman (Jan Breydel, an alderman and councillor). They were joined by Joris Metteneye, burgomaster, alderman and councillor, two jousters of the White Bear and the town sheriff. Such men might be considered the guild's upper class, yet the other five men at this table were not civic office holders. Only one of the five, Pauwels Boykin, appears in any civic documents, and then only as a collector of small water taxes, proving that standing outside of the guild was one factor in achieving high standing within the guild, but not the *only* factor.

---

[23] L. Crombie 'Honour, Community and Hierarchy in the Feasts of the Archery and Crossbow Guilds of Bruges, 1445–1481', *JMH* 37 (2011), 102–13.
[24] Brown and Small, *Court and Civic*, 54–87.
[25] Haemers, *Common Good*, 137–227.

The next table, seating twenty-three men, was headed by Jan Tsolles, noted above as an active archer and civic scribe. Also present was his son Melsior, still a young man in 1468, although by 1500 he had become a wealthy broker, likely with the assistance of his father's connections. The remaining twenty-one men were a diverse mix of trades: for five no profession can be traced, while the others comprised a blacksmith, a goldsmith, a potter, three brewers, an innkeeper, a shipper, a wool-merchant, a fletcher and, with them, four men from connected crafts – a skinner, a tanner, a bag maker and a glover – plus one man who collected small taxes on waterways and, finally, one town sergeant. The mix of crafts here is interesting: leather trades are closely connected, as are inn keeping and brewing, but such a diverse range of other professions indicates that there was a pronounced mix of socio-economic groups sitting and feasting together, and that guild bonds were not solely dependent upon profession.

The third table, of twenty-two men, was just as diverse. Seven of the guild-brothers professions' could not be found, but the remaining fifteen included three goldsmiths, four bakers, a barber-surgeon, a shearer, a shipper, a glover, a joiner, weaver, a bowyer and one (Williem Andries) who would later become a lock-gatekeeper (*spey-houder*) – a position of trust and standing if not wealth. Again there are a mix of professions here whose interaction can be inferred. It is also worth noting that two glovers attended the feast but did not sit at the same table, showing that craft identity did not necessarily supersede all others within guild feasts. The last table sat eleven men. Professions could be found for only five of these: two brewers, a painter, a basket-carrier and a weaver, while another of the men here would later become an alderman. That no clear pattern emerges among these tables is suggestive in itself, in that no craft or family groups dominate. The shooting guild's meals brought together men from across civic society, unified in guild membership on top of their socio-economic status, thus reinforcing the ideas of multiple identities raised in the previous chapter.

The *papegay* meal, held after the summer shooting contest, again reveals a mix of ranks at dinner. The top table was again headed by Jan Breydel and with him was the town sheriff, but no others at the top table were municipal office holders. One, Jeromyus Adornes, was related to numerous aldermen, but he is not recorded as holding civic office. At this meal Jan and Melsior Tsolles were seated at the top table along with a wool merchant, a brewer and a smith and five very active guild-brothers for whom no profession could be found. The feast following the shooting contest appears to be more representative of positions within the guild, recognising service and engagement with guild activities rather than wealth or status.

The second table, seating twenty-two, was headed by the new king, Jan de Bruneruwe – indeed, in other years the second table is called the king's table.[26]

---

[26] The abbreviations are difficult to interpret – it is unclear if this table is called the king's table (a table headed by the current king) or the kings' table (a table for current and previous kings).

Jan was an active guild-member and a skilled shooter, besides becoming shooter king in 1468, and he had also won the prize for best shot in a regional contest in Ghent in 1461. Also seated here was the 1467 king, Jacob Pots, and another former king, Jan van Rake. Among the remaining nineteen guild-brothers, fourteen professions can be firmly identified, with two barber-surgeons, a brewer, a joiner, a spice-seller, a shipper, a bag-maker, a tin-pot-maker, a bowyer, a sack-carrier, a washer, a smith, one guild-brother who would later become a councillor (but who in 1468 had yet to hold office or be recorded among a craft) and, finally, Jan Sijb, clerk of the Franc of Bruges. The presence of Sijb at the meal of 1468, and at nine others, indicates that communities extended beyond the town walls.

The third and fourth tables again constituted a diverse mix of socio-economic groups. Among the seventeen men at the third table eleven professions can be traced: two glovers, two cloth-merchants, a furrier, two goldsmiths, a corn-merchant, a glass-worker, a bowyer and Williem Andries, noted above as later a tax collector. Of the fourteen men at the final table, ten professions can be identified, comprising five bakers, two weavers, a cloth-merchant, a comb-maker and a painter. There are some patterns in these lower tables, particularly the number of bakers at the final table, but, in the main, men were not seated according to their professional groups; rather, these results suggest that guild-brothers feasted as a guild community, in recreational assemblies.

What comes through in the 1468 seating plans is not a hierarchy based solely on wealth or profession, but a guild community, with levels of engagement and skill determining a guild-brother's place. Jan Breydel is here not as a member of a 'civic elite' but as guild-headman; he is joined by several civic officials, but the number of 'elite' or very wealthy members at these meals is limited, and broadly corresponds to the percentages of officials within guilds. In 1463 Anthony the Great Bastard of Burgundy sat at the top table, but even he was present as guild-king, having won the shoot.[27] Anthony ate with the headman, Jan Breydel, the sheriff, the lord of Moerkerke and eight guild-brothers of various professions – the scribe Jan Tsolles, three tax collections, a baker and another three men for whom there are no details beyond the guild. Anthony's table, like the seating plan of 1468, illustrates very clearly that position within the guild was not determined by profession or by wealth. There are instances of members of the same, or of connected, professions sitting together, but these do not dominate. Each table represents a mix of standings and different levels of integration, helping to form a strong and representative urban community.

Unity and Disunity

Meals helped to emphasise unity and the sense of purpose that is clear in the guilds' regulations and registers. In terms of rights and actions, the guilds, like the towns around them, set out to create harmony and to keep the internal peace

---

[27] BASS, rekeningboeken, 1465–65, f. 30v.

for the benefit of all members. Despite such high ideals, however, the guilds could never be perfectly peaceful brotherhoods and disputes could and did break out. What is striking is not that militaristic guilds, well-supplied with wine, had fights but, rather, the ways in which they worked to limit disputes and restore peace and honour. In conflict resolution the guilds showed that they were capable of working for the peace that their ordinances envisioned: as has been observed of English guilds, the shooters had an active 'concern to foster among the members a loving friendship',[28] to maintain their common purpose.

Guilds were respected and rewarded by their town officials, but civic and ducal officials were not naïve and did not allow the guilds absolute freedom in their own towns. In the same charters in which he granted them the right to bear arms, Philip the Good stated that the archers of Sint-Winnoksbergen could not assemble without permission, not even for marriages, unless 'with the grant and consents of our said *bailli* or his lieutenant as it pleases us'. The same limitation was present in numerous fifteenth-century charters. One of the earliest surviving examples is in the charter to the crossbowmen of Estrées and Wattignies in 1405, and it was repeated in the charter to the crossbowmen of Aalst in 1494.[29] Ordinances in Lille even limited how many individuals could attend any wedding.[30] Clearly, civic officials were aware that guilds could create disorder and wanted to ensure a measure of control, as violence could and did happen.

The Lille judicial records, although imperfectly recorded and organised, include some fascinating case studies of guild-brothers who failed to uphold ideals of unity. In 1470, the archers' king, Jehan Poton, and another guild-brother, Roger Lobe, had a dispute. Poton had 'offered and said exceedingly bad things with much injurious language and many great and detestable oaths, and in doing so he went against the ordinance and constitution of the said garden'. As a result, he was forbidden entry to the archers' garden and expelled from the guild. Both Poton and Lobe were ordered to undertake pilgrimages, but this was not the end of the story. A few months later, in July 1471, Poton 'had been found in the garden where previously he had been reported for abuse', having entered 'against his oath'.[31] Poton's next punishment has not been recorded, nor has the reason for this squabble; perhaps his position as king gave Poton confidence to deal with an on-going struggle with Lobe. Whatever its cause, the dispute resulted in both men's being punished. Poton was removed from the guild for his disobedience, emphasising that guild-brothers had to be morally sound. Conflict between guild-brothers would not be tolerated by the community, nor

---

[28] Rosser, 'Finding Oneself in a Medieval Fraternity', 44.
[29] RAG, RVV, 7351, ff. 220–221; ADN, B1600, f. 26; ASAOA, 4 boek met den haire, ff. 87–88v.
[30] AML, OM, 397, in 1515 only 20 couples were to attend any wedding; in 1524 this was lowered to 10 couples, OM 397, 205v.
[31] AML, RM, 15919, f. 20, 35.

could the dishonour that such incidents risked for the guild. The guilds could not stop violence from happening, any more than society at large could, but they could bring Poton to justice and have him removed from the guild in order to uphold their honour and standing.

A few years earlier, in 1458, a rather different dispute had broken out within the crossbow guild. One guild-brother, Guilbin d'Ypres, 'with disorder and rebellion' injured another guild-brother, Jehan de Huernes, and refused to obey the king and constable.[32] D'Ypres was brought to trial but, unlike Poton, he appealed directly to the governor of Lille, who, as we have seen, was an important nobleman, and sought an exemption from civic punishment. Whether he received a pardon is not clear, but his case vanishes from civic records, strongly implying that he received an oral pardon from the governor. Nothing further is recorded. It is likely that d'Ypres had more power than Poton: he may have been related to, if not one of, the fifteen aldermen (as well as thirty-seven other municipal officers) from the d'Ypres family.[33] Unlike Poton, whom the archers were able to deal with, d'Ypres seems to have been an over-mighty *confrere* and beyond guild punishment. Although his appeal to the governor seems to have ensured no *civic* punishment, d'Ypres had nevertheless shown himself to be unworthy and was expelled from the guild, just as those who damaged civic society would be banished from their towns.[34]

In larger towns with multiple guilds, ideals of peace and community should have extended to keeping peace between guilds. In Ghent, the *jonghe* crossbowmen should have respected the *grote* – indeed their rules included the obligation to 'obey and respect' the greater guild. They even had to have a member of the *grote* guild as their headman, according to regulations issued in 1416 and reissued in 1449 and 1468.[35] The hierarchy and the obligation to be respectful and peaceful are clear, yet in 1446 a dispute broke out over precedence in shooting, with the lesser crossbowmen becoming dissatisfied with their subservient position. In 1467 the dispute seems to have become more serious, involving the revenues of the lesser guilds. However, the town decided in favour of the greater guild, requiring the lesser crossbowmen pay a large fine, and the aldermen worked to re-impose 'friendship' for 'the honour of the town'.[36] The reissuing of the 1416 statute in the months following these disputes emphasised the civic wish to maintain hierarchy and relative social positions.

Conflicts and disputes continued into the early sixteenth century, with unspecified 'squabbles' and even 'threats' being brought to the aldermen. The

---

[32] AML, RT, 15884, f. 137.
[33] D. Clauzel, 'Les élites urbaines et le pouvoir municipal; le "cas" de la bonne ville de Lille aux XIV et XV siècles', *RN* 78 (1996), 267.
[34] M. Moore, 'Wolves, Outlaws, and Enemy Combatants', in E. A. Joy, M. J. Seaman, K. K. Bell and M. K. Ramsey (eds), *Cultural Studies of the Modern Middle Ages* (New York: Palgrave Macmillan, 2007), 217–36.
[35] SAG, 301/27, f. 82v; 301/39, f. 63r; 310/49, ff. 19r and 110v.
[36] SAG, SJ, NGR, 20, 29, 42, 53.

aldermen of Ghent consistently sided with the greater crossbowmen, preferring to enforce urban hierarchy as it stood, rather than to allow a newer guild to gain power, just as in disputes between different craft guilds hierarchy and position were reinforced and standards maintained.[37] Disputes and violence within and between guilds do not negate the ideals of harmony and peaceful fraternity. Rather, the importance placed on removing the dishonourable and rebuilding bonds within and between communities emphasised the peaceful and communal purpose of guilds.

Guilds as devotional fraternities

Traditional scholarship tends to separate out the ideals of 'confraternities' and 'guilds', with the former categorised as (primarily) religious and the latter seen as being mostly focused on trade. Yet a good deal of recent work on craft guilds has shown that they, too, were devout, with attachment to patron saints, care for souls and efforts to maintain a chapel or altar. As noted, the guilds could be referred to as confraternities, and here they will be analysed using Black's definition of a devotional confraternity: a group of (mostly) lay people coming together for security and devotion, specifically for remembrance of the dead and the needs of salvation.[38] The devotions of guild-brothers, and even guild-sisters, constituted another aspect of communal identity and strengthened peace and harmony within the communities. Guilds did not develop religious functions as they grew; rather, devotional activities were an integral part of their activities from a very early point in their history. In Oudenaarde, few fourteenth-century guild records survive, but the crossbowmen's chapel of Saint George is recorded as attracting donations from 1348.[39] Mass and prayer were at the heart of almost all medieval communities, and from their earliest appearance the shooting guilds were no exception in ensuring spiritual security and a place for prayer.

---

[37] Dumolyn and Stabel, 'Stedelijkheid in harmonie en conflict', 56–71; M. Davies, 'Crown, City and Guild in Late Medieval London', in M. Davies and J. A. Galloway (eds), *London and Beyond: Essays in Honour of Derek Keene* (London: University of London, School of Advanced Studies, 2012), 241–61; idem, 'Governors and Governed: The Practice of Power in the Merchant Taylors' Company', in I. A. Gadd and P. Wallis (eds), *Guilds, Society and Economy in London, 1450–1800* (London: Centre for Metropolitan History, 2001), 67–83.

[38] Black, *Italian Confraternities*, 1–24; J. Bossy, *Christianity in the West, 1400–1700* (Oxford: Oxford University Press, 1985), 57–75; N. Terpstra, 'Introduction' to his *The Politics of Ritual Kinship*, 1–5. For the problems of definitions, specifically in Flanders, see P. Trio, 'Middeleeuwse broederschappen in de Nederlanden. Aan balans en perspectieven voor verder onderzoek', *Tijdschrift voor de Geschiedenis van het Katholiek Leven in de Nederlanden, trajecta* 3 (1994), 100–104.

[39] OSAOA, gilden, 507/II/2A.

Mass and Community

That mass and devotional interaction can promote unity within a community is well-known.[40] Charters and ordinances are full of examples of prescriptive devotional activities, showing the guilds' concerns to regulate moral behaviour and to reinforce bonds of community. The Lille archers required that on each Saint Sebastian's day a chaplain should sing 'ten songs of remembrance, at the cost of all, these humbly sung in the chapel'. Throughout the year, on twelve specified saints' days, masses would be said for all dead members, and candles would be brought into the church, all of this being funded by death-fees.[41] The crossbowmen of Douai were required to attend mass each week before they went to practise, and then to drink in recreational assembly in their garden, as were the crossbowmen and archers of the small town of Ingelmunster.[42] Numerous ordinances stress that all members should gather for mass at least once a year; others require those shooting each week first to pray together. Financial accounts, although rarer, reflect such ideals being put into practice.

The Aalst crossbowmen have not left accounts for long periods, but their 1461–62 account book goes into great detail on the guild's devotional costs and, by extension, practices within a smaller town. In Aalst, Saint George's day was an important one for guild society, with 14s being paid to priests for singing masses and all guild members required to be present. The day also saw the guild's *papegay* contest and its feast, which again all members were required to attend. Although in Aalst it is impossible to prove how many members did in fact attend, but it seems likely that, as in Bruges, most members attended the shoot and then a smaller number attended the feast. Drama was part of the celebration for Aalst, although its form is unfortunately slightly ambiguous. The guild put on what must have been a fairly elaborate *spel* (there is no hint at a script) of Saint George costing £7 12s. There is also a separate payment – presumably for a separate performance – of 8s to a man for telling the tale of Saint George. Such financial records cannot show where the events were performed, but it seems likely that these were two separate events on the same day, perhaps a larger event in the streets and a reading in the guild's own hall at its feast.

For the Aalst crossbowmen, their saint's day was a spectacular event, but it was not the only time they attended mass. A total of £24 was paid for 'diverse masses' throughout the year; some of these were funerals, but all were occasions on which to pray together. The Aalst guild-brothers recorded other small but important payments that highlight the importance of their chapel, including 8s

---

[40] Bossy, *Christianity in the West*, especially 60–67; C. Cross and P. Barnwell, 'The Mass in Its Urban Setting', in P. Cross and A. Rycraft (eds), *Mass and Parish Community in Late Medieval England: The Use of York* (Reading: Spire Books, 2005), 13–26; A. Thompson, *Cities of God: The Religion of the Italian Communes, 1125–1325* (Unversity Park: Pennsylvania State University Press, 2005), especially 103–40.
[41] ADN, 16 G 406.
[42] ADN, B1147-12.681; ADN, B 1358 (16026).

for flowers and another 8s for washing altar cloths.[43] This level of detail is unique in Aalst, but the pattern is not. The archers of Bruges had an agreement with the friars for their chapel of Saint Sebastian within the Franciscan monastery. The friars had to 'make a daily mass in the chapel of Saint Sebastian' and, if they missed any, they were to pay the guild one and a half groats. On twelve specified saints' days 'five friars of the convent will sing mass in the chapel', and again a fine was levied if any were missed. In addition to this arrangement, in 1461–62 the Bruges archers spent 18s 6d 'for the chapel' on Saint Sebastian's day, and 16s 11d for other masses and sermons during the year.[44]

That shooting events should be preceded by masses is not surprising. Chapters of the Golden Fleece were preceded by masses in a large urban church, although it is unlikely that the shooters copied this as a model, not least because they were considerably older. Rather, both groups drew on shared norms of community. Devotion was central to late medieval urban life and prayers were integral parts of saints' days and funerals, so they were to be expected before annual shooting contests, or even each week before shooting practice. These prayers emphasised the devout aspect of guild life and helped to reinforce the bonds of community and brotherhood that underlined so much of guild life.

Funerals and Spiritual Support

Guilds, like confraternities, were particularly concerned with remembrance of the dead and the needs of salvation, as manifested by funerals and mortuary payments. Such concerns are hardly surprising, as remembrance has been described by Van Bueren as 'a key organising principle' for much of medieval urban life.[45] Accordingly, charters emphasised the need for guild-brothers to leave money to the guild on their death, and this *dootghelt* is the most obvious evidence for the priorities of remembrance. In 1421 the archers of Aalst had to promise to leave their best bow to the guild or, if they did not have one fine enough, 8s. In return, the others promised to 'carry the brother to the sepulchre'. All guild-brothers should attend their dead brother's funeral, unless they were ill or away from Aalst, on pain of a 5s fine. Similarly in Dendermonde and Lille, crossbowmen and archers were required to leave the guild their best bow (or money) and, in return, the guild community promised to attend the funeral, praying for the deceased.[46] Funerals were important for individual salvation, but they were also part of the ritual of urban identity, demonstrating the care for

---

[43] ASAOA, 156, Rekeningen van de gezworenen van het Sint Joris gild, 1461–2.
[44] BASS, charter 2, 23 December 1416; Brown, *Civic Ceremony*, 140–85.
[45] T. Van Bueren, 'Care for the Here and the Hereafter; A Multitude of Possibilities', in T. Van Bueren and A. Van Leerdam (eds), *Care for the Here and the Hereafter; Memoria, Art and Ritual in the Middle Ages* (Turnhout: Brepols, 2005), 13; Black, *Italian Confraternities*, 1–24; Trio 'Middeleeuwse broederschappen in de Nederlanden', 100–104.
[46] *Ordonnances de Philippe le Hardi*, vol. 1, 296; AML, PT, 5883, ff. 28–31.

the soul of the deceased members as well as the identity and standing of those still living.[47]

So important were funerals – as one of the Seven Acts of Mercy – that taking responsibility for paying for them was common in devotional confraternities and even in some craft guilds.[48] Although they are rarer than rules for attending annual meals, provisions to pay for a funeral if the deceased was unable to do so appear in some shooting guild regulations. In Douai, from 1392, the crossbowmen and the town would combine resources to pay for a guild-brother's funeral if necessary. In the Hainaut towns of Enghien and Pecquencourt guild-brothers and town governors together undertook similar obligations.[49] Larger towns did not set out this requirement, either because it was an assumed unwritten custom or because, in Lille or Bruges, members had access to other support structures. But that smaller towns did undertake this care highlights the guilds' potential to act as a spiritual safety net.

Assistance could be informal, but by setting out what was required the guilds made it clear that death-duties were an important obligation for all members. Entrance fees could be waived, as entrance depended on an individual's ability to enhance guild and civic honour, but death-fees were closely related to remembrance and the needs of salvation, and so they were paid more regularly. On his death, a Bruges archer should have left the guild 2s plus his best bow and two dozen arrows, 'for the sounding of the bells and for the mass that the guild will celebrate in his memory'.[50] Seven archers died in 1455 and all left the guild sums between 2s and 5s, reflecting either that their bows had been sold and entered into the records as a cash value or that the guild was happy to accept money in lieu of bows. Payments in Aalst are also recorded as money, not bows, although both were required in ordinances. Five crossbowmen died in 1461–62: four of the deceased left the guild £3 each and the fifth left £12.[51] The Ghent crossbow guild took this further, enlisting the assistance of the aldermen and even the duke of Burgundy to try to ensure that the heirs of deceased members paid their death-fees.[52]

It is, of course, easy to be cynical and see these simply as enforcements of financial obligations. Yet it should be emphasised that entrance fees were not

---

[47] M. Boone, 'Réseaux urbaine', in W. Prevenier (ed.), *Le Prince et le peuple: images de la société du temps des Ducs de Bourgogne, 1384–1530* (Anvers: Fonds Mercator, 1998), 247–52.

[48] Black, *Italian Confraternities*, 104–6, 231–2, 258; Banker, *Death in the Community*, 95–100; C. Gittings, 'Urban Funerals in Late Medieval and Reformation England', in S. Bassett, *Death in Towns: Urban Responses to the Dying and the Dead* (London: Leicester University Press, 1968) 170–83.

[49] DAM, CC 202, f. 362; E. Matthieu, *Histoire de la ville d'Enghien*, 2vols (Mons: Dequesne-Masquillier, 1876–1878), vol. 2, 768–74; ADN, 1H 369.

[50] BASS, charter 1425.

[51] ASAOA, 156, Rekeningen van de gezworenen van het Sint Joris gild, 1461-2.

[52] SAG, SG, 155, 3; SAG, SJ, NGR, 17, 37, 38, 44.

enforced strongly, and, in addition, there is some evidence of sums being spent on care for members. The archers of Aalst received a charter from Philip the Good in 1421, said to be confirmation of an 'ancient custom' that if an archer fell ill or became poor though 'mishap' all of the other guild-brothers would pay for a mass to be said for him.[53] The Aalst crossbowmen seem to have provided more practical care for the widows of guild-brothers, although this type of aid is not mentioned in any of their surviving regulations. Accounts from 1461–62 show small payments made to the widows of recently deceased crossbowmen.[54] The amounts are tiny, none more than 12*d* a month, but such amounts were not designed to sustain an entire family but, rather, to augment a meagre income. Accounts and ordinances both demonstrate a genuine concern for the needs of salvation and care for the community.

Chapels and Saints

Chapels, whether free-standing buildings or altars within larger churches, gave form to the devotion and values of their guilds. The chapels were not only places for prayer and for remembrance, but spaces for guilds to come together and enhance their community.[55] Although the spaces themselves cannot be analysed, their meaning can be recreated to an extent by examining their decoration and the objects that once filled them. Frustratingly, little can be uncovered about what guild chapels in late medieval Flanders looked like. Art was certainly commissioned for them, but no works are known to have survived. In Brabant, a piece commissioned for the greater crossbow guild of Leuven and originally placed in its chapel within the church of Our Lady Outside the Walls (Onze Lieve Vrouw van ginderbuiten), decorating the High Altar, has survived. The piece's survival is due the unusual set of circumstances by which Mary of Hungary, the sixteenth-century regent of the Low Countries, 'asked' for it and provided a copy as a replacement. Sometime before 1564 it was taken from Mary's palace at Binch to Madrid, at the request of Philip II, and here it remains in the Prada. Thus the image was saved from the iconoclasm that destroyed the Leuven crossbowmen's chapel and numerous other devotional works across the Low Countries. It is an impressive piece, known as the *Deposition from the Cross*, painted by Rogeir van der Weyden, probably in the early 1430s. With its figures close to life size, the

---

[53] ASAOA, 3, peysboek ff. 152v–153.
[54] ASAOA, 156, Rekeningen van de gezworenen van het Sint Joris gild f. 2v.
[55] K. Giles, 'A Table of Alabaster and the Story of the Doom: The Religious Objects and Spaces of the Guild of Our Blessed Virgin, Boston (Lincs)', in C. Richardson and T. Hamling (eds), *Everyday Objects: Medieval and Early Modern Material Culture and Its Meanings* (Aldershot: Ashgate, 2011); C. Liddy, 'Urban Politics and Material Culture at the End of the Middle Ages: The Coventry Tapestry in St Mary's Hall', *Urban History* 39 (2012), 203–24; idem, 'The Palmers' Gild Window, St Lawrence's Church, Ludlow: A Study of the Construction of Gild Identity in Medieval Stained Glass', *Transactions of the Shropshire Archaeological and Historical Society* 72 (1997), 26–37.

work would have made a great impression on anyone who entered the guild's chapel – certainly it made an impression on both Mary and Philip. In its size and magnificence the works reflects the rising status of the guild. It is also a carefully planned commission: tiny crossbows in the side spandrels identify the piece with the crossbowmen. It has been argued that Mary Magdalene's unnatural position, and even Christ's curved body, are designed suggest the form of a crossbow.[56] The piece is hugely impressive but, in the words of Powell, would 'never have attracted to itself the undivided attention of the chapel's visitors', as the chapel featured numerous other works of art, including a fourteenth-century wooden Pietà and a late fifteenth-century carved retable of Saint George.[57]

There is no reason to suppose that the images in the Flemish chapels would have been any less spectacular. In Lille, the crossbowmen had a stained glass window of Saint George in their chapel inside the parish church of Saint Maurice. The window was purchased in 1480 with ducal support, and featured not just Saint George, but also images of Mary and Maximilian, emphasising ducal power as well as dedication to Saint George. Elsewhere, guilds undertook their own decorations. In 1509 in Cysoing, a small town about 15km south-east of Lille, the archers hired Gilles Contelie, a painter from Douai, to decorate their chapel with the legend of Saint Sebastian. In 1461–62 the Aalst crossbowmen paid an unnamed artist to paint the legend of Saint George for them.[58] Numerous chapels used images of Saint George, embodying the martial, masculine protector of their towns. The ubiquity of a patron saint, along with regulations requiring the guild-brothers to be in the chapel regularly, shows the importance of creating special guild sacred space to enhance identity and community.

Chapels were not just well decorated, they were also well lit. Candles, lamps and torches filled churches and illuminated all spiritual events, as well as important secular ones. Lighting candles on saints' altars, or carrying them in processions, were central parts of devotion for all levels of society[59] and, though they had practical purposes too, in the guilds' chapels the lights represent spiritual concerns. Inventories from Ghent and Bruges emphasised the

---

[56] A. K. Powell, *Depositions, Scenes from the Late Medieval Church and the Modern Museum* (New York: MIT Press, 2012), 143–57; M. Gold (dir.), *The Private Life of an Easter Masterpiece: The Descent From the Cross*. BBC2, 3 April 2010 (documentary); A. K. Powell, 'The Errant Image: Rogier van der Weyden's Deposition from the Cross and its Copies', *Art History*, 29 (2006), 540–52.

[57] M. Trowbridge, 'The *Stadschilder* and the *Serment*: Rogier van der Weyden's "Deposition" and the Crossbowmen of Louvain', *Dutch Crossing* 23 (1999), 5–28; Powell, 'The Errant Image', 543–4.

[58] ADN, LRD, B17734; Delsalle, 'La Confrérie des archers de Cysoing', 14–19; ASAOA, 156, Rekeningen van de gezworenen van het Sint Jorisgild, 1461–2, ff. 3v–5v.

[59] C. Vincent, *Fiat Lux, lumière et luminaires dans la vie religieuse du XIIIe au XVIe siècle* (Paris: Cerf, 2004), 9–22, 81–13; eadem, '"Protection spirituelle" ou "vigilance spirituelle"? Le témoignage de quelques pratiques religieuses des XIIIe–XVe siècles', *Cahiers de recherches médiévales (XIIIe–XVe siècles)* 8 (2001), 193–205.

importance of lights, listing many candelabras of various sizes. As payments for lights are rarely mentioned in guild accounts, it is likely that the guild-brothers and sisters provided them as needed, rather than the guild paying for them in annual sums.

In some guilds, candles were funded by fines for minor misdeeds. In Douai, from 1499, if a guild-brother failed to accompany the constable to church in his full livery in mid-Lent he would be fined 2s, with the funds going 'to the profit of the lights'. In Aalst, missing shooting practice also resulted in a fine for the lights. In Douai, the town itself provided additional funding for the guilds' lights,[60] emphasising the prestige of the guild. Numerous references to candles and candelabra can be traced in inventories, although they are rarely referred to in accounts, strongly implying that members funded them. In many other devotional confraternities candles were purchased by the voluntary donations of members, given either on specific days or for set masses or on a day of personal significance.[61] Lighting their candles, particularly if they did so before a saintly image, allowed guild-brothers to bring a part of themselves into their guild chapel and to build bonds with each other and their holy protector(s).

In choosing their protectors, and thereby how to represent their devotion and their identity, archery and crossbow guilds made standardised choices, just as several craft guilds did. Such choices did not reflect a lack of consideration, and all saintly protectors are important in understanding the ways that urban groups perceived themselves.[62] The standard shooting guild devotions were represented by Saints George and Sebastian. Saint Sebastian, a Roman soldier martyred by his own archers, was a fitting choice for archers, allowing the guilds to place themselves within divine images and highlighting the power of their weapons. On the other hand, Saint George had no clear connection to crossbowmen, but was an important military saint and very popular across Europe, usually represented killing a dragon and always distinctive, linking guilds with military heroism and the idea of protection.[63]

Both saints were, or became over the course of the fourteenth century, martial protectors of great status, and so they were fitting choices for guilds seeking honour and prestige. Not all Flemish archery and crossbow guilds were dedicated

---

[60] DAM, Arbalestiers de Douay, 24II232; ASAOA, 3, peysboek, ff. 152v–153; DAM, AA85.
[61] Vincent, *Fiat Lux, lumière et luminaires*; Banker, *Death in the Community*, 95–100, 161–7.
[62] Boone, 'Réseaux urbaines', *Le Prince et le peuple*, 233–47; A. Vauchez, 'Saint Homebon (†1197), patron des marchands et artisans drapiers à la fin du Moyen Age et à l'époque moderne', *Académie royale de Belgique. Bulletin de la classe des lettres et des sciences morales et politiques*, ser. 6, 15 (2004) 47–56; C. Phythian-Adams, 'Ritual Constructions of Society', in R. Horrox and W. M. Ormrod (eds), *A Social History of England, 1200–1500* (Cambridge: Cambridge University Press, 2006), 369–81.
[63] J. Jacobs, *Sebastiaan, martelaar of mythe* (Zwolle, 1993); H. Micha, 'Une rédaction en vers de la vie de Saint Sébastien', *Romania* 92 (1971), 405–19; S. Riches, *St George, Hero, Martyr and Myth* (Stroud: Sutton 2005), 1–35, 68–100; D. A. L. Morgan, 'The Cult of St George c. 1500: National and International Connotations', *PCEEB* 35 (1995), 151–62.

to Saints George and Sebastian. The crossbowmen of Douai were dedicated to Saint Martin, who, like Sebastian, was a Roman soldier who became bishop of Tours. Again, this was a prestigious military saint, well suited to represent the honour and ideas set out in guild ordinances, but Martin was also a saint whose life emphasised the importance of charity.[64] In representing their patrons as both honourable and militaristic, the guilds projected their sense of how members should behave and how they should be seen. Even in towns with two crossbow guilds, like Ghent and Bruges, both the *oude* and the *jonghe*, the greater and lesser, were dedicated to Saint George.

Beyond Flanders a number of archery and crossbow guilds were dedicated to the Virgin Mary, most famously Notre Dame de la Sablon of Brussels. The Brussels crossbowmen played a major role in the annual procession and escorted the miraculous statue of the Virgin that had been 'saved' from Antwerp in the mid-fourteenth century.[65] Their dedication to this statue demonstrated their place within the town and distinguished them from the other crossbow guild in Brussels, dedicated to Saint George.[66] The choice of different patron saints was probably strategic, to make clear that they were separate communities. In Hainaut, the crossbow guilds of Condé, Mons and Valenciennes were all dedicated to the Virgin, as were the crossbowmen in the Brabant town of Nivelles.[67] The Virgin was, of course, a hugely popular saint across Europe, and in Flanders numerous devotional confraternities were devoted this most powerful of intercessors.[68] Mary has no obvious connection to the crossbow, but her popularity across Hainaut and Brabant encouraged many guilds to associate themselves with her. It is hard to explain why no Flemish guilds record a dedication to the Virgin. It may be that they wished to remain distinct, to choose saints that were less common for their banners – only a few other groups were dedicated to George and Sebastian.[69]

---

[64] For example the crossbowmen of Courtrai were dedicated to the 'holy martyr and knight Saint George', RAK, 5800. Sint Jorisgilde. 1 stuk; DAM, Arbalestiers de Douay, 24II232, f. 1.

[65] In 1348 Beatrix Soetkens had a vision telling her to take the statue from Antwerp to Brussels, where it was placed in the church on the sands (*Sablon*) under the care of the crossbowmen; Brown and Small, *Court and Civic Society*, 242–3; Lecuppre-Desjardin, *La Ville des Cérémonies*, 88–9.

[66] Brussel Stadsarchief, AA/OA, reg. 1492, f. 1; Wauters, *Notice historique* 3–5.

[67] Devilliers, 'Notice historique sur les milices communales et les compagnies militaire de Mons', *ACAM* 3 (1862), 169–285; H. Stein, *Archers d'autrefois; archers d'aujourd'hui* (Paris: Longuet, 1925), 237–8; Willame, *Notes sur les serments Nivellois*, 8–12.

[68] Trio, 'The Emergence of New Devotions in Late Medieval Urban Flanders', 331–2.

[69] Saint Sebastian became associated with plague and, as a visually distinctive saint, is popular in art. Many Italian confraternities were dedicated to him as a plague protector, but few such confraternities existed in the North; L. Marshall, 'Reading the Body of a Plague Saint: Narrative Altarpieces and Devotional Images of St Sebastian in Renaissance Art', in B. J. Muir (ed.), *Reading Texts and Images, Essays on Medieval and Renaissance Art and Patronage* (Liverpool: Liverpool University Press, 2002), 237–72;

Just as no Flemish guilds were dedicated to the Virgin, none was dedicated solely to a female saint. Yet, toward the end of the fifteenth century some new saints are mentioned. The greater crossbowmen of Ghent had an altar to Saint Margaret. It had been founded by Charles the Bold and Margaret of York in 1474, but the chapel was still attracting donations in the early sixteenth century. The Ghent archers included Saint Christine with Saint Sebastian in their chapel by 1511, seemingly in connection with taking over a new part of the church from the Grey Sisters.[70] By the late fifteenth century the Ghent guilds included a number of female members, and so adding a new female patron may be a reflection of their changing identity as well as changing devotion. It could, of course, simply be a reaction to circumstances – the patronage of Margaret of York – but the continuing popularity of the Chapel suggests that it had, or had acquired, a deeper meaning for guilds, adding a new layer to their already complex identity.

The reasons for diversification are rarely ever given; rather, a new chapel or new dedication is simply recorded. In one town the change to female devotion is clearly explained and was pragmatic rather than driven by ideas of gender. At the end of the fourteenth century the archers of the small town of Armentières were dedicated to Saint Sebastian. However, in 1513 they received a 'portion of divinity and reliquary of the eleven thousand Virgins and Saint Ursula'.[71] Upon receiving the relic, the archers of Armentières rededicated themselves to Saint Ursula, although later documents refer to the archers of Saint Sebastian and Saint Ursula.[72] Such diversification shows a great deal of thought within the guilds about their heavenly protectors: their devotion was chosen and changeable and allowed for devotion to female saints. The Armentières case is also a warning against over-reading changing devotion, and it may be that changes in Ghent were similarly pragmatic rather than driven by changes in piety, but the ways in which guilds used their saints remain important.

Guilds used their patron saints in numerous ways to demonstrate their identity and as visual markers of devotion, the most obvious being on their seals. Seals, like all emblems, were carefully chosen and crafted to show the identity of the person or group who commissioned them. They 'express in a formal nature the legal entity and status of the sealer' and 'have specialised types of iconography'. In having seals at all, guilds made clear statements about their status: that they were independent and powerful groups, using their own seals to authenticate

---

V. Kraehling, *Saint Sébastien dans l'art* (Paris: Alsatia, 1938). Saint George was more popular, initially associated with the Jousters of the White Bear. In Bruges the cloth carriers were dedicated to Saint George, and a chapel to Saint George *ten distele* was established in the Church of Our Lady in Bruges around 1473; see Brown, *Civic Ceremony*, 321–5.

[70] SAG, SJ, NGR, 25; RAG, Archief van Sint Baafs en bisdom Gent, 3820.
[71] The relic was a gift from a nobleman, Thierry de Val.
[72] AAM, EE4.

their own documents.[73] Unfortunately, but perhaps unsurprisingly, the survival rate for shooting guilds' seals is poor. The only crossbow guilds seals I have found are those attached to invitations to competitions in Mechelen, Ghent and Oudenaarde. Attached to invitations, the seals would have been seen by regional audiences as the invitations were carried from town to town. Though small flecks of wax show that archery guild seals once existed, I have found none that provides any evidence of what was once represented on it. More small remnants of wax show that seals were once attached to guild documents, including ordinances and grants of property, but their conditions of storage have not allowed the seals themselves to survive. Copin's 1956 study of crossbow seals showed that guilds were using their saints to represent themselves and emphasised their place within towns through civic symbols.[74]

The following four seals (and more examples could be given) clearly show the interaction of the guilds' attachment to patron saint and to civic symbolism. The seal of the Sluis crossbowmen from 1497 (Figure 2), represents the guild, its saint and its town. Saint George here is a knight on horseback who tramples the dragon; his shield bears the cross of Saint George, making his identification clear. To the left is a crossbow and to the right is the civic badge of Sluis. The seal of Veurne from 1440 (Figure 3), is very similar. Again Saint George tramples a dragon, although not enough of the seal has survived for us to be sure whether a civic badge was once present. Both images, and others from Flemish guilds, represent Saint George not as a distant hero but as a contemporary knight, as did numerous fifteenth-century images. In a manner similar to chapel decorations, the seals of the Sluis and Veurne crossbowmen represent their devotion to Saint George, their links to a chivalric hero and their close connection with their town – that civic identity was part of their identity.

Seals from non-Flemish guilds again represent their holy protector and their civic pride, but through different saints. The seal of the crossbowmen of Condé (Figure 4) shows their patron saint, the Virgin, above the civic crest and flanked by crossbows, illustrating both guild devotional identity and civic status. The seal of the Tournai crossbowmen (Figure 5) is very similar to the civic seal, showing towers, plus a crossbow and a small arrow flying over the towers. Again the iconography of crossbow guilds' seals is military, strong and civic, like the guilds themselves, showing the honour and devotion of the guilds and their role as defenders of their towns.

---

[73] S. Abraham-Thisse, 'La représentation iconographique des métiers du textile au Moyen-Âge', and B. Bedos-Rezak, 'Du modele a l'image: les signes de l'identite urbaine au moyen age', both in *Le verbe, l'image et les représentations de la société urbaine*, 135–59, 196–8; J. Cherry, 'Images of Power: Medieval Seals', *Medieval History Magazine* 8 (2004), 34–41.

[74] J. Copin, 'Sceaux d'arbalétriers Belges', *Annales du XXXVIe congre de la fédération archéologique et historique de Belge* (Gand, 1956), 15–25.

Figure 2. Seal of the crossbowmen of Sluis, 1497[75]

Figure 3. Seal of the crossbowmen of Veurne, 1440[76]

---

[75] SAG, SJ, 155, 1.
[76] SAG, SJ, 155, 2.

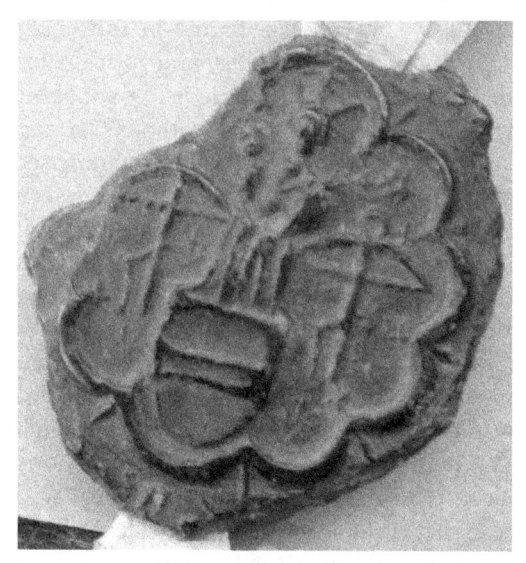

Figure 4. Seal of the crossbowmen of Condé, 1462[77]

Figure 5. Seal of the crossbowmen of Tournai, 1462[78]

---

[77] OSAOA, gilden, 507/ II/ 14 A.
[78] OSAOA, gilden, 507/ II/ 14 A.

The interaction between the devotion, identity and the military prowess of guilds is perhaps best shown on a badge in the Fitzwilliam Museum in Cambridge. It is tiny, less than 8cm across, and represents a crucifixion scene superimposed upon a crossbow. Sadly, little is known about the badge, which is thought to be early sixteenth century and perhaps German in origin. Another badge using the crucifixion crossbow motif is in San Francisco's Legion of Honor museum. Even less is known of this badge, which is referred to as belonging to a 'sharp shooters guild' and is probably German, again dated to the early sixteenth century. This badge is more elaborate, showing Saint Sebastian with a small hanging crossbow and crucifixion (Figure 6).[79] Both badges represent the guilds' devotion and their identification with military prowess, just as Weyden's image does in shaping Christ's body into the form of a crossbow. I have found nothing similar that can be proved to be Flemish, but badges do not generally survive in large numbers, having been either lost or melted down, as they were relatively cheap items.[80] The two crossbow crucifixions show how central devotion was to those who used these once diabolical weapons and, indeed, how far the crossbow had come in becoming an acceptable symbol to associate not just with saints, but directly with the Passion.

A final tool of the guilds' self-representation was their banners. All craft or social groups carried banners in processions, symbolising their dedication to the saint upon their banner, as well as to their craft. Like the banners of the nobility, those of the shooting guilds had a range of uses both in war and in peace. The military functions of banners remained unchanged, but the objects took on new social and cultural significances in the fifteenth century.[81] Banners were part of the guilds' iconography and their devotional choices and were a clear and public way of representing their identity to a broad audience. The banners that shooting guilds carried were often paid for with civic funds, again showing

---

[79] Badge of an Archers' guild, Fitzwilliam Museum, Cambridge, C. B. Marlay Bequest, MAR M.266-1912; Fine Arts Museums of San Francisco; de Young, Legion of Honor, inv. 60.2.6.

[80] J. Koldeweij, 'The Wearing of Significant Badges, Religious and Secular; The Social Meaning of Behavioural Patterns', in W. Blockmans and A. Jansese (eds), *Showing Status: Representation of Social Positions in the Late Middle Ages* (Turnhout: Brepols, 1999), 307–28; idem, 'A Pilgrim's Badge and Ampullae Possibly from the Chartreuse of Champmol', in S. Blick (ed.), *Beyond Pilgrim Souvenirs and Secular Badges: Essays in Honour of Brian Spencer* (Oxford: Oxbow, 2007) 64–74.

[81] J. Dumolyn and J. Haemers, 'Pattern of Urban in Medieval Flanders', in *JMH* 31 (2005), 389–90; R. Jones, '"What Banner Thine?" The Banner as a Symbol of Identification, Status and Authority on the Battlefield', *Haskins Society Journal: Studies in Medieval History* 15 (2006), 101–9; Arnade, 'Crowds, Banners and the Market Place', 471–97; S. K. Cohn, *Lust for Liberty, the Politics of Social Relations in Medieval Europe, 1200–1425* (Cambridge, MA: Harvard University Press, 2006), 177–204; M. Lupant, 'Drapeaux du Grand Serment Royal et Noble des Arbalétriers de Notre-Dame au Sablon', in *Fahnen, Flags, Drapeaux: Proceedings of the 15th International Congress of Vexillology, Zurich, 23–27 August 1993* (Zurich: Swiss Society of Vexillology, 1999), 130–34.

Figure 6. Pendant of Sharpshooters' Guild with St Sebastian, mother and child, and crucifixion, c.1500

how the towns valued their guilds. In 1451 the aldermen of Lille paid for a new banner for their crossbowmen, and in 1438 those Cambrai paid for the banners of both the archers and the crossbowmen to be repaired. Other guilds took care of the matter themselves – the Aalst crossbowmen paid £6 in 1462 to a painter to decorate the guild's standard with the legend of Saint George.[82] Banners were not simply military tools: they were carried in procession, taken to competitions and kept in guild chapels, symbolising social and devotional identities as well as the guilds' public representation.

Across Flanders, then, archery and crossbow guilds were social and devotional communities. They came together at least once a year to eat, to pray and to shoot. Numerous regulations emphasise the values of harmony and internal peace. The recorded practice, as shown in the Bruges records, is rather different, but the social side of guild life and the formation of bonds was a major part of their purpose. Of course, ideals of harmony were not always upheld, as disputes within the guilds of Lille and between the guilds of Ghent show, but in working to resolve conflict the guilds and their civic authorities worked for peace. Devotion was a major part of this emphasis on peace and harmony. Guilds across the region were dedicated to patron saints who represented their identity; they maintained chapels to the honour of their saints and placed their holy protectors on seals and banners. Archery and crossbow guilds were devotional groups concerned with funerals and mutual support within their own community, as well as overlapping with other civic communities. The value of the guild communities and their place within civic society is best understood through a case study.

Devotion in Ghent

Ghent was a town full of devotional opportunities, including the parish churches and several hospitals (some craft specific, others focused on a specific category of paupers, such the leper house), not to mention the Mendicants and the Beguines houses.[83] The four shooting guilds of Ghent, the greater and lesser archers and the greater and lesser crossbowmen, were able to interact with these, fostering a sense of community and an extra strand of devotion.[84] The shooting guilds of Ghent

---

[82] Espinas, *Les Origines*, vol. 2, 406; E. Gautier and A. Lesort, *Inventaire sommaire, ville de Cambrai* (Cambrai, 1907), 97; ASAOA, 156, Rekeningen van de gezworenen van het Sint Joris gild, 1461–2. f. 8.

[83] Stabel, 'Composition et recomposition', 56–8; Nicholas, *Metamorphosis*, 42–3; J. W. Brodman, *Charity and Religion in Medieval Europe* (Washington, DC: The Catholic University of America Press, 2009), 212–21.

[84] Also present was a culveriners (gunners) guild dedicated to Saint Anthony who appeared in the late fifteenth century; see STAM, Sint Antoniusgilde, register der doodschulden, inven.1091; V. Vanderhaeghen, *Jaerboeken van het souvereine gilde der kolveniers, busschieters en kanonniers, gezegd Hoofdgilde van Sint Antone te Gent* (Gent: Annoot-Braeckman, 1867).

stood, as did those elsewhere, at an intersection of complex devotion and civic protection that can be best understood through the analysis of guilds in one town. Ghent is taken as the case study here, partly for its own importance but mostly for the survival of excellent records detailing guild devotion and guild charity.

All four shooting guilds maintained chapels dedicated to their patron saints, the locations of which provide insight into the ways in which the shooting guilds interacted with civic society. Ghent, like most of Flanders, had far fewer parish churches than did most English towns, comprising four central parishes (Saint Jan's – now Saint Baaf's cathedral – Saint Nicholas's, Saint Jacob's and Saint Michael's) and three outlying parishes (Saint Veerle's, Our Lady's and Saint Saviour's). Each parish church provided Holy Ghost Tables to feed and clothe the poor and represented an institution that cared for an area larger and more diverse than an English parish. Each parish church had different associations, allowing each to develop its own identity, but each was linked to civic culture and to civic ideals. The boundaries of these parishes evolved during the eleventh and twelfth centuries and were established by the end of the thirteenth century, remaining largely unchanged until the religious reforms of the sixteenth century.

Each parish had a sense of identity and can be seen as a community in its own right. Most significant was Saint Jan's, the traditional centre of Ghent's devotion and the setting for strategic rituals, including the investiture of the Counts of Flanders and the swearing of oaths for new council members on the relics of Saint Blasius.[85] Like other parish churches, Saint Jan's was home to numerous craft guild chapels. It was home to two of the four shooting guilds, demonstrating their strong links to civic culture and to the devotional element of political power. The lesser crossbowmen were there by the early fifteenth century, while the archers initially met in the crypt in the fourteenth century before moving into the church itself. The latter gained more space in 1493 when the Grey Sisters gave, or possibly sold, them their chapel of Saint Séverin. Within the church community the shooters were prominently placed: in Ghent's annual procession the lesser crossbowmen were the first among the groups of Saint Jan's, implying that they had a prominent place within the church.[86]

The richest of Ghent's parish churches was Saint Nicholas's. Situated in the commercial heart of Ghent, Saint Nicholas's was home to numerous merchants and richer craft guilds involved in the supplying of food.[87] The richest shooting guild in Ghent – and possibly the whole of Flanders – was the Greater Crossbow

---

[85] L. Mills, 'The Medieval City', in Decavele et al., *Ghent, in Defence of a Rebellious City*, 75–9; A.-L. Van Bruaene and M. Bauwens, 'De Sint-Jacobskerk te Gent: een onderzoek naar de betekenis van de stedelijke parochiekerk in de zestiende-eeuwse Nederlanden', HMGOG 65 (2012), 103–25; Arnade, *Realms of Ritual*, 42, 53–4; Nicholas, *Metamorphosis*, 56–67, 115–18.

[86] Arnade, *Realms of Ritual*, 78–80; SAG, SJ, NGR, 7; RAG, Archief van Sint Baafs, 3820; RAG, Sint Pieter's, N1943; Archief van Sint Baafs en bisdom Gent, 7576; SAG, Serie 93, G/7, zwarten boek, f. 165v.

[87] Nicholas, *Metamorphosis*, 35–42, 71–9, 90–93, 280.

Guild of Saint George, which was closely connected to Saint Nicholas's parish church. It initially had an altar within the church, but later built a separate building nearby. Its new chapel received rights from the bishop of Tournai in 1356, including the right to celebrate mass. The first surviving reference to the chapel is in the 1339 will of Pieter vanden Moore, and Daniel Lievois has convincingly argued, based on property records, that the chapel had a priest from this date.[88] In addition, the crossbowmen had a chapel within their complex in the rich Hoogh-Poort area of Ghent, very close to the belfry in Ghent's 'centre of political decision making'. The crossbowmen's guild hall was the setting for several States of Flanders assemblies and, in 1477, hosted the delegation of the Estates General of the Burgundian Netherlands.[89] The guild was unusual in having a private chapel in its guild hall, as most guilds of all forms preferred to maintain a chapel outside their hall, in a nearby church.[90] Yet the crossbowmen's link to Saint Nicholas's remained, keeping them within a parish structure and their civic community.

Finally, the lesser archers had their chapel within Saint Jacob's church. Saint Jacob's was one of Ghent's newer parish churches, less connected with civic traditions than Saint Jan's and far less wealthy than Saint Nicholas's. Containing the Friday market place, Saint Jacob's parish was a more mixed area, with wealthy merchants living around the large market place, but with other, less-well-off areas around the church. The market place itself was associated with unrest, even rebellion, and with a martial tradition stretching back to the militia assemblies of the early fourteenth century.[91] This location, close to the military heart of Ghent, demonstrates that the lesser archers maintained martial identity and links to the captains and service to Ghent in times of crisis. A setting in Saint Jacob's church might, therefore, imply that the guild-brothers were less well off than the 'greater' guild, but the links to civic defence and martial culture should not be ignored.

The three chambers of rhetoric in Ghent were, like the shooters, located in three different parish churches. The Fountain (de Fonteine), the oldest of the chambers, had a chapel in the mercantile Saint Nicholas's parish church by 1446; the confraternity of Saint Barbara had its chapel in central and traditional Saint Jan's; and the chamber of Marien Thereen had its in the slightly poorer Saint

---

[88] UBG Hs, G. 61731; D. Lievois, 'Kapellen, huijse, fruit en bloemen bij de westgevel van de Sint-Niklaaskerk in Gent', *HMGOG* 59 (2005), 71–86.

[89] Boone and Prevenier 'The city state dream', 100; Nicholas, *Metamorphosis*, 67–119; Boone, *Gent en de Bourgondische*, 25–64; Lievois, 'Kapellen, huijse, fruit en bloemen bij de westgevel van de Sint-Niklaaskerk in Gent', 87–92.

[90] C. M. Barron, *London in the Later Middle Ages, Government and People, 1200–1500* (Oxford: Oxford University Press, 2004), 216–18.

[91] SAG, Serie 93, G/7, zwarten boek, f. 166; S. Hutton, 'Women, Men and Markets: The Gendering of Market Space in Late Medieval Ghent', in A. Classen (ed.), *Urban Space in the Middle Ages and the Early Modern Age* (Berlin and New York: de Gruyter, 2009), 427–30; Nicholas, *Metamorphosis*, 55–7; Arnade, *Realms of Ritual*, 47–8.

Jacob's. Van Bruaene has argued that the locations of the chambers of rhetoric suggest the three different guilds drawing members from the different areas of Ghent.[92] Similar motivations may well have been behind the Ghent shooting guilds' geographical diffusion, with guilds linking themselves to different urban geographical communities. The geographical spread of the shooting guilds may also help to explain the numerous conflicts between the guilds in a more convincing manner, rather than merely assuming them to be quarrels between youth and mature groups.

The iconoclasm of the sixteenth century destroyed the chapels and their contents, and no images of them have yet been found. Despite such losses, much can be gleaned from inventories about the practice of devotion within the guild chapels. Three inventories provide a window into the material culture of devotion: a late fourteenth- or early fifteenth-century inventory of the Greater Archers' chapel with additions made in 1465; one belonging to the greater crossbowmen in 1481; and one belonging to the lesser crossbowmen from 1528.[93] All three of these inventories show large quantities of precious objects, silver crucifixes, jewels and images of saints, many of them won as prizes in competitions. The greater crossbowmen had many prizes in their chapel, including sets of scales, among them two won in Dendermonde and three won in Brussels. They also owned precious objects, including the intriguingly described 'One holy dome with four small towers, those are the holy cross of our sweet lord and other saints, with crystal weighing three pounds and two ounces.' The guild further owned a sculpture of Saint George, made for the chapel in 1481. The lesser crossbowmen also kept prizes in their chapel, including one silver pot with the arms of Courtrai and another with the arms of Axele. That the guilds kept prizes, rather than melting them down, is in itself significant, showing that these objects had a cultural value beyond their financial one. That the objects were kept in the chapels shows not just that the chapels were the focus of identity, but that a display of civic honours was linked to the spiritual world of the guilds.

All three chapels also contained very large quantities of cloth and some cushions – items left to the chapels by guild members. As Eamon Duffy has shown for English parish churches, bequeathing a personal object to a church or chapel demonstrated a feeling of community.[94] Much of the cloth in the guild chapel was left by the female guild members, showing their wish to be associated with their guild through objects, such as bed sheets, that they had used in life. Not all cloth is identified as having been given by members. Some of it may have

---

[92] Van Bruaene, 'A Breakdown of Civic Community?', 280–1; Arnade, *Realms of Ritual*, 166–73.
[93] STAM, Sint sebastiaangilde; privilegieboek, inv. 1059, ff. 10–12; SAG, SJ, NGR, 6, 7.
[94] E. Duffy, *The Stripping of the Altars, Traditional Religion in England, 1400–1580* (New Haven, CT and London: Yale University Press, 2005), 183–6, 504–23; idem, *The Voices of Morebath, Reformation and Rebellion in an English Village* (New Haven, CT and London: Yale University Press, 2001), 36–46, 74–83.

been purchased by the guild, or even made by guild-sisters, but together the luxurious silverware and the simpler carpets, cushions and altar cloths attest to the care and attention that guild members lavished on their chapels, showing a deep attachment to them and a genuine concern for salvation.

Other objects recorded in the inventories do not just show what was being kept in the chapel, but hint at how the chapels were being used by the guild-brothers and sisters. The archers, for example, had a 'mass-book' on a 'book-stand with the arms of Saint Sebastian'. The lesser crossbowmen's inventory is more specific: their books included several prayer books and books of hours, 'one mass-book with sermons for reading, and with lessons for all', a 'book of ordinances, with black binding' and 'the hand book of the women'. Mass books and rule books, possibly books of instruction, indicate a real concern for the moral and religious education of the guild and offer insight into how devotionally minded guild members were investing in books to regulate and promote their care for salvation. Although only snapshots of guild devotion survive, it is clear that a complex and interactive devotion developed within the guilds in response to the demands and bequests of members. In addition, the greater archers and greater crossbowmen both left death registers. Unlike in Bruges, where membership lists record members on their entrance to the guild, the Ghent sources are death-lists, recording the deaths of members and the amounts they left to the guilds. Although some non-paying members are recorded, it is plausible that many who died without leaving money to the guilds are absent from these lists, even if they had been active in life. The Ghent records have not been used to attempt another prosopographical study, rather, they are analysed here in order to question the attachment members showed to their guild on their deaths, and what this reveals about the values the guild held for them and the guilds' place within civic communities.

The huge book of Saint George and the smaller one of Saint Sebastian reveal the importance of remembrance. The sheer size of the Saint George book, begun in 1498 and listing deceased members from 1468 to the late eighteenth century, with few dates, makes a full analysis impossible in this context. Moulin-Coppens has estimated there to be at least 150, 000 named men recorded. The book is divided into four categories; the first is 'Dukes, Counts, Knights and Nobles', and included the most powerful lords of the Low Countries, who often left very large sums of money to the guild. It seems that this list was begun slightly later than the others, as the first name is that of Maximilian, the Holy Roman Emperor, who left the guild 200 crowns on his death.[95] The second name is that of Margaret of York, widow of Charles the Bold. As already noted, she and Charles had given money to the guild for a new chapel, which explains her connection to the guilds but not why she is the only woman to be entered among the lords. After the lords, listed (it would seem) in chronological order comes

---

[95] STAM, Sint Jorisgilde, register der doodschulden, G 12.608; SAG, Sint Sebastian, 155/1, 22; STAM, G 12.608, f. 33.

by far the largest category, the 'men', who are arranged alphabetically by first name. Dates of death are imperfectly given and most men left the guild between 2s and 5s.

The memory book of the greater crossbow guild shows many rich and powerful members, as the location of their chapel would imply, but not an elite composition. The third category is 'Priests'. These are fewer in number but, as noted, their presence reveals how wide the appeal of the greatest Ghent shooting guild had become. The final section is simply 'Women' and includes several noble women as well as wives and widows, and women with no obvious connection to any guild-brother. The huge book was carefully planned and neatly set out, and is evidence that the guild perceived of itself as a prestigious group, one that would survive for generations.

The register created by the archers of Saint Sebastian is smaller and less ornate, and perhaps as a result it has received less historical attention. The only recent work to look at it, that of Arnade, did so briefly, stating that the 'register eludes statistical precision because it lists occupations only unevenly and is without dates'. Arnade surveyed only the first twelve folios of the register.[96] Professions are indeed imperfectly recorded and a full study of the register would be challenging, although, given the other sources available in Ghent, not impossible. A close scrutiny of the register shows that its 125 folios contain 4,863 names, in late fifteenth- and early sixteenth-century hands, including fifty-two lords, fifty-one women, thirty-five priests and two other ecclesiastical figures, providing potentially great insight into the make-up of the guild as well as the cult of remembrance. The register is a carefully planned memory book. Rather than listing the names alphabetically, as the crossbowmen did, members are organised by the amount they paid, with the greatest first. The necrology highlighted that membership did not end with the guild-brothers' demise, and that the dead were remembered within the guilds, and their death-fees were used for remembrance and charity. The death registers reveal the variety of the guild communities and their place within the wider civic community, but the guilds' interaction with civic society went further, through their charity.

Charity, including support networks and caring for others, was a civic virtue as well as a religious duty. Although many modern studies have been critical of the effectiveness of medieval charity, the majority of guilds were concerned for members who fell into hardship. The small amounts noted above as being paid in Aalst may well have been largely symbolic, yet they are still important demonstrations of community and of mutual aid, as well as tolls for maintaining social cohesion.[97] The study of charity is problematic, with *caritas* itself having

---

[96] Arnade, *Realms of Ritual*, 71.
[97] Nicholas, *Metamorphisos*, 41–58; W. P. Blockmans and W. Prevenier, 'Armoede in de Nederlanden van de 14e tot hetmidden van de 16e eeuw: bronnen en Problemen', *TVG* 88 (1975) 501–38; M.-J. Tits-Dieuaide, 'Les tables des pauvres dans les anciennes principauté's belges au moyen âge', *TVG* 88 (1975), 562–83; M. Galvin, 'Credit and

many definitions, but it must be remembered that care for others through alms was a central part of medieval Catholicism. Vincent has argued that the growth of confraternal hospitals in northern France highlights the importance of charity, just as in England guilds and confraternities worked for the *bonum commune* or *commen-welth*. In Flanders such groups likewise emphasised unity, with urban charity emphasising the body of the city working together and craft guilds caring for their members in poor-houses or hospitals. It is in this context, of numerous small efforts at charity stemming from strong, shared concerns, that the greater crossbow guild's charity needs to be understood.[98]

The Ghent crossbow guild is the only shooting guild known to have founded a hospital, caring not just for its brothers but for the urban poor. That the crossbow guild developed its own independent charitable institutions does not fit with Trio's assessment of other fifteenth-century Ghent confraternities which 'never used their means to develop a kind of poor relief of their own' with confraternities, Trio argues, showing apathy.[99] However, the Ghent crossbow guild, as evidence of the guild hospital suggests, behaved like the town governors, rather than like other devotional confraternities, in not becoming insular (as others did) but becoming more concerned with helping the poor of the town and more concerned with upholding and embodying civic values and even acting as good Christians as well as good townsmen.

The early history of the Ghent hospital of Saint George is poorly documented. It may have developed to help poor or elderly guild members, like the weavers' and fullers' hospitals.[100] The earliest detailed reference to the hospital is a charter granted to it by the bishop of Tournai in 1356. The hospital was not created in

---

Parochial Charity in fifteenth-Century Bruges', *JMH* 28 (2002) 131–54; S. Bos, 'A Tradition of Giving and Receiving; Mutual Aid within the Guild System', in M. Prak, C. Lis, J. Lucassen and H. Soly (eds), *Craft Guilds in the Early Modern Low Countries* (Aldershot: Ashgate, 2006), 175–8; M. Rubin, *Charity and Community in Medieval Cambridge* (Cambridge: Cambridge University Press, 1987), 1–2.

[98] C. Vincent, 'Les multiples forms de l'assistance dans les confréries du royaume de France à la fin du Moyen Âge', in Escher-Apsner, *Mittelalterliche Bruderschaften*, 71–3; C. Rawcliffe, 'Dives Redeemed? The Guild Alms-Houses of Later Medieval England', in L. Clark (ed.),*The Fifteenth Century, VIII: Rule, Redemption and Representations in Late Medieval England and France* (Woodbridge: Boydell, 2008), 1–27; I. W. Archer, 'The Livery Companies and Charity in the Sixteenth and Seventeenth Centuries', in A. A. Gadd and P. Wallis (eds), *Guilds, Society and Economy, London 1450–1800* (London: Centre for Metropolitan History, 2001), 15–28; Dumolyn, 'Urban Ideology in Later Medieval Flanders', 85–7; Nicholas, *Metamorphosis*, 47–51.

[99] Trio, 'The Social Positioning of Late Medieval Confraternities', 99–110.

[100] For craft guild hospitals see W. P. Blockmans and W. Prevenier, 'Opendare armenzorg te 's Hertogenbosch tijdens een groefifase 1435–1535', *ABVH*, XII, 1974, 19–78; ibid, 'Armoire in de Nederlanden van de 14e tot het midden van de 16e eeuw, bronnen en problemen', *Tijdschrift voor Geschiedenis* 88 (1976), 501–38; C. Vleeschouwers,'Het beheer van het O.L.Vrouw-hospitaal the Gent en de stichting van de Cisterciënserinnenabdijen O.L.Vrouw-ten-Bos (1215) en Bijloke (1228) door uten Hove's', *ABVH* 9 (1971).

1356, but in that year it was given the right to perform mass and ring bells.[101] With guild and civic support, the hospital grew, and by 1384 (when documents are more numerous) it was caring for the poor in general, not just for destitute guild members. This was not a health institution, as the hospital was concerned with spiritual care and providing hospitality for the poor, rather than physical care, as were most medieval hospitals.[102]

The main source of funding for the hospital was the *dootghelt*: the required death-fee. A charter from Emperor Maximilian explains that the crossbowmen needed the death-fees to fund the hospital, which 'maintained and further still maintains daily cares and celebrates six masses a day' as well as providing thirty beds for the poor.[103] The *dootghelt* was the foundation of guild charity, but many members were far more generous, leaving far more than the minimum set out in guild regulations. The surviving wills of a small number of Ghent crossbowmen show that some guild-brothers prioritised guild charity. Of course, because only a small number survive it cannot be argued that those who made wills and whose wills have been preserved by the guild are in any way representative. However, they do provide glimpses into the charitable impulses of the guild-brothers.

A telling example is that of Jan Burskin, who wrote his will in May 1384. Jan left his entire estate, including his house, to the guild of Saint George and, in particular, to the hospital. In return for his gift Jan would have been remembered and prayers would have been said for him, but this would have been the case had he left the guild a smaller sum and given his house to an established order. That he left his entire estate to the guild demonstrates how important his identity as a crossbowman was to him. In 1443 another guild-brother, Jooris Vander Jeeken, also left his house to the hospital. His will states that he did this out of great concern for 'those people in the hospital', implying that he knew something about the residents and was moved to pity for them. Neither man mentioned an heir or family in his will, but left everything to the guild and its hospital.[104] It is easy to be sceptical about the actions of these childless men and dismiss them as either tradition or the resort of guild-brothers who had no other option for their goods. Yet Ghent, as we have seen, was a large town full of devotional institutions. Neither Jan nor Jooris divided their goods, neither sold his house, nor did he leave money for alms. It is possible that for them the guild became an heir of last resort – as Italian confraternities did for members who lacked kin.[105] Both made a considered choice to give all they had to a small, focused charity administered by their own guild. Compassion for the poor, as well as care for salvation, informed their choices.

---

[101] UBG, Hs, G. 61731.
[102] S. Sweetinburgh, *The Role of the Hospital in Medieval England, Gift-Giving and the Spiritual Economy* (Dublin: Four Courts Press, 2004), 12–18.
[103] SAG, 155, Sint Joris, 3.
[104] SAG, SJ, NGR, 2, 13.
[105] Banker, *Death in the Community*, 114–33.

Large donations are the best-documented example of guild charity, but were not the only ones. Several women, most of them widows, left the hospital smaller, personal items, such as cloth – even bed sheets – as well as wax and candles.[106] Such items were given in addition to, not instead of, the required *dootghelt*. Small, personal gifts would probably have been used in the hospital, or even the chapel, rather than sold, and in the case of such small objects the choice of what to leave to the hospital is significant. Martha Howell has proved that elsewhere in Flanders women took great care in dividing their estates, even if only meagre ones, among friends, family and devotional groups.[107] The gifts left by guild-sisters to the hospital were personal, and show community, and compassion for the hospital.[108] Unlike Jan and Jooris, these guild-sisters gave most of their goods to family or friends and left smaller personal objects to the hospital, demonstrating a sense of community and perhaps a level of consideration for the needs of charity.

Twenty-eight women left personal objects to the hospital. Many left bed sheets, seven guild-sisters leaving two pairs and two guild-sisters leaving one pair (*slaaplakens*). One, Jonkvrouw Kerstine Gowaers, a 'zuster in het St-Jorisgasthuis' (a sister in the hospital), even left a small bed. Such domestic objects show a personal connection to the guild and that guild-sisters wanted to give something to their community that had meant to something to them – perhaps even something that would be useful to a hospital that cared for the poor. Among other textile gifts left by guild-sisters we find five women leaving *een serviette* – not quite a napkin, but probably fabric for use on the table, perhaps implying that within the hospital people ate at smaller, individual tables, rather than communally. But more generally this, like bed sheets, was a personal gift, showing personal connection. One of the five women who left a *serviette* was a sister in the guild hospital; another, Margriete de Langhe, is described as Mother of the Saint-George Cloister (*mater van het Sint-Jorisklooster*), indicating that the sisters were not property-less. Four guild-sisters left corporals, small items that can be defined as 'a cloth on which the chalice and paten are placed during the celebration of the Eucharist'.[109] Donations left by guild-sisters, and wills written by guild-brothers, show that many members of the community felt a real connection to their hospital and tried to care for the poor and to ensure that they would themselves be cared for and remembered by their guilds.

Wills are imperfect as sources for devotion, revealing only the wishes of those who had the wealth and right to create such a document, and further wishes

---

[106] SAG, LXVII, Sint Jorishospitaal, 4.
[107] M. Howell, 'Fixing Movables: Gifts by Testament in Late Medieval Douai', *PP* 150 (1996), 3–45.
[108] Analysed in greater depth in L. Crombie, 'Sisters of Saint George: Female Membership and Material Remembrance within the Crossbow Guild of Late Medieval Ghent', *Women's History Review* (forthcoming).
[109] Oxford Dictionary Online, accessed 02/02/16, http://oxforddictionaries.com/definition/english/corporal?q=corporals.

at the end of one's life. Despite such limitations, wills 'offer the historian a rare moment ... for listening to those who have had no intellectual history by the traditional standards'.[110] The guild-brothers who donated houses are well documented, the guild-sisters who left cloth are hinted at, but the residents of the hospital are harder to identify. The residents, the recipients of guild-charity, are not named, but by the end of the fifteenth century the hospital had thirty beds and provided for the spiritual care of residents with masses and funerals. There are several references in guild sources from the late fifteenth or early sixteenth centuries to poor women and children, but nothing more specific.[111] Fifteenth-century legislation for the Holy Ghost tables warned against giving aid to healthy young men, showing a fear of vagrancy and mistrust of a perceived lazy poor.[112] Although the Ghent hospital did not record rules on deserving or undeserving poor, similar motives may have – consciously or unconsciously – guided their choices in favouring poor women and children over men.

Despite the generalisations in charters, it is clear that not all residents in the hospital were destitute. In 1409 a married couple, Jan and Lysebette van Vracht (both guild-members), left their house to the guild on their deaths, on condition they would continue to live in their house for as long as possible and, if they could no longer live unassisted, would move into the hospital.[113] Jan and Lysebette mentioned no children, no kin, and so needed the guild hospital to act as their surrogate family. The guild would care for the van Vrachts in their old age and become their heir, praying for them after death and remembering them, acting as family when kin were lacking. Just as Jan and Jooris made conscious choices to give everything to the guild, Jan and Lysebette also made choices. That an aging couple in Ghent should guard against poverty in old age is not surprising: research in England has shown how common it was for the elderly to be at risk of poverty.[114] The hospital did look after guild-brothers and sisters in need, but it was not exclusively for them. The 30-bed hospital seems small relative to Ghent's size and the scale of urban poverty, but in helping a small number of deserving poor the guild was living up to civic values and promoting the common good of the urban community.

---

[110] S. K. Cohn, *Death and Property in Siena, 1205–1800* (Baltimore and London: Johns Hopkins University Press, 1988), 2.
[111] SAG, LXVII, Sint joirshospitaal, 3, 4, 8.
[112] P. Trio, *Volksreligie als Spiegel van een stedelijke samenleving. De Broederschappen te Gent in e late middeleeuwen* (Leuven: Universitaire Pers Leuven, 1993), especially 40–59, 271–4, 411–14; Nicholas, *Metamorphosis*, 41–66.
[113] SAG, SJ, NGR, 6.
[114] C. Dyer, *Standards of Living in the Later Middle Ages: Social Change in England c.1200–1520* (Cambridge: Cambridge University Press, 1989), 215–45; Barron, *London in the Later Middle Ages*, 295–301; E. Clark, 'The Quest for Security in Medieval England', in M. M. Sheehan (ed.), *Aging and the Aged in Medieval Europe* (Toronto: Pontifical Institute of Medieval Studies, 1990), 189–200.

How the hospital was administered in the fourteenth century is unclear, as early documents are simply financial records of sums given to it. For much of the first half of the fifteenth century guild officials again seem to have been keeping accounts. The situation was formalised in 1453 when another couple, Willem and Barbera de Rade, moved into the hospital to care for the residents. They were also given the care of the jewels and prizes that the crossbowmen had won, indicating that the guild regarded the hospital not only as a charitable institution but also as a safe house for the treasures that were not placed in the chapel. Willem and Barbera were guild members and relatively rich, property-owning citizens, but they lived in the hospital. Like the van Vrachts, Willem and Barbera do not refer to any kin in any of their documents. When he wrote his will in 1473, Willem arranged to leave all of his property, including the couple's house, to the hospital. Willem's will does not mention any other family, nor does it refer to Barbera, perhaps implying that she was dead or even that she had become a resident in the hospital and so did not need any additional provision.[115]

Willem is the last man recorded as running the hospital; after his death it became a female-run institution. The guild-sisters, with a guild-mother, took over the hospital administration. They lived in a 'cloister' or 'convent' attached to it, were forbidden to leave and were expected to earn money through their own work. A document of 1500 names the thirteen guild-sisters living in the hospital. No information is given as to their status, age or background, but it is striking that no guild-sister is given a title, nor are they identified as sisters, daughters or wives of guild-brothers. Each is named in her own right, whereas in membership lists for Aalst and Bruges women tend to appear as wives or widows. The guild lists are too large and not detailed enough for us to be sure that the women are not related to guild-brothers, but no relationship is made obvious, no status is displayed and no hierarchy is apparent between the guild-sisters. These thirteen guild-sisters are included in the death-list discussed above, indicating that they were seen as an integrated part of the guild community – and they may indeed have been a special part of the community, as they lived in the guild's cloisters, caring for the sick.

It is tempting to compare the Saint George sisters to Beguines, lay women who established convents across the Low Countries, lived by their own work and cared for the poor and the dying. Beguines were part of a movement, beginning in the thirteenth century, of women in textile and trading centres who formed themselves into enclosed communities.[116] Ghent, as both a textile centre and a centre of commerce, had numerous Beguine houses and it is possible that similar motives were felt by the women who became guild-sisters in the hospital. The Saint George sisters were not Beguines. They were involved in a property dispute with the convent of Saint Elizabeth – Ghent's largest Beguineage – in

---

[115] SAG, LXVII, Sint Jorishospitaal, 1–24; SAG, SJ, NGR, 10, 22.
[116] A. Winston-Allen, 'Women in Monastic Orders', in *Gender and Fraternal Orders in Europe*, 52–61.

which Charles V decided in favour of the hospital of Saint George in 1516.[117] Moreover, Beguines were part of a wider European community and, influenced by the Mendicants and wandering preachers, they 'turned their backs on the world'.[118] In contrast, the Saint George sisters were part of a small group focused on administering the charity of the Ghent crossbow guild in Ghent, for the poor of Ghent.

The Ghent sisters of Saint George were dedicated to a spiritual calling, especially charity and caring for the urban poor. The hospital became a sizable institution, and as well as maintaining thirty beds it became a property owner. In 1516, when Charles V granted it tax exemptions, the total annual income of the hospital from property rents was £49 10s.[119] The hospital's property is well recorded, but those who filled the thirty beds and what kind of charity they received are not recorded. Residents may have included former guild members, like the van Vrachts, or deserving urban poor, but references are imprecise and most are simply to 'the poor' or even 'the women'. The hospital of Saint George is an important example of urban charity, demonstrating that the guilds had the same concerns regarding the urban poor as did the civic authorities, and that they were concerned not just for the salvation of their own members but also for that of the poor whom they were honour-bound to protect, as was Saint George.

The Ghent guilds are unusually well documented, but in caring for each other, in having elaborate chapels and in prioritising charity they were not unique. The good of the guild was linked to the good of the town, and wills and bequests reveal an on-going concern for others in the last wishes of some guild members. Of course not all guild members would be as pious, just as not all Bruges archers attended the feast and not all Lille crossbowmen obeyed their constable. Guilds set up clear ideals of peace and harmony within social and devotional communities, using feasting and praying to bind brothers and sisters together into a strong community with a sense of purpose and unity. As we shall see, these communities were supported by both princely and urban powers and were able, through competitions, to extend their communities across and beyond the county. Guild devotion and care for fellow members was an integral part of the purpose of guilds and highlights the fact that guilds, like other urban communities, were focused and acting as brotherhoods.

---

[117] SAG LXVII, Sint Jorishospitaal, 1.
[118] W. Simons, *Cities of Ladies, Beguine Communities in the Medieval Low Countries, 1200–1565* (Philadelphia: University of Pennsylvania Press, 2001), 2–54, 91–119.
[119] SAG LXVII, Sint Jorishospitaal, 4, 1.

4

'For the honour of the duke and of the town'

Guilds and Authority

We have seen that guilds were militarily significant for their town and their prince and that their membership came from across civic society to form members into a unified socio-devotional community. The guilds must now be placed within their civic and wider political context(s). The purpose of the present chapter is to look at the support given to guilds by towns and by lords and to try to explain their place within both civic culture and court–civic interactions. The significance of civic honour – indeed, honour as a concept – will be discussed and the guilds will be used to offer new insight into relationships between nobles and towns and, in particular, the rule of the dukes of Burgundy as counts of Flanders. The guilds were part of civic culture and part of their urban communities, but they were also part of the shared society and shared forms of cultural expression that developed between the ducal court and urban activities.[1]

'Honour'

Before analysing the archery and crossbow guilds' relationship to civic honour, and indeed why the guilds were perceived as bringing honour to the dukes, the term itself must be considered. In medieval sources 'honour' is an even more

---

[1] Brown and Small, *Court and Civic Society*; P. Arnade, 'City, State in Public Ritual in the Late Medieval Burgundian Netherlands', *Comparative Studies in Social History* 39 (1997), 300–18; M. Boone, 'Entre vision idéale et représentation du vécu: nouveaux aperçus sur la conscience urbaine dans les Pays-Bas à la fin du Moyen Âge', in P. Johanek (ed.), *Bild und Wahrnehmung der Stadt: Kolloquium des Kuratoriums für vergleichende Städtegeschichte* (Köln: l'Allemagne Böhlau Verlag 2012), 79–98; J. Braekevelt and J. Dumolyn, 'Diplomatique et discours politiques?: une analyse lexicographique qualitative et quantitative des ordonnances de Philippe le Bon pour la Flandre (1419–1467)', *RH* 662 (2012), 323–56; H. Brand, *Over macht en overwicht. Stedelijke elites in Leiden 1420–1510* (Leuven: Garant, 1996); Brown, 'Bruges and the "Burgundian Theatre-State"', 573–89; A.-L. Van Brauene, 'The Habsburg Theatre State; Court, City and the Performance of Identity', 131–49.

ubiquitous term than 'community'. A 1443 civic charter from the Lille aldermen on the occasion of the 'reunion' of the two crossbow guilds – the *grand* and the *petit* – gave the guild rights organised for the 'honour, fortune and grace' of the duke of Burgundy and the town of Lille. The guild-brothers were to uphold 'good and honour' in their conduct and at all times behave in an 'honourable' manner. If a competition was to be held in another town, then the best men must be sent 'for the honour' of the confraternity and of the town. The guild officials were to be 'suitable for the good and honour of the town' and all of the guild-brothers must be sufficiently armed and skilled 'for the honour of the town' and were to follow their regulations 'profitably and honourably for the good and honour of the town and of the duke'.[2]

Honour can be understood in numerous different ways and it is likely that the term meant different things to different writers, even within the towns of the late medieval Low Countries. In the following, honour is understood in an anthropological sense, drawing on definitions put forward by Julian Pitt-Rivers. Honour is linked not just to an individual's (or in this case a group's) self-worth, but also to values seen as honourable, or valuable, by his (or their) society. Each group has its own idea of honour, but it is connected to power as well as to conscience, and with great honour comes great responsibility, as honour has to be defended. When discussing the guilds' 'honour', or indeed civic 'honour', this is taken to be a 'validation of the image which they cherish of themselves' and a concept that 'provides a nexus between the ideals of a society' and the ways in which those ideals are represented. Collective honour was a delicate matter: it could be and was lost through actions, like running away, or visiting a brothel in guild livery, or through words, like insults. This explains why guild-brothers had to be good and worthy men. For guilds, honour was a system of conduct and a standard of behaviour, it meant being true to their word, following their rules and winning victories, whether in war or in competition. Civic and ducal 'honour', when linked to urban groups as it is in the following, is a greater authority, as the dukes could bestow honour. Princely honour was about status and legitimacy, and it could be reinforced through ritual.[3]

---

[2] AML, RT, 15883, f. 134r–v.

[3] J. Pitt-Rivers, 'Honour and Social Status', in J. G. Peristiany (ed.), *Honour and Shame: The Values of Mediterranean Society* (Chicago: Chicago University Press, 1974), especially 21–38; J. Pitt-Rivers and J. G. Peristiany, 'Introduction', to their *Honor and Grace in Anthropology* (Cambridge: Cambridge University Press, 1992), 1–17; T. Fenster and D. Lord Smail, 'Introduction', to their *Fama: The Politics of Talk and Reputation in Medieval Europe* (London: Cornell University Press, 2003), 1–11; W. Prevenier, 'The Notions of Honour and Adultery in the Fifteenth-Century Burgundian Netherland', in D. Bicholas, B. S. Bachrach and J. M. Murray (eds), *Comparative Perspectives on History and Historians: Essays in Memory of Bryce Lyon (1920–2007)* (Kalamazoo: Medieval Institute Publications, 2012), 259–78. These ideas have benefited greatly from teaching an MA seminar on 'honour and shame' for three years at the University of York, and I am grateful to all participants.

Civic Support and Civic Honour

Civic support is the earliest and best-documented form of support for the guilds, so it is sensible to analyse the relationship between civic honour and guilds first. It was civic support that gave guilds the security and the firm financial base that they needed so as to be able to build their regional and urban–aristocratic networks. Civic support can even be seen as the foundation of guild culture. Guilds received rights from their towns; they also received wine, money and even land, allowing them to become representatives of civic honour. The idea of 'civic patriotism' or a civic sense of pride will be discussed more fully in the following chapters. As we have seen, the towns of the Low Countries were large and had developed a sense of pride as shown in their walls, seals and urban buildings. Although it has been argued that only Florence could develop a sense of 'urban ideology', sponsorship of guilds and their competitions – as well as jousts and other events – embodies the same sorts of values and indicates self-worth and a strong self-image.[4] From the thirteenth century, and in a more pronounced way in the fourteenth century, civic authorities across Flanders promoted the good of the town. Civic jurisdiction was a huge part of this but so was urban protection, in the widest sense.[5] The civic authorities' support to the guilds fits these broader concerns of self-sufficiency and independence, with the guilds forming part of an urban defence force, but also being part of the civic pride and even ideology. The guilds were a way for towns to assert their power and honour.

Early civic support makes clear that the guilds were often patronised and promoted in part for their military skills and for civic protection. In 1348 the aldermen of Oudenaarde granted rights to the Saint George crossbowmen 'for helping our lord' and so that Oudenaarde would be better defended. From the 1380s civic motives for supporting the shooting guilds reflect honour alongside defence. In September 1383 the crossbowmen of Douai had their 'customary' rights confirmed by aldermen for the 'honour, profit and aid' of the town. In 1423 the Ghent guild of Saint George 'honourably received' money for the 'profit' of the town when electing officials.[6] By 1493 the guild-brothers of Saint George

---

[4] G. Holmes, 'The Emergence of an Urban Ideology at Florence c. 1250–1450', *Transactions of the Royal Historical Society Fifth Series*, vol. 23 (1973), 111–34; Arnade, 'Crowds, Banners and the Market Place', 417–97; J. Dumolyn, 'Urban Ideologies in Later Medieval Flanders, Towards an Analytical Framework', in A. Gamberini, J.-P. Genet and A. Zorzi (eds), *The Languages of Political Society, Western Europe 14th–17th Century* (Rome: Viella, 2011), 69–96.

[5] M. Boone, *A La Recherche d'une modernité civique. La société urbaine des anciens Pays-Bas Moyen Âge* (Bruxelles: Université de Bruxelles, 2010), 79–83; B. Chevaliers, 'Corporations, conflits politiques et paix sociale en France aux XIVe et XV siècles', in his *Les Bonnes villes, l'État et la société dans la France du XVe siècle* (Orleans: Paradigme, 1985), 271–98.

[6] OSAOA, gilden, 507/II/12; DAM, Arbalestiers de Douay, 24I1232, f. 1; SAG, 301/27, f. 82v, 17.

of Ghent were being given funds 'for the honour and reverence' of God, Saint George and Ghent.[7] From the late fourteenth century onwards towns all over Flanders favoured their guilds for civic honour, emphasising that the guilds were protectors as well as becoming part of civic identity. The repetition of 'honour' in civic grants emphasised that guilds were part of what made towns strong and gave them self-worth: guilds brought might, and might was bound up with honour.

Civic support quickly became an annual matter, granted to guilds whether they served in war or not, and whether they attended competitions or not. That their funding became an established part of urban budgets, never cut even in years of dramatic civic deficits and huge expenses on other civic projects, demonstrates the prominence of the guilds in the eyes of civic authorities. So ubiquitous is support for guilds that it is difficult to analyse and may simply be taken as an accepted norm. No other group received this kind of annual funding, and that the guilds did so is extremely important for understanding their place in urban ideology.

The town accounts of Lille are particularly detailed for tracing the importance of 'honour' in civic support to urban groups. As we have seen, the crossbowmen were given annual gifts of wine before the archers, implying that they were older and perhaps more prestigious. The crossbowmen first received wine for their 'games and establishment' in 1332. As new guilds emerged, hierarchy became more apparent. In 1397 both the archers and the lesser crossbowmen received twelve lots of wine for their annual shooting contests, their *papegay*, while the greater crossbowmen received twenty-four lots. Until 1405 amounts remained constant, but in 1406 the wine given to the archers was raised to sixteen lots, while the crossbowmen still received twenty-four lots. The lesser archers did not receive annual grants of wine until 1437, when the greater crossbowmen received eighteen lots, the lesser crossbowmen twelve lots, the greater archers twelve lots and the lesser archers nine lots. All of this wine was presented for the 'honour' of the town.[8]

A hierarchy had clearly been established, with the crossbowmen receiving more than the archers, implying they were of a higher status. It is also striking that the *grand* and *petit* guilds received separate gifts of wine, in different quantities, again implying that they were separate adult groups of different status, not co-dependent youth and adult guilds. Although not all guilds were equal, all guilds received annual grants of wine for the honour of the town. No other group, not even the jousters of the Epinette, enjoyed such grants, demonstrating the prestige of guilds and their recognition as groups that could protect and represent their towns.

Patterns of hierarchy and gift-giving changed surprisingly little over the fifteenth century and do not seem to have provoked any complaints in Flanders.

---

[7] SAG, 155, SJ, 3.
[8] AML, CV, 16021, f. 39v; 16130, f. 36r–v; 16148, f. 40v; 16178, f. 50r–v.

In contrast, Tournai did see signs of resentment of the guilds' privileged position and civic funding. In 1429, when the town was in a financial crisis, the 'commun peuple' objected to exemption from the watch for churchmen, to the men of law being paid for looking after the gate keys and to the £20 that the crossbowmen received each year for five feast days.[9] In Flanders there were no recorded complaints about sums of money given to the guilds, and their support was maintained across the fourteenth and fifteenth centuries for the prestige and honour they brought to the town.

Towns wanted their guilds not just to be prestigious but to be communities that could enhance civic honour in display as well as in martial potential. In 1447 the Lille archers were given 8s a week 'for being in recreational assembly every Sunday for the purpose of shooting'. The crossbowmen received 12s a week for the same reason.[10] The guilds each received a further £6 for being in 'recreational assembly' on the day of the procession.[11] The guild-brothers were expected to practise, in groups of ten, in their garden each Sunday and afterwards would be rewarded with drinks paid for by the town, emphasising that the civic authorities valued the shooters for their skill. The gift of wine endowed status and emphasised community, as the wine would be consumed by many guild-brothers. Wine was the standard civic gift, given to messengers, lords or any other important visitors to the town. Yet no other groups received weekly gifts of wine. On top of this, the guilds received extra money and wine when they 'won honour' in competitions. Jousters or drama groups, especially those associated with procession, received funds for their events and, as in France and England, wine was given freely during special events like town entrance ceremonies.[12] Most rewards were given for specific events and were not a standard annual and weekly grant as was received by the shooting guilds. The guilds received grants from their towns in recognition of the honour they brought through validating the towns' civic self-image as independent and powerful, and of their potential as defenders.

Many Flemish towns also gave their guilds cloth each year. The accounts of Oudenaarde are particularly useful for references to cloth, as they record in detail the quantity and the cost of cloth given to the guilds. Civic gifts of cloth, as Blockmans observed when looking at councillors, proclaimed both the honour of the town and the wearer's position within civic hierarchy. To take this further, van Uytven has argued that place within a procession and gifts offered by urban governments including cloth and travel expenses were key ways by which to understand medieval 'rank'.[13] The Oudenaarde accounts make clear that the

---

[9] Vandenbroeck, 'Extraits des anciens registres', 283.
[10] AML, CV, 16188, f. 71–71v.
[11] AML, CV, 16225, ff. 107–109v.
[12] R. Hilton, 'Status and Class in the Medieval Town', in T. R. Slater and G. Rosser (eds), *The Church in the Medieval Town* (Aldershot: Ashgate, 1998), 14–16.
[13] Blockmans, 'The Feeling of Being Oneself', 13; R. Van Uytven, 'Showing off One's Rank', in W. Blockmans and A. Jansese (eds), *Showing Status: Representation of Social Positions in the Late Middle Ages* (Turnhout: Brepols, 1999), 20–21.

cloth was given to be made into clothing, as it was often listed as 'for costume' or 'for hoods'. Regulations also make clear that guild-brothers were expected to look after their liveries and wear them on special occasions and that they occupied a high place and important rank. Flanders, perhaps because it was a cloth centre, seems to have been more generous in giving full costumes than were other areas. In sixteenth-century Germany, towns gave trousers or money for trousers (*hosengeld*), rather than full costumes, to their shooting guilds.[14] In giving liveries to the guilds the towns made clear the status of the guild-brothers and proclaimed their link to civic honour and civic independence.

From the earliest town accounts, in 1407, Oudenaarde lists gifts of cloth made to the most important civic groups, much like present-masters in Ghent. The list includes aldermen, messengers, even some lords, and, in the middle of the list, the crossbowmen of Saint George.[15] Early accounts are in poor condition, but from 1418 onwards this gift took the annual form of costume for sixteen sworn shooters, at a cost of £60. There were more than sixteen crossbowmen in Oudenaarde, but the cloth changed very little from year to year and the guild-brothers would maintain their costume for many years. The archers did not begin to receive cloth until 1486, and this is very likely to be connected to the ducal 'request' to give them wine the same year.[16] Between 1418 and 1486 only the crossbowmen and the aldermen received a civic livery every year. Individuals or occasionally messengers might receive cloth, but no other social, devotional, festive or political groups were *consistently* given cloth each year. In granting cloth to the crossbowmen and aldermen, Oudenaarde made a statement about which groups and individuals were valued for their sense of society and civic honour.

As in Lille, when the archers began to appear in Oudenaarde's civic accounts a hierarchy was apparent. In 1486 the crossbowmen received cloth for the uniform of sixteen sworn shooters, costing £30; the archers received cloth for twenty-five shooters, but worth only £25. From 1490 onwards the crossbowmen received cloth for sixteen guild-brothers worth £60; in 1514 the archers' cloth for twenty-five guild-brothers was raised from £25 to £30.[17] The crossbowmen did not just receive more money but, crucially, a higher quality of cloth, demonstrating that they had been chosen as representatives of civic ideology. The pattern in Oudenaarde is clear evidence that the guilds were not equal, but were all a part of civic society and all able to contribute to the whole body politic.

Like the right to bear arms, gifts of wine and cloth must be understood within their civic context. Guild-brothers looked prestigious with their weapons because no one else was allowed to bear arms; annual gifts of wine and cloth

---

[14] Tlusty, *The Martial Ethic*, 204–5.
[15] AGR, CC, Microfilm 684, ff. 45v–47.
[16] AGR, CC, Microfilm 684, f. 97v; OSAOA, 1148, stadsrekening, 16, 1483–4, f. 164v.
[17] AGR, CC, 31788, f. 31; OSAOA, 1148, stadsrekening 17, 1490–94, f. 34; AGR, CC, 31802, F. 33; 31809, f. 55v; 31810, f. 30v.

demonstrated their desirable status and honourable position because no other group received this level of support. In their full civic liveries, the guild-brothers were comparable to the civic messengers, who were often given a full costume at civic cost because they would go out of the town representing the community.[18] Grants of livery were particularly significant because other groups were banned from distributing liveries, just as they were banned from bearing arms. In 1420 Lille banned 'confraries' in 'assembes illicities.' In 1450 the Lille aldermen reacted angrily to unauthorised groups behaving 'like the archers and of crossbowmen, giving robes and liveries and costume in great number to many simple companions'. Strict penalties were set out and anyone except authorised guild-brothers found to be wearing livery or carrying arms would be fined £60. Ducal charters, like that of 1412, forbade nobles from distributing livery, reflecting the value of liveries and their potential for creating disorder: they were as dangerous as unauthorised arms. In granting the guilds liveries, towns emphasised and enhanced their civic and corporate honour by supporting small, enfranchised and morally worthy groups.[19]

Guilds could also receive extra grants when additional honour was available, as a study of competitions will shortly show. In leaving their town, in travelling across Flanders in their civic liveries, guilds won honour and represented the wealth and standing of their town, but they did not have to leave their towns to bring honour to their urban communities. In 1427 the Lille archers were given wine 'for the honour that ... they had held ... the feast of the *papegay*'. Indeed, simply by becoming established, guilds brought honour to their towns. In 1484, Lille granted lands to a new guild, the archers of pleasure, 'considering that the said bow is honourable for young men and profitable for the guard and defence of the said land and the said town'.[20] This was by no means unique to large towns, for in 1408 the crossbowmen of Aalst received wax and money for the 'honour' that they took part in the procession; and in the Hainaut town of Ath the crossbowmen were given £10 for maintaining their guild and their annual shoot 'for the honour and reverence' that they brought.[21] Civic authorities gave their guilds privileges and rights for security and for honour. The guilds were civic protectors, but regular gifts of wine, cloth and money make clear that guilds could bring honour to their town simply by being active there, often on civic land.

The value that urban communities placed upon their guilds is further shown by gifts of lands. Towns paid for stages and galleries for jousts and plays. Such events were often held in the market place, but no other groups were given land at civic cost for their 'recreational assemblies'. The English situation was

---

[18] Lowagie, 'Stedelijke communicatie in de late middeleeuwen', 273–95.
[19] ADN, B17667; J. Braekevelt, F. Buylaert, J. Dumolyn and J. Haemers, 'The Politics of Factional Conflict in Late Medieval Flanders', *Historical Research* 85 (2012), 23.
[20] AML, CV, 16170, f. 52; AML, CV, 162223, f. 86v.
[21] AGR, CC, 31419, f. 53v; AGR, CC, 39239, f. 22v.

very different, with public butts at which everyone was required to practise.[22] The gardens of the Flemish shooting guilds were enclosed and were for the guild-brothers only. Gifts of civic land were important in terms of their value, but their location is also revealing of the guilds' status, with land grants being given in some of the most symbolically powerful parts of the town. As noted in the previous chapter, in Lille both the archers and crossbowmen had gardens outside the Porte de Courtrai, a rich and prestigious part of town.[23] The archers of Armentières had a garden outside the prestigious Houpline-gate, near the Franciscan church. The crossbowmen had a garden on the other side of the same church, nearer to the Erquinghem gate. Both guilds' leading place in civic society was demonstrated by these grants of land in a prestigious and affluent part of town.[24] Virtually all guilds were given land. In Douai the archers received their garden, rent free, for a hundred years at a time, as first recorded in 1445 and renewed in 1545. The garden ran just outside the town walls and the archers were expected to make it secure and to plant trees.[25] Such long-term, but nonetheless temporary, support is unusual, implying that the civic authorities of Douai were unwilling to alienate civic property, despite the prestige of the guild. The gardens of the archers and crossbowmen rarely survive, but their traces can still be found in street names – for instance, in Douai the Ruelle des Archers and Ruelle des Arbalétriers follow the old town walls. Grants of municipal land marked out the shooting guilds as special and privileged – no other group was given civic land in such a standardised fashion.

Although civic space is a useful indicator, the best way to understand the place of the archery and crossbow guilds within civic society is to analyse their place within urban processions. Processions brought the entire community together in devotional celebration, often in a demonstration of peace.[26] Most Flemish towns focused on one annual procession to build unity and 'spared no expense' in making it a great event. The events demonstrate a shared spirituality, with the entire community on show and ranked. The place of each group in the procession was a physical manifestation of its social standing.[27] In processions,

---

[22] Gunn, 'Archery Practice in Early Tudor England', 53–81.
[23] AML, RT 15884, ff. 134–135v; AML, RM, 16973, f. 79.
[24] AAM, EE4.
[25] DAM, 2 II 2/ 5; 2II2/ 10; Espinas, *Les Origines*, vol. 2, 543–4.
[26] M. Jurdjevic, 'Voluntary Associations Reconsidered: Compagnie and Arti in Florentine Politics', in N. A. Eckstein and N. Terpstra (eds), *Sociability and its Discontents, Civil Society, Social Capital, and Their Alternatives in Late Medieval and Early Modern Europe* (Turnhout: Brepols, 2009), 253–6.
[27] Trio, 'The Emergence of New Devotions in Late Medieval Urban Flanders', 332–3; B. Ouvry, 'Officieel ceremonieel te Oudenaarde, 1450–1600', *Handelingen van de geschieden oudheidkundige kring van Oudenaarde* 22 (1985), 25–64; Brown, 'Civic Ritual: Bruges and the Count of Flanders in the Later Middle Ages', 277–99; Brown and Small, *Court and Civic Society*, 239–52; Lecuppre-Desjardin, *La ville des Ceremonies*, 165–97, 23–43; Black, *Italian Confraternities*, 108–16.

guilds demonstrated their strong associations with civic culture and the value that towns placed upon guilds, with several towns helping their guilds to look spectacular. In Douai, from 1390 the guild of Saint George received 12lb. of wax, 'as is the custom for the candle of that guild', to be carried in the procession.[28] In Aalst too, from 1408 the crossbowmen received wax, here 9lb., given 'with honour' for the procession.[29] Gifts of cloth and wax would have made the guilds some of the most visually striking parts of the greatest urban events, placed at the heart of civic hierarchy and paid to be there.

Flanders's most famous procession was the Holy Blood Procession of Bruges. As Trio has shown, Bruges used the procession more and more for its own purposes, making the event a great demonstration of civic prestige.[30] The focus of the event was a vial of Christ's blood, supposedly brought back from the Holy Land in the mid-twelfth century by Count Thierry d'Alsace (although possibly brought a century later from Constantinople), which became a central part of civic culture. The route of the procession around the town walls made a clear statement of civic pride and brought the community together, demonstrating urban strength as well as hierarchy. The relic emphasised both civic identity and links to the counts of Flanders and, by extension, the dukes of Burgundy. The crossbowmen and archers flanked the relic – indeed they still do in the modern procession, guarding it as well as demonstrating their central place within civic culture, at the very heart of civic devotion and of civic society.[31]

Bruges is not unique in placing its guilds at the centre of a great urban procession to promote civic peace. In Lille the procession of Notre Dame de la Treille had been established by 1270 and was linked to the countess of Flanders and a miraculous statute of the Virgin.[32] The procession brought together the entire town; ordinances were passed to keep the day peaceful and 'honourable'.[33] The centre of the procession was a statue of the Virgin and, like the Holy Blood, she was protected by the archery and crossbow guilds, although by the sixteenth century they had moved to the front of the procession.[34] The civic governors

---

[28] DAM, CC 201, f. 293.
[29] AGR, CC, 31419, f. 53v.
[30] Trio, 'The Emergence of New Devotions in Late Medieval Urban Flanders', 332–3.
[31] Brown, 'Civic Ritual: Bruges and the Counts of Flanders', 277–99; idem, 'Ritual and State Building; Ceremonies', 1–24; idem, *Civic Ceremony*, 37–52; Brown and Small, *Court and Civic Society*, 213; SAB, 385, Sint Jorisgilde, register met ledenlijst enz. 1321–1531, f. 54; Rekeningen 1445–1480, f. 14v, BASS, rekeningboeken, Volume 3, 1, 1454–1456, f. 31v.
[32] Lecuppre-Desjardin, *La Ville des Cérémonies*, 88–9, 94–7.
[33] In 1382 immoral or illicit games and assemblies on the day of the procession or the night before were banned, AML, OM, 373, f. 12; an ordinance of 1462, reissued numerous times, emphasised the need for all who attended the procession to behave 'with honour', AML, OM, 378, f. 98v.
[34] A. E. Knight, 'Processional Theatre in Lille in the Fifteenth Century', *Fifteenth Century Studies* 13 (1988), 99–109; idem, 'Processional Theatre and the Rituals of Social Unity

placed the guilds in a prestigious position, flanking the Virgin as civic protectors, and rewarded them for their service. From 1415 the crossbowmen were given £4 by the town for taking part and the archers received 40s. The guild officials saw this great civic event as important and wanted the best of their community on display. From 1443, all crossbowmen had to 'promise to have and wear their cloaks on the day of the procession of Lille' and march with their king at their head; any guild-brother who failed to do would be fined 10s. The Lille guilds also took part in general processions, marching with the clergy of Saint Peter's for the procession called in 1469 'for praising God our creator and for the peace' made between Louis XI of France and Charles the Bold.[35] In great civic spectacles the guilds occupied some of the most important places, protecting relics just as they protected the town, representing civic values and promoting their own status.

The importance of processions as moments of civic unity, as demonstrations of urban devotion and as opportunities to show guild status was just as significant in smaller centres. Smaller towns would not draw in regional audiences as Bruges would, but their events would bring in people from surrounding villages. In these small towns with limited festive options, the procession demonstrated unity and that they, too, were centres of culture. By 1397 the crossbowmen and archers of Ninove had been granted civic funds for attending the Corpus Christi procession, as were those of Caprijk from 1407.[36] In every town, large and small, for which records can be found guilds demonstrated devotion and status through paid participation in civic processions, carrying their weapons not to war but for peace. In marching, and in being paid to march, at the centre of great civic processions, guilds demonstrated their devotion and their central place within their civic communities.

Noble Support and Noble Guild-Brothers

Guilds were central to their urban communities; they were also a central part of the communities that existed between nobles and civic society. For some minor lords, interaction with the guilds could be used to demonstrate their role at the head of their local communities. Other lords built more complicated networks with guilds across Flanders, integrating themselves into various urban communities and, in doing so, gaining civic support. It must be emphasised that most Flemish nobles were not a world apart from towns. The Flemish nobility as a whole was, to use Buylaert's phrase, 'strengthened with urban families' and their wealth. Numerous urban groups contained noble members. Just as numerous devotional confraternities included nobles among their ranks, the jousters of the White Bear of Bruges and the Epinette of Lille were often led

---

in Lille', in *Drama and Community: People and Plays in Medieval Europe* ed. A. Hindley (Turnhout: Brepols, 1999), 251–2.
[35] AML, PT, 5883, ff. 28–31; AML, CV, 16208, f. 121.
[36] AGR, CC, 37076, f. 17; 33009, f. 7v.

by nobles, building bonds and forms of interaction that helped to strengthen political power. The existence of such links undermines the traditional view of a weakening of noble power in the Low Countries. On the contrary, noble power did not 'erode' in the face of growing civic power; rather, nobles engaged in commerce, tax farming and other projects. By kin, by finances, by politics and by culture, nobles were integrated into the urban world. Thus, placing themselves within archery and crossbow guilds through charters and joining urban festivals was a natural step in order to strengthen urban–aristocratic networks.[37]

Nobles could act as patrons to urban groups, placing themselves at the head of the guild community and, by extension, leading a section of urban society. Such relationships are common in the smaller towns and can be glimpsed through ducal charters. On 16 July 1405 John the Fearless granted a charter to the archers and crossbowmen of Wattignies and of Estrées at the 'humble supplication of our friend and loyal knight, messier Rolland de la Hovarderie, lord of Wattignies and of Estrées'. Both guilds, the charter makes clear, had been active 'during the life of his late father' and the ducal grant was to 'renew' and 'sustain' the eighty crossbowmen and forty archers.[38] The father referred to was Mathieu de la Hovarderie, who had served first Louis of Male and then Philip the Bold in the Ghent war from 1379. Rolland, like his father, showed himself to be part of his town's urban society and helped the guild to assemble 'for the giving of prizes', placing them on a par with guilds in larger towns. The charter was also part of a relationship between John the Fearless and Rolland. By granting a charter at Rolland's wish to his guilds, John was assured of Rolland's loyalty. A few weeks later, in August 1405, Rolland would take the field as one of the leaders of the force John led into France in preparation to march against the duke of Orléans, thus demonstrating the political value of these social networks of support between town, lord and prince.[39]

Rolland de la Hovarderie was a powerful figure, able to use ducal influence to assert his position at the head of two guilds. The families of Lannoy and Commines were even more prestigious and even more powerful, and both used their influence at the court of Philip the Good to obtain rights for shooting guilds within their towns. The history of the town of Lannoy is interlinked with that of the lords who ruled it, a family who obtained great power as ducal servants.[40] In a charter of 1459 Philip the Good stated that he had received the 'humble

---

[37] F. Buylaert, 'The Late Medieval "Crisis of the Nobility" Reconsidered: The Case of Flanders', *Journal of Social History*, 45 (2012), 1117–34; idem, *Eeuwen van Ambitie*, 83–140; Van den Neste, *Tournois, Joutes, pas d'Armes*, 123–44; Brown, *Civic Ceremony*, 141–62, 222–59; Brown and Small, *Court and Civic*, 1–28, 210–36.

[38] ADN, B1600, ff. 25v–26.

[39] K. de Lettenhove, *Histoire de Flandre*, 6 vols (Bruxelles: Vandale, 1847–1855), vol. 3, 60.

[40] W. Ossoba 'Jean de Lannoy', in R. de Smedt (ed.), *Les chevaliers de l'ordre de la Toison d'Or au XVe siècle, notes bio-biographique* (Frankfurt am Main; New York: P. Lang, 2000), 109–10; B. Sterchi, 'The Importance of Reputation in the Theory and Practise of Burgundian Chivalry; Jean de Lannoy, the Croys and the Order of the Golden Fleece',

supplication of our friend and loyal knight, councillor and chamberlain, lieutenant in our lands of Holland, Zealand and Friesland, and governor of Lille, Douai and Orchies, My Lord Jehan, lord of Lannoy', stating that Jehan has 'a great desire and wish to augment and strengthen his house, town, land and lordship of the said Lannoy' and surrounding area. Jehan, therefore, humbly requested Philip's permission to establish a guild of archers 'for the maintenance of the guard and defence of the said town', and Philip granted the request.[41] The charter brought privileges to the guild, allowing it to bear arms across Flanders and to wear a livery of its – or possibly Jehan's – choosing. The charter makes clear the influence of Jehan over the guild and implies his authority over the town, but it also makes clear the power of Philip over both lord and town of Lannoy.

The town of Commines was likewise linked to a noble dynasty, having been rebuilt by Colard de la Clyte at the end of the fourteenth century. The Clytes, who became Commines (or Commynes), were not as ancient as the Lannoys, although they became as powerful in the Burgundian period. The Clytes were Ypres patricians who had been ennobled for their service to the counts of Flanders, and are a fitting example of urban families strengthening the nobility.[42] In 1455 Philip the Good granted rights to the crossbowmen of Commines at the request 'of our friend and loyal esquire, councillor and chamberlain, Jehan, lord of Commines'. As in Wattinges, the crossbowmen were not new, and the charter adds that 'the lord of Commines, father of the supplicant, played often and many times with the said guild without contradiction or impeachment'.[43] The father referred to is Jean de la Clyte (d. 1443), grandson of Colard who rebuilt the town. Jean was a knight of the Golden Fleece and he had fought with the French at Agincourt and led Flemish troops in the Burgundian army in the 1420s, as well as the Ghent militia at Calais in 1436. The Jehan who obtained this charter did not enter the Order of the Golden Fleece but was nevertheless an important ducal councillor and military leader and was the uncle of Philippe de Commines, the famous court memoirist.[44]

Charters are not the only sources that demonstrate the bonds built between lords and archery and crossbow guilds. Shooting with guilds in larger towns,

---

in J. D'Arcy, D. Boulton and J. R. Veenstra (eds), *The Ideology of Burgundy*, (Leiden: Brill, 2006), 99–116.

[41] AML, RT, 15884, f. 171.

[42] L'abbé L-T. Messiaen, *Histoire chronologique, politique et religieuse des seigneuries et de la ville de Comines* (Courtrai:Collectie Vliegende Bladen, 1892), 121–5.

[43] AML, RM, 16977, f. 135.

[44] J. Paviot, 'Jean de la Clite, seigneur de Comines', in R. deSmedt (ed.), *Les chevaliers de l'ordre de la Toison d'Or au XVe siècle, notes bio-biographique*, (Frankfurt am Main; New York: P. Lang, 2000), 35–7; 11–12; J. Dumolyn, 'Philippe de Commynes et les discoures politiques en Flandre Médiévale', in J. Blanchard (ed.), *1511–2011, Philippe de Commynes, Droit, écriture: deux piliers de la souveraineté* (Genève: Librairie Droz, 2012), 38–40; Buylsert, *Repertorium van de Vlaamse adel*, 168–76.

or interacting with them socially, could bring prestige to lords, as is shown by a poem commissioned by Philippe de Croy to commemorate his victory in a competition of 1525 that made him king of the Mons crossbowmen.[45] The Croys were another of the great families of the Burgundian Netherlands, having served the dynasty loyally and been rewarded with titles and lands. Philippe was governor of Hainaut and was clearly strengthening his ties with the county in interacting with the Mons guild. He would later become one of Charles V's leading generals and is often referred to as his 'cousin'.[46] The poem shows the prestige that Philippe hoped to gain by interacting with the guild. He is described as 'a flower of nobility', and in taking part in the event he was praised for guarding his inheritance. The guild of Notre-Dame was his 'advance guard' and his 'very wise guard' and they had come together 'as friends'. In being 'crowned king of your crossbowmen' Philippe had achieved a 'great triumph' 'in very noble assembly' which allowed him to 'sustain in peace all your supporters'. The poem praised both Philippe and the guild, and emphasised he was the head of its community; they were *his* crossbowmen, *his* guards. In shooting with the guild Philippe had not just shown his prowess and glory, but worked to ensure future support and ingratiated himself with Mons's civic society.

Another great nobleman found a less literary way to demonstrate the attachment he placed on interacting with a guild and to place himself at the head of guild communities. In 1463 Philip the Good, at the 'humble supplication of our friend and loyal esquire Jan, lord of Dadizeele', allowed him to establish 'a guild of archers in his said lordship of Dadizeele' with the rights to bear arms and immunity from prosecution, as others had. In his memoirs, Jan recorded the obtaining a charter for the archers, along with service with Simon de Lalaing and the birth of his children, as one of his proudest achievements.[47] That he remembered founding a guild as a worthy achievement and noted it in his rather short memoir highlights the value that lords placed upon guilds as means of building support networks with towns and augmenting their relationship with civic powers. The placement of the guild foundation here – indeed the publication transcribes the charter – may imply that Jan saw the guild as another of his offspring, or another military achievement. Jan was no humble figure; he became one of most important military leaders after the death of Charles the Bold, and was one of Mary's most trusted councillors. He was one of few figures who remained popular with the towns and influential at court during Mary's

---

[45] Devilliers 'Notice Historique sur les milices communales', 169–285.
[46] B. D'Ursel, 'Princes en Belgique (1ère partie): Croÿ Aerschot', *Le Parchemin* 74 (2009), 170–205; M. Wittek, 'Note sur le monogramme de Philippe de Croy', *Scriptorium* 57 (2003), 272–6.
[47] RAG, RVV n 7351, ff. 230v–231r; *Mémoires de Jean de Dadizeele*, 3–4. Based on the only edition of these memoirs, it has been suggested that the editor, Baron Kervyn de Lettenhove, reordered the details and made some omissions, but it has not been possible to check the original manuscript, which is still held by Jan's descendants and is not available for consultation.

short reign, being appointed commander-in-chief of Flemish forces in 1478. His murder in 1481, in which Maximilian may have been complicit, caused uproar.[48]

As in the Mons poem, the guild-brothers were *his* guild in *his* town. Jan had obtained important rights for a guild and saw it, or wanted to see it, as *his* men, to ingratiate himself with urban society and to be the leader of a powerful civic group. Jan was also active with other urban communities: he was a member of the Ghent crossbow guild, one of several connections he maintained with the great Flemish town, and also served as Grand Bailly of Flanders and kept Ghent informed of military events. Jan also had less direct connections to the Bruges shooting guilds through his wife, Catherine Breydel. Her father was an important and active member of the archery guild and it is very likely that Catherine and her mother are the 'my lady the wife' and children of Jacob recorded as paying 2*d* each per year by 1465.[49] Such levels of interaction between great lords and guilds in large and small towns fostered a steady strengthening of complex urban–aristocratic networks across fifteenth-century Flanders.

Of course, guilds also benefitted from such interactions by gaining rights and prestige. Every surviving guild membership list includes a number of nobles, usually listed first, emphasising their special place within guild community. Members of the greater guild of Saint George included Maximilian and Margaret of York, and some of the most powerful nobles of the fifteenth and early sixteenth centuries. As has already been noted, this was a death-list, so dates of entrance into the guild are not given. Other names here include Adolf and his son Philip of Cleves, Jan van Gruuthuse, son of Lodewijk and later, Engelbert Count of Nassau.[50] Adolf was the younger son of Adolf I, Duke of Cleves and of Marie of Burgundy (thus a grandson of John the Fearless and nephew of Philip the Good) and was brought up at the Burgundian court along with his elder brother John. Adolf married Beatrice of Coimbra, niece of Isabella of Portugal, strengthening his links to the ducal family and, after Beatrice's death in 1462, he married Anne of Burgundy, one of Philip the Good's illegitimate daughters and thus his cousin. He participated in the Feast of the Pheasant in 1454 and became a Knight of the Golden Fleece two years later. Adolf served Philip and Charles the Bold and continued to serve the dynasty under Mary – indeed he died in 1492 loyally serving Maximilian and Philip the Fair; Vale describes him as 'the head of those Netherlandish nobles who sustained Mary's cause'.[51]

---

[48] J. Haemers, 'Le Meurtre de Jean de Dadizeele. L'ordonnance de Cour de Maximilien d'Autriche et les tensions politiques en Flandre (1481)', *PCEEB* 48 (2008), 227–48; idem, *Common Good*, 72–4.

[49] Haemers, 'Le Meurtre de Jean de Dadizeele', 227–47; Lowagie, 'Stedelijke communicatie in de late middeleeuwen', 273–95; Jan married Catherine Breydel, daughter of Jacob; her brother Corneille married Marguerite van Niewenhove, sister of Jan; BASS, Rekeningen, 1465–7, 3.4 f 69; Volume 3 t. 4, f. 20v.

[50] STAM, G12.608, ff. 33–34.

[51] M. Vale, 'A Burgundian Funeral Ceremony: Olivier de la March and the Obsequies of Adolf of Cleves, Lord of Ravenstein', *EHR* 111 (1996), 920–3; Haemers, *Common Good*,

It is no exaggeration to say that Adolf was one of the most important figures in Mary's court, and as well as his participation in the Ghent crossbow guild he built communities with shooting guild across Flanders. In 1471 the aldermen of Lille gave him large amounts of wine as 'king' of their crossbowmen, implying that he had attended and won their annual shoot. Adolf was also part of the guild community of Bruges, actively leading the crossbowmen in a competition to Damme in 1447.[52] Adolf may also have had a connection to the Brussels crossbow guild – during his funeral, paupers gathered in the garden of the guild to queue, in an orderly fashion, for alms.[53] As noted above, tracing how active members were in guilds is very difficult, and these numerous hints at interaction with guilds across the region are very interesting when considering Adolf's position within civic society and his part in urban–aristocratic relationships.[54] With such powerful nobles in their ranks, guild-brothers gained in prestige and moral credit; they had a greater chance of obtaining special rights and would be seen as more worthy. Noble participation brought validation, increasing the guilds' self-worth and, as a result, their honour, as well as enhancing broader connection between lords and urban cultures.

Noble guild-brothers could bring guilds prestige as well as privilege, and many nobles were part of multiple guilds, building up networks of interactions. Most notable here was Lodewijk van Gruuthuse. It is difficult to overstate the importance of Lodewijk, sometimes called Louis of Bruges in English historiography. He was created earl of Winchester by Edward IV and had been at the court of Philip the Good since 1445; he was knighted in 1452 and entered the order of the Golden Fleece in 1461. Having loyally served Philip the Good and Charles the Bold, under Mary of Burgundy he became first chamberlain, and he remained a loyal servant to Philip the Fair (despite conflicts with Maximilian) until his death in 1492.[55]

As well as being a great court figure, Lodewijk was a powerful civic figure. His family had built up its fortune by controlling the beer trade in Bruges and he was active in numerous Bruges urban groups, including the White Bear, the Dry Tree and Our Lady of the Snow; he even acted as a god-father to one of Anselmus Adornes' sixteen children.[56] With his many connections to Bruges,

---

106–109; idem, 'Kleef (Adolf van)', *NBW* 18 (2007), 540–7; 178–215; W. Ossoba, 'Adolphe de Cleves', in *Les chevaliers de l'Ordre*, 120–1; Cools, *Mannen met Macht*, 107–11, 121–5; Lecuppre-Desjardin, *La Ville des Cérémonies*, 206–10.

[52] AML CV, 16214, f. 77v; SAB, 385 Sint Joris, rekeningen, 1440–8, f. 13.

[53] Vale, 'The Obsequies of Adolf of Cleves', 937.

[54] Vaughan, *Philip the Good*, 129–35, 162–3, 290–1; Vaughan, *Charles the Bold*, 17, 115, 240–4, 320; Soisson, *Charles le Téméraire*, 93, 117, 320–3; Haemers, *Common Good*, 1–5, 53, 73–8, 103–9.

[55] Vale, 'An Anglo-Burgundian Nobleman and Art Patron: Louis de Bruges', 115–31; Haemers, *Common Good*, 103–13.

[56] Despars, *Cronijke van den lande ende graefscepe*, 248, 288, 425; SAB, 505, gilde droogenboom, ledenlist, f. 1; Buylaert, *Eeuwen van ambitie*, 133–7, 236–8.

Lodewijk's participation with the shooting guilds in Bruges is not surprising. He led the crossbowmen to a competition in Sluis in 1452; three years later he was given a guild livery (and he received another in 1465); and he was elected headman of the Saint George guild in 1479. Alongside his participation with Bruges guilds, he was also a member of the Oudenaarde crossbow community, taking part in its competition of 1462, and a member of the crossbow guild of Aalst. He further took part in events with the Ghent crossbowmen, although his name does not appear in their death-list, and he attended their feast in 1477 with 'other lords and ladies'.[57]

For Lodewijk, interacting with guilds across Flanders strengthened bonds with urban communities. He acted just as Adolf of Cleves and Jan van Dadizeele had done, all three building bonds with urban groups, all three using guilds to integrate themselves with different Flemish towns. The political significance of urban support for Jan, Lodewijk and Adolf, became clear after 1477. It was these lords who held Flanders, and the Low Countries, together in the face of rebellion and invasion. Ghent maintained close communications with Adolf of Cleves, and both Bruges and Ghent enlisted the help of Adolf and Lodewijk in choosing new baillies to replace those 'imposed' by Charles the Bold. Haemers described Lodewijk and Adolf as 'the most influential noble courtiers' in 1477, not only 'protecting the young duchess' but also leading armies against Louis XI. Lodewijk became Mary's 'knight of honour', while Adolf of Cleves was her 'closest relative'. Jan was a military leader, remaining popular with the towns and the court and rising quickly in Adolf's entourage.[58] That all three powerful men, Lodeweijk van Gruuthuse, Jan van Dadizeele and Adolf of Cleves, maintained strong levels of interaction with the guilds is no coincidence. Their membership in multiple urban shooting guilds helped them to build and maintain strong urban connections that allowed them to remain popular among townsmen while simultaneously serving as influential courtiers. Support networks with honourable urban groups helped them to work for the Common Good of Flanders, or at least to be seen to be acting for the good of Flanders during Mary's reign.

Such networks and influences lasted beyond the short reign of Mary of Burgundy. After her death, the four men selected as the Flemish regency council were Adolf of Cleves, Philip of Burgundy (son of Anthony the Great Bastard), Lodewijk van Gruuthuse and Adrien Vilain, lord of Rasseghem. Adrien was a Ghent native and a member of the Saint George guild, continuing the tradition of building honourable bonds of brotherhood with court and with the city as

---

[57] Geirnaert 'De Adornes en de Jeruzalemkapel', 23; OSAOA, gilden 507/II/4B; ASAOA, 155, Register Sint Jorisgilde, f. 6v; A town-sponsored 'great feast', town accounts quoted in De Potter, *Jaarboek*, 116.

[58] Haemers, 'Le Meurtre de Jean de Dadizeele', 228–34; idem, *Common Good*, 106–9; idem. 'Adellijke onvrede: Adolf van Kleef en Lodewijk van Gruuthuse als beschermheren en uitdagers van het Bourgondisch-Habsburgse hof (1477–1482)', *JMG* 10 (2007).

represented by the guilds.[59] The social interactions between the guilds and the influential councillors of Mary's reign and those on the regency council for her son are particularly fascinating. Nobles' interaction with guilds across Flanders, but especially in Ghent and Bruges, implies that they used guilds to bolster urban support for themselves and their parties in the large towns in particular, but across Flanders they used urban bonds to build communities, and in this the guilds were an important part.

Guilds and the Rulers of Flanders

Guilds were funded by their towns and built bonds with nobles, but the support they received from the rulers of Flanders was in many ways the most significant. The guilds benefited in clear and obvious ways from princely support, in particular in obtaining privileges. In addition, as has already been shown in the case of noble membership, the princes also benefited from their promotion and privileging of the shooting guilds. The interaction between princes and guilds will be examined in two ways. Firstly, the charters issued by the rules of the Low Countries will be analysed, as these brought rights and prestige to the guilds, from immunity from prosecution for accidental deaths to the 'privilege' of wearing ducal livery, and, in doing so, strengthened relationships. Secondly, the relationships between princes and shooters will be analysed as they grew and developed over the later Middle Ages to allow for the strengthening of links between the dukes and their subjects through cultural interactions as well as potential military preparations.

Charters

Charters and ordinances are a useful starting point for understanding the relationships between the rulers of Flanders and urban groups. Charters reveal much about legal developments and the growth of rights and are administrative and legislative documents, but those issued to shooting guilds show relationships at work. They can be interpreted as written records and as expressions of power, as well as being issued in response to the 'humble requests' of guilds or, more broadly, through representative institutions.[60] As Braekevelt and Dumolyn have

---

[59] H. G. Koenigsberger, *Monarchies, States Generals and Parliaments, the Netherlands in the Fifteenth and Sixteenth Centuries* (Cambridge: Cambridge University Press, 2001), 60–1; W. Ryckbosch, *Tussen Gavere en Cadzand, de Gentse stadsfinancien op het eide van de middeleeuwen (1460–1495)* (Gen: Maatschappij voor geschiedenis en oudheidkundet, 2007), 13–15; STAM, G3018/3, ff. 33r–v.

[60] D. Bates, 'Charters and Historians of Britain and Ireland; Problems and Possibilities', in M. T. Flanagan and J. A. Green (eds), *Charters and Charter Scholarship in Britain and Ireland* (Basingstoke: Palgrave Macmillan, 2005), 1–8; M. Boone, 'Langue, pouvoir et dialogue. Aspects linguistiques e la communication entre les ducs de Bourgogne et leurs sujets flamands (1385–1505)', *RN* 379 (2009), 9–34.

shown, charters issued by the dukes of Burgundy, especially Philip the Good, were the result of negotiation and were not mere written records. Burgundian charters carried a significant aural quality, with charters and legislation being read out at town *bretèches*, in churches or at important civic events, as well as being displayed. This sensory element of publishing charters made their repetition of 'honour' more weighty and added emphasis to representations of civic and ducal values.

Not only did charters help to establish a Burgundian state, linking numerous urban groups to a Burgundian ideology, they also allowed the duke to represent himself as an ideal prince, one who cared for his people and worked to maintain peace.[61] Charters were displayed prominently; indeed one charter issued to a shooting guild was on display in a rather too prominent position: in 1463 Philip the Good had to issue a new charter to the crossbowmen of Oudenaarde because the original, granted by John the Fearless in 1408, had been left out in the rain.[62] Charters were visible, aural and symbolic demonstrations of ducal power and ducal honour granted to the guilds and in this way recognised their contribution to Burgundian strength.

In setting out her vision of an ideal prince, Christine de Pisan wrote that a prince should be virtuous, raise his children with care and look after his people. He should behave as a good shepherd and love the 'bien publicque'. He should, further, be liberal with gifts, as this 'libéralité' would benefit his soul and his reputation and bind his subjects to him through love.[63] In their charters to archery and crossbow guilds, the dukes of Burgundy made sure not just to assert the power of the Burgundian dynasty but to show themselves as ideal, even independent, princes, caring for the public good and enacting generously. Pisan's prince also guards his people, mindful of the 'deffence et garde de son pays et peuple', with good soldiers who will be bound to him by an oath ('par serment') and who will be ready to go out against enemies to stop damage and pillage, *chiens a colères ferrez*.[64] The guilds, often called *serments*, represented such a force for Flanders.

The virtue of defending the Flemish towns was emphasised in several charters, showing the dukes as good princes using the guilds to secure the 'Public Good'. In 1423 Philip the Good granted rights to the archers of Courtrai for the 'great need and necessity for the security and defence'. The charter depicts Philip as a concerned lord, fearing that Courtrai could become 'less secure and badly defended' and granting rights to the archers to provide 'convenient remedy'.[65]

---

[61] J. Braekvelt and J. Dumolyn, 'Diplomatique et discours politiques. Une analyse lexicographique qualitative et quantitative des ordonnances de Philippe le Bon pour la Flandre (1419–1467)', *RH* 662 (2012); OSAOA, gilden 507/II/ 15B.

[62] OSAOA, gilden 507/II/ 15B.

[63] Christine de Pisan (ed. A. J. Kennedy), *Le Livre du corps de policie, Edition critique avec introduction notes et glossaire* (Paris: Honoré Champion, 1998), 13–15, 23–6.

[64] *Le Livre du corps de policie*, 13–15.

[65] RAK, 478. Register van de gilde van Sint-Sebastiaan f. 2r–v.

Here the archers become ducal officers, protecting their town for the good of their own communities but enabled to do so by Philip's actions. Phrases like 'garde, tuicion et deffence' appear in numerous charters granted to shooting guilds across and beyond Flanders; for example, to archers in Arras in 1437.[66] As we saw in chapter one, the guilds were soldiers and were valued across the fourteenth and fifteenth centuries for their military potential. Such concerns show the dukes bringing their lands together and caring for the common people, acting as good shepherds and binding their subjects to them.

Other charters were more specific in their attention to security. In 1447 the archers of Sint-Winnoksbergen received new rights because the town 'is located on the frontier of Calais' and 'in the times of wars and commotions that have been in our lands' the guild had been, and would be, necessary for 'good fortification' of the town. The archers of Biervelt received new privileges in 1446 because the town 'is on the frontier by the sea' and so 'in need of guarding'.[67] None of these charters created guilds. As we have seen, all had been active in military service, and had been taking part in competitions, for generations. Yet, in creating a narrative of new rights and new empowerment, Philip placed himself as civic protector and bound guilds to his generosity and, indeed, his honour.

A good prince should not just protect in case of war, but reward those who have served him well. Numerous charters to shooting guilds recognised their past service and rewarded it liberally with 'gifts'. These charters also recognised that the shooting guilds could serve in the future and so should be kept in a state of readiness. In 1398 Philip the Bold granted rights to the crossbowmen of Dendermonde for their service 'in times past, in the times of our dear lord and father the count of Flanders'. In 1405 John the Fearless confirmed the rights of the Lille archers because the guild had served 'well and diligently, each and every time they have been summoned and requested by our predecessors, counts and countesses of Flanders, in many places'.[68] Legislation affirmed the dukes as protectors and as patrons of the guilds, and by extension of the common good, rewarded the guilds for service, showing that such service was valued.

Ducal charters had a subtler benefit, emphasising the dukes' right to issue charters and to grant privileges independently and so strengthen their rule. The idea of a 'Burgundian State' as a separate political entity removed from France remains debatable because, for all their power, the dukes were not independent princes. The efforts of the dukes, in particular Charles the Bold, to be recognised as kings, perhaps of Lotharingia or of Burgundy, imply a wish to make their status clearer and to increase their standing on the European stage.[69] In issuing charters

---

[66] Espinas, *Les Origines*, vol. 2, 129.
[67] RAG, RVV, 7351, ff. 220–21; f. 239.
[68] *Ordonnances de Philippe le Hardi* vol. 2, 296–300; *Ordonnances du Jean Sans Peur*, 24.
[69] J. Dumolyn, 'Justice, Equity and the Common Good', and G. Small, 'Of Burgundian Dukes, Counts, Saints and Kings, 14 C.E.–1500', both in J. D'Arcy, D. Boulton and J. R. Veenstra (eds), *The Ideology of Burgundy* (Leiden: Brill, 2006), 1–20, 151–94.

as dukes 'by the grace of God', and without having them confirmed by the kings of France, Philip the Good and Charles the Bold made a statement of independence within Flanders. In contrast, in Philip the Bold's charters he styles himself 'son of the king of France', while John the Fearless tends simply to give his titles. Only one surviving charter to the guilds is recorded as being confirmed by a French king; the rest, it seemed, could exist without royal confirmation.[70] In granting charters to their own guilds, in their own county, without reference to French royal power, the dukes were able to use the guilds – and other urban groups – as extensions of their authority.

Charters allowed the dukes to depict themselves as protectors of civic rights and as independent rulers. For the guilds, benefits were rather more obvious and immediate. The most common rights granted to guilds were permission to bear arms, immunity from prosecution if someone should be killed in practice and permission to wear ducal emblems. For guild-brothers, the right to carry arms was not just symbolic, for it came with the obligation to use them should the need arise. The right to bear arms both in and beyond the town was almost ubiquitous in ducal charters. In 1405, recognising the loyal service of the Lille archers on his joyous entry, John the Fearless granted the guild the right 'to travel and to bear their arms and armour, at all times as it pleases them, in assembly or alone … in and among our town and castellanies of Lille and land of Flanders'. The right was confirmed by Philip the Good in 1419 and again by Charles V in 1516.[71] In Aalst, meanwhile, Philip the Good granted the archers the right to 'freely carry their arms and armour, suitable bows, as is befitting for archers, throughout our land and County of Flanders' in 1431. In a nearly identical charter granted to the archers of Zuienkerke, a pike was added to the list of permissible arms in a ducal charter of 1456.[72] The weapons guild-brothers were carrying were not simply related to their service as archers. As Tlusty has shown of military groups in Germany, the arms they bore were both military pieces of kit and 'important symbols of power, status and individual sovereignty', perhaps even corporate honour.[73]

The significance of weapons as symbols of status was particularly powerful in towns that passed regular legislation against anyone else bearing arms. In Lille in 1382, for instance, the magistrates declared 'that no one, neither individuals nor groups, neither those of humble status nor grand, may henceforth engage in any shooting of the crossbow or the bow of the hand', except authorised guilds. In the same year ordinances were passed that no one could go out armed – except guild-brothers or nobles – and these ordinances were repeated in 1426.

---

[70] In 1464 Louis XI confirmed a charter of John the Fearless to the crossbowmen of Lille that if anyone should be killed by the crossbowmen shooting in their garden, they 'will have no impeachment or damages perpetually from those responsible for our justices'; ADN, B1601, f. 157; B1608, f. 277; AML, affaires generale, 5.

[71] *Ordonnances du Jean sans peur*, 24–5; AML, PT, 15879, f. 215; RM, 16973, 90; RM, 16977, 139.

[72] RAG, RVV, 7351, ff. 209–210, ff. 205v–206.

[73] Tlusty, *The Martial Ethic*, 10, 133–65.

In 1472, even harsher ordinances were passed, specifying 'that no one, not any person of any sort, whether bourgeois or resident' might 'carry with him day or night' any weapons, unless a noble or guild-brother, and offenders would be fined 60s.[74] Together, these ducal charters and civic ordinances made clear that the guilds were not just powerful but were trusted and prestigious, while others in their towns were not.

Dukes and towns allowed guilds to be armed and to wear livery where others were forbidden to carry weapons, marking them out as honourable and trustworthy. The guilds' position was enhanced further by immunity and by exemptions. In 1417 John the Fearless granted a charter to the Lille crossbowmen stating that 'if it should happen by mistake' that any 'companion' should 'injure, strike, hurt or kill ... any person of any condition estate or position', they would suffer no 'punishment or impeachment, neither in body nor in goods'. John's charter was far from unique: similar charters were granted across the fifteenth century, becoming an essential part of guild life. In 1505 Philip the Fair reconfirmed that the archers and crossbowmen of Enghien would not be pursued, punished or molested if they should 'by misadventure or misfortune' during their shooting 'hurt or kill' anyone. The charter was a confirmation of ancient rights, granted because the original had been lost in a fire.[75] In allowing the guilds immunity from prosecution for 'accidental' injuries, even deaths, the dukes showed again the trust placed in the guilds and their high moral standing.

The guilds' standing was emphasised and augmented still further by another important exemption. The town watch was vital for defence, but more than this, it was part of urban identity. We have seen that the walls and buildings represented on seals were part of civic representation, and those who patrolled the walls could be just as important. Indeed the watch was metonymic of civic security, vital not just to civic safety but to the *perception* of civic safety. Watching the walls was one of the most important way of defending the town and, in theory, everyone in a medieval town was responsible for watching the walls. Small has stated that 'the watch mobilised the population like no other civic organisation'.[76] The watch was a burden borne by almost all in a medieval town; often only small number of churchmen and nobles were exempt from serving. Like all townsmen, guilds were part of the civic watch. For instance, in 1398 the Dendermonde crossbowmen were required by Philip the Bold to 'make the guard for the defence of our said town by the order of the said bailey or others or by us and by the said law, so much by night as by day'. But, unlike other townsmen, they would be paid 2s a day for their service.[77]

---

[74] AML, OM, 373, f. 3v; 373, f. 15v; 376, f. 55v; AML, OM, 378, ff. 98v–99v.
[75] ADN, B1601, ff. 157–158v; Matthieu *Histoire de la ville d'Enghien* vol. 2, 766–7.
[76] G. D. Suttles, *The Social Construction of Communities* (Chicago, IL: University of Chicago Press, 1972), 21–43, 189–232; Tlusty, *The Martial Ethic*, 31–4; G. Small, *Late Medieval France* (Houndmills: Palgrave, 2009), 200–202.
[77] *Ordonnances de Philippe le Hardi*, vol. 2, 296–300.

As the guilds grew in significance, and as they obtained more rights and recognitions, their position within the civic organisation and the watch changed. In Bruges, from 1425, 'each guild-brother will be free and quit of the watch, on the conditions stipulated by the communal authority'.[78] By 1488 Maximilian and Philip the Fair were referring to the exhaustion of the crossbowmen of Douai. During the previous twenty years the guild-brothers 'had continually been constrained to keep watch and guard the gates, towers and walls of our said town', and were greatly depleted. As a result, the guild-brothers 'will be made free, quit, and exempt of all services', including watching the gates.[79] Guilds were required to watch and to serve in times of crisis, especially if an attack was likely, but otherwise were freed of the onerous responsibility that all townsmen were obliged to fulfil. Rather than contradicting the military defensive responsibilities discussed in chapter one, these exemptions make clear the value of the guilds as civic powers and the requirement for them to be ready as needed, and not to be exhausted by day-to-day service.

The dukes valued the guilds and assisted them in becoming powerful groups, both parties gaining honour as a result, yet financial assistance from the dukes is rather more complicated. Dukes rarely granted money directly to any urban groups; rather, they allowed towns to collect extra taxes to fund events like jousts or processions, or to sell rents in order to fund new building projects.[80] Similarly, the dukes did not give gifts of money to guilds; rather, they 'gave' them the right to raise their own money, from their own town, through lotteries. Lotteries are not unknown in the fifteenth century Low Countries. The town accounts of Bruges first refer to lotteries being held in 1411 and they became a semi-permanent source of municipal funds in the following years; twenty-seven were held between 1450 and 1474. Elsewhere, a few wealthy individuals organised lotteries (one of the earliest was the Antwerp merchant Thiemann Claussone in 1446), and lotteries developed into an efficient way of raising extra income.[81]

The crossbowmen of Bruges held lotteries at least twice, in 1457 and 1486, although why they needed the extra funding is not recorded. Later, other guilds followed their example, with the crossbowmen of Ypres organising a lottery in 1509 and those of Mechelen in 1520.[82] References to lotteries are not uncommon, but only in Ghent are the details of their organisation and an explanation of the needs for funds set out. In 1469 Charles the Bold allowed the great guild

---

[78] BASS, charter 3.
[79] DAM EE18; Arbalestiers de Douay, 24II232, ff. 6v–7.
[80] Clauzel, *Finance et Politiques de Lille*, 153–60.
[81] Gilliodts-Van Severen, *Inventaire des archives de la ville de Bruges*, vol. 5, 212–19; vol. 6, 465; A. K. L. Thijs, 'Les loteries dans les Pays-Bas méridionaux (15e–17e siècle)', in I. Eggers, L. de Mecheleer and M. Wynants (eds), *Geschiedenis van de loterijen in de Zuidelijke Nederlanden (15de eeuw–1934)* (Brussels: Algemeen rijksarchief, 1994), 7–11.
[82] SAB, 385, Sint Joris, Rekeningen, 1445–1480, f. 118; 1481–1507, f. 20v; Thijs, 'Les loteries dans le Pays-Bas', 10–12.

of crossbowmen to hold a lottery to fund its hospital, maintain its chapel and expand its guild hall, and it held a lottery twice a year, for two years. Almost five decades later, in 1517, the guild-brothers were again spending beyond their means. They had begun to build a *'belle et magnifique galerye'* and, as a result, they were 'greatly in need'. They told Charles V that it was impossible for them 'to pay for or even to undertake the said works which they have started in their court'. Charles granted them permission to hold a lottery, with 'many fair prizes of money and further of pots, glasses, goblets and other similar pieces of finery', to be held for six years, the first being in 1517.[83] Lotteries could imply that guilds were impoverished, perhaps because few members were paying fees, but that they were nonetheless granted this privilege reveals once again that they inspired trust for the duke and the urban community that supported them.

Guilds were supported and rewarded by dukes, but they were not all-powerful groups – they were ducal servants and, as such, were required to obey and to show loyalty. Several charters, such as that of Philip the Bold to Douai, emphasise that the guild-brothers 'cannot go to serve outside the town without the consent and authority of the aldermen' or the duke.[84] A 1382 charter to the crossbowmen of Douai commanded them to 'be ready to go, for reasonable wages', to serve town and duke. John the Fearless required the crossbowmen of Wauvrin to be 'always ready to serve us or our successors, Counts and Countesses of Flanders', in a charter of 1412. In 1441 the archers of Houthem were required by Philip the Good to be 'ready to serve well and ably' whenever he called upon them. Even as late as 1518, when issuing a new charter to the archers of Annappes, Charles V wished them to 'aggrandise the guard and defence of our lands' so that the archers could be relied upon 'for summoning in our wars and armies when they will be needed'.[85] The numerous rights that were conferred on the guilds elevated their status and marked them out as important figures within their towns were granted in return for service, and guilds were expected to be ready and able to serve whenever called on to do so.

Above all, the guilds had to show their *colères ferrez* (iron collars). Philip the Good wished to make the guilds' allegiance to himself and his successors visible to all through the use of emblems. Guilds were not the only recipients of ducal emblems: under Philip the Good numerous civic buildings were stamped with his insignia of a flint or fusil, as well as the Burgundian cross of Saint Andrew.[86] Philip's policy of having his supporters wear his symbols may have been influenced by

---

[83] SAG, SJ, NGR, charter 25; SAG, SJ, NGR, charter 51.
[84] DAM, AA94, ff. 70v–71v; RijksArchief Kortrijk, Oude stadsarchief Kortrijk, 5800. Sint Jorisgilde; Godar, *Histoire des archers*, 163–71.
[85] DAM, AA94, ff. 70v–81; AML, RM, 16973, f. 47; RAG, RVV, 7351, ff. 202–3; AML, RM, 16978, 7.
[86] The on-going work of J. Braekvelt will shed more light on this practice; the present work has benefited from the examples in his 2012 paper, delivered at the International Medieval Congress in Leeds.

his father's actions during the French civil war, when he distributed badges and symbols, including the Saint Andrew's cross, to partisans.[87] Among nobles, the distribution of emblems, badges, even collars, was well understood as a sign of support and status. Distribution of emblems to the guilds and allowing them to wear these in and beyond their urban environments should be understood in the same way. Clothes carried layers of meaning and can be considered 'a potent means of communication', even as 'systems of signs that derive meaning from context'.[88] Certainly the guilds of archers and crossbowmen used their liveries to communicate not just status but also the honour they derived from their loyalty to the dukes of Burgundy.

The first surviving charter to refer to ducal insignia comes from 1446. In March of that year the archers of Biervelt were granted permission to wear on 'their robes our sign of the fusil and of two arrows in a cross of my lord Saint Andrew'.[89] Three months later, the archers of Nieuwpoort were permitted to 'wear on their robe, hood or cloak, our device and fusil of the two arrows in the form of the cross of Saint Andrew'. By July the archers of Ypres were permitted to wear 'for the finery of the said guild our device of the fusil, and the two arrows, amongst them in the form of the cross of Saint Andrew'. The next year guilds in Sint-Winnoksbergen, Cassel and Tielt received nearly identical charters, and by the end of Philip's reign Menin, Cockelare, Douai, Dadizeele and Zuienkerke had also received this 'right', or perhaps obligation.[90] Many of the towns in which guilds received the right to wear ducal emblems were in coastal or eastern Flanders, again reflecting defensive concerns: loyalty and ducal influence needed to be more visible in areas that could be contested.

Philip was the first, and the most active, of the dukes who granted this right, but his successors continued his practice. In 1508 the archers of Béthune were 'advised' to wear the cross of Saint Andrew, and in 1518 Charles V granted the same privilege to the archers of Annappes. Late sixteenth-century militias preserved the 'Burgundian flag' on their uniforms, demonstrating not just

---

[87] E. J. Hutchison, 'Partisan Identity in the French Civil War, 1405–1418: Reconsidering the Evidence on Livery Badges', JMH 33 (2007), 250–74.

[88] M. Pastoureau, 'Emblèmes et symbole de la Toison d'Or', in C. Van den Bergen-Pantens (ed.), L'Ordre de la Toison d'Or, de Philippe le Bon à Philippe le Beau (1430–1505). Idéal ou reflet d'une société?, (Turnhout: Brepols 1996), 99–106; C. Shenton, 'Edward III and the Symbol of the Leopard', in P. Cross and M. Keen (eds), Heraldry, Pageantry, and Social Display in medieval England (Woodbridge: Boydell Press, 2002), 69–81; M.-T. Caron, 'La noblesse en représentation dans les années 1430; vêtements de cour, vêtements de joute, livrées', PCEEB 37 (1997), 157–72.

[89] RAG, RVV, 7351, f. 239.

[90] RAG, RVV 7351, ff. 217–217v; f. 199v; ff. 220–221; Archives Municipales de Cassel, AA1, ff. 117–118; RAG, RVV, 7351, ff. 222v–223, original in Stadsarchief Tielt, Oud Archief, n 846; ADN, B17696; RAG, RVV, 7351, ff. 226v–227; AGR, chartes de l'audience, 21; RAG, RVV, 7351, ff. 230v–231; ff. 205v–206.

regional identity but the durability of this symbol.[91] Guilds' liveries were part of their identity; through colours and luxury they communicated to all observers that the guilds were special, privileged groups. In incorporating ducal emblems on their livery they demonstrated that they represented not just their urban communities but their duke's quasi-princely power.

Princes and Guild Communities

Not all of the interaction between guilds and their lords was in written form. The rulers of Flanders formed bonds with their towns and reinforced their rule by shooting with the guilds, being members and attending social events. As with military service, such networks were not new with the beginnings of Burgundian influence in 1369 or Philip the Bold's accession in 1384. The last of the Dampierre counts, Robert (d. 1322), Louis of Nevers (d. 1346) and Louis of Males (d. 1384), had interacted with the guilds, using them to strengthen relations with their towns. The efforts of the Valois dukes to build communal ties with urban groups are better documented, but it is clear that they drew on traditions established by the Dampierre counts. Nor did such communities end in 1477. Maximilian and, to a lesser extent, Philip the Fair used the guilds as a way to integrate themselves into urban society.

From an early stage, these links were strategically important and, like the guilds themselves, they are likely to be older than any written record of them. Upon his accession, Count Robert had the task of rebuilding the community that had been shattered in the wars of his father's reign. The year 1302 is perhaps the most famous date in Flemish history, with the heroic victory of the urban militia over the 'flower of French chivalry' at the battle of the Golden Spurs, which was seen not just as a nationalistic victory but as the beginning of an 'infantry revolution'.[92] The battle was a dramatic victory, and helped the craft guilds to enter civic governance, but success did not last. With the signing of the treaty of Athis-sur-Orges, Flanders was a much weakened county. Robert spent much of his reign in Flanders, but the towns did not always support his efforts to resist France, which makes his attempts to interact with military groups all the more significant.[93]

Robert needed military support from his towns but, just as importantly, his authority was strengthened by civic acceptance of his rule. Civic connections

---

[91] Espinas, *Les Origines*, vol. 2, 251–4; AML, RM, 16978, 7; A. Duke, 'The Elusive Netherlands; The Question of National Identify in the Early Modern Low Countries of the Eve of the Revolt', *BMBGN* 119 (2004), 14.

[92] C. Oman, *A History of the Art of War in the Middle Ages* (London: Methuen, 1921, first published 1898), 113–21; Verbruggen, *De krijgskunst*, 196–7; C. J. Rogers, *The Military Revolution Debate: Readings on the Military Transformation of Early Modern Europe* (Boulder, CO: Westview Press, 1995).

[93] T. Luykx, 'Robrecht van Béthune en zijn tijd', in *Iepers kwartier: Driemaandelijks tijdschrift voor heemkunde*, 9:2–3 (1973) 116–29; Nicholas, *Medieval Flanders*, 209–58.

were therefore important for Robert in allowing him to portray himself as part of the urban communities. Unfortunately, few civic records that would show such interaction survive for the early fourteenth century, but Robert belonged to at least one crossbow guild, that of Oudenaarde. His date of entrance is unknown, but his name is the first on the guild's death-list, hinting at least that in the generation after Courtrai the ruler of Flanders tried to link civic power to his rule.[94]

Robert's grandson and successor, Louis of Nevers, was a rather different figure. Loyal to the French crown, he spent most of his life in France, and indeed, he died in the French host at Crécy.[95] His reign saw the rebellion of maritime Flanders between 1323 and 1328, with the county turning against its count. The rebels even briefly imprisoned Louis, driving him closer to his sovereign and protector. With French assistance, Louis was able to reclaim his county at the battle of Cassel in 1328. Another rebellion, led by Jacob van Artevelde, began in Ghent in 1337.[96] Louis may have tried to build bonds with the Ghentaars, and de Potter believed that he shot with the Ghent crossbow guild in a competition in Halle in 1331, although I can find no archival proof for such a claim.[97] In the first years of his reign Louis did try to involve himself in urban culture and with the towns, and in building links between Flemish and French towns, as he took part in the procession of Tournai with a Ghent delegation.[98] The violence of Louis's reign, and the antagonisms between ruler and ruled, meant that he did not interact with his county as his grandfather had, and he took little interest in archery or crossbow guilds, or indeed the civic cultures of Flanders.

Louis of Male, who succeeded his father as count in 1346, worked hard to keep the peace with both France and England and to win support from his towns. Louis spent more time in Flanders than his father had done, although at the end of his reign the county, especially Ghent, rebelled once again. Louis worked to build bonds with his towns, recognising that he needed Flemish

---

[94] OSAOA, gilden, 507/II/6A.
[95] Nicholas, *Metamorphosis*, 2–10; M. Vandermaesen, 'Kortrijk in vuur en bloed. De gevangenneming van graaf Lodewijk II van Nevers omstreeks 17 juni 1325', *De Leiegouw* 32 (1990) 149–58; idem, 'Toverij en politiek rond de troon van Lodewijk II van Nevers graaf van Vlaanderen. Eden merkwaardige aanklacht (1327–1331)', *HMGOG* 44 (1990), 87–98.
[96] Boone, *A La Recherche d'une modernité civique*, 70–71; L. Crombie, 'The Low Countries'.
[97] De Potter, *Jaarboeken*, 19, states Louis was present; town accounts refer only to the crossbowmen attending '*feesten*', in Halle, SAG, 400, 1330-1, f. 16. It is, of course, possible that a source existed in the 1860s that has since been lost; Potter's only footnote is the town accounts, but he did not always provide references for his information.
[98] M. Boone, 'Les Gantoise et la grande procession de Tournai; aspects d'une sociabilité urbaine au bas moyen âge', in J. Dumoulin and J. Pycke (eds), *La Grande Procession de Tournai (1090–1992), Une Réalité religieuse, urbaine, diocésaine, sociale, économique et artistique* (Tournai: Fabrique de l'Église Cathédrale de Tournai, 1992), 52.

support rather than French or English, and he made the shooting guilds part of those efforts. He was a member of the Ghent guild of Saint George, shooting with it at least once, as well as granting charters, in Flemish, to the guilds.[99] Louis of Male needed to be strong in his own county. We have seen how the guilds and towns supported his military campaign of 1356, so it is no surprise that he strove to build cultural and social bonds with the towns as represented by the guilds.

The dukes of Burgundy, like their fourteenth-century predecessors, interacted with the towns of Flanders. Although they spent varying amounts of time in the Low Countries, the wealth of the Flemish towns ensured that the dukes could never ignore civic demands and the need to maintain civic support. They built urban courts and held the greatest events of their reigns in Flemish towns. Interaction with urban groups allowed the dukes to use splendour, space and symbols to communicate not just their power over the civic world, but their part in it – indeed Van Bruaene has called their attempts to integrate themselves with urban political and cultural networks 'exceptional'.[100] Even before he became count of Flanders in 1384, Philip the Bold interacted socially with the shooting guilds, seeing them as a way for him to ingratiate himself with his new subjects. He shot with the Ghent crossbowmen in 1371 and those of Bruges in 1375, and in the same year he was given a livery by the guild of Ypres. Philip, like every later duke, was a member of the Ghent greater guild of Saint George.[101] The dukes understood the power of building bridges between themselves and the powerful Flemish towns, and used the guilds' devotion to civic values to build strong court–civic connections.

Philip's chief focus was Paris, not Flanders, as he strove to control his nephew, the often mad Charles VI. Philip's successor, John the Fearless, began his reign

---

[99] De Potter, *Jaarboeken*, 23–4; STAM, Sint Sebastiaangilde; privilegieboek, inv. 1059, ff. 1v–3; for the importance of language, with Louis's charters almost all in Flemish, see le Comte T. De Limburg-Stirum, *Cartulaire de Louis de Male, comte de Flandre / Decreten van den grave Lodewyck van Vlaenderen 1348 à 1358*, 2 vols (Bruges: De Plancke, 1898–1901., introduction to vol. 1.

[100] A. L. Van Bruaene, 'A Wonderfull tryumfe, for the wynnyng of a pryse', *Renaissance Quarterly* 49 (2006), 386–7; Brown and Small, *Court and Civic Society*, 36–85, 165–209; R. Van Uytven 'Splendour or Wealth? Art and Economy in the Burgundian Netherlands', in his *Production and Consumption in the Low Countries, 13th–16th Centuries* (Aldershot: Ashgate 2001); J. Landwehr, *Splendid Ceremonies; State Entries and Royal Funerals in the Low Countries, a Bibliography* (Nieuwkoop: De Graaf, 1971); M. Boone, 'Langue, pouvoirs et dialogue. Aspects linguistiques de la communication entre les ducs de Bourgogne et leurs sujets flamands (1385–1505)', *RN* 91 (2009), 9–33.

[101] Boone, 'Réseaux urbaine', in W. Prevenier (ed.), *Le Prince et le peuple, image a la société du temps des ducs de Bourgogne, 1384 – 1530*, ed. W. Prevenier (Anvers: Fonds Mercator, 1998), 247; M. de Schrijver and C. Dothee, *Les Concours de tir à l'arbalète des gildes médiévales* (Anvers: Antwerps Museum en Archief Den Crans, 1979), apendix and lists; Vaughan, *Philip the Bold*, 19; Arnade, *Realms of Ritual*, 71; Moulin-Coppens, *Sint Jorisgilde te Gent*, 34–9.

with much the same priorities.[102] John spent much of the early part of his reign in Paris, attempting to maintain influence over the king, and it is tempting to see his hand in many of the royal ordinances granted to French shooting guilds in the early fifteenth century.[103] He returned to Flanders only in moments of crisis in France. When in Flanders, he recognised the importance of urban support and, like Robert of Bethune, he chose Oudenaarde as the setting in which to involve himself with urban culture. In 1408, just a few months after John had been forced to flee from Paris, a great shoot was held in Oudenaarde. Not only did John allow the event to take place, but he attended the competition and shot in person, as recorded in both the chronicle of the abbey of Eename and an anonymous civic chronicle. The monastic chronicles describe entrances made into the town and

> 'Then the dean of the Saint George guild, and the guild wardens, and the twelve shooters who would shoot in the name of the town, who were all similarly dressed, and all the *poorters* and all the other people of the town, those that were rich, they all had great cloaks of green and white. Then Count John of Flanders, Duke of Burgundy, and my lady the Duchess his wife, were with the shooters. Then Count John shot with the town of Oudenaarde and with him many other noble men ... Then Count John himself carried his own bow up to his turn to' shoot the targets.[104]

The civic writer recounts the same scene but adds the details that

> The Count of Flanders John Duke of Burgundy and my lady his wife were clothed like the shooters and Count John shot with the town of Oudenaarde, like a man of the guild of Saint George of Oudenaarde, and Count John like the rest carried his own bow and won the first prize of 2 silver jugs.[105]

In 1408 John was not acting as a distant lord granting privileges, nor as an inactive member simply enrolled in the membership list. He shot with the guild, dressed like a guild-brother, part of the guild urban community, festively promoting civic values and strengthening urban–aristocratic communities. It is striking that both chronicles refer to 'Count John' not 'Duke John', making it clear

---

[102] Philip's immediate successor in Flanders would have been his wife, Margaret of Male, who was countess in her own right from the death of her husband in April 1404 until her own death in March 1405. These eleven months of female rule are sadly understudied, but Margaret issued no charters to the guilds and so cannot be analysed here.

[103] Lecuppre-Desjardin, *La Ville des Cérémonies*, 31–2; Vaughan, *John the Fearless*, 67–102; ORF, vol. 9, to Parisian crossbowmen, August 1410, 522–6; to Rouen Crossbowmen, April, 1411, 595–8.

[104] Cauwenberghe, 'Notice historique sur les confréries de Saint Georges', 281–3.

[105] OSAOA, gilden 241/2, ff. 89–92v; Cauwenberghe, 'Notice historique sur les confréries de Saint Georges', 279–291; UBG, Hs434, Vredesverdragen, ff. 92–100.

that, although he held a great many other titles, when he shot in Oudenaarde, in interaction with the urban community, he was acting as count of Flanders.

Philip the Good, as we have seen, was a member of the Bruges crossbow guild, entering it shortly after 1437 and attending a feast in 1454.[106] He was also a member of the Ghent crossbow guild and interacted with guilds beyond Flanders. In November 1435, less than two months after signing the treaty of Arras, which gave him control of the Somme towns, Philip the Good and his wife attended the feast of the Amiens crossbow guild.[107] He seems to have been using the Amiens guilds as he and his ancestors' had used the Flemish ones, to integrate himself into civic culture and to depict himself as part of the urban world rather than as just a conqueror. His charters to the guilds allowed him to appear as an ideal prince, and in competitions he, like his father, could portray himself as part of the urban world.

Philip took part in urban events, yet he did not quite follow his father's example in shooting as a guild-brother. Rather, in taking part in a Ghent competition in 1440, he brought a special ducal team to the spectacular civic competition. Philip's team included his cousin, Charles, count of Nevers, and Jehan Villiers, lord of l'Isle-Adam, whose father had been killed in the Bruges rebellion of 1436–37.[108] Despite the power of such men, and of Philip himself, the ducal team is poorly documented in Ghent sources – unlike the Oudenaarde sources, which emphasised John's participation. The *Bouc van Pieter Polet*, an important account of the Ghent shoot drawn up by 1506 by a crossbowman and civic official, gives no more space or emphasis to the ducal team than to any other civic team.[109] Such a lack of attention strongly suggests that the Flemish observers were focused on the shoot and saw Philip the Good as part of the community rather than as the centre of attention, as John had been. Philip's participation in the Ghent competition demonstrates that just four years after his failed siege of Calais – discussed in chapter one – he did not see the towns as enemies; rather, he cultivated social relations with civic society, in particular with the powerful crossbowmen, in order to restore peace to Flanders and to ensure that he had urban support. Philip's entrance into Bruges a few months later expressed the same ideals of peace and harmony, of rebuilding communities and building bridges between court and city. By the middle of the fifteenth century

---

[106] SAB, 385 Sint Joris.
[107] Arnade, *Realms of Ritual*, 71; G. Durand, *Ville d'Amiens, Inventaire sommaire des archives communales antérieures à 1790*, 7 vols (Amiens: Imprimerie Typographique et Lithographique Piteux Freres, 1891–1925), vol. 2, 64–5.
[108] The list of names in UBG, Hs 6112, *Dit es den bouc van ... Pieter Polet*, f. 34v; for the shoot, Arnade, *Realms of Ritual*, 91–4; for the death of Jehan Villiers, Vaughan, *Philip the Good*, 87–94; for Philip's cousin, Charles Count of Nevers, W. Paravicini, *Die Hofordnungen der Herzöge von Burgund. Band 1: Herzog Philipp der Gute 1407–1467* (Ostfildern: Thorbecke, 2005), 131, 151.
[109] UBG, Hs G 6112, *Dit es den bouc van ... Pieter Polet*, f. 34v; Arnade, *Realms of Ritual*, 84–93; SAG, SJ, NGR, Charters en diverse losse documenten, 30.

the relationship between duke and towns was constantly being performed and reaffirmed in spectacles, and the shooting guilds were an important part of these performances.[110]

Charles the Bold's relationship with the Flemish towns was rather less harmonious. Arnade's description of his joyous entry in 1467 calls it a fall from 'unity into discord'.[111] Charles did not interact with guilds as count of Flanders, although he did take part in events in Bruges and Mechelen as count of Charolaise. As we have seen, he issued charters and made donations to the hospital and altar of Saint George in Ghent alongside Margaret of York in 1473. In Brabant he founded the archery guild of Linkebeek and perhaps a chapel to Saint Sebastian in 1469. Members of the new archery guild included two of his illegitimate brothers and other courtiers; indeed, so many noble members in such a small place implies that this was a ducal guild rather than an urban one.[112] Charles was also, of course, preoccupied with wars far from Flanders, spending little time in the North. Although the great events of his reign were held in an urban setting he did not feel that he needed the towns as his predecessors had done, and did not try to use the guilds to build communities. However, he did not ignore the guilds. He confirmed Lille's wine privileges in 1476, required the guilds to declare numbers in 1469 for his wars and rewarded Mechelen for its participation at the siege of Neus.[113] Charles understood the value of guilds, but he was not part of their world as his father and grandfather had been, and he did not build urban networks.

Although he was not a legitimate member of the family, Anthony the Great Bastard of Burgundy was an important figure in his own right and a popular representative of his father and half-brother. Anthony's role in urban societies is significant; indeed, the popularity of his half-brother may have given Charles the Bold the confidence to remove himself from relationship with the guilds. After the death of his brother Corneil, Anthony was Philip the Good's eldest son, jousting with Anthony Woodville (brother of Elizabeth Woodville, wife of Edward IV) at Smithfield in a long-awaited event in 1467 and representing his dynasty on an international stage.[114] Anthony was an active member of the archery and crossbow guilds of Bruges, attending dinners and winning *papegay* shoots. He also interacted with the Ghent crossbowmen as he did in Bruges. He feasted

---

[110] Lecuppre-Desjardin, *La Ville des Cérémonies*, 284–7.
[111] Arnade, *Realms of Ritual*, 127.
[112] Schrijver and Dothee, *Les Concours de tir*, appendix; Godar, *Histoire des archers*, 110–25; SAG, SJ, NGR, 25; Stein, *Archers d'autrefois*, 17–19; C. Theys and J. Geysels, *Geschiedenis van Linkebeek* (Linkebeek: Drukkerij A. Hessens, 1957), 73–90; A. Wauters, *Histoire des environs de Bruxelles*, vol. 10 (Bruxelles: C. Vanderauwera, 1855), 348–9.
[113] ADN, B17724.
[114] C. Van Den Bergen-Pantens, 'Antoine, Grand Bâtard de Bourgogne, bibliophile', in her *L'Ordre de la Toison d'Or, de Philippe le Bon à Philippe le Beau (1430–1505). Idéal ou reflet d'une société?* (Turnhout: Brepols, 1996), 198–200; J. Clement, 'Antoine de Bourgogne, dit le Grand Bâtard', *PCEEB* 30 (1990), 165–82.

with both guilds and even became a guild-king of the crossbowmen of Ghent and archers of Lille. Anthony took part in events in small towns too, becoming king of the Ninove archery guild in 1457. Like his father and grandfather, he also took part in crossbow competitions, leading the Lille crossbowmen to the 1455 Tournai competition.[115]

His participation with Lille at Tournai, in a French competition designed to celebrate the victory of the French king in driving the English out of France, is noteworthy. It is likely that his participation was a way for the ducal family to use the prestige of the Flemish guilds to demonstrate to Tournai the honour of Burgundy and the power of Flanders. Had a legitimate member of the ducal family taken part in the Tournai shoot, it might have disrupted the delicate balance between Tournai and the dukes. As a bastard, and a hugely popular figure, Anthony was able to represent his dynasty and the county of Flanders in urban–aristocratic communities. Further, Anthony received wine from Lille for attending its crossbow competition in 1457, implying that his participation at Tournai had a lasting significance for Lille. His interaction with guilds and other urban groups enhanced both his own popularity and that of his dynasty across Flanders, even advertising the honour of his family beyond the Burgundian Low Countries.[116]

The strength of community between prince and guilds did not end with the Valois dukes. In common with previous duchesses, no personal interaction can be traced between Mary and the guilds, yet Mary's husband and son continued the tradition of festive communication. Following Charles the Bold's violent death in January 1477, his lands passed to Mary, his only child. The period of instability that followed saw towns demanding lost liberties and Mary being forced to sign the Great Privilege. Her marriage to Maximilian Habsburg brought in German armies and German money to stop the French assault, but it also brought in conflicts and tensions. On Mary's death in 1482, her lands passed to her young son, Philip the Fair. Flanders was willing to recognise the young count, but not the regency of his deeply unpopular father. Such tensions made building bonds between the court and the towns, as represented by the guilds, an important concern for the new rulers. Maximilian had shot in urban

---

[115] S. Kemperdick, *Rogier van Weyden* (Cologne: Konemann Verlagsgesellschaft, 1999), 102–5, argues that the famous van Weyden picture of Anthony holding an arrow is based on his position as king of the Ghent shooters; de Cock, *Geschiedenis van het Koninklijk Handbooggild*, 5–12.

[116] Brown and Small, *Court and Civic Society*, 219–25; G. Small, 'Centre and Periphery in Late Medieval France: Tournai, 1384–1477', in C. Allmand (ed.), *War, Government and Power in Late Medieval France* (Liverpool: Liverpool University Press, 2000); AML, CV, 16198, f. 44v; for his popularity with other urban groups see H. Cools, 'Antoon: "de Grote Bastaard", van Bourgondië', *Het Land van Beveren* (2007), 205–55; ibid., 'In het spoor van 'de grote bastaard', 42–55.

crossbow competitions in Germany before he came to the Low Countries, and he remained active with German guilds in the early sixteenth century.[117]

In Flanders Maximilian followed the Burgundian tradition of shooting with the guilds. Like Philip the Bold a century earlier, he tried to use the shooting guilds to win over urban support and show himself to be part of the urban world, not simply a foreign ruler on its peripheries. Maximilian was a member of the Ghent crossbow guild and became 'king' of the Bruges archers in 1479.[118] The crossbowmen of Aalst received extra money and wine from their town in 1485 when Maximilian, King of the Romans, shortly to become Holy Roman Emperor, 'with many other lords and good men' ate with them.[119] Maximilian was not entirely successful in his efforts to win Flemish support, but that he understood the potential of the guilds to bring him into urban–aristocratic communities, and his efforts to win the guilds over, reveals their status and the high regard they enjoyed at court. Indeed Maximilian's efforts to use guilds to build up civic support may be the reason why his campaigns in 1477–79, as discussed in chapter one, attracted such civic support.

So important were the guilds for court and civic cooperation that the infant Philip the Fair was brought into the urban–aristocratic network of guilds. In 1481, represented by Guilliame Estu, the three-year-old became king of the Brussels crossbowmen.[120] As an adult, Philip would continue the tradition of ducal participation in guild competitions, taking part as a guild-brother in another Ghent shoot in 1498.[121] He made his entrance with the guild of Bruges, and shot with the Ypres guild, making as many bonds as possible. The competition was described in great detail in the *Excellent Chronicle of Flanders*, printed by Voosterman in Antwerp in 1531. The competition, and a poem describing the entrances, is given far more attention than other urban events and included a woodcut that is not used elsewhere in the chronicle. The image probably shows Philip the Fair shooting, with the Habsburg eagle and lion of Flanders prominently displayed between the Belfry and Sint Jan's church. In the chronicle other woodcuts are used repeatedly, with battle scenes and royal figures used dozens of time, as woodcuts were expensive to produce. That a woodcut seems to have been made for this one event, combined with the unusually long account that includes a poem describing the event, demonstrates the significance of the event and the way it was remembered a generation later.[122]

---

[117] F. Unterkircher, *Maximilian I, 1459–1519* (Wien: sterreichische Nationalbibliothek, 1959), appendix; Tlusty, *The Martial Ethic*, 202.
[118] Godar, *Histoire des archers*, 122.
[119] AGR, CC, 31479, f. 47.
[120] Wauters, *Notice historique*, 9.
[121] SAG, SJ, 155, nummer 2; P.Van Duyse, 'Het groot schietspel en de Rederijkersspelen te Gent in Mei tot Juli 1498', *Annales de la Société Royale des Beaux-arts et de Littérature de Gand* 6 (1865), 273–314; F. De Potter, 'Landjuweel van 1497', *Het Belfort* (Gent, no date).
[122] *Dits die excellente cronike van Vlaanderen*, f. 286; for the attribution of Philip see Arnade, *Realms of Ritual*, 183.

Princely participation in shooting events should not be seen as unusual; rather, it was part of the wider relationship between prince and town. As Dumolyn has shown in analysing civic letters, for the urban ruling classes in Flanders 'a crucial piece of their city's worth lay in good relations with the princes of the land'. Towns and dukes were bound up in a mutually dependent relationship: towns needed dukes and the dukes needed their towns, as, for all their royal aspirations, they were not absolute rulers of Flanders. Just as ducal entrances and their expressions of symbolic communication helped to link the duke and his citizens, so too did personal interaction with shooting guilds.[123] The personal nature of connections formed in shooting and in feasting may have made for stronger bonds between the dukes and the towns. Philip's participation in the 1498 Ghent competition is particularly important, as was the competition itself, and shows that the duke and the towns were working together for honour and for harmony at the end of the fifteenth century.

Archery and crossbow guilds became prestigious and powerful urban groups through civic maintenance, through noble membership and, most importantly, through ducal support. Across Flanders, urban authorities gave the guilds durable support, showing that towns felt their guilds to be important and that they valued them above other social or cultural groups. The repetition of honour throughout these charters, and the central place of the guild in civic celebrations, makes clear that the guilds were crucial to civic self-representation. The flowering of this self-representation in the form of regional competitions and civic communities will be the focus of the final two chapters of this book. In interacting socially with the guilds, as well as in helping them to obtain rights and charters, lords could form bonds with the urban communities. In using their influence at court to obtain charters, lords could place themselves at the head of guilds and, by extension, at the head of smaller urban communities. Such urban–aristocratic connections helped lords, particularly Adolf of Cleves, Lodewijk van Gruuthuse and Jan van Dadizeele, to govern in periods of crisis. Ultimate power for rights over the guilds, as with so much else in the Low Countries, lay with the dukes of Burgundy, who privileged the guilds, interacted with them and stamped their authority on the guilds through liveries in order to emphasise their part within civic community and to make the honour of the guilds clear to all observers. Archery and crossbow guilds became a central part of ducal–civic interactions, allowing the dukes to represent themselves as perfect princes and as integral parts of civic communities.

---

[123] Dumolyn, 'Urban Ideology in Later Medieval Flanders', 82–4; J. Gilissen, 'Les villes en Belgique, histoire des institutions, administration et judicaires des villes belges', *Recueil de la société Jean Bodin* 6 (1954), 547–601; Lecuppre-Desjardin, *La Ville des Cérémonies*, 284–92.

5

'For friendship, community and brotherhood'

Archery and Crossbow Competitions as Part of Civic Honour and Identity

Shooting guilds were military groups, were diverse social and devotional communities and maintained important links to their lords. All of these elements of guild identity, with their ideals of peace and the centrality of civic honour, are best illustrated by an analysis of the spectacular competitions that guilds staged across the fourteenth and fifteenth centuries.

By 1498, when an elaborate event was held in Ghent, the competitions had become some of the largest and most impressive urban spectacles put on in Flemish towns. Competitions could last for months, as compared to the day or two given to princely entrances or to jousts, their size possible only with civic and ducal support. The events grew quickly from simple shooting contests, beginning before 1330, to become huge events that involved hundreds of competitors, thousands of followers, musicians, play wagons, silver forests, a wooden dragon and even an elephant.

The competitions, like jousts and entrance ceremonies, were not simply about pomp and show; rather, they carried layers of meaning and communicated urban honour and the guilds' values. In the civic support they received and in their symbolic communication they are fascinating examples of urban identity – the same 'urban panegyric' analysed by Lecuppre-Desjardin in her study of processions.[1] This chapter will first look at the origins of archery and crossbow competitions and provide an overview of what the competitions consisted of and how they were funded and organised. Following this, it will consider the role of honour and friendship in competitions. As noted, guild ordinances emphasised honour and community, and these same priorities become clear in a close analysis of some of the letters of invitation sent out by guilds in advance of their great events. The mechanics of civic representation and the forms that guild spectacle could take will be analysed with reference to the entrances made into Ghent in 1498, drawing on the ideals of civic honour expressed in the last chapter as well as the forces for community set out in chapter three. The centrality of community

---

[1] Lecuppre-Desjardin, *La Ville des Cérémonies*, 1–12, 184–9.

also becomes apparent through a discussion of the prizes given at shooting competitions, and the prominence of drink and drinking vessels confirms what has already been observed about the power of commensality to build bonds of brotherhood. The next chapter will build on this to look at the regional communities that were enhanced by shooting guilds and their competitions, and the ability of guilds to act as forces for peace and stability.

Development of Archery and Crossbow Competitions

The earliest competition for which found archival evidence can be found was held in Oudenaarde in 1328. No description of the event survives, but both Lille and Ghent gave their crossbow guilds civic funds to attend.[2] However, it is unlikely that the Oudenaarde competition was the first to be staged; indeed, other scholars have provided earlier dates for the 'first' shooting competition. The nineteenth-century Ghent historian Frans de Potter referred to two earlier crossbow competitions, at Ypres in 1323 and Ardenbourg in 1326; other writers believed that a competition in Bapaume in 1326 was the first. More broadly, Breiding is likely to be correct in stating that 'informal gatherings [of shooters] had taken place since the early Middle Ages', but no firm arguments can be made for events for which no written records survive.[3]

Archery and crossbow competitions, like the guilds themselves, probably have older and more informal origins than the oldest surviving written reference to these events. Shooting competitions began to be recorded, and began to receive civic funding, in the third decade of the fourteenth century. As we have seen, it was in the 1330s and 1340s that town accounts became more detailed and better recorded, meaning that events like shooting competitions are more likely to have received civic funds and are more likely to have been recorded. Like the guilds themselves, no exact 'foundation' or 'inception' date can be provided for archery and crossbow competitions. However, it is, important to understand that shooting competitions are first recorded in the same generation as the guilds themselves are first recorded. Guilds and competitions appeared at the same moment of civic confidence and development of civic identity in early fourteenth-century Flanders.

The earliest competitions for which records survive were held in Flanders, but events were also staged elsewhere. In the following discussion, examples from Hainaut and France will be brought in for comparison, as the competitions

---

[2] AML, CV, 16018, f. 29v; Vuylsteke, *Gentsche stads en balijuwsrekeningen, 1280–1336*, vol. 2, 664.

[3] D. H. Breiding, *A Deadly Art; European Crossbows, 1250–1850* (New York: The Metropolitan Museum of Art, 2012), 12–13; De Potter's *Jaarboeken*, 10–16; Arnade, *Realms of Ritual*, 80; Schrijver and Dothee, *Les Concours de tir*, 2; Cauwenberghe, 'Notice historique sur les confréries de Saint Georges', 273; Boone, 'De Sint-Josrigilde van kruisboogschutters', 28–31.

across the Low Countries were remarkably cohesive and shared the same sorts of values and ideas and, indeed, networks extended far beyond Flanders. Competitions held in L'Île de France and in Normandy are less well documented, but certainly merit further study; in particular it would be interesting to analyse the changing nature of loyalty and urban pride in Valois and Lancastrian Normandy.[4] Competitions in Germany had much in common with those in Flanders, but had a somewhat less honourable tone to them. In Augsburg in 1470 a crossbow competition included 'prostitutes, who had a special hut on the shooting grounds', perhaps explaining why the competition turned a profit of 1,120 *gulden*.[5] The power of bows to keep peace was understood across a wide area, but Flanders emphasised honour and respectability, while German events seem to have become more carnivalesque and to have had more entertainments. Such differences between German and Flemish events may be why disputes and feuds within competitions seem to have been more prevalent in sixteenth-century Germany than in fifteenth-century Flanders.

In studying the guilds and their competitions, it is tempting to set out a chronology of a group of men serving in war, forming a guild and then attending competitions. In Ghent we have seen that 'zelscutters' were paid from around 1301, a crossbow guild received funding by 1315 and the guild hosted its first competition in 1331, seeming to fit such a simple chronology. However, it must be remembered that the 'zelscutters' cannot be assumed to have been guild-brothers. Ghent's records are far earlier and more methodical than those of most Flemish towns; for numerous other centres, guilds appear in records as receiving civic funds to attend competitions before they are attested in any other civic sources. The Douai crossbowmen were given £92 to attend a competition in Tournai in 1350 and hosted a smaller event the next year, but regular references to guilds in the town accounts and in charters to the guilds are attested only from the 1380s.[6] The details provided in Ghent, Bruges and Lille record their guilds as visiting other towns for competitions before any surviving documents from the host's town refer to the guilds. For instance, the first surviving reference to a crossbow guild in Tournai comes from a payment made by the Lille aldermen to their guild to attend a shoot in that French city in 1344.[7]

For some towns, references to the competitions are the first references to guilds. For some others, the competitions may even have been the inspiration

---

[4] Guilds from these areas attended Flemish shoots, though only while under French royal authority. Such events are touched on in P.-Y. Beaurepaire, 'Les nobles jeux d'arc à la fin de l'Ancien Régime; miroir d'une sociabilité en mutation', in *Société et religion en France et aux Pays-Bas XV*ᵉ*–XIX*ᵉ *siècles, mélanges a l'honneur d'Alain Lotin* ed. G. Derengnaucourt (Arras: Artois presses université, 2000), 539–51; Delaunay, *Étude sur les anciennes compagnies*; V. Fouque, *Recherches historiques sur les corporations des archers, des arbalétriers et des arquebusiers* (Paris: Dumoulin, 1852).
[5] Tlusty, *The Martial Ethic* 192–6, 207–9.
[6] DAM, CC200 ter, roll 1; DAM AA94, ff. 70v–71; AML,CV, 16057, f. 14.
[7] AML, CV, 16040, f. 13v.

behind guild incorporation. As we will see, the competitions were extremely successful in winning honour and communicating values, and it is likely that civic governors saw or heard about competitions. As a result, civic officials in some towns seem to have been inspired to enfranchise and patronise informal groups of shooters. An interesting example of this comes not from Flanders but from the neighbouring French-controlled Tournesis – the region around Tournai. The archers of Euregnies informed Charles VII that 'many of the said inhabitants have applied themselves to the sport and establishment of the shooting of the bow' and further 'are reputed to be the best shooters' of their region, but 'they have no confraternity between them and they have neither rules nor oaths' and, as a result, they have been unable to visit the 'surrounding towns, when they will have feasts'.[8] The Euregnies archers made clear that they were an informal group seeking rights and incorporation not on the basis of service or the needs of defence, nor indeed for their own community. Rather, they were great shooters, had been in existence for at least a generation and wanted to become a recognised *serment* or guild so that they would be able to attend competitions in order to win civic honour and represent Euregnies.

Competitions began before 1330 and were quickly recognised as opportunities to build communities and win civic honour. So as to understand their ability to communicate such ideals, the mechanisms of organisation and funding both hosts and attendees must be set out. Towns paid for the events, but competitions could be staged only with ducal permission, and such permission was granted to the town as a whole, not just to the guild. How consent was sought in Flanders and where the initiative came from is not recorded, but the deliberations of the magistrates of Tournai are revealing. In 1384 and 1443 the guild of crossbowmen requested permission to hold a shoot, and the magistrates refused. In other years, such as 1455, the request was granted.[9] Records of negotiation on whether or not to hold an event do not survive in Flanders, although it is likely that such negotiations were performed orally across the Low Countries. Ducal letters of permission to hold shoots provide evidence of such civic negotiations at work and emphasise that the guilds themselves did not ask for permission to hold their own shoots. In 1462 Philip the Good allowed the crossbowmen of Oudenaarde to hold a competition because he had 'received the humble supplication of our friends the burgomasters, aldermen, councillors, king, deans, leaders and others, the companions of the guild of my lord Saint George in the town of Oudenaarde'.[10] The letter goes on to explain that the guild and town wish to hold a crossbow competition not just in order to encourage the shooting of the crossbow, but also for the great honour that will be brought to

---

[8] *ORF*, vol. 13, 456–7.
[9] Vandenbroeck 'Extraits des anciens registrers', 4–7; Grange, 'Extraits analytiques des registres', 89–91, 209–11. In 1455 the aldermen decided it would be 'good and expedient' to hold a shoot and gave the guild £200.
[10] OSAOA, gilden, 507/II/12 A.

the town, as had happened at other events in Brussels, Leuven and Tournai.[11] It seems that these early events had achieved their aim of winning honour and splendour for the guilds and their towns, and Oudenaarde hoped to follow suit as it had done in 1408.

As noted in the previous chapter, dukes allowed guild competitions to happen and even attended the shoots, but they did not directly fund the events. The events were expensive, with the above-mentioned Oudenaarde competition costing £4,925 15s. In giving his consent for the competition to be held Philip the Good allowed a special tax to be levied on all beer, wine and mead sold during the shoot, and this tax raised the impressive sum of £3,954 16s. The shortfall of funds was made up by the towns that hosted the events. The sums to fund archery and crossbow competitions came not just from the aldermen but from civic society as whole, underlining the central place that the guilds played in civic honour and an urban sense of self-representation.

The Oudenaarde aldermen, as a corporate body, contributed to the 1462 competition, giving the guild the significant sum of £149. The rest of the funds came from different urban groups, eager to support this great event for the honour that it would accrue – and possibly also for the customers it would bring to them. The butcher's guild was the most generous, giving £60 'for aid and help in the aforesaid shoot'. Butchers' guilds, some of the more exclusive guilds, were often powerful, even militaristic, and might logically be expected to be interested in bringing honour to their town and they were generous in funding the shoot. The mercers gave £24, the brewers contributed £36, but most of the craft guilds, including the smiths and many textile trades, gave less, generally between £6 and £10. A further £225 was raised from the 'good people of good towns and parishes outside' Oudenaarde.[12] All of the craft guilds, all of the civic community, gave money to help pay for the crossbow competition, showing that it was a civic effort and would benefit the entire urban community. Similarly, in Ghent for its great crossbow competition in 1440, numerous craft guilds gave sums of money, some small and some large, to help fund the competition, and there were far larger grants from the civic accounts. Contributions from all groups, as well as directly from the aldermen, emphasised that the great shoots were staged with the support of a wide cross-section of civic society.[13]

Money was not the only way in which towns showed their support for competitions, as details for Ghent from the *Bouc van Pieter Polet* make clear. For the shoots in 1440 and 1498 all guildsmen and organisers of the shoot received

---

[11] The Brussels reference could refer to the recent, but relatively small, shoot of 1461 or the huge event of 1444; Leuven held several small shoots, but none for which evidence survives as spectacular as those in Ghent or Brussels; the large shoot in Tournai of 1455.
[12] OSOA gilden Nummer 507/II/4B.
[13] SAG, Cousemakers, Rekeningen, 165, f. 40; UBG, Hs G 6112*Dit es den bouc van ... Pieter Polet*, ff. 36–37v.

civic liveries from civic funds. Significant amounts of civic money were also spent on practical matters, such as building galleries, setting up targets and, later on, replacing windows in the town hall that had been broken by arrows. In 1440 the alderman had to settle a dispute between the guilds of Liège and Amiens over who had travelled the farthest. Two municipal messengers were despatched to find out which town was furthest away and it was assumed that whichever messenger returned first would have visited the closer town.[14] The messengers were civic officials, sent at civic expense, thus showing once again how seriously host towns took the competitions and how important it was for them to be seen as honourable and fair. Ghent gave money, cloth, space and civic messengers to the guild, ensuring that the competitions would be memorable and honourable.

Once permission had been obtained, letters of invitation were despatched. The invitations made clear when the event would begin, where and when guilds should enter and the types of prizes that would be awarded. In Tournai in 1394 at least two, more likely four, messengers were sent out. The letter to the guilds in Holland and Northern Brabant was transcribed by Chotin in 1840 (it was destroyed a century later). The letter the Chotin described had seals attached from Brabant and Holland towns, including 's-Hertogenbosch, Antwerp, Amsterdam, Haarlem and Gouda. Other sources make clear that many attendees came from the southern Low Countries and France, and so other invitations must have been sent out to these southern areas.[15]

In 1404 Mechelen sent out four messages to invite guilds to attend its competition. In Mechelen, all four of letters of invitation have been kept and each bears the seals of guilds for different regions. When messengers visited different towns, the guilds would attach their seals if they intended to attend the competition.[16] Not all of the seals attached to the Mechelen invitation can be identified, as many are little more than fragments of wax, but enough survive to show that one messenger went to France and the southern Low Countries, visiting Paris, Laon and Reims, another to Flanders, a third to Brabant and Luik and a fourth to northern Brabant and Holland.[17] In 1440 Ghent again sent out four messengers, to broadly the same four areas. Only one letter of invitation has been preserved – perhaps only one was deemed necessary to be kept by either the guild or a later archivist. In addition to the one surviving invitation, lists of

---

[14] UBG, Hs G 6112, *Dit es den bouc van … Pieter Polet*, f. 5.
[15] Whether or not other invitations existed in 1840 is not clear; certainly none survived the 1940 bombing. Chotin, *Histoire de Tournai et du Tournésis*, vol. 1, 349–58; those invited are discussed in Stein, 'An Urban Network in the Low Countries', 54; L. Crombie, 'French and Flemish Urban Festive Networks: Archery and Crossbow Competitions Attended and Hosted by Tournai in the Fourteenth and Fifteenth Centuries', *French History* 27 (2013), 157–75. For the destruction see L. Verriest, 'La perte des archives du Hainaut et de Tournai', *RBPH* 21 (1942), 186–93.
[16] See above, pp. 108–12.
[17] Stadsarcheif Mechelen, IX, 4, no. 128 bis, 1–4.

the gifts that the messengers received in the towns they visited were copied into the *Bouc van Pieter Polet*, as will be discussed in greater depth below in analysing the invitation.[18] Such detailed records do not survive elsewhere, but it is likely that towns did all they could to attract guilds to their great events so as to ensure that the competitions would be as large and as spectacular as possible.

In Ghent, Mechelen and Oudenaarde invitations from other towns were kept, as were descriptions of competitions elsewhere. The guilds were working not just to spread the word of their own events, but also to record in detail events of their neighbours.[19] The rivalries in hosting great competitions were similar to the rivalries and patterns of towns in attempting to outdo one another as observed by Blockmans and Donckers in the planning of princely joyous entrances. Fifteenth- and sixteenth-century towns worked to gather information about entrances elsewhere, competing not just to put on the greatest show for their sovereign but also to put on the greatest show for the urban crowds that witnessed these entrances.[20] In keeping not just their own letters of invitation but those from elsewhere, reports of other shoots and descriptions of prizes, Ghent, Oudenaarde and Mechelen showed an interest in the development of competitions and strove to outdo their neighbours in their own spectacular events so as to enhance their own civic honour.

As will be shown, entrances and displays became more important over time, but from as early as 1331 a special day was set aside for entrances.[21] Once all of the guilds had entered, the order in which guilds were to shoot was established, and even in this opening event of the competition, equality and fairness were emphasised. The order in which teams would shoot was decided not by ideas of precedence or hierarchy, as in jousts, but by chance; the competitions strove for the same 'strong fiction of equality' that Van Bruaene has described for drama competitions. The order could be chosen simply by drawing lots, as in Oudenaarde in 1408. In 1455 the crossbowmen of Tournai devised a far more elaborate way of determining the order of shooters. A large 'wax meadow' was constructed, at municipal expense, and a 'beautiful young girl' chose apples, each representing a guild, in order to determine to the order in which the guilds would shoot.[22] The hosts were clearly making a great effort to ensure that all of these events were honourable and memorable and emphasised fairness and community.

---

[18] UBG, Hs G 6112, *Dit es den bouc van … Pieter Polet*, ff. 36r–38v.
[19] SAG, SJ, NGR; UBG *Vredesverdragen*, ff. 92–100, f. 89v; Stadsarcheif Mechelen, IX, 4, nos 5, 6, 13, 14.
[20] W. Blockmans and E. Donckers, 'Self-Representation of Court and City', in *Showing Status: Representations of Social Positions in the Late Middle Ages*, ed. W. Blockmans and A. Jansese (Turnhout: Brepols, 1999), 81–111.
[21] Vuylsteke *Gentsche stads en balijuwsrekeningen, 1280–1336*, vol. 2, 765–6.
[22] Van Bruaene, 'A Wonderfull tryumfe', 390; Cauwenberghe, 'Notice historique sur les confréries de Saint Georges', 218–21; Brown and Small, *Court and Civic Society*, 219–25.

Of course it was not just the aldermen of the host town who recognised the potential that elaborate shooting competitions held for civic honour and the representation of urban prestige. Honour and prestige could certainly come from hosting an event, but guilds' leaving their town and travelling to competitions could also enhance their own reputation, and also enhance the honour of their town. Some towns not only helped their guilds to attend competitions elsewhere but even made it clear that their attendance was expected. When the statutes of the Douai crossbowmen were first recorded by the aldermen, they made clear that if the guild heard of any competition in any *bonne ville* or lordship, the guild was to take its best men.[23] The significance for the guilds of hosting and attending shooting competitions was recognised by civic authorities as an opportunity to demonstrate their identity and to compete for honour.

Civic financial assistance for attending competitions is very common. Indeed, details in town accounts give far more figures than can be analysed here, but a few examples are provided here, to show that simply attending brought honour, but winning prizes meant more honour, and so greater reward. In 1394 Douai gave its crossbowmen £26 for a competition in Tournai. When it received news that the guild had won prizes – two silver pots weighing 6 marks – the aldermen gave the guild an additional £41 17s and 6d 'for the honour of the town'.[24] In 1451 the archers of Douai attended a competition in Béthune. The town accounts note that they went there 'winning notable prizes and did so well and honourably for the honour of this town' and received £36.[25] The town accounts of Tournai take the idea of rewarding honour with material wealth even further. In 1432 the archers went to a shoot in Roubaix. They requested money from their town for this event, but the magistrates delayed giving them anything until they had news of what prizes they had won.[26] Civic authorities wanted the guilds to go out and be honourable, to represent them and to showcase urban values on a regional stage and, in doing so, to show honour and the values that the guilds strove to maintain. They funded them to attend competitions 'for the honour of the town', just as they helped the guilds to become prominent within their own civic societies through grants of land, wine and cloth 'for the honour of the town'.

Douai encouraged both the archery and crossbow guilds to attend competitions and win honour. Lille's records show a more nuanced pattern of support. We have seen in the previous chapter that Lille gave the crossbowmen more annual assistance, and more wine for their annual events, than it gave to the archers. A similar division appears in the civic funding granted to the guilds for attending competitions. In 1359 the archers received 72s for attending a shoot in Tournai and the same year the crossbowmen received £4 plus wine worth

---

[23] DAM, Arbalestiers de Douay, 24II232, f. 2.
[24] DAM, CV, CC203, f. 454, the later payment on f. 479.
[25] DAM, CV, CC219, f. 64.
[26] Grange, 'Extraits analytiques des registres des consaulx de la ville de Tournai', 13.

6s 11d for shooting in Douai. In 1392 the crossbowmen went to a competition in Avesnes (near Montreuil-sur-Mer) and received £24 16s. In the same year the archers travelled to Mons and received £12. In 1403 the crossbowmen attended a competition in Chièvres in Hainaut and received eight lots of wine plus £24, while the archers travelled to Ypres and were granted £12. In 1427 the crossbowmen were given an unusually large grant of £80 to go to a competition in Saint Omer. The same generosity was not shown to the archers, who in 1432 received only six lots of wine for travelling to the nearby town of Roubaix. Distance was not the only issue here, for in 1439 the archers received only 16s to go to a competition in Saint Omer. To give one final and very emphatic example of this disparity between the archers and crossbowmen, in 1454 the archers of Lille received £8 to go to a shoot in Lens. The next year the crossbowmen received £192 to go to the spectacular Tournai shoot.[27]

Distances, and the size of the Tournai shoot, are important, but across our period it is clear that the aldermen of Lille made consistent choices about the hierarchy of honour and support. For Lille, the crossbowmen were the more prestigious representatives, but both guilds were granted funds and were rewarded: the guild-brothers had become urban ambassadors, representing the status and values of their town on prestigious urban stages. To represent the town in the best light possible, good behaviour was important. In Aalst, if a crossbowman broke the rules or otherwise misbehaved while there, he would be fined 5s. If he misbehaved or did anything dishonourable while at or travelling to a competition he would be expelled from the guild, being no longer worthy to represent civic status. As we have seen, honour had to be protected and defended, and threats to honour removed.[28] Hosts, similarly, had to make sure that attendees would be impressed by their town, and some were concerned about the impression certain townsmen would make. For the 1498 shoot the Ghent aldermen set out harsh penalties for quarrels or disobedience – not for the guild-brothers, who had their usual grants of immunity, but for the rest of the Ghent population, who should not upset the prestigious visitors.[29] Competitions were about the ideals of the guilds, about inviting guilds in friendship and in honour and about building spectacular events with civic support – and for such ideals to have any hope of coming to fruition, good behaviour was crucial. Across Flanders, the civic powers invested in their guilds, ensuring that they were well armed, skilled and well dressed. Sending the guilds to competitions for the honour of the town was their next logical step and they did all they could to ensure that the guild-brothers lived up to the honourable image. The next

---

[27] AML, CV, 16072, f. 16, ff. 32v–33; 16122, ff. 22, 35; 16143, ff. 37v–38; 16170, f. 54v; 16174, f. 47; 16180, f. 56v, 16195, f. 13v; AML, CV, f. 45v, the 102s of wine given to Anthony the Bastard of Burgundy, who led the shooters in the Tournai competition, could be added to this total.
[28] ASAOA, Den boek met den haire, 7, 72.
[29] UBG, Hs G 6112, *Dit es den bouc van ... Pieter Polet*, f. 40r–v.

chapter will explore in more depth a few examples of rules' being broken; but the ideal is important because the aldermen sent out their guilds at civic expense and in civic cloth to uphold a civic self-image and to demonstrate and augment civic honour.

The events would be planned, the invitations would be sent out, on the appointed day the guild would enter the town and then the shooting would begin. Just as time and space were allotted for the entrances for a show of status, so too were they set aside for the martial displays at the heart of competitions. Evidence from the early fourteenth century is limited, but by the late fourteenth century it was normal for up to three teams to shoot each day – fewer on a Sunday or saint's day. In Tournai in 1455 crossbow guilds entered the town on 11 August, took part in a procession and performed plays on the 12th, chose the order in which to shoot with their elaborate wax meadow on the 13th and began the shooting on 14 August. The last of the fifty-nine guilds took their turn to shoot on 18 September. The Ghent competition of 1440 lasted even longer, as no more than two teams shot each day. Teams usually consisted of ten to twelve men, with each guild-brother shooting horizontally at a large circular target at the other end of the market place, each man shooting three to five times and each shot being recorded and measured if necessary.[30] Prizes were awarded for the best individual and best team, as well as for other displays (the form and significance of the prizes will be discussed below).

The shooting competitions took over central market places for weeks at a time, dominating civic space. Such a location was in part pragmatic, as the market places were the largest open spaces within towns. But market places were in many ways the heart of most cities and the focal point of urban life. Not only were they in the city centre, but they drew meaning from the interactions between town dwellers and others, such as merchants and traders, and as places of interaction and integration. Market places were also symbolic spaces, frequently the settings for numerous civic rituals that again emphasised interaction, such as princely entrance ceremonies.[31] Urban jousts also took place in these urban spaces. In this way the competitions linked ludic and commercial networks.[32]

---

[30] UBG, Hs G 6112, *Dit es den bouc van ... Pieter Polet*, ff. 16–16v.

[31] Van Bruaene, 'A Wonderfull tryumfe', 374–405; P. Stabel, 'The Market Place and Civic Identity in Late Medieval Flanders', in M. Boone and P. Stabel (eds), *Shaping Urban Identity in Late Medieval Europe* (Leuven: Garant, 2000), 43–64; M. Boone, 'Urban space and Political Conflict in Late Medieval Flanders', *Journal of Interdisciplinary History* 32 (2002), 621–40.

[32] Brown and Small, *Court and Civic Society*, 165–209; Arnade, *Realms of Ritual*, 127–58; J.-M. Cauchies, 'La signifiance politique des entrée princières dans les Pays-Bas; Maximilien d'Autriche et Philippe le Beau', *PCEEB* 24 (1994), 19–35; Blockmans, 'Le Dialogue imaginaire', 37–53; E. Strietman, 'Pawns or Prime Movers? The Rhetoricians in the Struggle for Power in the Low Countries', in S. Higgins (ed.), *European Medieval Drama, 1997. Papers from the Second International Conference on Aspects of European Medieval Drama*, Camerine, 4–6 July 1997 (Turnhout: Brepols, 1998), 211–22.

During the competitions the guild-brothers gathered to shot in turn at the targets, often in large wooden galleries. The galleries offered some protection for the audience and were built at municipal expense, providing further evidence of the care and attention that the alderman paid to the competitions. Yet, despite the organisers' best efforts, the competitions were dangerous. In 1462, in his letter of consent for an Oudenaarde crossbow competition, Philip the Good made clear that 'if it should happen, that God does not wish, that in the said shoot anyone should by mishap or by mischief, be between the butts and targets and be killed or injured or struck in any manner by any of the crossbowmen, those that have made the said strike or harm will be quit and free, without being in any way apprehended'. In addition, Philip granted free passage to anyone to attend the shoot, excepting his own and the French king's personal enemies, in this way emphasising the prestige of the guild-brothers and the value placed on their competitions. Although no cases of death are recorded in Flanders, the repair bill for broken windows in Ghent following the 1440 crossbow competition highlights the danger of the events, either from bolts that missed their mark or from others that ricocheted toward buildings and, presumably, spectators.[33]

Elsewhere, arrows did cause harm. In 1353 French King Jean II issued a letter of remission to Codart le Gurvelier for the 'involuntary' killing of Robert Bagas 'in the game of the crossbow' in Amiens. Although the letter is not particularly detailed, it is clear that Codart had been participating in a shoot and his shot had missed the target and struck Robert. The king was satisfied that Codart had not meant to harm Robert and was also satisfied that the competition had been properly ordered and held for civic honour, and so he pardoned Codart, ensuring that he would not face any punishment. In Brussels the crossbow guild had immunity from prosecution for accidental deaths in competitions, as did the Flemish guilds. This right was called into question in 1423 when an unnamed crossbowman fled the town after 'accidentally' killing another man during a competition. Although the crossbowman had feared prosecution and so had fled, the ducal court quickly recognised that he was a guild-brother and therefore could not be prosecuted. The privilege was renewed by Maximilian in 1478, possibly because the freedom from prosecution had been called into question by another accident.[34] Despite the dangers, events were celebrated, ending with feasting and the awarding of prizes and with displays of honour and friendship. All archery and crossbow competitions had this basic format, with civic support, ducal permission, invitations and prizes – although, as we shall see, the size and splendour of competitions could differ a great deal across the fourteenth and fifteenth centuries and across Flanders.

---

[33] OSAOA, gilden, 507/II/12 A; SAG, SJ, 155, 1, f. 6.
[34] E. Maugis, *Documents inédits concernant la ville et le siège du bailliage d'Amiens*, 3 vols (Amiens: Yvert et Tellier, 1908), vol. 1, 17–22; Wauters, *Notice historique*, 3–5.

Letters of Invitation and the Language of Community and Honour

The values for which competitions strove, their efforts to build communities and to show honour, are clearest in the invitations sent out by the guilds in advance of their events. Invitations should not be mistaken for an account of how competitions unfolded, but they are an invaluable source for analysing the hopes and ideals of both aldermen and guild-brothers for their competitions and they make very clear what the hosts hoped to gain from their competitions. No letters of invitation survive from the early years of shoots and it is very likely that messengers delivered the early invitations orally. In 1359, when a messenger from Douai arrived in Lille to tell the crossbowmen about a *jeu* to be held that same year the aldermen of Lille rewarded him with wine, but there is no hint that he carried a letter or that a copy of one was made or required in Lille.[35] It may be that written invitations became necessary only as events grew and became more elaborate and more complex and as rules on numbers of competitors and shooting distances became formalised. Once again, no firm conclusion can be drawn from the silences of the early fourteenth century. Although it is clear from a very early date that competitions were being funded for civic honour, invitations do not survive until the 1380s.

To understand these priorities, and how they developed over time, six letters of invitation will be analysed here. The six are a letter from Mons in 1387, Tournai in 1394, Oudenaarde in 1408, Ghent in 1440, Hulst in 1483 and Ghent in 1498.[36] These are not the only letters to have survived from Flanders, but they are taken here as representative of the development of more elaborate language over time, as well as allowing for consideration of towns of different sizes. The Hulst invitation is the only such document known to have survived for a small town and so it provides a useful counterbalance to the far more plentiful sources coming from Ghent and Oudenaarde. No comparable letters of invitation to archery events have survived, although archery competitions could be just as spectacular, as is indicated by town accounts. The lack of invitation to archery events is unlikely to indicate that none existed: Ypres held some of the largest archery contests of the fifteenth-century and, had its archive survived, it is likely that archery invitations would have been found.

The values – predominantly friendship and honour – expressed in the letters of invitation are part of a wider discourse, with drama competitions emphasising 'harmony and honour', just as processions and entrance ceremonies emphasised order, unity, loyalty and obedience.[37] The same values appear in other civic

---

[35] AML 16072, f. 22.
[36] Devillers, 'Notice Historique sur les milices communales', 169–285; UBG Hs 434 (76) *Vredesverdragen* ff. 85–87; Chotin, *Histoire de Tournai et du Tournaisiens*, vol. 1, 349–58; UBG, Hs 434, *Vredesverdragen*, ff. 92–100; SAG, SJ, 155, nummer 2; SAG, SJ, NGR, Charters en diverse losse documenten, 30; SAG, SJ, 155, no. 3.
[37] Van Bruaene, 'Harmonie et honour en jeu', 227–78; 'Introduction', to Lecuppre-Desjardin and Van Bruaene, *De Bono Communi*, 1–9.

written records. In looking at the account books of the major Flemish towns and analysing their use of keywords, Dumolyn has proved the importance of social unity, with frequent expressions like 'unity', 'friendship', 'mutual love' and 'concord' providing evidence that the 'Members always aspired to unity'.[38] Events might fall short of such unity and honour, as the next chapter will explain, but the values of unity and the centrality of honour appear in every surviving letter of invitation. The desire for honour, unity and friendship, clear in drama, procession and account books, is equally evident in letters of invitation to crossbow competitions.

Mons 1387

Mons was the capital of Hainaut and had been ruled by the counts of Flanders for much of the twelfth and thirteenth centuries, but by 1387 was ruled by the Bavarian family that were also counts of Holland and Zealand. It would later pass into Burgundian hands via the infamous Jacqueline of Bavaria and a number of complicated successions.[39] Count William of Holland and Hainaut had married Philip the Bold's daughter in 1385, linking the lands politically, and Hainaut had been commercially and culturally connected to Flanders for some time. Like its northern neighbours, Mons was a major cloth centre and the river Haine connected the town to Valenciennes and, eventually, to the Scheldt, and so to Ghent and Tournai. The town had a population of around 8,000, including men with aspirations toward nobility.[40] It was, then, an important centre outside of Flanders that chose to reach out to guilds in and beyond Flanders for its competition of 1387, using this spectacle to enhance regional links and demonstrate its own status.

Little notice was given to guilds that wished to attend, perhaps implying the letter was not carried too far. The letter of invitation is dated 13 June and the competition was to start on 13 July. The crossbowmen of Mons wrote to all 'honourable men,

---

[38] Dumolyn, 'Urban Ideology in Later Medieval Flanders', 81–3.
[39] For Jacqueline, her four marriages and war with her uncle, see R. Nip, 'Conflicting Roles: Jacqueline of Bavaria (d. 1436), Countess and Wife', in. M. van Dijk and R. Nip (eds), *Saints, Scholars, and Politicians: Gender as a Tool in Medieval Studies. Festschrift in Honour of Anneke Mulder-Bakker on the Occasion of her Sixty-Fifth Birthday* (Turnhout: Brepols, 2005), 189–207; E. Pluymen, 'Jacoba van Beieren als vorstin', *Spiegel Historiael* 20 (1985) 321–5, 362; Vaughan, *Philip the Good*, 32–52.
[40] V. Flammang, 'Anoblissement des élites urbaines en Hainaut (1400–1550)', *Mémoires et publications de la Société des sciences, des arts et des lettres du Hainaut* 104 (2008), 37–64; D. Dehon, 'Mons/Mons: étude archéologique du sous-sol et archéologie du bâti de la tour Valenciennoise', *Chronique de l'archéologie wallonne* 12 (2004), 64–7; J.-M. Cauchies, 'Mons et Valenciennes devant le Grand Conseil du duc de Bourgogne: un conflit de longue durée (1394–1446)', *Bulletin de la Commission royale des anciennes lois et ordonnances de Belgique* 38 (1997), 99–171; M. Bruwier, 'La foire de Mons aux XIVe et XVe siècles (1355–1465)', *PCEEB* 23 (1983), 83–93.

courteous and wise' guild-brothers, inviting them to a very friendly game with bows (*jeu des arcs*). The invitation emphasised that the competition was being held for the pleasing of God and their patron saint, the Virgin Mary. Perhaps as importantly, the competition was organised with the permission of 'our very dear and redoubtable lord, my lord the Duke Albert of Bavaria, lord, heir and successor to Hainaut, Holland and Zealand' and with the consent of 'the venerable and very wise dear lords, the mayor and aldermen' of Mons. The letter invites all '*bonnes villes fermées*' (walled towns) to the competition and goes on to describe all the prizes that will be awarded and how these may be won.

The Mons letter is relatively short, providing all the information that guilds needed in order to attend, with a small amount of rhetoric. The competition had received the blessing of God, of the count of Hainaut and of the aldermen, but the letter uses little by way of elaborate language or honourable expressions, although love and honour are emphasised, as are the bonds of friendship that, the men of Mons hope, will be created and strengthened through the competition.

Tournai 1394

We have seen that Tournai was a French episcopal city close to and soon to be surrounded by Burgundian lands. It was a rich city, economically bound to Ghent, as well as politically and culturally extremely loyal to the French king. The invitation sent out by the crossbowmen of Tournai in 1394 shows a growth in the language of honour and uses more elaborate terms. It begins with a similar greeting to the Mons letter. All 'honourable and wise' members of all crossbow guilds in '*bonnes villes*' are invited to the shoot. The guild explains in more elaborate terms its motivation for organising the event:

> Considering that the holy scriptures say and testify that sloth is the mother of all vice and injurious to all virtues, and that all human creatures should flee it and occupy themselves in good works, so that Satan does not find mankind idle and that they are well occupied in doing what can be done properly and does little or no harm, but pleases everyone greatly, and so that humans may be inclined to occupy themselves as it pleases each of them differently, with some enjoying one activity and others another.

To avoid sin, suitable guild-brothers, those from established and sworn guilds, are invited to take part in 'our very noble, beloved, gentle, gracious, pleasing, kind and very recommended game' of the crossbow. During the event the participants must 'deport themselves without blasphemy', as the game of the crossbow 'cannot have any hate, vanity, trouble or pillage, greed nor any other pain or mortal sin, but humility, charity, fraternity, largesse and love, sobriety, chastity and all virtues' and can never be played by 'a man of bad life or of perverse condition', for the crossbow 'is great and notable in comparison to all other games'.

The letter continues to emphasise the honour both of the game of the crossbow and of the guild of Tournai, stating that the 'game and occupation are exalted' and that 'it pleases the king our lord that as many persons as possible take up this occupation'. This is likely to be a reference to the numerous French royal ordinances banning ball games and other sports and ordering all able men to take up archery. The first surviving such ordinance was issued by Charles V in May 1369.[41] Civic documents only hint at a connection between royal encouragement and the competition, but the *Chronique des Pays-Bas, de France, d'Angleterre et de Tournai* makes more of the royal connection, recording that the competition was held with 'a great desire to be in the grace of the king'.[42] In linking the 1394 competition to French royal ordinances and to pleasing the king, the crossbowmen emphasised their honour and, as part of this honour, their loyalty to the French king. The letter is longer and more elaborate than the Mons letter, and makes clear the virtue of crossbows and crossbowmen, as well as their hopes for love and community in the event.

Like that of Mons, the Tournai letter was written in French. In the fourteenth century it was the southern French-speaking towns that led the way in creating a narrative for grand competitions. The next four letters in our study were sent out by Flemish-speaking towns. Some invitations were sent out in both French and Dutch and it is of course possible that bilingual messengers were sent out with invitations – but for early shoots the invitations survive in one language only. There are hints here at multilingual communities, with Flemish-speaking guilds responding to French invitations and French-speaking guilds responding to Flemish invitations.[43]

Oudenaarde 1408

The letter sent out by the crossbowmen of Oudenaarde in 1408 shows a similar desire for reputation, prestige and love. The 1408 letter is the first surviving bilingual letter of invitation and is addressed to 'the honourable, discrete and wise, all those Lords, kings, constables, deans, governors and to all other companions' of sworn guilds 'of the noble game of the crossbow' in cities and walled or privileged towns.[44] Honour is demonstrated through exclusivity, the letter emphasising that rural groups are not welcome; teams from '*hammeaulx, villes champestres ou chasteaulx*, supposing that they have a guild or a company

---

[41] ORF, vol. 5, 172–3.
[42] Smet, *Collection des chroniques*, vol. 3, 289–295.
[43] Multilingualism has been explored in more depth in Crombie 'Target Languages', in *The Multilingual Muse*. A. Armstrong and E. Strietman (eds) (forthcoming).
[44] Chartered or walled towns. For the use and meaning of *bonnes* and *enferme villes* see B. Chevalier, 'Les Bonnes Villes and the King's Council in Fifteenth-Century France', in *The Crown and Local Communities in England and France in the Fifteenth Century*. J. R. L. Highfield and R. Jeffs (eds) (Stroud: Alan Sutton, 1981), 110–128; idem, 'Loches, une bonne ville au bailliage de Touraine à l'aube de la Renaissance', *Loches aux XVIe* (1979), 1–12.

or *serment'*, will not be welcomed. If any such should appear in Oudenaarde they 'cannot play in the said games nor win the said prizes'. Although the previous letters had emphasised that guilds had to be '*serment*' and from good towns, the Oudenaarde letter is more emphatic. Only townsmen are honourable enough to attend; villagers will be not welcome. Such clauses are important in understanding the perception of civic honour – the identities of the guilds that took part in competitions was *urban* and they strengthened urban networks and urban honour through the exclusion of rural groups.

Honourable men from suitable places were invited to play the 'excellent, very noble and loved game, and above all other games, the most pure and honourable', which 'cannot and must not be bad nor villainous'. The letter emphasised the importance of the 'very noble game' before describing the shooting and prizes. As in earlier competitions, the men of Oudenaarde make clear that they have princely permission from the 'very high and very excellent, our very dear and very redoubtable lord and prince, my lord the Duke of Burgundy…'. Friendship and community are again central, and because the invitation is bilingual it appeals to an even larger community and even more guilds are invited to come to Oudenaarde for peaceful games.

Ghent 1440

The crossbow competition held in Ghent in 1440 was one of the largest and most spectacular yet staged. Civic sources show that a great deal of planning and care went into it as a celebration of Ghent and of harmonious communities. The invitation was again bilingual and full of elegant and peaceful language: the guild-brothers wished to make peace and to build communities. Guilds had longer to prepare for this shoot, perhaps in expectation of staging yet more spectacles or larger and more elaborate entrances. The invitation was written on 13 March for entrances to be made in June and was addressed to 'all good privileged and free towns' and called them to the 'honourable game of the crossbow' by virtue of 'their honourable and worthy ancient rights and renown'.

Crossbowmen were asked to come in friendship. The letter from the Ghent guild-brothers emphasised that 'this feast of ours is for the good honour of God and His Holy Mother, wishing all for the good of the community, for the honour and love that we wish to be given on this our oath'. It letter stated that the competition was to be held with 'the consent, ordinance and grant of our high noble lord and natural prince' the duke of Burgundy. The language in the invitation emphasised Ghent's efforts to rebuild unity in Flanders, to keep the peace through a great competition and to use martial prowess to rebuild war-torn communities. As noted in chapter one, Flemish guilds were dishonoured by the retreat from Calais and disunified by the Bruges rebellion that followed.[45] The references to the great competitions in 'olden times' that 'maintained'

---

[45] Boone, 'De Sint-jorisgilde', 30–31.

community and their 'ancient and worthy rights' make clear the desire for peace and the hope for past successes to be repeated. The letter further emphasises that the competition should bring 'joy' and all sworn guilds should attend with 'good wishes' and 'act honourably' throughout the event.

Ghent took great care in spreading the word about its competition, with four messengers being sent to over a hundred towns. The detailed list of the messengers and their routes was added to Pieter Polet's book, no doubt to help plan the routes of messengers in 1498.[46] The list of towns invited to the shoot provides great insight into the ability of competitions to demonstrate civic status and build communities even before the start of the event. The first messenger, Martin van Eerdbiere, travelled to the ducal court and then across eastern and southern Flanders. He received numerous gifts including silver scales, cloth and wine, indicating that towns respected the Ghent messenger and understood the importance of the guild he represented. A second messenger, Gillis de Mueleneegh, travelled south on the Scheldt to Oudenaarde and then into Hainaut and parts of Brabant. Like Martin, he was well received and presented with silver objects and some jewels. All gifts should have been carried back to Ghent, but at least some, notably large quantities of wine, were 'lost' by Martin and Gillis.

In Holland a third messenger, Jan Maeaert, received far fewer gifts. Dordrecht paid his costs and gave him a small jewel, but he received nothing at all in Rotterdam or Amsterdam, and neither town attended the shoot. This could imply that guilds in Holland were less developed than those in Flanders, but it is more likely that Jan's cooler reception was linked to wider networks and political integration. Had the towns of Holland given a gift to Jan, it could have been the start of a relationship with the Ghent guild and perhaps they did not want such bonds, as they had only recently, and bitterly, been brought under the political hegemony of the dukes of Burgundy in 1433.[47] For all the ideals of friendship and community expressed in letters of invitation, the competitions could not single-handedly create bonds; rather, they were just one aspect of regional networks. The fourth, unnamed messenger travelled even further, eastward into Germany through parts of Brabant, and received a rather mixed reception. In Liège he was received with a great show, as he was welcomed by pipers, trumpeters and even a small procession. But many smaller towns were less enthusiastic; in Bovyins (a small town near Dinant) he received nothing because, as the accounts state, there were no shooters. In nearby Fleurus (closer to Charleroi) he received nothing, as *'daer zijn de scutters al doot'* (there the shooters were all dead). While such statements might have been true, they are also likely to indicate that not all towns believed in the unity and honour expressed by Ghent. In all, 107 towns were invited but only fifty-six guilds attended. Not all the invited guilds accepted the ideals of friendship and honour set out in the letter of invitation and not all

---

[46] UBG, Hs G 6112, *Dit es den bouc van … Pieter Polet*, ff. 17–20v.
[47] Vaughan, *Philip the Good*, 32–51.

wanted to build community with Ghent, but the desire of the Ghent guild and aldermen for a specular, honourable and memorable event is clear.

It is possible that Ghent's huge demonstration of civic culture, especially with Philip the Good as an active participant, can be linked to a wish to show Ghent as more reliable than Bruges, and thus a worthy capital of the emerging Burgundian state. The messengers and their reception make clear that the degree of integration in civic networks was shaped by attitudes toward Ghent and toward crossbow competitions. Many towns grasped the opportunity to (re)connect with Ghent and, in order to demonstrate their status on a regional stage, to use festive networks as a means to augment commercial and political ones. Not all towns wanted to interact with Ghent and build bonds with Flanders, and not all guilds or civic authorities were keen to enter into the community Ghent envisaged – a community built on honour and friendship, and looking to old and worthy traditions to recreate bonds and restore honour.

Hulst 1483

The small town of Hulst organised a crossbow competition in 1483, one of many smaller events held in the crisis years of the early 1480s.[48] With the death of Mary of Burgundy in March 1482, the estates had recognised her son, Philip, as count of Flanders, but the regency of his father, Maximilian Habsburg, remained unpopular. Hulst had hosted archers in 1462, but its 1483 letter of invitation is the first surviving invitation sent out by a small town. The letter demonstrates that the communities desired and valued by guilds were not limited to the great towns, or to years of peace. Small and medium-sized towns shared the same ideas of civic honour and urban harmony. Hulst's population in the fifteenth century was less than a tenth of Bruges's, with fewer than 3,000 residents. The town was in the far north of Flanders (and in the modern Netherlands) and, as Stabel has shown, was far closer economically to Holland than to Flanders.[49] Given Hulst's size and location, its crossbow competition could not match those of Ghent or Oudenaarde in spectacle, yet the event held in this small community was set out on the same model and with the same ideals of honour and friendship as observed by the guilds in Ghent.

As earlier letters had done, the Hulst invitation claimed divine support. The competition would be held 'to the honour of God and all the saints of the church'. In 1483 the Hulst competition had no access to earlier competitions' second source of consent and prestige – princely authority. The Hulst invitation makes reference

---

[48] An event was held in Bruges in 1477, De Potter, *Jaarboeken*, 113–14; in Brussels, in 1479, Wauters, *Notice historique*; *De Brugse kruisbooggilde*, 72–4. Chronological patterns will be discussed in more depth in the following chapter.

[49] Stabel, 'Composition et recomposition', 58; idem, 'Van schepenen en ontvangers, politieke elite en stadsfinancien in Axele en Hulst', *TVSG* 18 (1992),1–12; idem, *De kleine stad in Vlaandered*, 112–18.

to its festivities having been 'begun with our lady the duchess', but no letter of consent from Mary survives – although, given how few records survive from medieval Hulst, it is far from impossible that some informal instructions have been lost. Nothing in the town or from central bureaucracy gives any indication that this 'lady the duchess' could be the dowager duchess Margaret of York. The Hulst crossbowmen recognised that their competition was taking place in an unstable period. Despite this, there is no mention of military training or war; rather, the invitation emphasises honour and love. Many elements common to the earlier shoots are repeated, with the crossbow guilds being invited to compete in 'the most honourable and greatest game'. The crossbowmen of Hulst refer to 'the great friendship' and 'brotherly love' they have for other guilds. Such similarities are to be expected and show that even in this period of great instability the crossbowmen of Hulst wanted to emphasise the nobility of crossbow shooting and, in doing so, to bring great honour and prestige to their town. The Hulst letter aspires to the same values of peaceful community and harmony through honourable conduct as had been made clear in invitations from larger towns during the previous century. Competitions in smaller towns would, of course, be different, but their values and their sense of honour and civic pride indicate the same wishes and the same hopes for peace and friendship.

Yet differences do emerge in this small town during this period of instability. Hulst's letter was addressed to all free and good towns, areas around castles (*cateeles*) and even villages (*dorps*). Such an open invitation is in stark contrast to Oudenaarde's 1408 statement that *only* urban guilds could attend and that villagers, if they did have guilds, would not be welcomed. Such openness is partly pragmatic: given its size and its northerly position, Hulst was never going to attract as wide an audience as the competitions in Ghent or Oudenaarde. Yet it may also reflect that in smaller towns the contrast between urban and rural was less strongly felt and less divisive than it was in the greater towns. Their views on rural shooters aside, that the Hulst crossbowmen wrote a letter full of noble language emphasised the prestige of their guild and the loving community of shooters that they felt themselves to be a part of and able to enhance. The guild was still searching for honour and prestige through games, indicating not just the strength of competitions but also the importance of sport and festivities even during times of war and hardship, and even in a small, peripheral town.

Ghent 1498

The Hulst crossbowmen faced many difficulties in their 1483 competition, from the status of their town and the political situation around them. By contrast, the Ghent shoot of 1498 had every opportunity to be spectacular, and the invitation emphasised the need for unity and for honour, with the hope that Flanders would again be unified and strong. The invitation, indeed the competition as a whole, drew heavily on the 1440 event for inspiration, as Pieter Polet's detailed plans show. In 1498 the town and crossbow guild of Ghent were not seeking innovation or to reinvent competitions; rather, they wanted a great event in order to restore civic honour. By 1498 Flanders was returning to some form of stability, as Philip the Fair had been declared of age and able to rule in his own right at the age of sixteen in 1494. Two years later he enhanced the international standing of his dynasty, as well as helping to secure the future of the Habsburgs, by marrying Joanna (later known as Joanna the Mad), daughter of Ferdinand and Isabella of Spain. The late 1490s saw the end of an unpopular regency, hopes for the calming of international tensions and the possibility for Flanders once again to be a community that worked for peace and unity, under a count who supported Flemish ambitions and hoped for internal peace.

The competition of 1498 looked to great events of the past and set out to restore peace and loving brotherhood both in and beyond Flanders. The competition was to begin in May 1498 and the letters of invitation were sent out in January, allowing ample time for guilds to plan spectacular entrances into Ghent by land and water. The invitations were addressed to 'all emperors, kings, lords, constable and princes, *jures*, deans and brothers and other honourable persons and companions of the great and special guilds of the noble and honourable game of the crossbow, in all good towns and free or walled communes where they are accustomed to use the said high crossbow' in sworn associations. The guild-brothers whom Ghent hoped to attract were described as 'very noble and gentle guilds, special companions in peace, playing the very joyous and very honourable game, in friendship and communities of brotherhood'. The invitation also emphasised the honour of 'the noble game of the crossbow (which) is above and before all other games in morality and nobility' for all suitable and honourable persons, and that 'this honesty and highly renowned (game)' will 'stop all debates' as the competition will be held in 'honour and friendship'. The ideals of community and peace are expressed time and again in this relatively long invitation, making clear the guild's hopes to strengthen regional bonds and demonstrate honour through their great event.

As well as friendship, claims of divine and princely support are important factors in ensuring that the competition will be honourable and spectacular. The guild-brothers make clear that their competition will please 'God in Paradise, His Blessed Mother, and further our gentle patron my Lord Saint George and all the saints and angels in Heaven'. Further, the event had 'the consent and grant of our very honourable lord and natural prince my Lord of Austria Duke of Burgundy'. The honour of the duke – who was to attend – and the competition are again linked and share the same values of friendship and honour. Rural guilds were excluded, as they had been in Oudenaarde, making clear that the larger towns looked down on rustic guilds. The Ghent guild strove to attract as wide a geographical audience as possible, from honourable towns, with more prizes than previous events and more elaborate invitations, offering even more prizes than in 1440.[50] The guild in 1498, just as it had done in 1440, tried to draw

---

[50] UBG, Hs G 6112, *Dit es den bouc van … Pieter Polet*.

in as large an audience as possible and to make its shoot a truly great peace-keeping exercise. The invitation of 1498 returned to the peaceful and elaborate language of earlier invitations emphasising the continuity that guilds wished to project, as well as the centrality of community within competitions and the honour of taking part in the events.

Entrances and Prizes as Statements of Identity

The letters of invitation make clear the value that the hosting guild placed on honour and friendship. Competing guilds and the civic authorities that supported them could express their civic honour and guild identity in their entrances into shooting competitions, while prizes awarded for best shot and for other events again reminded all guilds of the values of community. Guild entrances drew on many influences and must be considered in the context of other forms of semiotic communication utilised across the Low Countries. In the jousts of the Epinette, competitors were welcomed at specified gates; they made great entrances with musicians, banners and even *tableaux vivants*. Individual riders then jousted in a specific order corresponding to rank. Van den Neste has emphasised that the jousters entering the towns projected an image of a rich and flourishing city. Princely entrances to cities were even more spectacular, funded by civic authorities and demonstrating the glory of the prince and the power of the town. Entrances can thus be understood as negotiations between court and city, with both being able to express their status and power.[51] The use of civic space was part of these events, with messages being transmitted between urban and aristocratic groups, but the messages presented to the urban community as a whole were just as important. Shooting competitions set aside a day, or days, for entrances, allowing each guild the opportunity to express its civic pride and individual identity. Together, the guild entrances promoted the unity and brotherhood of the events as well as the individual prestige of the town that each guild represented.

From at least 1331 a day was set aside and dedicated to entrances to the Ghent shoot.[52] Later, at least two if not three days were needed for entrances, with land entry by Flemish teams, then land entry by non-Flemish teams and, for some competitions, a third day for entrances by water. That 'Flemish' and 'non-Flemish' teams entered separately and won separate prizes emphasises that guilds and their towns were aware of their county and shared an ideal of

---

[51] Van den Neste, *Tournois, joutes et pas d'armes*, 89–90; S. Nadot, *le Spectacle de joutes, sport et courtoisie à la fin du moyen âge* (Rennes: Presses Universitaires de Rennes, 2012), 198–214; Brown and Small, *Court and Civic Society*, 165–7; Murphy, 'Between Court and Town: Ceremonial Entries in the Chroniques of Jean Molinet', 155–61; Van Bruaene, 'The Habsburg Theatre State; Court, City and the Performance of Identity', 131–40; eadem, 'A Breakdown of Civic Community?', 276–8.

[52] Vuylsteke *Gentsche Stads – En Baljuwsrekeningen, 1280–1336*, vol. 2, 765–6.

regional unity. Rewards for splendour and honourable entrances began very early in the evolution of shooting competitions. No specific prizes are noted for the 1331 event but they had become a feature of competitions two decades later.

In 1350 in Tournai, Bruges won the prize for best entrance, being described as *lucratus* by Giles le Muisit is his account of the competition. Le Muisit's account is relatively short, but that he mentions the event at all in a narrative that is preoccupied with great events of state is in itself significant in demonstrating the growing prestige of shooting competitions. How Le Muisit, who was blind by 1350, obtained his information is not recorded; presumably another canon of the cathedral described the event to him, but in any case the ideal of guilds being luxuriously displayed to demonstrate urban identity is important. From then on, it seems that prizes for best entrance became a standard part of shooting competitions, with prizes being given for specular and for fine displays as well as for shooting prowess. In Mons in 1387, a large silver bowl was given to the 'most noble and elegant company'. The importance of winning prestige through elaborate entries is again shown at the Tournai shoot of 1394, where again Bruges won the prize for best entry and the crossbowmen of Paris were rewarded for having travelled the greatest distance.[53] The guild entrances to competitions were not simply extravagant, but cultural statements. The clothing worn during competitions, like other medieval clothing, was part of the show, linking civic products to civic identity. The ability of such entrances to display and even augment honour is best shown by an analysis of well-documented entrances into one great competition, that of Ghent in 1498.

Although fragmentary notes on the form of entrances made to this and other competitions survive in numerous medieval sources, the most detailed and cohesive account of entrances comes from an early sixteenth-century printed chronicle. The *Excellent Chronicle* is part of a tradition of Flemish chronicle writings and is a massive work. Various manuscript traditions exist, covering Flemish history from a semi-mythical past to the sixteenth century. The version used here is that printed by Vosterman in Antwerp in 1531.[54] The chronicle covers the shoot in incredible detail and it is likely that the description draws on an account written in or close to 1498, but I have been unable to trace a manuscript version of the account reproduced by Vosterman. The crossbow competition of 1498 fills almost thirteen folios and includes an elaborate poem describing the entrances, as well

---

[53] le Muisit, *Chronique et Annales*, 272–3; Deville, 'Notice Historique sur les milices', 169–285; Chotin, *Histoire de Tournai et du Tournisses*, vol. 1, 350–2.

[54] *Dits die excellente cronike van Vlaanderen*; for the longer tradition see J. Oosterman, 'De Excellente cronike van Vlaenderen en Anthonis de Roovere', *Tijdschrift voor Nederlandse taal – en letterkunde* 11 (2002) 22–37; J. Dumolyn and E. Lecuppre-Desjardin, 'Propagande et sensibilité: la fibre émotionelle au cœur des luttes politiques et sociales dans les villes des anciens Pays-Bas bourguignons. L'exemple de la révolte brugeoise de 1436–1438', in E. Lecuppre-Desjardin and A.-L. Van Bruaene (eds), *Emotions in the Heart of the City (14th–16th Century). Les émotions au cœur de la ville (XIVe–XVIe siècle)* (Turnhout: Brepols, 2005), 44–6.

as the woodcut described in chapter four. The detailed printed account presents a perfect opportunity to analyse the guilds' representation of civic values and its emphasis on community. The chronicle may well exaggerate and is certainly not taken here as an absolutely accurate account; rather, the description printed by Vosterman shows how the entrances into Ghent in 1498 were remembered and what details seemed worth including a generation after the event, and provides insight into how contemporaries watched and understood the events.[55]

In recording the entrances, the chronicle described each town in the order in which it entered Ghent, those that entered by land being described in verse and a shorter, prose note being added on those that entered by water. In all of the descriptions cloth was the most striking element in the shooters' entrances, indicating the power of cloth to communicate and to be remembered. Much of this cloth was linked to civic traditions; for instance, the Ypres guild wore 'fine red cloth'. This is very likely to have been Ypres Scarlet, one of Ypres's signature products.[56] The Ypres crossbowmen in scarlet can be understood as a statement of the town's continuing hopes for wealth and the ability to produce luxurious and desirable products, even in an era of economic decline. The guild had given red cloth to the Ghent messenger of 1440, and again this was very likely to have been Ypres Scarlet, showing the ability of cloth to communicate wealth as well as identity and, here, civic pride.[57]

Cloth was used, and commented upon, in all of the entrances made in 1498. The Lille men entered in 'precious cloth covered in regal lilies' and the guild-brothers of Dendermonde came in 'properly', each carrying an arrow and 'clothed in fine attire'. Oostende's clothing was 'fine and fair'. The men of Hulst's clothing had been made using 'dye of Hulst' and had 'lettering'. Each guild entered in a carefully considered style and was recorded by our anonymous poet in deliberate and laudatory language. The dominance of cloth in the descriptions is perhaps not surprising, given the dominance of cloth in Flemish industry, but each guild used its materials to impart a message to the gathered audiences about its civic identity and about the honour of its guild. Remembering the entrances made into Ghent in poetry, rather than prose, is unusual and significant in itself, adding a layer of prestige to the event long after it had finished.

---

[55] All of the following on the 1498 entrance is based on the description in *Dits de Excellente Chronijke van Vlaanderen* ff. 289–291v.

[56] Boussemaere, 'De Ieperse lakenproductie', 131–61; S. Abraham-Thisse, 'Kostel Ypersch, gemeyn Ypersch: les draps d'Ypres en Europe du Nord et de l'Est (XIII–XIVe siècles)', and P. Chorley, 'The Ypres Cloth Industry 1200–1350: the Pattern of Change in Output and Demand', in M. Dewilde, A. Ervynck and A. Wielemans (eds), *Ypres and the Medieval Cloth Industry in Flanders: Archaeological and Historical Contributions* (Zellik: Instituut voor het archeologisch patrimonium, 1998), 111–24, 125–38.

[57] S. Abraham-Thisse, 'la Valeur des draps au moyen âge. De l'economique au symbolique', in M. Boone and M. Howell (eds), *In but not of the Market; Movable Goods in the Late Medieval and Early Modern Economy* (Brussel: Koninklijke Vlaamse academie van België voor wetenschappen en kunsten, 2007),17–19.

Cloth was important, but several towns used other, often less subtle, means of communication. The Brabant town of 's-Hertogenbosch (the name means ducal forest) staged a notable event: its entrance included wagons with cloth and fine silver objects, as well as what might be *tableaux vivants* or possibly wooden figures. A wagon is described as having a lion in each corner, a maiden in white damask and a wild-man. It is likely that the lions are references to the lions of Flanders and Brabant, and the wild-man and maiden may have been part of a story, but the poem is not clear as to what, precisely, they were doing. The most memorable part of 's-Hertogenbosch's entrance, however, was a silver forest, a pun on its name and a way of making sure that its entrance would be striking and would be clearly linked to the town and so demonstrate civic honour through a display of wealth.

Water entrances could be just as elaborate. Although fewer guilds entered by water, those that did so made the most of the opportunity to travel down the Scheldt toward a large crowd. Diest's water entrance featured a tree, possible a reference to the guilds' gardens. The crossbowmen of Menin were judged to have made the finest water entrance, their entrance including a ship covered in leaves – possibly another reference to gardens and to nature. More elaborate was another part of their entrance – a target set up on one of the barges, perhaps a representation of the competition itself, or at least a representation of the guild doing what it did best: competing in community and winning honour.

Many guilds made use of symbols of one form or another to make clear to all observers which town was being represented. At least one town seems to have favoured splendour over symbolism. The Antwerp entrance was incredibly large and expensive, but no coherent message can be discerned from the account reproduced by Vosterman. The entrance included 200 men dressed half as rustics, and 900 others half dressed in arms. This is very likely to refer to men dressed half in costume and half not in costume. The Antwerp entrance also featured fifty carts, 230 other figures, pipers, a local nobleman and many other individuals. There seem to have been two plays or *tableaux vivants*, a 'spectre' of good and evil and an 'establishment' of Julius, presumably a Roman play. The Antwerp entrance even featured an elephant, very likely to have been the sort of wooden one used in procession. The elephant was *bedriven*, which implies pulled, although the text is no clearer on the Antwerp elephant than on the 's-Hertogenbosch lions. It is just possible that it was a living elephant, as a local history of Antwerp describes the arrival of a live elephant in the town in August 1480.[58] As well as the entrance described in verse, the chronicle adds a prose description of 'another fine thing for Antwerp', recounting that the next day all members attended mass and afterwards gave the cloth that had covered their wagons to the poor of Ghent. The Antwerp spectacle was the largest of the Ghent entrances, but it did not win first prize.

---

[58] J. Wegg, *Antwerp, 1477–1559, from the Battle of Nancy to the Treaty of Cateau Cambrésis* (London, Methuen & Co, 1916), 77–8.

The guild from outside Flanders that was seen as the best was Brussels. Its entrance seems, from Vosterman's account, to have been less elaborate, although as the chronicle was printed in Antwerp this may be local bias and evidence of continuing local pride. The Brussels entrance included a wagon with jesters, and a further fifty wagons with pipers and flowers, and a wagon with towers, perhaps a representation of the town walls or an allegorical castle. The guild-brothers identified themselves by carrying the banners of Saint Michael, patron saint of Brussels, and of Saint George, patron saint of their guild. The entrances made to the 1498 competition were elaborate: each guild is described in some detail and each clearly made an impression on the audience. Some entrances were larger than others, and described in more depth than others, but the unity of the event is emphasised by the account in the *Excellent Chronicle*, where all guilds are described in the order in which they entered Ghent.

Entrances were made with the assistance of civic funds and, as we have seen, some towns invested more heavily than others in elaborate entrances. Oudenaarde seems to have prided itself on a tradition of great entrances and was regularly recorded as the winner of best entrance and best play. In Ghent in 1498 it did not win best entrance. Bruges, with Philip the Fair as part of its entrance, won the prize. The Oudenaarde entrance seems to have been spectacular, featuring 130 wagons covered in cloth, trumpeters, four 'fair maidens', an elaborately dressed guild king and a fine procession of horses. It may be that it *would* have won, had Philip not been with Bruges, with the ducal presence adding to Bruges's display.

Oudenaarde seems also to have lost out to a princely participant in an earlier event. In 1455 in Tournai, the Lille guild-brothers won the prize for best entrance and were accompanied by Anthony the Great Bastard of Burgundy. It is possible that Lille won *because* of Anthony's presence. In an account of the shoot written in Tournai, the anonymous author describes the entrances made by the various guilds, noting that 'the finest of which was Lille ... The company from Oudenaarde were also very fine, but in honour of the Bastard of Burgundy they were happy with second place', which seems to imply that without Anthony's presence, Lille would not have won. Oudenaarde won a silver ewer for its entrance, while Lille won two.[59] Oudenaarde kept up this tradition of luxurious entrances. It may be that because Oudenaarde remained a textile centre and moved into luxury products, particularly tapestries, it found its guild decked out in civic cloth to be a useful vehicle for showing off both its cloth and its status. For the Ghent competition in 1440 the Oudenaarde aldermen gave their crossbow guild the incredible sum of £751 18s to send its men to the competition.[60] The aldermen had spent large sums investing in honour; they wanted to make sure the guild did well and that they would receive an honourable return on their large investment.

---

[59] Brown and Small, *Court and Civic*, 221.
[60] OSAOA, 1436–1448, on microfilm 686, f. 202v; to put this huge figure in perspective, the town income that year was £10,209 17s 7d, and total expenditure was £12,476 19s 7d.

Two town messengers were sent on the same day to ascertain that the guild had won the prize for best entry – which it did.

Just as princely entrances can be considered as powerful tools for communicating identities and politics,[61] the shoots must be interpreted as opportunities for towns to communicate their standing, splendour and status. As Van Bruaene has shown in analysing the competitions staged by chambers of rhetoric, the dense urbanisation of the Low Countries allowed for an exchange of ideas that can be viewed as an economy of symbolic exchange.[62] In the same way, archery and crossbow competitions allowed towns to make statements about their identity to larger audiences. Civic governors were concerned not just for the political good of their town, but to represent its honour and identity on a large scale. In addition to the entrances, shooting competitions offered further opportunities for performance, with drama quickly becoming part of archery and crossbow events. It is likely that the drama in shooting competitions encouraged the rise of the chambers of rhetoric and their own competitions.[63] By encouraging drama and display in their competitions, the shooting guilds made their shoots more spectacular, just as the civic authorities boosted the prestige and magnificence of processions by encouraging the introduction of plays.[64] Drama was part of all civic rituals, and part of urban symbolic communication and festive traditions in the Low Countries, highlighting the vibrancy of urban culture, with its own system of values.[65]

In 1408 the crossbow competition in Oudenaarde rewarded not only entrances but also the best two plays. A prize was given for the best French play and another for the best Flemish play, performed 'without villainy'.[66] Two prizes, like the bilingual invitation, make clear that the guild and its civic sponsors were trying to bring in as large an audience as possible and to celebrate both French- and Flemish-speaking cultures in one event, in one community. In a shoot including 15–20 guilds in Courtrai in 1422, the crossbowmen of Oudenaarde won a prize for best play, continuing the tradition observed above for finery and for spectacle. Not all guilds participated in drama competitions, despite the prizes and encouragement, and some focused on shooting or on display. In 1440 Ghent gave separate prizes for the best plays in French and Flemish, and a prize for the best jester. Yet, among the fifty-six crossbow teams in attendance, only three French-

---

[61] Van Bruaene, 'The Habsburg Theatre State, Court, City and the Rhetoric of Identity in the Early Modern Low Countries', 131–40.
[62] Van Bruaene, 'A Wonderfull tryumfe', 377–7.
[63] Van Bruaene, *Om Beters Wille*, 27–50.
[64] B. A. M. Ramakers, *Spelen en figuren, toneelkunst en processiecultuur in Oudenaarde tussen Middeleeuwen en Moderne tijd* (Amsterdam: Amsterdam University Press, 1996), 1–4, 5–22, 75–83.
[65] Van Bruaene, 'A Wonderfull tryumfe', 378–9; H. Pleij, *Het gilde van de Blauwe Schuit. Literatuur, volksfeest en burgermoraal in de late middeleeuwen* (Amsterdam: Meulenhoff, 1979).
[66] Cauwenberghe, 'Notice historique sur les confréries de Saint Georges', 279–91.

speaking towns (Arras, Tournai and Béthune) and four Flemish-speaking ones (Courtrai, Wervick, Oudenaarde and Geraardsbergen) are recorded as bringing a play with them. Oudenaarde won the prize in Ghent in 1440, as it did at an archery contest in Berchem in 1441, perhaps drawing on the plays that formed an important part of its Corpus Christi procession.[67] Fifteenth-century shoots continue to award prizes for the best individual and best team shot, but they also rewarded an increasing number of other events, bringing more spectacle to the competitions and more opportunities to win honour. Not all guilds took part in all events. Larger towns may have tried compete in all categories, while smaller towns focused on just one category.

What the plays consisted of in Flanders is poorly recorded. It does not seem that themes were specified, beyond regulations to avoid villainy, blasphemy and slander. In Tournai in 1455 plays were encouraged on the theme 'of the great, miraculous and victorious deeds of the King of France' in the reconquest of Normandy.[68] No comparable instructions survive from Flanders, although a few details can be gleaned from archival evidence. In 1462, for a large crossbow competition in Brussels, the crossbowmen of Aalst constructed a large wooden dragon and pulled it across Flanders and Brabant, suggesting a Saint George play. As noted above, drama was part of many entrances to the Ghent 1498 competition as recorded by Vosterman.[69] Rather than plays having a unifying theme, it seems that during Flemish shooting competitions guilds were given great freedom to create their own sense of honour and identity.

Honour and reputation could be won in different ways, and they could also be recognised and rewarded in different ways. The variety of prizes and gifts given at shooting competitions is in itself evidence of the centrality of civic status and the promotion of urban identity and community. The most common prizes were wine or tableware, although more elaborate prizes could be won too, like silver monkeys or unicorns. The dominance of prizes related to community and dining is particularly striking when compared to the prizes awarded to urban jousters. Prizes for urban jousts were often aristocratic and individual in nature, and included hunting animals or armour, emphasising the individual skill and the individuality of the jousts, in contrast to the communal nature of shooting guilds.[70] Prizes, like the wine and cloth given to guilds each year, were not just expensive, they were statements of civic identity and of the prestige of the guilds. Expensive silver objects could have been melted down or pawned, but inventories from Ghent, Bruges and Oudenaarde show large quantities of

---

[67] Ramakers, *Spelen en figuren*, 1–4, 5–22, 75–83, 43–93; de Rantere, *Geschiedenis van Oudenaarde*, vol. 2, 29, 71; Ouvry, 'Officieel ceremonieel te Oudenaarde, 1450–1600', 25–64; E. Vanderstraeten, *Recherches sur les communautés religieuses et les institutions de bienfaisance a Audenarde*, 2vols (Audenarde: Bevernaege, 1858–1860) vol. 1, 21–35.
[68] Brown and Small, *Court and Civic Society*, 222–3.
[69] ASAOA, 156, Rekeningen van de gezworenen van het Sint Joris gild, 1461–2, f. 9–9v; *Dits de Excellente Chronijke van Vlaanderen*, f. 290v.
[70] Van den Neste, *Tournois, joutes, pas d'armes*, 92–3.

silverware being kept in guild halls or chapels in the fifteenth and even the early sixteenth centuries.[71] The splendid objects were lasting reminders of the glory of the competitions, the reputation of the host and the honour of the winners.

Certain host towns gave visiting guilds wine for simply attending, just as they gave wine to all important visitors. As Uytven, Damen and Boone have all shown, the amount of wine given to different visitors by civic governors indicates the rank of the visitors and the value that the governors placed on building a relationship with them.[72] Like gifts given to important civic visitors, the wine given to all the guilds who attended a shoot emphasised the value of taking part and that honour could be obtained, and community enhanced, simply by being together. Further, wine given to all emphasised that all guilds were welcome even if they did not win a prize. In 1331 the aldermen of Ghent gave all those who came to shoot high-quality red wine.[73] Like the wine given to noble visitors, it is likely that the wine given to shooting guilds was in municipal jugs, bearing the town's crest, in this way making a statement of the town's generosity, even largesse, to its visitors. At the early fourteenth-century shoots wine was given to all, but over time different amounts were given to those visitors who seen as more honourable or more prestigious. At a competition in Ypres in 1422 guilds from both large and small towns attended. Several guilds from larger towns, including those of Lille, received four kannes of wine; most guilds received three kannes, but one, the archers of the small town of Croy, received just two kannes.[74] The competitions built community and emphasised harmony, but like the guilds feasts analysed above, they were not about equality and honour remained exclusive and hierarchical in regional competitions.

Wine continued to be liberally distributed at shooting competitions, for attending as well as for winning. In addition, lasting drinking vessels were available for skilled shooters and impressive displays. In Ghent in 1440 prizes were given for the best land entry from within Flanders (won by Oudenaarde), best land entry from beyond Flanders (won by Brussels) and best water entry (won by Mechelen). Each guild won two silver pots weighing 7 marcs. Amiens won a jug for travelling the greatest distance, again a drinking vessel, emphasising community for the entire guild. For the shooting there were seven prizes for best individual and best team shot. The best team shooters, Bergen op Zoom, won five silver cans weighing 36 marcs. In addition, anyone who hit the centre of the target would win a silver rose, worth 10s. With the exception of the rose, all prizes were for use at table in one form or another, and all prizes were

---

[71] SAG, SJ, NGR, 7; Gilliodts-Van Severen, *Inventaire des archives de la ville de Bruges*, vol. 4, 542–9; OSAOA, gilden 507/II/2B.

[72] Van Uytven, 'Showing off One's Rank', 20–4; Boone, 'Dons et pots-de-vin', 471–9; Damen, 'Giving by Pouring; The Functions of Gifts of Wine', 83–100.

[73] Vuylsteke *Gentsche stads en balijuwsrekeningen, 1280–1336*, vol. 2, 765–6.

[74] AGR, microfilm 1772/2, ff. 39v–41v.

made of silver.[75] The value of these objects went far deeper than their cost: for their winners, the silver pots would be evidence to a larger home audience of their glory and prestige in winning prizes, as they would be placed in a semi-public location, often the guild chapel, and emphasise the skill and prestige of the guild.

Regulations make clear that prizes should have been placed in a shared space, either the guild hall or the guild chapel. Most guilds also made clear that their prizes would be held in common; even the prize for best shooter was a guild honour, not an individual award for the shooter to take home.[76] Objects won as prizes may even have been used in the guilds' communal events. Certainly, most guilds owned an impressive quantity of cups, bowls and, especially, very large pots and jugs, and it is possible these were used in guild meals. There is no evidence for how such objects were used, but their potential to be used at feasts, with their emphasis on community, is important in understanding guild values. Even if the objects were not used, their potential for use and for building community through commensality emphasises the brotherhood of the guilds.

Prizes emphasised the honour of the community that had won, just as they spread the renown and largesse of the host. All of the prizes available at the 1408 competition in Oudenaarde were engraved with 'the arms of my lord Saint Georges', 'of our aforesaid very redoubtable lord and prince' and 'of this said town of Oudenaarde'. In Tournai in 1455 all prizes 'bore the arms of Saint George, of the king and of the city'.[77] The same arrangement of prizes honouring saint (and, by connection, guild), lord and town was seen in the prizes at the crossbow competitions in Dendermonde in 1450, Mechelen in 1458, Oudenaarde in 1462 and both the Ghent shoots of 1440 and 1498.[78] Inventories such as those mentioned above record not just the weight and value of an object but where it was won. Such objects in prestigious guild locations would remind the winning guild of the honour of the host, the prizes serving as physical reminders of the splendour and honour of competitions for generations to come.

While wine and/or tableware were the most common form of prizes, other objects also appear and could serve as reminders of the host's honour and the winning guild's success. The Oudenaarde shoot of 1408 is the first to record impractical objects – that is to say, objects that could not be used for a dinner or similar event – being offered as prizes. The team that made the best entry won a silver unicorn, those who had travelled the furthest won a silver crown,

---

[75] UBG, Hs G 6112, *Dit es den bouc van ... Pieter Polet*, f. 8–8v.
[76] DAM, Arbalestiers de Douay, 24II232.
[77] Brown and Small, *Court and Civic Society*, 220.
[78] J. Dauwe, *De Kruisboogschutters van St.-Joris te Lebbeke (1377–1796)* (Gent: Koninklijke bond der Oostvlaamse volkskundigen, 1983), 8–12; J. Vannerus, 'Trois documents relatifs aux concours de tir à l'arbalète, organisés à Malines en 1458 et en 1495', *BCRH* 97 (1933), 203–54; Vanhoutryve, *De Brugse Kruisbooggilde*, 30–32; SAB, 385, Sint Jorisgilde, Rekeningen 1445–1480, f. 171; UBG, Hs G 6112, *Dit es den bouc van ... Pieter Polet* ff. 7, 41v–42.

the best play won a silver monkey and the best lights won jewels. Such objects would be unusual in a guild hall or chapel. In 1408 the Bruges crossbowmen won the silver unicorn for best entrance into Oudenaarde, and in the 1470s it was still the only unicorn in their collection.[79] The unicorn was kept, and noted as being from Oudenaarde, preserving the memory of Bruges's win and Oudenaarde's largesse and, thus, the honour of both. Silver animals also represented a conscious choice of symbolism, with greater care being taken to choose appropriate prizes. Unicorns indicated wealth and status and were mythical creatures representing honour and standing. Oudenaarde's prizes were the earliest to be recorded, but the town were certainly not the only one to award impractical prizes. A Bruges inventory written before 1435 contains not just the unicorn, but also a dragon, won at Sluis, 'a Saint George', a pair of trumpets, an engraved *papegay*, '2 solid lilies', two engraved crowns and an impressive collection of cups, plates and crosses.[80]

Mythical creatures, especially unicorns, embodied chivalric symbolism and status. The meaning of the monkey in Oudenaarde is less clear, the 1408 prize being the only instance of such a creature. Monkeys had traditionally been seen as evil creatures, but by the late fourteenth century were also seen as playful, mimicking animals.[81] Oudenaarde rewarded the best play with a monkey, showing a conscious choice to reward an enjoyable play with a playful prize. Other guilds were less subtle. In Tournai in 1455 the prize for the second best play praising the glory of the French king and the Dauphin was a silver dolphin.[82] In giving elaborate prizes and engraving them with civic emblems the host town made a conscious choice to invest in the guilds and invest in their communication networks as a representation of their status. Silver prizes would be carried far beyond the towns and, potentially at least, seen by large audiences. Whatever form they took, elaborate silver animals or objects emphasised the prestige of the winning guild and would be noticeable in the guild hall, enhancing the memory of both the host and the event.

Archery and crossbow guilds held annual shoots in their own towns from at least the 1330s. In the same years, small regional competitions began to be staged between guilds. This natural competitive element allowed for the same sorts of bonds to be made between guild-brothers in different towns as we observed being formed between guild-brothers in chapter three. No exact foundation date can be ascribed to the competitions, but by the mid-fourteenth century they were well-established events, allowing guilds to come together in friendly

---

[79] Gilliodts-Van Severen, *Inventaire des archives de la Ville de Bruges*, vol. 4, 542–9.
[80] SAB, 385, Sint Jorisgilde, register met ledenlijst enz. 1321–1531, ff. 76–82.
[81] H. W. Janson, *Apes and Ape-Lore in the Middle Ages* (London: Warburg Institute, University of London, 1952), 29–54; W. B. Clark, *A Medieval Book of Beasts* (Woodbridge: Boydell, 2006), 7–8, 42–4. I am grateful to Dr Debra Higgs-Strickland for these references.
[82] Brown and Small, *Court and Civic Society*, 222–3.

communities for the honour of their town. Letters of invitation emphasised the honour of the events and of the guilds and their lords, and the events themselves became a celebration of urban identity in the guilds' entrances and in opportunities for display and honour. Towns used competitions as they used ducal entrances, processions and other events, to pull their own civic population together and celebrate their standing, and to advertise their prestige and power, through their guilds, to a regional audience. Prizes of wine and jugs emphasised the power of community, as well as the role of community in creating memorable experiences to augment the honour of both host and guests. The competitions were important opportunities to practise shooting and to compare skills with other towns, but they were far more than simple sport. In competing together, emphasising honour and celebrating civic splendour, competitions brought together hundreds of shooters, representing numerous towns, to celebrate honour and to enhance communities. Through their repetition of friendship and honour the competitions could also help to restore peace after war and to strengthen regional networks, as the next chapter will explore. Although not all who were invited participated in the competitions, the desire on the part of the organisers to reach out and create community is important.

6

Archery and Crossbow Guilds and their Competitions in Regional Networks and as Tools of Social Peace

For who does not know that the provinces of these Netherlands have always derived the greatest advantage from being united with each other? Has this union not been the origin of the old custom they have always observed, of assembling towns and provinces for the meeting of the archers and crossbowmen and bearers of other old-fashioned arms, which they call *landjuweel*? Why else have the towns and provinces always met for public repast and plays by order of the authorities unless it were to demonstrate the great unity of these provinces, as Greece showed her unity in the meetings of the Olympic Games?[1]

Writing in 1574, and looking back on the growth of unity in the Low Countries, the significance of archery and crossbow guilds, and their *landjuwellen* – their great competitions – was clear to the governor of Veere in Zeeland. Just as the Olympic Games had built unity between the city states of ancient Greece, so shooting competitions shared values and, in competing together in large shoots, the guilds demonstrated and strengthened their inter-urban networks. Networks were vital to the Low Countries; the towns of Flanders were powerful in their own right, but gained from regional networks and from the ideals of social peace.

Archery and crossbow competitions benefited from established networks, especially those of trade and interactions along rivers, but they also served to strengthen regional communities. Small networks grew out from large towns into their hinterlands, bringing economic and political benefit, but also the possibility of tensions. In looking at charters granted to shooting guilds in smaller towns and analysing the guilds' festive interactions, it becomes clear that shooting guilds were part of small networks, used by the civic powers to

---

[1] E. H. Kossmann and A. F. Mellink (eds), *Texts Concerning the Revolt of the Netherlands* (Cambridge: Cambridge University Press, 1974), 123.

demonstrate authority and to emphasise community with smaller neighbours. In considering regional networks, many recent works have shown not just the high level of urbanisation in Flanders, but also the strength of urban networks and desires for the 'Common Good'.[2] The shooting competitions present an exciting lens through which to analyse such networks in action. The location of and attendance at competitions reveal the significance of rivers, as well as the efforts that civic governors went to in order to build and maintain politically and economically powerful links through festive bonds.

Unity was an ideal of civic networks and regional cooperation, but an ideal that did not always represent the situation in Flanders. The county saw numerous wars and rebellions across the fourteenth and fifteenth centuries and, as we have seen, shooting guilds served in many of these conflicts. Yet competitions were not about military training; rather, they were used to rebuild bonds, as an analysis of the chronological pattern of events will demonstrate. For all their ideals of harmony and unity, disputes did arise within shooting guilds and within shooting competitions. However, examples of disunity are extremely rare and do not negate the ideals of peace. By analysing one dispute within Flanders, and one that involved a Brabant guild in Flanders, the overwhelmingly peaceful nature of competitions will be demonstrated.

Guilds' competitions were spectacular events, as the previous chapter has made clear, and it should come as no surprise that these events have been studied before. Numerous antiquarian studies have been produced looking at one or more such events. Some, like Chotin's account of the Tournai shoots, have been heavily drawn on here because the original sources were lost during the twentieth century.[3] Many other studies, in particular Van Duyse's account of Ghent and Cauwenberghe's of Oudenaarde are excellent, but they consider just one guild and are connected to the splendour of the host town.[4] Other writers have looked at one or more competition(s) as part of a narrative of the growth and prestige of a single town and these, as such, are an important part of local history.[5] More recent studies have attempted to list all events that a town's guilds hosted or attended.[6] However, the networks within competitions have not been examined

---

[2] Van Bruaene, 'The Habsburg Theatre State', 131–51; Marnet, 'Chambers of Rhetoric and the Transmission of Religious Ideas', 274–96; Lowagie, 'Stedekijke communicatie in de Late Middeleeuwen', 273–95; 'Introduction', to Lecuppre-Desjardin and Van Bruaene, *De Bono Communi*, 1–9; Haemers, *Common Good*, 2–9.

[3] Chotin, *Histoire de Tournai et du Tournésis*, v. 1, 349–58.

[4] Van Duyse, 'Het groot schietspel en de Rederijkersspelen te Gent in Mei tot Juli 1498', 273–314; Cauwenberghe, 'Notice historique sur les confréries de Saint Georges'.

[5] Matthieu, *Histoire de la ville d'Enghien*, vol. 2, 754–8; idem, 'Concours d'arc à la main à Braine-le-Château en 1433', *Annales de la société archéologique de l'arrondissement de Nivelles*, 3 (1892); Willame, *Notes sur les serments Nivellois*; Vannerus, 'Trois documents relatifs aux concours de tir' à l'arbalète', 203–54; Stein, *Archers d'autrefois*, 249–61.

[6] Brown and Small, *Court and Civic Society*, 219–25; Arnade, *Realms of Ritual*, 84–94; D. Coigneau, '1 Februari 1404. De Mechelse voetboogschutters schrijven een wedstrijd

in depth using the wealth of available archival sources, although Stein touched on competitions in Tournai as part of an excellent study of cultural networks in the Low Countries.[7] Here, there will be greater focus on using the numerous shooting competitions, their locations, their participants and their dating to start to trace urban networks in action and the efforts of civic authorities to maintain or restore regional harmony. So numerous are references to competitions in civic accounts that the present study cannot hope to be complete. Rather, by selecting examples from across the region, from large and small towns, competitions will be set in the context of regional networks and wider civic hopes for peace. Such treatment may seem naïve, especially given the numerous wars and rebellions that Flanders witnessed over the fourteenth and fifteenth centuries, but, as will be shown, the ideal of peace was central to shooting competitions, to the guilds and the towns that funded them.

Towns, Hinterlands and Smaller Networks

As we have seen, within their own towns archery and crossbow guilds worked to build community through feasts, devotion and annual shooting matches. It was therefore natural that guilds should start to compete with each other, holding feasts and competitions, to build small and regional networks and compete for honour. Lille's relationship with the towns of its hinterland, and its changing relationship with larger towns further afield, are evidence of such networks in action. Of course, the shooting guilds were just one part of the commercial and festive networks that spread out from the town. The shooting guilds' interactions, funded by Lille's civic officials, allow for an appreciation of the civic bonds between the town and its hinterland, as well as some insight into Lille's reintegration into Flanders.

Lille, like the rest of Walloon Flanders, had been removed from the county in 1305, and returned in 1369. The town was a centre of commerce and more luxurious textile production, producing a smaller quantity but higher quality of cloth than the more industrial towns of northern Flanders, and remained an important city in trade networks between France and the Low Countries. Under the dukes of Burgundy Lille grew in influence, and a *chambre des comptes* was established there by 1386, meaning that surrounding towns needed to build connections with Lille and were often required to send copies of their accounts

---

uit. Stedelijke toneelwedstrijden in de vijftiende en zestiende eeuw', in R. L. Erenstein (ed.), *Een theatergeschiedenis der Nederlanden. Tien eeuwen drama en theater in Nederland en Vlaanderen* (Amsterdam: Amsterdam University Press, 1996), 30–35; Schrijver et Dothee, *Les Concours de tir*; Stein, *Archers d'autrefois*, 71–7; Godar, *Histoire des archers*, 53–7, 61–8; Wauters, *Notice historique*, 7–9, 11–14; Baillien, 'De Tongerse schutterijen van de 14de tot de 16de eeuw', 16–23; Lemahieu, *De eerste Vlaamse schuttersgilden*, 4–6, 30–37; R. van de Heyde, *Vijf eeuwen vereningsleven te Leftinge Deel twee, de Schuttersgilden* (Middelkerke: Heemkring Graningate, 1985), 12–18.

[7] Stein, 'An Urban Network in the Medieval Low Countries', 51–4.

to the *chambre*. The dukes also spent time in Lille. John the Fearless fled there after the assassination of the duke of Orléans and Philip the Good built a palace in Lille which played host to events like the Feast of the Pheasant, giving Lille greater wealth as well as access to princely power.[8] Lille is a useful case study for the role of the guilds in civic relations, showing the influence of a larger town on charters and the interweaving of festive connections with economic and political ones.

Networks and the influence of a larger town over its hinterland are perhaps easiest to see in the granting of rights and charters. When civic or ducal powers granted charters to shooting guilds in smaller towns, the charters granted by the larger towns naturally served as a model. This is not surprising, as the same pattern has been observed in the granting of rights to craft guilds and even in the granting of town foundation charters.[9] Guilds either looked to Lille as an example, or the ducal and civic powers issuing the charters used the existing Lille models when enfranchising new guilds. In either case, the influence and prestige of Lille as a town and of its guilds as civic representatives is clear. The governor of Lille appears in many such charters; he was a ducally appointed official, ruling for a long time, usually for life, and often from one of the noble families that held great influence at court, such as the Lannoys. The governor had control not just over Lille itself but over much of its hinterland – indeed, over much of Walloon Flanders – yet he was based in Lille and this gave prestige as well as authority to the town.

The influence of both Lille and its governor are clear in a charter granted by John the Fearless to the crossbowmen of Croix in 1410. The Croix crossbowmen were granted the right to bear arms, to wear their own livery, to travel across Flanders and even immunity from prosecution for accidental deaths. The Croix charter is very similar to the rights granted to the Lille guild by John the Fearless just five years earlier. The men of Croix were dedicated to Saint Nicholas rather than Saint George, perhaps hoping in this way to show their own identity as separate from that of Lille, yet the influence of Lille remains clear. The charter was copied into the Lille *Registre aux Mandates*, a collection of rights and charters of civic interest, emphasising that Lille were aware of and took an interest in the guilds of nearby towns.

Lille's influence over Croix is clear from the form and location of the 1410 charter. The interaction, even control, of Lille went further still. Rather than having the Croix guild swear loyalty to a local official of its own, or indeed a local lord, the Croix crossbowmen were required to swear an oath in the presence of the governor of Lille, in his 'halle' in Lille.[10] Croix was bound to Lille economically, depending on the larger town for market access – a common relationship among

---

[8] Clauzel, *Lille*, 13–17; Trenard, *Histoire de Lille*, vol. 1, 219–34.
[9] Small 'Centre and periphery in late medieval France', 148–51; K. D. Lilley, *Urban Life in the Middle Ages, 1000–1450* (Houndmills: Palgrave, 2002), 44–55.
[10] AML, RM, 16973, f. 15.

the small towns of Flanders – meaning that the relationship between shooting guilds mirrored the relationship between the towns.[11] Lille worked politically and commercially to ensure its hegemony, in the same way as craft guilds were extending their monopoly over the town's hinterland. The archery and crossbow guilds were establishing their superiority over surrounding areas through display, oaths and, in the recording of names, control.

The influence of Lille over its hinterland, as revealed through shooting guild charters, is clear throughout the fifteenth century. The archery and crossbow guild-brothers of Wattignies, who, as we have seen, gained a charter from John the Fearless confirming their rights through the mediation of Rolland de la Hovarderie, were also required to swear oaths to the governor of Lille. Like the guild-brothers of Croix, those of Wattignies were required to come to Lille and to make a display – presumably demonstrate their ability – and have their names recorded by the Lille governor, as well as swear an oath of loyalty to him.[12] In 1440 the archers of Cysoing received a charter confirming their 1429 rights from Philip the Good. The charter was granted at the request of the Lady *Seneschaless*[13] of Cysoing, but the influence of Lille was emphasised. The archers of Cysoing were granted rights, in part for the defence of Lille, and were required to take their oaths in the presence of the governor of Lille.[14] Even as late as 1518 the influence of Lille is demonstrated and strengthened through shooting guild charters. The archers of Annappes, a village near Ascq, received a charter from Charles, King of Castile (soon to become Charles V, Holy Roman Emperor) granting the new guild the same 'rights and franchise as those in our town of Lille', again requiring the swearing an oath of loyalty to the Lille governor.[15] The charter is important in demonstrating that even a village with a population of some 500 individuals[16] could maintain a guild with the same rights and same values of those of Lille, and in demonstrating the lasting influence of Lille and its culture over the surrounding area.

There is no record of the smaller guilds asking Lille for these models or for such support. It is possible that they did not ask and, rather, that the Lille model was imposed upon them or, more likely, that due to their proximity such negotiations took place orally. Elsewhere, however, guilds did ask for help and advice from other towns in moments of potential crisis or when guidance was needed. In 1456 the archers of Nieuwpoort sent representatives to Bruges to find out the best way to organise and regulate a large shooting competition.[17]

---

[11] R. Vandenbussche et al., *Croix, la mémoire d'une ville* (Paris: Martinière, 2006), 5–25.
[12] ADN, B1600, ff. 25v–26.
[13] The feminine form of Seneschal, or sénéchal.
[14] AML, RM, 16973, 215, 231.
[15] AML, RM, 16978, 7. The names of the first 38 guild-brothers are also recorded.
[16] T. Leuridan, *Annappes (Notice historique sur), Monographies des villes et villages de France* (Paris: Res universis, 1989 (reproduction en fac-sim de 'Notice historique sur Annappes', 1881), 12–18.
[17] Godar, *Histoire des Archers*, 106–7.

A small town naturally looked to a larger one for a suitable model for shooting, even though, as we shall see, Bruges did not hold large events. Nieuwpoort, a small coastal city linked with English trade, wanted to stage large events like those of the greater towns and, rather, than ask the far closer towns of Veurne or Oostende, it looked to the great market centre of Bruges, showing the link between commercial and festive networks. It was not, however, simply the case that small towns looked to larger ones for advice. In 1523 a Bruges guild-brother, Arnould Neyson, broke guild rules and would not obey the officials; the crossbowmen asked their guild-brothers in Mechelen how they should handle the situation.[18] When guilds needed help or wanted advice, they looked to each other for assistance, implying that they saw other guilds in other towns as part of a shared community, not as rivals.

The relationships between Lille and its environs may have been, like those of Bruges, based on requests for help and advice, although there was also the potential for conflict. In extending the control of Lille and requiring other guilds to swear loyalty to the governor of Lille, disharmony could be interwoven with the efforts for harmony and community emphasised in charters. The Cysoing archers were to be 'pleasing' and of 'good loyalty', to meet 'pleasantly and profitably', but in the requirement for them to recognise the control of Lille over their guild there was a clear potential for discontent. Harmony could be strengthened through social interactions between the archery and crossbow guilds of Lille and those of the surrounding area, building community in a small local network. In such interactions, the shooters were behaving in the same way as the participants in the drama events analysed by Van Bruaene. She notes that drama competitions 'celebrated the relations among different cities and towns within the urban networks' and that urban culture cannot be understood without reference to a town's hinterland.[19]

The shared cultures and the strength of the connection between towns and their hinterland are clear from a short study of shooting interactions between Lille and its neighbours.[20] The Lille aldermen gave their crossbow guilds thirteen lots of wine to travel to Croix in 1415 for 'the honour of the town' and to take part in an 'establishment'. Such an event just five years after the Croix guild received their charters and, presumably, five years after its first trip to Lille to swear loyalty and have the guild-brothers' names recorded, shows efforts at commonality and friendship. The guild of Lille visited its neighbours not to demonstrate control, but to take part in a friendly event as equals, with civic wine to ensure that the event built bonds. The guilds of Lille took part in numerous small events like these with the towns of their hinterland, showing that they were part of the same community, upholding the same values. Almost every event was funded by the Lille town accounts 'for the honour of the town', and often for 'peace' with the nearby towns.

---

[18] van Doren, *Inventaire des archives de la ville de Malines* vol. 4, 95.
[19] Van Bruaene, 'A Wonderfull tryumfe', 388.
[20] Based on analysis of town accounts from 1317 to 1517, AML, CV, 16012–16253.

In 1432 the archers of Lille were in Roubaix, a small town north-east of Lille, and were granted six lots of wine by their civic officials. In 1454 the archers visited Lens and were again rewarded with wine for making a *jeu*. Three years later the archers travelled to Wauvrin, again being given wine and again forming communities through shooting in a game together.[21] Numerous small notes such as these appear throughout the town accounts of Lille and make clear that the civic governors gave small but regular grants of wine to the shooting guilds to go to nearby towns and take part in small events. The sums here are far smaller than the grants for attending the great shoots discussed in the previous chapter, but the local networks that stretched out from Lille into its hinterland were important enough to the civic officials for grants of wine and money to be made, emphasising that the shooting guilds showed the unity of the castellany of Lille.

By looking at the towns which the Lille guild-brothers hosted and visited beyond their castellany, Lille's part in wider networks can be observed. Douai appears regularly as a host and a visitor across the period. Given that both were large towns in Walloon Flanders, and were located close together, it is not surprising that the civic officials of both towns used their shooting guilds as a means to maintain bonds. Archers and crossbowmen from Lille and Douai regularly took part in small events and received generous amounts of wine and small amounts of money to do so. The crossbowmen of Lille visited Douai in 1352, and again in 1359, and on both occasions they were given wine from the Lille aldermen as a 'courtesy'.[22] In the early fourteenth century, before being returned to Flanders in 1369, Lille interacted mainly with other French towns. Douai and Tournai feature prominently and show the town using festive events to strengthen links between neighbouring areas that traded with each other and that even sought each other's advice in diplomatic matters.[23]

The Lille guilds attended some events in Flanders before 1369. The crossbowmen of Lille visited both Courtrai and Oudenaarde in 1362, but they received no visitors from Flemish towns.[24] Or at least, no visitors from Flanders received civic funds. The possibility that the shooting guilds of Lille hosted other visitors without municipal funding cannot be entirely discounted. Yet, as we saw in the previous chapter, towns and guilds could not stage competitions without princely support, and it may be that the rulers of Flanders were not prepared to issue the generous rights of free passage that would have allowed such interaction or enabled the guilds to travel outside of the county or into the lands of a potential enemy.

After the reunification of Flanders in 1369 Lille gradually began to integrate itself with the county. The shooting guilds were part of the efforts to rebuild links with Flanders and to establish Lille's place with the Flemish community.

---

[21] AML, CV, 16174, f. 47; 16194, f. 41v; 16198, f. 49v.
[22] AML, CV, 16057, f. 14; 16072, f. 33.
[23] Small, 'Centre and Periphery in Late Medieval France', 148–51.
[24] AML, CV, 16078, ff. 15, 15v.

By the fifteenth century, Ypres had become the most common Flemish town for Lille to visit for small shoots, and guilds were often given more wine for going to Ypres than to other towns. The archers visited Ypres for a small shoot in 1400 and were given eight lots of wine by their civic officials. They visited again in 1403 and were given twelve lots of wine, and again in 1415 for a larger shoot where they won second prize 'for the honour of the town'. Both the greater and lesser crossbow guilds attended a large Ypres competition in 1422 and were given, respectively, £13 4s and £7, and both were present for another crossbow competition in 1428.[25] The links with Ypres demonstrate Lille's engagement with Flemish networks, the use of guilds to show community and the shared values across the later Middle Ages. As one of the Three Towns and as a Flemish power, Ypres was an important centre and its relative proximity to Lille made it an easier target for festive networks and social bonds than either Ghent or Bruges. The growing festive links between Lille and Ypres reinforced political and economic ones, and Lille's place as a Flemish town.

Of course Lille did not interact only with the Ypres guilds. In 1415 the archers were given four lots of wine to go to and shoot in Courtrai, and guilds also took part in small shoots in Courtrai in 1387, in Verdun in 1413 and in Veurne in 1420. Examples of Lille interacting with guilds in Flanders, both in small-scale shoots and at larger events, proliferate across the fifteenth century. Yet the favouring of its close neighbours Douai and Ypres remains clear, highlighting that competitions were not *just* large and spectacular, but were carefully construed events designed to enhance various networks with the support of civic funds. As Lille became better integrated into Flanders and interacted less with French towns, festive and social links grew, with the guilds and their competitions representing civic networks and the priorities of civic rulers.

In understanding Lille's place in inter-urban networks, the shoots organised by the newer hand-gunners' guild, the culveriners, provide examples of the bonds between towns of the southern Low Countries.[26] From 1465 onwards culveriners' guilds from Lille, Douai, Valenciennes, Tournai and Arras met once a year and were given small amounts of wine by their towns to do so. It was unusual for all five to attend, but rare for fewer than three teams to be present. The hand-gunners' competitions moved around the five towns with no discernible pattern. It cannot be proved from town accounts, but it is likely that, as in the *landjuwellen* of the chambers of rhetoric, the winner of an event hosted the next competition. From 1487 Ypres regularly sent its culveriners' guild to events, but no other towns joined this small club until Cambrai in 1509. The culveriners may have had less choice in their networks, as fewer towns had culveriners' guilds and gunpowder was more expensive and more dangerous that bolts or arrows. The stability of the small competitions, with two Flemish

---

[25] AML, CC, 16137, f. 40; 16143, f. 37v; 16159, f. 42v; 16166.

[26] For the gunners' guilds see A. de Meanynck, *Histoire des Canonniers de Lille*, vol.1 (Lille, 1892); Vanderhaeghen, *Jaerboeken van het souvereine gilde der kolveriniers*.

towns, a French one, an Hainaut one and an Artois guild, shows that towns worked to find new ways of maintaining their networks and inter-urban links. Gunners' guilds used urban networks in a way that seems to have deliberately copied the archery and crossbow guilds – certainly, they copied their rights and their organisation, so as to grow and evolve.

As the culveriners' guilds were newer and could not look to ancient foundations as the archers and crossbowmen did, their first charters of privileges are illuminating for urban communication. In the case of archers and crossbowmen, the larger towns tended to have charters first, or at least to have rights written down earlier, and then the same or very similar rights were granted to smaller towns. For culveriners' guilds this is not the case, with the novelty of the equipment encouraging towns to look for the best models, rather than simply looking to their prestigious neighbour. In 1482, when the Lille town authorities decided to grant rights to their gunners' guild, they sent out messengers to the towns they shot with regularly to inspect the privileges granted to their guilds. The above festive interactions meant that the Lille culveriners and officials knew about other guilds and could look to smaller towns as models. The Lille officials decided that Douai's charter granted to its culveriners in 1452 – which itself borrowed heavily from the Douai crossbowmen's privilege of 1383 – was the best model. In 1483 the Lille aldermen granted a charter of rights and privileges to their culveriners' guild that was almost identical to that granted to the Douai guild.[27] Rather than a smaller town copying the rights of a larger one, or simply being given the rights of its nearest powerful neighbour, festive networks had allowed for a different sort of model within the gunners' guilds, and a regional conversation about forms of rights and about what it meant to be a guild.

Lille is far from unique in using the guilds to build bonds with its immediate neighbours and with the rest of Flanders. The archers of Bruges, as we have seen, used their meals to build community across socio-economic groups within the town. The archers also created and enhanced links with the nearby small towns of Damme and Dudzele. Damme's origins go back to a twelfth-century dam, but it became Bruges's outpost as the Zwin silted up, emerging as a power in its own right by the fifteenth century. Damme was only three miles from Bruges and had many cultural links with the town, and the Bruges guild of Hulsterlo had a chapel there. Dudzele remained a village, but a canal linked it with Bruges by the thirteenth century and made it an important part of the peat trade. In addition, groups and individuals from Bruges purchased a large amount of land in and around both Damme and Dudzele, emphasising that great towns needed the support of their hinterlands.[28] The archers built on this tradition of developing links to Damme and Dudzele (not to be mistaken for Dadizeele, discussed in the

---

[27] Espinas, *Les Origines*, vol. 2, 456–60.
[28] Murray, *Cradle of Capitalism*, 196–8; Brown, *Civic Ceremony*, 136–7, 174–6, 232; Nicholas, *Medieval Flanders*, 110; the on-going research of Kristof Dombrech, at Ghent University, on villages around Bruges and their social groups, including the archery guild of

chapter four). In each year for which accounts survive, the Bruges feast of the *papegay* included representatives from these areas. It seems that the two archers from Damme and two from Dudzele, who are never individually named, watched the *papegay* shoot, but did not shoot themselves, and then attended the feast afterwards.[29] In this way, the guilds from nearby centres worked for lasting connections with the archers of Bruges, sharing the same values.

Bruges invited small towns to its feast every year, and these were not its only guests. The Bruges archers also hosted the king of the Lille archers in 1470 and 1480. Unfortunately the accounts for 1490 have not survived, so it is not possible to see if this is a pattern or coincidence. The archers were also visited by representatives from Ghent and Wervick, showing a range of regional connections being strengthened through feasting together and including honoured guests in guild events.[30] Scattered references to guilds from different towns drinking, eating and shooting with each other hint at the regional communities being built or strengthened, and the role of shooting guilds as part of such networks. Only in Bruges have guild accounts survived to show commensality at work, although it is unlikely that they were unique in inviting others to their feasts. In lieu of guild regulations, town accounts from the smaller Flemish centres can be used to chart the development of low-level networks.

No descriptions of competitions in small towns can be traced. Yet the payments for them are numerous in financial records and provide enough information to suggest that smaller competitions were a well-recognised, even ubiquitous, part of cultural interactions between smaller towns. Just as Hulst held a shoot in 1483 that set out to demonstrate the same values and same ideas as the far larger competitions, so too could small towns work for the same sort of networks and regional bonds that were being built by Lille and Bruges. Events held in small towns provide insight into a different level of regional networks, as the example of Ninove, a small town in eastern Flanders on the River Dender, a tributary of the River Scheldt, will show. Ninove's population in 1450 has been estimated at just 1,700 but its riverine location between Geraardsbergen and Aalst gave it access to wider festive and commercial networks.[31] The town accounts, surviving from 1389 to 1436, show the importance of cultural connections and that guilds of archers and crossbowmen were a central part of low-level festive networks.[32]

Each year the archers and crossbowmen jointly received £18 from the civic budget for their *papegay* and for taking part in the procession. The guilds attended large competitions, including the great Oudenaarde shoot of 1408, for which the crossbowmen received £24. Yet many of the *schietspelen* mentioned in the Ninove

---

Dudzele, will provide new details on the function of guilds within the village of Dudzele.
[29] BASS, rekeningboeken, 1465–77, f. 27v.
[30] BASS, rekeningboeken, 1465–72, ff. 62v–64, accounts 1472–80, f. 97; 1460–65, f. 6 bis 1v.
[31] Stabel, 'Composition et recomposition', 56–8; idem, *De kleine stad in vlaanderen*, 15–17.
[32] AGR, CC, 37076–37103.

accounts are far smaller, indicating a local and more focused level of inter-urban communication. In 1408 the archers received £3 12s for attending a shoot in a town that may have been Poperinghe, although the name is heavily abbreviated. In 1416 the archers went to a shoot in the small Brabant town of Lenneke, winning 'fair prizes', and received £8, a large sum for Ninove and a sign that winning prizes and honour was as important for small towns as it was for the great urban centres. In contrast, the crossbowmen attended a shoot in Ypres in the same year but did not win a prize, and received only 8s. As in the larger towns, honour and winning prizes were strong motivating factors for funding participation in shooting competitions and investing in urban networks. As in Lille, the civic officials of Ninove sent their guilds to small and large shoots with support and with wine to emphasise that their town was part of the Flemish community and to demonstrate their part in commercial networks.

The priorities of the civic officials in building local networks are demonstrated by a competition held in Ninove in 1426. The event was attended by archers from Geraardsbergen, Lessines and Menin, and all the visiting guilds received wine worth 18s. The event was not as spectacular as the Ghent event described above, yet it shows the same efforts at strengthening networks. Travelling south down the River Dender, the next town after Ninove is Geraardsbergen, and a few miles later one would arrive in Lessines. The bond between these three small towns was vital for their trade, with Brussels to the east, Aalst to the north and Oudenaarde to the west making cooperation necessary. The three towns were united economically, so it is not surprising to see the bonds being strengthened in shooting competitions. Menin is further away, just north of Lille, so its connection with Ninove is less clear but indicates that although festive and commercial bonds were influenced by rivers and geography, these were not the only considerations. Ninove could not attract large numbers, as Ghent could, but it is clear that in hosting three guilds from other small towns the town officials of Ninove were using their guilds to demonstrate urban honour and strengthen urban networks in the same ways as the larger towns hoped to do with their far larger competitions.

Regional Networks

Examples from Lille and Ninove demonstrate the significance of local networks for large and small towns. For the larger competitions far more documents can be used to demonstrate the links that guilds worked to build and strengthen, and how these connected to other inter-urban connections. As Peter Stabel has argued, the Low Countries were not typical European regions and their extremely high level of urbanisation and density of population gave them a unique character. Towns were prosperous, but not were stand-alone giants, in the way that London or Paris were; rather, inter-urban trade and regional communications, as well as national and international trade, helped Flanders to prosper. Such a tradition of inter-regional communication, as well as the excellent waterways and road networks of Flanders, encouraged what Marc Boone has called 'a very intense inter-urban traffic', with the rivers in particular promoting the 'trafficking [of] people, material goods and cultural products. Many of these 'cultural products' have been analysed and the role of rivers as 'cultural highways' is well understood, and the addition of archery and crossbow competition further demonstrates unity and communication.[33]

The following discussion does not seek to challenge the well-argued case for the strong bonds between towns across Flanders. Rather, it seeks to place the archery and crossbow guilds and their great competitions within these networks and, in so doing, to add a new strand to analyses of Flemish networks. Stein's study of the durability of urban networks, Lowagie's work on messengers, Van Bruaene's analysis of drama competitions, Blockmans' work on the ability of inter-urban activities to promote honour and Boone's study of civic space, as well as studies analysing the ideals of 'Common Good' have all shown that Flemish towns and Flemish urban cultures are better understood as networks.[34] Here, such values will be analysed through crossbow competitions, which, as was understood in the sixteenth century, showed Flemish unity, just as the Olympic games showed Greek unity. In comparing Flanders and Ancient Greece, and the shooters and the Olympic games, the governor of Veere was emphasising the status of the competitions and their hosts as well as the connections between the glorious events and the unified region.

A glance at any map will make clear the importance of rivers for the Low Countries in general, and for Flanders in particular. Rivers had helped to create powerful economic networks.[35] Such networks are particularly clear along the River Scheldt, a vital French and Flemish trade artery connecting Valenciennes, Tournai, Oudenaarde and Ghent before flowing east to Antwerp. The Scheldt was

---

[33] Stabel, 'Composition et recomposition', 29–30; idem, *De kleine stad in vlaanderen*, 15–17; Boone and Porfyrion, 'Markets, Squares, Streets', 227–39; H. Pleij, 'De late triomf van een regionale stadscultuur'; B. A. M. Ramakers, 'Rederijkers en stedelijk feestcultuur in her laatmiddeleeuwse Noord-Brabant', both in A.-J. A. Bijsterveld (ed.), *Cultuur in het Laatmiddeleeuwse Noord-Brabant. Literatuur, boekproductie, historiografie* ('s-Hertogenbosch: Stichting Brabantse Regionale Geschiedbeoefening, 1998), 8–12, 37–54; A. Cowan, 'Nodes, Networks and Hinterland', *Cultural Exchange*, vol. 2, 28–38.

[34] Stein, 'An Urban Network in the Low Countries', 43–68; Lowagie, 'Stedekijke communicatie in de Late Middeleeuwen', 273–95; Van Bruaene, *Om Beter Wille*, 11–17, 27–35; Marnet, 'Chambers of Rhetoric and the Transmission of Religious Ideas', 274–96; Blockmans, 'Stedelijke netwerken in de Nederlanden voor de industrialisatie', 59–68; idem. 'Loyalteitskonflikten in een process van staatsvorming; Vlaanderen in de 14de en 15de eeuw', *Handelingen van het Vlaams filologencongres* 31 (1977), 259–64; Lecuppre-Desjardin and Van Bruaene, 'Introduction', to their *De Bono Communi*, 1–9; Haemers, *Common Good*, 2–9.

[35] Boone and Porfyrion, 'Market, Square, Street', 227–39; H. Pleij, 'De late triomf van een regionale stadscultuur'; Ramakers, 'Rederijkers en stedelijk feestcultuur in her laatmiddeleeuwse Noord-Brabant', both in Bijsterveld, *Cultuur in het Laatmiddeleeuwse Noord-Brabant. Literatuur*, 8–12, 37–54.

the Flemish highway of both trade and festive networks. It may have encouraged the early growth of these cities, and certainly it boosted their economies.[36] Despite being the official border between France and the Holy Roman Empire from the ninth century, the river united rather than divided towns and communities.[37] That all of these towns held large competitions is no coincidence: towns that had evolved through trading on the river were more likely to host large competitions that attracted great attendance, thus strengthening their networks.

Oudenaarde is worthy of particular attention. Its population in 1450 has been estimated at around 6,500, far below the estimated 50,000 of Ghent, and below even the estimated 20,000 of Mechelen and estimated 8,700 of Ypres.[38] Yet Oudenaarde could hold competitions on the same scale as, if not even larger than, all of those communities. Oudenaarde's festive dynamism was possible only by virtue of its central position in Flanders on the River Scheldt, just south of Ghent. By the fourteenth century Oudenaarde was flourishing, deriving great wealth from textiles, especially tapestry production and trade.[39] Like many other late fifteenth-century Flemish economies, that of Oudenaarde had gone into decline, yet the town's textile wealth was still used for numerous civic festivities, like the Corpus Christi procession and play cycle.[40] A town dependent upon trade and regional markets naturally encouraged its shooting guilds to play a leading role in regional communities. The Oudenaarde crossbow guilds, with civic support, used the town's position on the Scheldt to maintain urban networks, as is shown by spectacular competitions in 1408, 1462 and 1497.

We saw in the previous chapter the lengths to which the guilds and civic powers of Oudenaarde went in staging great entrances to shooting competitions across the Low Countries. The competitions they held were just as impressive and are evidence of networks being formed and the power of shooting competitions to bring civic representatives together and, in doing so, to celebrate unity. As we have seen, the 1408 competition was attended by John the Fearless, who took part with the hosts as a guild-brother of Oudenaarde. Constructing attendance lists for this competition is difficult, but the town accounts list thirty-five guilds that attended and were given gifts of wine simply for attending. The vast majority of these, twenty-five of the thirty-five guilds, were Flemish. Many guilds were from

---

[36] A. Verhulst, 'An Aspect of the Question of Continuity between Antiquity and Middle Ages: The Origin of the Flemish Cities between the North Sea and the Scheldt', *JMH* 3(1977), 175–205; A. Maesschalck and J. Viaene, 'Het vervoer van de natuursteen op de binnenwateren van het Scheldebekken in het midden van de 15de eeuw, met het oog op de bouw van het Leuvense stadhuis', *BTG* 82 (1999), 187–200; P. Stabel, 'Demography and Hierarchy', 206–17.

[37] S. T. Bindoff, *The Scheldt Question* (London, 1945), 6–81; C. Terlinden, 'The History of the Scheldt', *History* 16 (1920) 185–97.

[38] Stabel, 'Composition et recomposition', 58.

[39] M. Vanwelden, *Het tapijtweversambacht te Oudenaarde, 1441–1772* (Oudenaarde: Stadsarchief Oudenaarde, 1979), 15–47.

[40] Ramakers, *Spelen en figuren*, 25–80.

large towns like Bruges and Ghent, but those from many smaller places, including Commines and Hulst, were given money simply for attending. Ghent received wine worth 40s, more than twice as much as the next highest amount, reflecting the close bond between the neighbouring towns and their trade connections.

Oudenaarde's trade connections expanded beyond Flanders, but were not as numerous, and so more Flemish attendees should be expected. Other guilds that received gifts simply for attending included three from Hainaut, one from Limburg, four from Brabant and one each from Holland and Friesland. Other guilds attended, including the Hainaut small town of Maubeuge, which won second prize but was not given a gift simply for attending.[41] The 1408 list is not complete, but De Rantere's seventeenth-century chronicle states that forty-six guilds attended, although he records only the winners. The civic authorities considered thirty-five visiting guilds to be more important than the others that attended. It may be that, like Maubeuge, they were non-Flemish towns, although of course nothing can be proved in the absence of evidence. What is clear from the gifts of wine and money given to selected guilds is that connections with Flanders dominated. The Oudenaarde guild, with civic support, was working to demonstrate its prestige to a large audience, but it was the Flemish guilds that received gifts because it was within Flanders that networks were the most important to it. In the shoot of 1408, Oudenaarde made the most of its location on the River Scheldt, and its situation in central Flanders, to strengthen bonds with Flemish towns, over and above French towns or other parts of the Low Countries.

Attendance at the next great competition in Oudenaarde the shoot in 1462, cannot be fully recovered. The five prizes for the best shooting went to Tournai, Courtrai, Ardenbourg, Lier and Enghien. The guild-brothers of Bruges were also present, led by Lodewijk van Gruuthuse, as were Ypres and Aalst. The younger and older guilds of Brussels had been invited, but no list of those who attended, nor of those who were invited, has been found. The event was specular and, as noted in the previous chapter, well funded, with all civic groups contributing to the total outgoings of £4,925 15s. It may be that a larger number of guilds took part, and certainly the town seems to have invited many guilds, sending out four town messengers for between forty and fifty-nine days.[42]

The shoot of 1497 was, according to the town accounts, attended by thirty-one guilds. Just six are named in the accounts themselves, but all thirty-one are named in De Rantere's seventeenth-century chronicle, which copied a now lost fifteenth-century description. Two of the place names De Rantere gives (Biquay and Suspel) cannot be linked today to any specific place, but the remaining twenty-nine show a Flemish bias in the Oudenaarde event, but slightly different networks than had existed in 1408. Fifteen of the twenty-nine

---

[41] OSAOA, gilden, 707/II/8A.
[42] de Rantere, *Geschiedenis van Oudenaarde*, vol. 2, 128–9; OSAOA, Gilden, 507/II/4B; 507/II/3B; 507/II/12 A; 507/II/16.

identifiable guilds came from Flanders (sixteen if Mechelen is included). The Ghent guild-brothers were not there, probably because the town was investing a great deal in its own 1498 shoot. Otherwise a mix of large and small towns from within Flanders, including Bruges, Dendermonde and Damme, dominated the event. Also present were eight guilds from Brabant, including Maastricht,[43] three from Hainaut and the guilds of the French city of Tournai and from the bishopric of Utrecht, which had, until 1496, been ruled by David, one of Philip the Good's illegitimate sons. Competitors from a French city surrounded by Burgundian lands and from a bishopric with a tradition of Burgundian rulers demonstrate the links between political networks and the guilds that took part in cultural events. Flemish guilds dominated events in Oudenaarde in 1408 and in 1462 because Oudenaarde, in central Flanders and on the River Scheldt, needed Flemish connections. The slightly more Brabant guilds present in 1497 than in 1408 no doubt reflect the integration between the two regions that had occurred since they were both absorbed into the Burgundian state, as well as the economic growth of Brabant. The Scheldt was not just a Flemish river: also in attendance were Antwerp and Tournai, both of them towns that were connected to Oudenaarde by water, indicating the networks the civic officials wanted to strengthen in 1497.

In a consideration of rivers as part of festive and commercial networks, the Scheldt is not the only waterway worthy of analysis. Ghent's dominant position is at least partially explained by its location at the confluence of the Scheldt and the Lys rivers. Along the Lys there are many other relatively small towns with extremely rich festive traditions. One such town was Courtrai, which in 1450 had in an estimated population of around 8,500 and was home to archery and crossbow guilds.[44] Most of the early shoots, those before 1350, include Courtrai as attendees and, often, winners. The civic officials and guilds of Courtrai also hosted events in 1411 and 1415, hinting at links between rivers and festive networks.[45] Like Oudenaarde, they interacted mostly with guilds from within Flanders, although a few attendees from Hainaut do appear, as does the French guild of Tournai. Courtrai used its guilds to build connections with Flanders and with Tournai, using festive interactions to shore up regional networks. Similarly the small town of Roubaix, on a branch of the River Lys, was able to attend numerous shoots, even hosting an impressive competition in 1432 that was attended by guilds from Flanders and the archers of Tournai.[46] Courtrai and Roubaix, like Oudenaarde, relied on a river for trade and communication, and

---

[43] Maastricht was, in theory, ruled by both the bishop of Liège and the duke of Brabant, but in describing Maastricht's entrance into Ghent in 1498 the *Excellent Chronicle* identified Maastricht as being in Brabant; f. 290.
[44] Stabel, 'Composition et recomposition', 57–8.
[45] De Potter, *Jaarboeken*, 34–5; Ypres gave their guildsmen £68 to attend, AGR, CC, 38641, f. 57.
[46] AML, CV, 16174, f. 47.

so encouraged their guilds to visit neighbouring towns. Guilds and civic powers used the river communication networks to strengthen civic bonds, with archery and crossbow competitions being an important strategy for maintaining, even augmenting, urban networks.

The only town to hold significant competitions that was not located on a part of a larger river open to ships in late medieval Flanders was Ypres. In contrast to Oudenaarde and Ghent, which gave centre stage to their crossbow guilds, Ypres focused on its archers. More importantly for our purposes, Ypres's strong place within festive networks cannot be explained by rivers but, rather, by Ypres's diplomatic links to both north and south. By the fifteenth century, Ypres's economy had been deep in recession for perhaps two centuries and the city had shrunk in production and population. Despite such set-backs, its festive culture remained strong during the period covered by surviving town accounts.[47] The town's archives were lost in 1914, so the present study relies on the copies of town accounts sent to the ducal *chambre des comptes* from 1406 onwards, as well as earlier sources in other civic records. Ypres shot regularly in Tournai, taking part in great events in 1350, 1394 and 1455 – indeed, Ypres seemed to work harder than Oudenaarde or Courtrai to build links to the francophone south. In 1399 Ypres was the only Flemish-speaking guild to be given a gift of wine for attending an archery contest in Douai.[48]

As well as the small events attended by Lille, as noted above, Ypres held larger events, including an archery competition in 1415 and a crossbow event in 1422. The former gave gifts of wine to twenty guilds for attending and, as in Oudenaarde, it is possible more came to shoot but were not given gifts. Among the guilds to receive civic gifts of wine and money, perhaps unsurprisingly a Flemish majority can be seen, with eleven out of twenty guilds from the county. It must be noted, however, that this was not as large a majority as in Oudenaarde, and indeed Flemish towns that might be expected to shoot are absent, including Oudenaarde itself, Bruges and Courtrai. Far more towns from the hinterland of Ypres, like Poperinghe, or the south, like Lille and Douai, were given wine for attending. Also present were four guilds from Hainaut, two from Artois, one each from Picardy and Brabant and the French guild of Tournai. The list of guilds rewarded for attending the shoot of 1415 shows that Ypres, like Oudenaarde, favoured its fellow Flemish guilds, but not in exactly the same way. Each town used its competitions in a similar yet nuanced way to enhance the networks that were important to it economically, culturally and politically. Ypres built the bonds to its immediate hinterland and to the south, using the guilds to strengthen networks and to ensure that economic partners were also part of cultural communities

---

[47] Haemers, *Common Good*, 248–64; Stabel, *Dwarfs among Giants*, 28–9; 208–9; AGR, CC, 38635–38733.

[48] le Muisit, *Chronique et Annales*, 272–3; Crombie, 'French and Flemish Urban Networks', 157–75; DAM, CC, 204.

The Ypres 1422 event is noteworthy for the number of greater and lesser guilds attending. As noted in chapter two these were unlikely to be adult and youth teams but, rather, were guilds of differing statuses. Ghent, Lille, Courtrai, Nieuwpoort, Bruges, Veurne and Mechelen all sent both their lesser and greater guilds and, in addition, a handful of towns sent just their lesser guild. The event is again dominated by Flemish guilds, including small-town guilds like Armentières and large ones like Bruges and Ghent, as well as a good number of southern francophone guilds.[49] In ensuring that towns sent two guilds, Ypres was able to stage a larger competition, with more competitors and more events, but without needing to bring in larger geographical areas, making the bonds with those in attendance stronger through commensality. Ypres built bonds with Flanders through its shooting events, but also with the French-speaking south, highlighting civic choices and the importance of strong urban networks building on commercial and cultural relationships.

In the analysis of networks built and enhanced through archery and crossbow competitions, towns that did not host great events are more intriguing than those that did. It is easy to understand why Ghent, Oudenaarde and Ypres held great shoots in order to win honour and build bonds across and beyond Flanders. All three were centres of production, all relied on trade networks and all used their shooting guilds to strengthen their inter-urban networks. Lille and Bruges both funded their guilds to attend large competitions and to host guests from nearby towns in order to build local bonds, as we have seen. Yet neither Lille nor Bruges hosted any large competitions in the fourteenth or fifteenth centuries. Neither can be described as a centre of production, although both had manufacturing sectors. Lille was not on one of the Flanders river-highways, but was a vital trade link between France and Flanders; its position made it a powerful secondary market place.[50] Despite the silting up of the once-powerful Zwin, Bruges remained one of the most important market places in Western Europe in the fifteenth century.[51] Oudenaarde and Ghent can be considered industrial centres; in contrast, Bruges and Lille were markets, and favoured urban jousters over the shooting guilds.

When staging spectacular events within their walls, both Bruges and Lille represented their civic values, their ideals, through rather more aristocratic pursuits. The towns were the two greatest supporters of urban jousters, the White Bear and the Epinette, as well as staging two of the most spectacular Flemish processions, the Holy Blood and Notre-Dame de la Trielle.[52] The jousts

---

[49] AGR, CC, 38640–1, ff. 48v–49; 38647, 39v–40v.
[50] Stabel, *De kleine stad*, 116–38, calls Lille a *Handelsknooppunter*.
[51] Van Uytven, 'Stages of Economic Decline; Late Medieval Bruges', 259–69; Brulez, 'Brugge en Antwerpen in de 15e en 16e eeuw', 15–37; R. Degrijse, 'Brugge en de organisatie van het loodswezen van het Zwin op het einde van de 15de eeuw', *ASEB* 112 (1975), 61–130.
[52] Van den Neste, *Tournoi, Joutes et pas d'armes*; Lecuppre-Desjardin, *La Ville des Cérémonies*, 80–99; Brown, *Civic Ceremony*, 37–72.

were hugely expensive, so it is possible that Bruges and Lille could not afford to host great shooting competitions. We have seen that, in Bruges at least, shooters could also be jousters, with both groups upholding similar values and requiring significant investment of both time and money. Like shoots, the jousts were great events staged in market places, giving prizes for skill and ending with feasts that included nobles as well as townsmen. It is quite possible that in both Bruges and Lille large shooting competitions were seen as superfluous. It is likely that jousts brought Bruges and Lille great status, and so their shooting guilds had to take second place. In addition, we have seen that shooting competitions lasted for many weeks, while jousts and processions took only a few days. As both towns were market centres, the civic governors of Bruges and Lille may have been less keen than their counterparts in Ghent and Oudenaarde to allow the market places to be dominated for weeks at a time by potentially dangerous shooting competitions. Urban networks, shown in the hosting and attending of archery and crossbow competitions, emphasise the strong links that held Flanders together and the ability of towns and networks to adapt and develop, just as they worked to keep the peace. But, just as not all of those invited to Ghent in 1440 attended, so not all towns hosted their own very large competitions.

The guilds emphasised strong regional cultural networks linked to regional economic bonds. In analysing the region, Martha Howell has commented that the great textile centres and regional markets the Low Countries were 'precociously saturated by trade' and that the towns were geared towards commerce.[53] In Flanders, especially in Ypres, Ghent and Oudenaarde, this trade meant textiles, with much of the urban populations engaged in textile production. All three towns used their archery and crossbow guilds to promote their cloth industry, particularly in entrances to competitions. All three centres of cloth production invested in their guilds as symbols of their industry, and their own men wearing their fine cloth advertised their skills in the best possible way. Such an idea should not be taken too far, because most of Flemish towns had important textile industries, but the dominance of textile centres among the hosts of the greatest shoots and the winners of best entrances is striking.

Competitions and Making Peace

Shooting competitions grew geographically on the foundations established by trade and by other cultural interactions between towns. The previous chapter made clear that events idealised peace and unity, and we have seen above that crossbow competitions were bound up with socio-economic networks. But how could events of such a size, with hundreds of shooters, thousands of followers, all granted large quantities of wine and often immunity from prosecution for 'accidental' deaths hope to make peace? How far can the expressions of friendship and honour in letters and descriptions be taken as more than empty rhetoric?

---

[53] Howell, *Commerce Before Capitalism*, 2–6.

Competitions held the potential for violence, and indeed disputes did happen. Yet an examination of the chronological patterns of competitions shows that they can be linked to the will to restore order and rebuild peace in and beyond Flanders. Competitions were staged across the fourteenth and fifteenth centuries, becoming larger and more spectacular. This is a true, but simplified statement. Events were held after wars and rebellions, after towns had been in conflict – even engaged in physical battles – with each other. In the wake of war, competitions were used by civic authorities to rebuild bonds and, as the events grew in size and splendour, their ability to promote unity increased and the events became agents of social peace.

Desires to remake peace are clear from the earliest references to shooting competitions, although, as already noted, it is impossible to identify a starting date for competitions. The events are first documented and first receive civic funds in the years following the suppression of the so-called 'Peasants' Revolt' of 1323–28.[54] It is possible, although it cannot be proved, that in the wake of war the existing informal shoots came to civic attention and obtained municipal funding as a means to restore the fractured networks that were so important to Flanders. The first event to be described in any detail was the Ghent crossbow shoot of 1331. It began with a separate day for entrances, which was followed by several days of shooting, and ended with the presentation of prizes. The decades that followed the great Ghent shoot cannot be described as either peaceful or conducive to large competitions that necessitated travel across Flanders. War, rebellion or plague could have stifled the growth of competitions, yet the competitions grew in spite of these challenges, and indeed they may have grown *because* of the need to rebuild bonds in the wake of such events. The following is not a full chronology, rather it is a summary of the competitions interspersed between the wars and rebellions of the late medieval Low Countries, providing proof of their role in building peace.

War and rebellion, suppressed in 1328, returned with the Ghent uprising of Jacob van Artevelde and Flemish support for England's Edward III in his wars with France. An 'extraordinary government' was established in Ghent in January 1338 and an alliance was made with England. In January 1340 Ghent went so far as to recognise Edward as king of France. The same year saw a naval battle at Sluis and an Anglo-Flemish siege of Tournai.[55] Years of war and rebellion damaged regional networks and any feeling of friendship between Ghent and French towns. Instability could have ended the competitions, and the turmoil of the late

---

[54] W. H. TeBrake, *A Plague of Insurrection: Popular Politics and Peasant Revolt in Flanders, 1323–1328* (Philadelphia: University of Pennsylvania Press 1993), 108–38; S. K. Cohn, *Popular Protest in Late Medieval Europe, Italy, France and Flanders* (Manchester: Manchester University Press, 2004), 36–40; Nicholas, *Medieval Flanders*, 211–16.

[55] Nicholas, *Metamorphosis*, 2–4; H. Van Werveke, *Jacob van Artevelde* (Den Haag: Kruseman, 1982); N. De Pauw, *Cartulaire historique et généalogique des Artevelde* (Brussels: Hayez, 1920).

1330s and early 1340s did limit the growth of the newly developed competitions. No competitions are documented between 1338 and 1343, and yet war did not put an end to them. Large shoots were held in both Tournai and Antwerp in 1344, with the spectacles and festivities being used to re-establish vital trade links that had been damaged in war.[56] The years following Artevelde's rebellion, and the siege of Tournai, saw larger events held across the Low Countries in order to restore civic networks and work for peace and unity.

Rebellion was, of course, not the only threat to Flemish unity and prosperity. The Black Death struck Flanders in the late fourteenth and early fifteenth centuries, and the areas least affected in 1349–51 were hit hard in 1361.[57] The plague killed and terrified, and it threatened to pull societies apart. Yet survivors, as Italian studies have particularly emphasised, became more optimistic and wished to celebrate life and their triumph over death.[58] Large-scale shooting competitions were part of this new vitality, even part of the late medieval celebration of life. By 1350 the guilds were a recognised part of civic life, with their gardens, weekly shoots and annual *papegay* matches; they took part in procession and were beginning to be granted rights and even land, and the plague may even have acted as a catalyst to the process of guilds gaining rights and funds.

Such a celebration of life, with the guilds as a part of the triumph over death, is clear in Tournai. The city had been hit hard by the first wave of the plague in 1349, in which perhaps half of the city's population had perished,[59] but festive and convivial displays survived. As Stein has shown, the procession of Tournai grew in the months following the plague and the procession of 1349 was larger than any previous event. This was perhaps to be expected, as the procession had been established in 1098 in thanksgiving to the Virgin for having saved the city from the late eleventh-century plague. Hundreds of flagellants appeared from all over the Low Countries, whipping themselves in public for thirty-three and a half days, making the procession of 1349 a memorable event.[60] And just as men came from all over Flanders, and from France, to the procession of Tournai in 1349, so in 1350 another large audience gathered for a rather different festive event. In August 1350 a great crossbow shoot was held in Tournai, one of the

---

[56] AML, CV, 16040, f. 13v.
[57] S. K. Cohn, 'After the Black Death: Labour Legislation and Attitudes towards Labour in Late-Medieval Western Europe', *Economic History Review* 603 (2007), 451–62; W. Blockmans, 'The Social and Economic Effects of Plague in the Low Countries', *RBPH* 58 (1993), 833–63; M. Aubrey, 'Les Mortalities Lilloise (1328–1369) *RN* 65 (1987), 327–42; A. Derville, 'La Population du Nord au Moyen Âge, I; avant 1384', *RN* 80 (1998), 524–7.
[58] S. K. Cohn, 'Triumph over Plague: Culture and Memory after the Black Death', in *Care for the Here and the Hereafter*, 35–54; idem, 'The place of the Dead in Flanders and Tuscany: Towards a Comparative History of the Black Death', in *The Place of the Dead: Death and Remembrance in Late Medieval and Early Modern Europe* B. Gordon and P. Marshall (ed.) (Cambridge: Cambridge University Press, 2000), 17–43.
[59] S. K. Cohn, *The Black Death Transformed* (London: Arnold, 2003), 152–67.
[60] Stein, 'An Urban Network in the Low Countries', 54.

largest that the Low Countries had seen. The size and fame of the spectacular shooting competitions and their place within urban networks helped to restore communities in the wake of threats and to re-establish urban networks. No attendance list survives for the Tournai shoot, but Giles le Muisit, the blind monastic chronicler, praised the event. He records that thirty-five guilds attended the competition, which lasted for a week, beginning on the feast of the assumption of the Virgin (15 August). Le Muisit notes that Bruges won the prize for best entrance and Ypres was also very fine, while the Douai town accounts noted that 'many bonnes villes' attended.[61]

Events of the 1340s and 1350s celebrated peace and the triumph over plague, and continued in the 1360s, but did not grow in size until the 1380s. Ghent and other towns again rose in rebellion in 1379 and the uprising was not fully put down until the peace of Tournai in 1385. The 'Ghent war' of 1379–85 had been particularly divisive. Despite appeals, Bruges and Ypres did not support Ghent, with the result that the Ghent militia attacked Bruges during the procession of the Holy Blood in May 1382. Other Flemish towns, including Oudenaarde and Dendermonde, actively supported Louis of Male in his siege of Ghent in 1380 and the tension continued for the next five years. The last major event of the rebellion was Ghent's seizure of Damme in August 1385, which caused further tensions within the county and between the towns.[62] Flanders had not just been in rebellion against a count: the towns had been at war with one another. In the months following the peace of Tournai, competitions were staged to rebuild the communities of the Low Countries and to bring unity back to the urban networks. In 1386 the Bruges crossbowmen attended a small competition in Ghent, referred to in the accounts as a *'thoorlement'*. A year later the guilds of Brabant and Holland, as well as those of Lille, Bruges, Ghent and many towns attended the crossbow competition in Mons. As we have seen, the invitation to the Mons shoot of 1387 makes clear that the event, larger than those of the 1360s, was designed to rebuild peace and community between the towns and with princely authority.[63] It is unlikely to be a coincidence that the Mons event was the first to record the prizes given for plays and for drama and to give large quantities of silverware, in particular jugs and bowls, that emphasised community. Competitions were larger after the rebellions than during the preceding years of relative peace: after disunity, greater events that lasted longer, with larger displays and more wine and prizes, helped to restore networks.

War divided Flanders, setting towns against each other not just in rivalry and tension but physically, in battle. After peace was made the shooting guilds used their martial skills to rebuild bonds of peace across Flanders. As we have seen, in remembering service in warfare, particularly in the wars of the late

---

[61] le Muisit, *Chronique et Annales*, 272–3; DAM, CC 200 ter, roll 1.
[62] Nicholas, *Metamorphosis*, 9–11; idem, 'The Scheldt Trade and the "Ghent War" of 1379–1385', *BCRH* 144 (1980), 189–359.
[63] Devillers, 'Notice Historique sur les milices communales', 169–285.

fourteenth and early fifteenth centuries, towns celebrated their guilds as military representatives. Guilds themselves, when recording their past and their loyal and prestigious service in their own guild registers, noted military success and loyalty to their lords. This juxtaposition of remembering service and working for peace may seem like a contradiction, but the different audiences for these sources should be kept in mind. Guild books can be considered as semi-private – they would have been seen only by the guild-brothers and visitors to their halls. For a guild audience, loyalty and successful service were remembered, but in more public documents and in displays, peace was emphasised. As we saw in the previous chapter, letters of invitation were carried across a larger region and were seen, and probably heard, by large audiences. These letters were opportunities for guilds to display another side of their identity and to emphasise peace. Entrances and the shooting competitions themselves placed great weight on harmony and civic honour. They performed the ideal of unity on a prominent urban stage and demonstrated the desire for community.

The late 1380s saw ever larger events in Flanders that celebrated peace and restored bonds damaged during the Ghent war. By 1394 the French city of Tournai had a new reason to celebrate and to rebuild peace. A truce had been signed between Richard II and Charles VI in 1389 that brought a pause, if not peace, in the Hundred Years' War, allowing the civic authorities of Tournai to turn toward building bonds with their neighbours. The Tournai crossbow competition of 1394 was commemorated in several prose chronicles and in a poem which is likely to have been composed by a Tournaisian rhetorician, as it praises the town as well as the visiting guilds. In 1394, forty-eight guilds came to Tournai for the 'noble feast of the crossbow' and a competition that lasted from 5 June to 8 August. The guilds came from a wide area, reflecting the fact that networks were still strong and would be strengthened and rebuilt by means of this great event. As might be expected of a French town, French guilds were well represented, with twelve from the kingdom of France,[64] eleven from Hainaut, three from Artois, eight from Brabant and ten from Flanders, plus two guilds from lands controlled by the prince-bishop of Cambrai and a guild from the town of Namur. That such a diverse range of guilds gathered in Tournai, all with the support of their civic officials, demonstrated that the towns wished to rebuild peaceful bonds and restore trade and political links in this fractured northern region.

Similar ideals of peace and community building are apparent in events throughout the early fifteenth century. A large shoot was held in Ghent in 1400, and another in Mechelen in 1404, both emphasising bonds and community, with Mechelen inviting guilds from across France and the Low Countries in the hope to celebrate brotherhood. As we saw above, impressive events were staged

---

[64] Arguably, parts of Flanders south of the Scheldt and Artois were French fiefs, but for the purposes of this discussion 'Flanders', is seen as a county separate from France, as is Artois; Crombie, 'French and Flemish Urban Networks', 157–75.

regularly during the 1410s, 1420s and 1430s, with competitions in Oudenaarde in 1408 and Ypres in 1415 and 1422. Events continued in years of peace, but there was no step up in grandeur: the standard had been set in 1387 and 1394. It was not until after the wars and instability that competitions again became bigger and gave a renewed emphasis to community, as was shown in the Ghent crossbow competition of 1440. This spectacular event, with its bilingual letter of invitation, more elaborate prizes and more time for preparing entrances, was far larger than the events of the previous decade. The Ghent shoot was held less than four years after several militias, including those of Ghent, had fled Calais, and only two years after the end of the Bruges rebellion. The late 1430s had seen disputes across Flanders as well as the economic tensions caused by the switching of allegiances during the Hundred Years' War and the resulting loss of English contacts. The great crossbow guild of Ghent, with the support not just of its alderman but of most of its urban community, set out to stage a great event celebrating peace. In their shoot of 1440 the guilds and civic powers of Ghent were working to create a new memory and, in doing so, to distance Ghent from the dishonourable and unpleasant memory of 1436. The town and crossbow guild of Ghent wanted to ensure that their sense of self was prestigious and honourable; but, just as importantly, they wanted to ensure that when others thought of Ghent they thought of wealth, of honour, of spectacle, and not of military dishonour and divisions.

The Ghent guild succeeded in making its event memorable and, in doing so, helping to cancel the memory of 1436. The event of 1440 was not only used as a model for the later shoot of 1498, but was referred to and remembered across the Low Countries. Local chronicles, which rarely mention shooting competitions but, rather, focus on aldermen's elections, princely visits and portents, give a good deal of attention to the 1440 shoot. The *Brabandsche Kronijk*, the *Chronycke van Nederlant, Besonderlyck der Stadt Antwerpen*, Nicholas Despars' chronicle with its focus on Bruges and the Ypres chronicle attributed to Olivier van Dixmuide all note that their guilds went to Ghent in 1440, most of them adding small details (like the number of horses or colour of livery) not found elsewhere in order to demonstrate civic pride as represented by the guilds.[65] Such a wide range of reporting suggests that the Ghent guild and the civic community had succeeded in their ambition to stage a great and memorable urban event that emphasised the prestige of Ghent and the unity of the Low Countries. The events of the 1440s, like those of the 1380s and 1390s, increased in splendour after the violence and conflict partly so as to demonstrate status, but also to build peace and recreate unity through competition.

---

[65] *Brabandsche Kronijk* and *Chronycke van Nederlant, Besonderlyck der Stadt Antwerpen*, both in C. Piot (ed.), *Chroniques de Brabant et de Flandre* (Bruxelles: Hayez, 1879), 57, 76; Despars, *Cronijke van den lande ende graefscepe*, 422; Olivier van Dixmuide, *Merkwaerdige Gebeurtenissen*, 170.

A celebration of peace was needed once again just over a decade later, after the end of the Ghent war in 1453.[66] This complex uprising divided Ghent from the rest of Flanders. The Ghent rebels appealed for aid to Bruges and other Flemish towns, and even to Brussels and Brabant, but, in Richard Vaughan's words, 'Flanders as a whole stood firm for the duke'.[67] Despite the animosity that the war must have caused, particularly with Ghent's pillaging of Aalst, Dendermonde and Geraardsbergen and besieging of Oudenaarde in 1452, the shooting guilds soon re-established festive relations with Ghent. The renewing networks might be partially for the 'Common Good' and for the ideal of brotherhood and harmony, but it was also a practical matter to restore networks. As noted, most Flemish towns depended on commercial and political connections with their neighbours, and so investing in festive and cultural bonds to shore up such networks was sensible and pragmatic, and connections to Ghent were too important to be neglected. The crossbowmen of Lille hosted the Ghent crossbowmen for a small shoot in summer 1454, and the Ghent archers hosted those of Bruges a year later. In 1454, small archery and crossbow contests were also held in Lens, Dixmuide and Dendermonde.[68] Small events helped to take the first steps toward rebuilding bonds damaged in a particularly violent and long-lasting conflict, bringing Ghent back into a community with its neighbours and former enemies, and to maintain the 'Common Good' of Flanders.

The Tournai crossbow competition of 1455 was one of the most splendid of the fifteenth century, again demonstrating large competitions working for peace. The Tournai event was attended by both the *jonghe* and *oude* guilds of Ghent and both of Bruges's crossbow guilds as well as teams from Brussels, Lille, Oudenaarde – in all, over fifty other guilds.[69] The Tournai event can be linked to other reasons for rebuilding social and economic bonds and regional communities, as 1453 marked the end of the Hundred Years' War and Charles VII's final reconquests of Normandy. Peace in Burgundy and royal success gave the French city of Tournai a dual reason to celebrate peace and rebuild communities. Although Flanders had officially accepted Charles VII as king of France from the time of the treaty of Arras in 1435, strong links between Flanders, especially Ghent, and England remained, as was demonstrated by the towns' reluctance to attack Calais in 1436. In 1455 the towns of the Low Countries gathered to celebrate unity and to build peaceful communities through elaborate crossbow competitions and an event that was even larger than the Ghent shoot of 1440 and its efforts at unity.

---

[66] J. Haemers, *De Gentse opstand, 1449–1453: de strijd tussen rivaliserende netwerken om het stedelijke kapitaal* (Kortrijk: UGA, 2004); M. Populer, 'Le conflit de 1447 à 1453 entre Gand et Philippe le Bon. Propagande et historiographie', HMGOG 44 (1990), 99–123.

[67] Vaughan, *Philip the Good*, 316–17.

[68] AML, CV, 16195, f. 21v; SAG, stadsrekeningen, 400/17, f. 386; Godar, *Histoire des archers*, 105; AML, CC, 16195; BSA, 385, Sint Joris, 84; AGR, CC, 31448, f. 36.

[69] Brown and Small, *Court and Civic Society*, 219–25.

Tournai had maintained links with Flanders, as was shown by their attendance in Ghent in 1440. Yet, the Hundred Years' War, as well as the Ghent war, had damaged relations between the French city and the Flemish networks. Tournai was surrounded by Burgundian lands, and so cordial relations with Flanders were of great importance for security as well as for trade. To enhance their networks and to rebuild peaceful links with their Flemish neighbours, the civic authorities of Tournai used the great shoot of 1455 to bring in a large audience and to (re)build communities and unity. The event of 1455 began with a drama event, featured elaborate entrances and a huge amount of spending by the town itself. The route into Tournai was bedecked in cloth, and to decide the order of shooting the guild devised an extra elaborate event. As noted, competitions emphasised fairness from the outset, and usually lots were drawn to decide who would shoot first. In Tournai

> a portable meadow had been installed in the town hall, complete with bushes and flowers ingeniously made from wax, and in the meadow stood wax female figures representing the companies in attendance. To the heads of these female figures were attached missals bearing the names of the cities and towns which had sent companies to the contest. A beautiful young girl dressed in a bright red tunic embroidered with the emblem of the Tournai crossbowmen stood beside the meadow. The girl held a little rod in her hand which she used to touch each of the wax figures in turn.

The elaborate method of choosing an order of shooting followed the awarding of a silver dolphin for the second-best play praising the dauphin, as well as entrances with drama and lights. The 1455 event was spectacular and seems to have been the largest event yet held – indeed, it was to remain among the largest events of the fifteenth century, and celebrated peace.

The events of 1440 and 1455 did not simply continue a tradition of elaborate shoots. They made the shoots grander and more spectacular and, in doing so, used competitions to restore urban networks across a wide region, emphasising the ideals of peace and honour. The 1455 shoot may have been the largest of the fifteenth century, but events continued in the next two decades, with competitions in Mechelen in 1458, Oudenaarde in 1462 and Lier in 1466, yet none was as large as that of Tournai.[70] With the peace that characterised the last two decades of Philip the Good's reign, more competitions were held. There was an increase in the quantity of events, but not in the size of individual shoots, and every year there were at least one if not three or four shoots of various sizes. Like the events held in the 1420s and 1430s, the competitions of the 1450s and 1460s were important for maintaining communities, but did not grow to rebuild such communities. Numerous smaller shoots were important for maintaining civic

---

[70] SAB, 385, rekening st Joris; ADN, LRD, B 17879; OSAOA, gilden 507/II/16; AGR, CC, 31460, f. 42; CC, 31770; CC, 38690, f. 37v.

communities and winning honour, but no individual shoot was as elaborate or drew in as large an audience as had those of 1440 and 1455.

If competitions became slightly smaller and less elaborate during long years of peace, they shrank dramatically in prolonged years of crisis. Small events continued during the reign of Charles the Bold but they were not huge spectacles to rebuild peace, perhaps because the uprisings of Charles's reign did not divide Flanders. It must also be remembered that Charles's reign saw far more taxation than his father's had, and towns had less money available to invest in spectacles, as well as having more reason to invest in fortifications. After Charles's violent death before the walls of Nancy in January 1477, competitions continued in their smaller forms. In the crisis years of Mary's short reign and the long and divisive regency for Philip the Fair, travel became difficult.[71] In addition, guilds were militarily important, as we have seen, and towns may not have wanted their potential defenders to be far away, shooting for prizes, should the town come under threat.

Yet, just as archery and crossbow competitions had survived wars and plague in the fourteenth century, and had helped to restore peace after 1436–38 and 1453, so too they continued in these years of crisis, maintaining fragile inter-urban bonds. An archery competition was held in Bruges in 1477, another in Brussels in 1479, two in 1480 and three in 1481.[72] The Hulst event of 1483 was not unique; rather, it was part of the continued efforts on the part of civic authorities to maintain regional fraternities and keep peace across Flanders. The competitions of the 1480s were smaller than those of the 1450s and 1460s, but, as with the events of 1350, the fact that the competitions were held at all is important. The numerous smaller events show that the desire for peace and community remained even in periods of crisis and that shooting guilds continued to be seen as a useful tool in maintaining networks.

War, instability and uncertainty for Flanders ended, or at least there were hopes that such troubles would end, when Philip the Fair reached majority in 1494. With Maximilian's removal, Philip's international marriage and hopes for peace, the towns again used crossbow competitions to reaffirm bonds with other towns and, indeed, with the count himself. Two great events were held at the end of the 1490s: an event in Oudenaarde in 1497 and one in Ghent in 1498. Oudenaarde and Ghent were emerging, or at least trying to emerge, from a period of intense political conflict and rebellion and a severe economic downturn. Both needed once again to replace dishonourable memories with new, honourable events, and to rebuild Flemish unity. Oudenaarde, as it had done previously, staged an elaborate shoot that was attended mostly by Flemish

---

[71] J.-M. Cauchies, *Philippe le Beau, le Dernier duc de Bourgogne* (Turnhout: Brepols, 2003), 3–15.

[72] De Potter, *Jaarboeken*, 113–14; Transcription of Brussels documents in apendix of Wauters, *Notice historique*; for some participants, including Bruges, see Vanhoutryre, *De Brugse kruisbooggilde*, 72–4; AGR, CC, 31474, f. 75v.

guilds. Philip the Fair was invited to participate, but he does not seem to have done so, although other lords did lead shooting guilds.[73] The 1497 shoot was not as large or as specular as those of 1440 or of 1455, but was far larger than anything in the previous decades, again using spectacle and competitions to restore unity.

As we saw in the previous chapter, the Ghent crossbow competition was remembered long after 1498. It is clear that, as at Oudenaarde a year before, the guild and civic authorities of Ghent were working to use the crossbowmen to restore peace in Flanders. The competition was described in chronicles that celebrated the entrances and the success of the event and the numerous prizes – and the entrances, which surpassed anything recorded earlier, were certainly elaborate. Yet, on closer inspection, the competitions begin to look, to use Huizinga's famous term, like the *Herfistij*[74] of these events – a competition at its most developed and fullest, and yet about to decay. The 1498 competition was beautiful and was remembered as stunning and impressive, but was attended by far fewer guilds than the earlier events had been. In all, fifty-six guilds came to Ghent in 1440, fifty-nine to Tournai in 1455, but only thirty to the 1498 competition. Of these, sixteen came from within Flanders, nine from Brabant and three from Hainaut, with the men of Tournai and Utrecht also in attendance. The pattern here is very similar to that of the Oudenaarde competition discussed above, although in earlier years Ghent's shoots had been far bigger than those staged by their smaller neighbour. The Ghent shoot of 1498 was a celebration of peace and of hopes for a unified region, and with larger entrances and an even greater number of prizes than at previous shoots it had the potential to be an extraordinary event. Yet far fewer civic authorities chose to fund or to allow their guilds to take part. The same ideas of unity were expressed both in 1440 and in 1498, but in 1498 they were not so well received. Perhaps, given a decade of peace, the events could have recovered, and those staged in 1507 or 1508 would have been as elaborate – perhaps even more elaborate – as the events of the mid-fifteenth century, had Philip's reign continued and restored the 'promised lands' of his great-grandfather's reign.

Although the competitions of 1497 and 1498 were not as well attended as previous events, their potential to build and restore unity was recognised by civic authorities. Archery and crossbow competitions gathered hundreds of armed men together, gave them large (often very large) quantities of wine and granted immunity from prosecution for accidental deaths or injuries – surely a potential for violence. Yet it is clear from their timing, as it is clear from

---

[73] AGR, CC, 31783, 36r–v.
[74] J. Huizinga, *Herfsttij der Middeleeuwen* (Haarlem: H. D. Tjeenk Willink 1919), reprinted many times and translated into English as the 'Waning' or 'Autumn' of the Middle Ages. For the influence of the work see W. Simons and E. M. Peters, 'The New Huizinga and the Old Middle Ages', *Speculum* 74 (1999), 587–620, and for an argument against the term see J. Koopmans, 'Einde van het Herfttij der Middeleeuwen', *Rapports: Het Franse boek* 65 (1995), 101–9.

the language of letters of invitation, that peace was one of the major goals of competitions. Using archery and crossbow competitions as ways of keeping social peace fits with studies that have demonstrated a widespread wish for *'paix civile'* in the later Middle Ages.[75] Guilds had been given rights for the honour and protection of their towns, and their competitions looked to the Flemish common good, to peace and order, and to work toward building unity and demonstrating community across the region.

Guilds worked for unity, and their competitions promoted peace and harmony, but did the events live up to these expectations? As Van Bruaene has shown, chambers of rhetoric similarly emphasised honour, brotherhood, peace in their competitions. Yet in the drama events such ideals were, more often than not, marred by conflict, and disputes were submitted to the provincial court of Flanders in 1494.[76] Jousts were not so idealised for peace, but they should have promoted community and enhanced civic prestige. Yet, at the end of the thirteenth century a joust in Douai led to continued violence between Douai and Lille. The conflict typified in jousting came close to war.[77] Given the violent potential of archery and crossbow competitions, a similar picture of violent reality failing to live up to idealised community might be expected. Yet remarkably few disputes were recorded, and none was submitted to higher authorities. The possibility that disputes occurred, but that the civic powers that funded the shoots chose not to record them, cannot be dismissed. It is entirely possible that violence did break out in shooting matches, but in records of the events and in all the depictions of them it is peace and harmony that are dominant, and only two examples of disputes have been found. Conflicts involving Liedekerke and Brussels, and Courtrai and Dixmuide, occurred, but seem to have been the result of local tensions that spilled over into shooting competitions. Such a small number of disputes, like the small number of conflicts within the guilds, is evidence not of the failure of guilds to create unity but of an overwhelming success in keeping the peace.

Competitions were held between urban guilds and, as we saw in the previous chapter, several invitations made clear that villagers were not welcome. Although there were exceptions, such as the Hulst shoot of 1483, the anti-rural bias of shooting competitions fits with the anti-rural bias evident in urban literature.[78] Competitions built communities and networks between *towns*. Guilds in villages certainly existed, but were not allowed to attend the most prestigious shooting

---

[75] A. Vauchez, 'La paix dans les mouvements religieux populaires', in *Pace e guerra nel basso medioevo. Atti del XL Convegno storico internazionale* (Spoleto: Fondazione Centro italiano di studi sull'alto Medioevo), 313–33; Tlusty, *The Martial Ethic*, 6–8, 11–20.

[76] Van Bruaene, 'A Wonderfull tryumfe', 392.

[77] L. Feller, 'La fête faillie: les événements de mai (1284, Lille-Douai)', *RN* 334 (2000), 9–34; G. Espinas, *Une Guerre sociale interurbaine dans la Flandre wallonne au XIIIe siècle, Douai et Lille, 1284–5* (Paris: Sirey, 1930).

[78] H. Pleij, 'Restyling "Wisdom," Remodeling the Nobility, and Caricaturing the Peasant: Urban Literature in the Late Medieval Low Countries', *JIH* 32 (2002), 689–704.

events; they were seen as rustic and unworthy of the honour offered by the great competitions. No records of violence by urban groups against villagers have been found, but the rules banning villagers from attending were used against one town. Liedekerke is a small town in western Brabant, between Aalst and Brussels. Although small, Liedekerke had shooting guilds, confraternities, municipal governors and an impressive procession, and would seem to fit any definition of urban.[79] The crossbow guild of Liedekerke had attended the crossbow competition in Ghent in 1400 without any trouble, and a messenger visited it in 1440.[80] Even though a small town, Liedekerke was part of the fifteenth-century festive networks, even hosting its own small competition in 1433, which attended by Ghent and Oudenaarde, among others.[81] In 1460 members of the Oudenaarde Saint Sebastian guild travelled to Liedekerke and were granted £5 by the town authorities for the 'honour of the town' in doing so.[82] Yet they were not always welcomed as part of the peace-keeping brotherly community outlined above; rather, they seem to have become particularly unwelcome.

In 1440 the Liedekerke crossbowmen complained to the Ghent crossbow guild that they had been attacked by the crossbow guild of Brussels. The neighbouring and far larger town had ridiculed the Liedekerke guild-brothers and had called them villagers on their way to the Ghent shoot. Despite their inauspicious start, Liedekerke did compete in 1440, with ten shooters listed and named, like every other guild, by Pieter Polet.[83] The guild did not win any prizes, but once it had entered Ghent it was treated like every other urban guild who took part. In 1462, on its way to another great shoot in Oudenaarde, it seems to have been treated even more harshly. Not only did the Brussels guild insult it; it robbed the king of the Liedekerke guild of some of his jewels. The men of Liedekerke wrote to the hosts; they claimed that they would have won best entry, had Brussels not robbed them, and they appealed to the Oudenaarde guild officials to obtain justice for them.[84] Small towns had their own guilds, and they wanted prestige and honour in the same way that guilds from great towns did, but they did not always achieve such high reputations in competitions in urban centres. Peaceful communities were desirable, and were worked for in guild regulation and guild competitions, but competitions were honourable because they were exclusive.

Liedekerke's crossbowmen were attacked and insulted as outsiders, emphasising that the communities were not open to all, but only to respectable

---

[79] E. de Reuse, 'Processies te Liedekerke', *Eigen Schoon en de Brabander: Driemaandelijks Tijdschrift van het Koninklijk Geschied – en Oudheidkundig Genootschap van Vlaams-Brabant*, 62 (1979), 353–63.
[80] UBG, Hs G 6112, *Dit es den bouc van ... Pieter Polet*, f. 12v.
[81] AGR, CC, CV, 37101, f. 18; OSAOA, microfilm 685, accounts 1432–3, f. 145v.
[82] Rantere, *Geschiedenis van Oudenaarde*, vol. 2, 127–8.
[83] Letter published in De Potter, *Jaarboeken*, appendix, no. 1; the document has recently been purchased by the municipality of Liedekerke, but does not yet have an archival reference; UBG, Hs G 6112, *Dit es den bouc van ... Pieter Polet*, ff. 12v, 33v.
[84] OSAOA, gilden 507/II/4B.

urban communities. What made Liedekerke acceptable in 1400, but a target for violence in 1440 and 1462, is not clear from the surviving sources. Liedekerke *was* a town, and not even the only small town attending the Ghent shoot; it was certainly not smaller than other towns visited by messengers in 1440. Despite the violence, it is important to note that Liedekerke did not respond with violence; rather, it appealed in both cases to the hosts of the competitions, just as guild-brothers in dispute should appeal to their constable. Liedekerke wanted to be part of the peace-building festive network that the crossbow guilds were part of, and the crossbowmen expected the hosts to restore peace within that community and treat them fairly. Liedekerke did not get what it wanted. Ghent seems to have ignored its letter completely, the Oudenaarde guild promised to look into the matter but no action seems to have been taken. Liedekerke emerge as a victimised participant and seems to have been badly treated by a far larger town.

Liedekerke's treatment seems unfair, especially as no other town helped it in its struggles, but this is the only documented case of a town being victimised. One other case of dispute can be traced in Flanders, and this seems to have been a more complicated one involving two towns, and probably other underlying tension that cannot now be recovered. The archery guilds of Dixmuide and Courtrai, medium-sized towns of central Flanders with estimated populations in the mid-fifteenth century of 2,200 and 8,400, respectively, had a long-running conflict. The loss of the Dixmuide archives in 1914 means we have only one side of this dispute, but it is nevertheless revealing. Each guild had a long tradition of taking part in shoots, with the archers and crossbowmen of Courtrai winning many prizes in the fourteenth century.[85]

There seems to have been a misunderstanding in 1462. The archers of Courtrai arrived for a shoot in Dixmuide, only to find the city in the middle of an unrelated festival. Enraged, the Courtrai men attacked and damaged several buildings and stole some 'finery'. The teams met next in Eecloo in 1468. The archers of Dixmuide objected to the men of Courtrai's presence, and Eecloo sent the Courtrai guild-brothers home in dishonour. This had still not been resolved in 1494, when both teams attended a shoot in Menin. Again, the host decided in Dixmuide's favour and sent the Courtrai men home, although the Courtrai guild-brothers felt that they should have won the prize for best entrance.[86] In 1496 both teams held separate shoots, and neither attended the event held in the other's town. This is the last known mention of the dispute. Why the Dixmuide archers invited Courtrai to a non-existent competition, and how they settled the squabble between themselves, is impossible to know. The Dixmuide–Courtrai dispute was a local tension, unconnected to wars or rebellions, and was the only

---

[85] Chotin, *Histoire de Tournai et du Tournisses*, vol. 1, 349–358; UBG, Hs G 6112, *Dit es den bouc van ... Pieter Polet* ff. 111v–113v.

[86] E. Hosten, 'Notes et documents, un différend entre archers au 15e siècle', *ASEB* 68 (1925), 77–83; RAK, 982; 4389; 4863.

long-running dispute between guilds recorded in any Flemish archive that I have encountered. We must conclude, then, that despite their military service, despite civic tensions, guilds of crossbowmen and archers were agents of social peace, building honour and friendship through skill and spectacle in great competitions. Conflict was recorded in a tiny minority of competitions, and not in any of the great competitions.

Archery and crossbow competitions, like the guilds that staged them, were representative of Flemish values and of Flemish towns. Guilds and towns emphasised community between towns, and the centrality of urban networks for both trade and cultural activities. The great events gave guilds, and the towns that sponsored them, an opportunity to demonstrate their civic identity and to win urban honour on a public stage. Powerful as they were, the Flemish towns were not islands. They must be understood as part of networks and as part of a community that wished to uphold peace and unity. Archery and crossbow competitions became means to strengthen economic and political networks, to use rivers to emphasise the strength of regional communities and the necessity for Flanders to work together. Small networks show the connections between larger towns and their hinterlands, as well as bonds between smaller towns and the ways in which civic powers could use guilds to enhance existing connections. Large events used rivers as well as civic connection to demonstrate and to strengthen the networks that ran across the Low Countries, maintaining and rebuilding communities. Archery and crossbow competitions were great spectacles in later medieval Flanders, but they were more than great shows: they were meaningful events, demonstrating and winning status and enhancing the Common Good and unity of Flanders. Disputes did happen, just as violence within guilds happened, but these were minimal and, in the vast majority of events, the ideals of unity and community were upheld. In planning, describing and remembering the competitions, civic authorities and guilds created a history of competitions that emphasised the use bows and crossbows as tools for social peace in the years following their use as weapons of war.

Conclusion

Guilds in Civic Society

This study has situated the archery and crossbow guilds of late medieval Flanders within their civic societies. The analysis of guilds as civic defenders, civic organisations and civic representatives in aristocratic and regional networks has demonstrated that the guilds acted as the embodiment of the urban 'Common Good'. The guilds built on existing ideals of brotherhood and commensality, on evolving and often ardent devotions and, fundamentally, on the variations in the meaning of membership, to create strong communities both within towns and across Flanders. That war and instability were driving forces for urban men to take up archery seems obvious, but the guilds were not militias; their development and evolution was linked to civic self-representation and desires on the part of townsmen to demonstrate their prominence and augment their honour, and even to keep the peace.

Guilds were military groups. They served in war throughout the period, representing their communities on the town battlements and on the battlefield, but they were valued as far more than this by their civic societies. Guild-brothers were small but significant groups and recognised parts in the army that Louis of Male led into Brabant in 1356, and supported Maximilian at Guinegatte in 1479, proving the potential of their expertise by winning a swift victory. Yet the guilds were far more than soldiers or militias and the present study has proved that community and desires for peace were more important than war for the Flemish towns.

The ability of archery and crossbow guilds to bring individuals from different socio-economic backgrounds together to form communities was central to their formation and functions. Within their own towns, guilds built communities around saints, around socialising and around spiritual aid. They invested in devotion, allowing their members to demonstrate corporate and individual identity. The location of guilds' chapels, their concern for charity and the role in them of women and children all demonstrate the guilds fulfilling civic values. Guilds, like towns, were not perfect; disputes and even violence happened; but, just as towns worked to maintain the 'good' and peace of their town, so too did guilds, expelling disobedient members and encouraging all members to eat and drink together to build bonds of community. Guild communities included all ranks of the nobility, with local lords and the dukes of Burgundy placing themselves at the head of guild communities to emphasise their own status and sense of their own lordship. In interacting with the guild-brothers in shooting or recreational assembly, lords used guilds to strengthen their bonds with civic society; in return, guilds gained greater honour and greater recognition.

Guilds as a force for peace and for community can be appreciated through our study of their spectacular competitions. Despite the threats of the wars, rebellions and plagues of the fourteenth century, competitions grew and became stronger. Indeed, threats and instability helped competitions to grow and evolve, because after war and violence invitations and competitions emphasised wishes for peace, for friendship and for honour. Archery and crossbow competitions allowed for a reaffirmation of regional networks and unity, as well as a strengthening of friendly connections. In bringing so many men together, competitions held the potential for great conflict. Hundreds of armed men together in a town for weeks, even months, all being given large quantities of wine and with comparatively little to do beyond watch others shoot, seems like an explosive mix, yet the competitions brought peace, not war. Through varied membership, with strong emphasis on community and with civic support, the guilds became influential groups in late medieval Flemish towns, representing their towns and civic ideology, a part of urban life.

Guilds represented ideals of civic honour and civic community in fourteenth- and fifteenth-century Flanders. How far they 'waned' or evolved over the next five centuries is another matter. The Bruges guild of Saint Sebastian will celebrate the six hundredth anniversary of its papal recognition in 2016 and make clear its claim to be the oldest sporting group in Europe.[1] As we have seen, it was not the first guild to receive rights, but it is unusual in having maintained those rights and its place in civic society across the centuries. The Ghent Crossbowmen of Saint George – who celebrated their seven hundredth anniversary in 2014 – lost their rights and their property during the Calvinist period in Ghent.[2] The Lille guilds, who are also attested in civic sources before the Bruges archers, lost their rights in the French Revolution, although a new guild was established in the early nineteenth century. The Brussels crossbow guild, who still form part of the bi-annual Ommegang and who own and meet in a hall under Saint Jacques church, very near to their medieval shooting range, also lost their rights and much of their silverware in the French Revolution. The opportunity I had to be

---

[1] The celebration and exhibition will result in a new study of the guilds: . M. Lemahieu en J. Dumolyn (eds), *Koninklijke Hoofdgilde Sint-Sebastiaan binnen Brugge. 600 jaar gildearchief* (2017); for the modern history of the guild see Lemahieu, *De eerste Vlaamse schuttersgilden*; idem, *De Koninklijke Hoofdgilde Saint-Sebastiaan Brugge* and the guild's wesbite, http://www.sebastiaansgilde.be.

[2] Van Bruaene and Coessens, 'Weerbare mannen?'; for the modern 'Souvereine Hooftdgilde van St. Joris' in Ghent see its website, http://www.sintjorisgilde.be/nl/home.php.

in their guild hall to watch the guild-brothers prepare for the 2009 Ommegang offered an incredible insight into the bonds within guilds, the rivalry between crossbow guilds and the civic pride that is palpable in civic events.[3] The pride felt by twenty-first-century guilds is a testimony to the vibrancy of the shooting guilds and the continuing importance of community and drinking in recreational assembly for all ranks of society.

Archery and crossbow guilds suffered in the traumas of early modern and modern conflict, just as their towns did, yet they survived and were usually refounded and re-created after wars and instability. In 1618 the Infanta Isabella took part in a crossbow competition in Ghent, the town of her grandfather's birth. She successfully shot the *papegay*, becoming 'queen' of the Greater Guild of Saint George, and her triumph was recorded in a monumental picture in the town hall. The guilds of 1618 had changed greatly from those of 1500: no longer did they serve in war, and their devotional activities had become far less involved, most chapels having been destroyed in the iconoclasm of the sixteenth century. They had lost most of their obvious characteristics, but even in 1618 the guilds were prestigious urban groups and they represented the best way for the new governor of the Low Countries to integrate herself into urban culture. Isabella's victory was seen as significant, and the imagery of her victory and of the parrot was used in the following royal procession. Just as her ancestors had done two centuries earlier, Isabella used the guilds to show herself to be part of urban culture, as integrated into civic communities and as upholding civic values.[4] The guilds of the Spanish Netherlands represented the power of tradition and the continuity needed for community within towns and between court and civic societies. Archery and crossbow guilds represented urban honour and urban wishes for peaceful communities; these values survived far beyond the fifteenth century, even if the military potential of their weapons and the attachment to saints did not.

---

[3] I am extremely grateful to Luc Bernaerts, Doyen et Archiviste de la Gilde, for this opportunity; for the modern history of the Brussels guild see L. Bernaert, *Chronologie du Grand Serment Royale et de Saint George des Arbaletriers de Bruxelles A partir de 1830* (Brussels, 2007) and its website, http://www.arbaletriers-saintgeorges.be/.
[4] M. Twycross, 'The Archduchess and the Parrot', 63–90; Arnade, *Realms of Ritual*, 65–7.

Bibliography

Archival Sources

Aalst, Stadsarchief
Oude archief	3 Peysboek
	7 Den boek met de haire
	55 Register Sintjorisgilde
	123 Scheppenboek
	127 Rentenboeken
	156 Rekenigen Sintjorisgilde
Kerkerchief	622, Broederschappen

Archives Départementales du Nord (Lille)
Séries B (chambre des comptes)	319, 671, 731, 885, 888, 937–8, 1060, 1116–89, 1218–337, 1358, 1916–41, 1633, 1639,1650–8, 1675, 1964,1843, 2021, 2153, 2352, 2817, 5361
Registre aux Chartres	1600–30
Expéditions militaires	835, 1188, 1418–19, 1380, 3495, 3516–20, 3533
Lettres reçues et dépêche	17724, 17734, 17751, 17758, 17762–7, 17644, 17869, 17832–3, 17875–9, 17883, 17875, 17879, 17888, 17790, 17896, 17904, 19165
Séries E–J, autre communes	J 471/289, 471/403, 847/1, 1438, 1674–748
Séries G (religieuses)	16, 86, 275, 369, 406 125/ 1465 339/5841

Archives Générales du Royaume (Brussels)
Chambre des comptes, comptes des villes	Anvers	30886–8
	Alost	31412–595
	Audenarde	31762–848
	Biervliet	32061–147
	Blankenberge	32148–566
	Bruges	32827–42

Caprycke	33009–70
Courtrai	33147–252
Damme	33544–871
Dixmude	33912–93
Eecloo	34355–433
Haerlebeke	35532–79
Loo	35903–86
Ninove	37076–157
Renaix	37887–92
Ypres	38635–780
L'audiencier (inv 52/2)	219, 1550
Famille van der Noot (fonds 144)	244, Bruges, pièce du procès de la gilde des arbalétriers contre la gilde des archers, 16e siècle

Armentières, Archives Municipales

EE, Affaires militaires	4–6

Brugge, Archief van de gilde van Sint-Sebastian

Charters	
Rekening	1454–6, 1460–65, 1465–72, 1472–80, 1486–7, 1506–12
List des confrères de la gilde, débutant en 1514	

Brugge, Archief van de Biscop

Acta capitali	A 49–52
Ambachten en hun kapellen in de st Donaaskerk	D 4
Broederschappen	S 289, 335, 344, 377, 386, 534–5

Brugge, Rijksarchief

Ambachten	33, 75, 116, 117, 118, 123–32, 138, 143, 146–8, 170–1, 173–4, 182–4, 196–9, 224–5, 237, 256–306, 311, 356, 375, 386, 447–53, 470, 487–8, 511–12, 553, 603, 635, 636
Onze Lieve Vrouw (inv. 91)	134, 250, 338, 1217–18, 1496, 1501, 1531

Brugge, Stadsarchief

Sint Joris en Jongehof	385
Gilden	46, 299, 314, 324, 336–7, 345, 456, 505, 524
Westvernieuwingen	114
Stadsrekening	216

Douai, Archives Communales
Séries AA	84, 94, 97
Séries BB	1–3
Séries CC	200, 262–497 (années 1391–1508)
Séries EE	13–18, 21
24II232	Registre 'Arbalestiers de Douay, 1382'

Gent, Rijksarchief
Fonds Sint-Baaf	03820, 7576, 7634, 7792, 7793
Fonds Sint-Pieter	1163, 1943, 1989

Gent, Stadsarchief
Reeks Sint Joris	155
Reeks Sint Sebastiaan	155/1
Reeks Sint Anthonius	155/2
Sint Jorisgilde, niet genummerde reeks	
Sint Jorishospitaal	LXVII
Cartularies	93–7
Jaarregister	301
Actes en keuren	302
Stadsrekening	400

Gent, STAM
Sint Jorisgilde, Register der Doodschulden	G 12.608
Sint Sebastiaangilde; Privilegieboek	inv. 1059

Gent, Universiteitsbibliotheek
Sint Joris Charters	Hs. G 3018/3, Hs. G. 61731
Archief Sint Joris	Hs. G 19580/9
Dits es den bouc vander scutters tobehoorende Pieter Polet ende Sint Joris Gilden te Gent	Hs. G 6112
Kronijke van Audenaerde	Hs. 708
Inventaire des chartes des deux confréries d'arbalétriers de Saint Georges qui existèrent en la ville de Gant	HS 610–11
Traites de paix/ Vredesverdragen	Hs 434

Kortrijk, Rijksarchief
Notulenboek van de Sint-Sebastiaansgilde	464
Register van de gilde van Sint-Sebastiaan	478
Stukken m.b.t. de Sint-Sebastiaansgilde	1087
Stukken m.b.t. de Schuttersgilden	3896

Reglement voor de Kortrijkse Schuttersgilde 5341
van Sint-Sebastiaan
Sint-Jorisgilde. 1 stuk   5800

Lille, Archives Municipales

Fonds Anciens, Affaires Generales	Arbalétriers	7–9
	Archers	5–6
Registre aux Mandates	16.973–992	
Ordonnances de Magistrates	373–80	
Pièces aux Titres	1066–787	
Comptes de la Ville	16012–270 (années 1317–1536)	

Oudenaarde, Stadsarchief

Gilden	507/II Sint Joris Gilde
	507/III Sint Sebastiaan Gilde
Stadsrekening	microfilm 684–7
Chronickes van Oudenaarde	241
Bartholomeeus de Rantere	microfilm 1484–6

Roubaix, archives municipales
Affaires Militarisés, EE   1–4

Printed Primary Sources

Batselier, A. (ed.), *Kroniek van het toneel en van het letterkundig leven te Geraardsbergen (1416–1808)* (Geraardsbergen: Koninklijke rederijkersgilde Sint-Pieter Vreugd en deugd, 1976).

Bonenfant, P. (ed.), *Ordonnances de Philippe le Hardi et de Marguerite de Male du 17 janvier 1394 au 25 février 1405* (Bruxelles: Ministère de la justice, 1974).

Brown, A. and Small, G., *Court and Civic Society in the Burgundian Low Countries c1420– 1520* (Manchester: Manchester University Press, 2007).

Cauchies, J-M. (ed.), *Ordonnances de Jean Sans Peur, 1405–1419* (Bruxelles: Ministère de la Justice, 2001).

——, *La législation princière pour le comté de Hainaut: ducs de Bourgogne et premiers Habsbourg (1427–1506)* (Bruxelles: Publications des Facultés universitaires Saint-Louis, 1982).

Commynes, Philippe de, *Mémoires*, 2 vols, ed. J. Blanchard (Genève: Droz, 2007).

Dadizeele, Jean de, *Mémoires inédits de seigneur Jean de Dadizeele*, ed. A. Voisin (Bruges: Vandecasteele-Werbrouck, 1850).

Despars, N., *Cronijke van den lande ende graefscepe van Vlanderen van de Jaeren 405 tot 1492*, 4 vols, ed. J. de Jonghe (Bruge: Messchert, 1839–42).

Dits die excellente cronike van Vlaanderen, beghinnende van Liederik Buc tot keyser Carolus, W. Vosterman (Antwerp, 1531) [Konilijke Bilbiotheek, Brussels VH 27.525].

Dixmude, Olivier van, *Merkwaerdige gebeurtenissen, vooral in Vlaenderen en Brabant, en ook in de aengrenzende landstreken: van 1377 tot 1443*, ed. J-J. Lambin (Ypre: Lambin, 1835).
Dynter, Edmond de, *Chronique des ducs de Brabant*, 4 vols, ed. P. F. X. De Ram (Bruxelles: Hayez, 1854-60).
Espinas, G., *Les origines du droit d'association dans les villes de l'Artois et de la Flandre française jusqu'au début du XVIe siècle*, vol. 2, Documents (Lille: Raoust, 1941).
Gailliard, E. and Gilliodts-van Severen, L., *Inventaire des archives de la Ville de Bruges*, 9 vols (Bruges: Gailliard, 1871-85).
Grange, A. de la, 'Extraits analytiques des registres des consaulx de la ville de Tournai, 1431-1476', *Mémoires de la Société historique et littéraire de Tournai* 23 (1893), 1-396.
Hennebert, F., 'Extraits des registres des Consaux de la ville et cite de Tournai' (1477-1482) *Mémoires de la Société historique et littéraire de Tournai* 3 (1856), 57-285.
Klerk, Jan de, D'Anvers, *Les Gestes des ducs de Brabant*, 4 vols, ed. J. F. Willems (Bruxelles: Hayez, 1839).
Lettenhove, K. de (ed.), *Istore et croniques de Flandres, d'après les textes de divers manuscrits*, 2 vols (Bruxelles: Hayez, 1879-80).
——, *Chroniques relatives à l'histoire de la Belgique sous la domination des ducs de Bourgogne*, 3 vols (Bruxelles: Hayez, 1870-76).
Marche, Olivier de la, *Collection complète des mémoires relatifs à l'histoire de France, Olivier de la Marche*, 2 vols, ed. M. Petitot (Paris: [s.n.]: 1825).
Muisit, Giles le, *Chronique et Annales*, ed. H. Lemaitre (Paris: Renouard, H. Laurens, 1906).
Nicholas, D. and Prevenier, W., *'Gentsche stads- en baljuwsrekeningen (1365-76)*' (Bruxelles: Palais des Académies, 1999).
Nicolay, Jehan, *Kalendrier des Guerres de Tournay (1477-1479)*, ed. F. Hennebert (Bruxelles: Aug. Decq, 1853).
Pauw, N. de, *De rekeningen der stad Gent: tijdvak van Jacob van Artevelde 1336-1349*, 3 vols (Gent: Hoste, 1874-85).
Piot, C. (ed.), *Chroniques de Brabant et de Flandre* (Bruxelles: Hayez, 1879).
Preud'homme, G., 'Extraits des registres des Consaux de la ville de Tournai (1455-1472); complément a l'édition de la Grange', *Mémoires de la Société royale d'Histoire et d'Archéologie de Tournai* 1 (1980), 297-341.
——, 'Extraits des registres des Consaux de la ville de Tournai (1488-99)', *Mémoires de la Société royale d'Histoire et d'Archéologie de Tournai* 2 (1981), 91-106.
Rantere, Bartholomeus de, *Geschiedenis van Oudenaarde, van 621-1397* (Oudenaarde, 1986), and *1397-1468*, ed. E. Dhoop and M. De Smet (Oudenaarde: Vereninging voor Vreemdelingenverkeer en Monumentenzorg, 1986).
Richebé, M. A., *Compte de recettes et dépenses de la ville de Lille, 1301-1302* (Lille: Leleu, 1894).
Smet, J. J. de (ed.), *Recueil des chroniques de Flandres/ Corpus chronicorum Flandriae*, 4 vols (Brussels: Hayez, 1837-65).
Stavelot, Jean de, *Chronique*, ed. A. Borghet (Bruxelles: Hayez, 1861).
Vandenbroeck, H., *Extraits analytiques des anciennes registres des Consaux de la ville de Tournai, 1385-1422)* (Tournai: Mémoires de la Société historique et littéraire de Tournai, 7, 1861).

——, *Extraits des anciens registres aux Délibérations des Consaux de la ville de Tournai, 1422–30* (Tournai: Mémoires de la Société historique et littéraire de Tournai, 8 (1863).
Vuylsteke, J., *De rekeningen der stad Gent: tijdvak van Philips van Artevelde 1376–1389* (Gent: Hoste, 1891–93).
——, *Gentsche stads- en baljuwsrekeningen 1280–1336*, 3 vols (Gent: Meyer-van Loo, 1900–8).
——, *Gentsche stads- en baljuwsrekeningen. 1351–1365* (Gent: s.n., ca. 1916).

Secondary Works

Abeele, A. Van den, *Het ridderlijk gezelschap van de Witte Beer: steekspelen in Brugge tijdens de late middeleeuwen* (Brugge Walleyn, 2000).
Abraham-Thisse, S., 'Kostel Ypersch, gemeyn Ypersch: les draps d'Ypres en Europe du Nord et de l'Est (XIII-XIVe siècles)', in *Ypres and the Medieval Cloth Industry in Flanders: Archaeological and Historical Contributions*, ed. M. Dewilde, A. Ervynck and A. Wielemans (Zellik: Instituut voor het archeologisch patrimonium, 1998), 111–24.
——, 'La représentation iconographique des métiers du textile au moyen-âge', in *Le verbe, l'image et les représentations de la société urbaine au moyen âge*, ed. M. Boone, E. Lecuppre-Desjardin and J.-P. Sossons (Anvers: Garant, 2002), 135–59.
Acker, L. van, *Geschiedenis der Ardooise schuttersgilden* (Kortrijk: [s.n.], 1952).
Ainsworth, M. W. (ed.), *Petrus Christus in Renaissance Bruges* (Turnhout: Brepols, 1995. 1995).
Aert, E., Blockmans, W. et al., *Brugge en Europa* (Antwerp: Fonds Mercator, 1992).
Alamichel, M.-F., 'Brutus et les Troyens: une histoire européenne', *RBPH* 84 (2006), 77–106.
Allen, V., 'Playing soldiers; tournaments and toxophily in late medieval England', in *Studies in Late Medieval and Early Renaissance Texts, Studies in Honour of John Scattergood*, ed. A. M. D'Arcy and a. J. Fletcher (Dublin: Four Courts Press, 2005), 35–52.
Alvin, F., *Les anciens serments d'arbalétriers et d'archers de Bruxelles, leur sceaux, leur médailles et leur jetons* (Bruxelles: J. Goemaere, 1901).
Amos, M. A., "Somme Lordes and Somme others of Lowe Estates', London's urban elite and the symbolic battle for status', in *Traditions and Transformation in Late Medieval England*, ed. D. Biggs, S. D. Michalove and A. Compton Reeves (Leiden: Brill, 2002), 159–76.
Anon., 'Tireurs d'arc', *Le Petit journal du musée, d'art, d'histoire et de folklore de Cassel* 1 (1994).
Anon., 'Le Sceau des archers du serment de Douai (1460)', *Souvenirs de Flandre Wallon*, 2e série 1 (1881), 103–7.
Arnade, P., 'Crowds, Banners and the Market Place; Symbols of Defiance and Defeat during the Ghent War of 1452–3', *Journal of Medieval and Renaissance Studies* 24 (1994), 471–97.
——, *Realms of Ritual, Burgundian Ceremony and Civic Life in Late Medieval Ghent* (Ithaca, NY: Cornell University Press, 1996).
——, 'City, State in Public Ritual in the Late Medieval Burgundian Netherlands', *Comparative Studies in Social History* 39 (1997), 300–18.

—, *Beggars, Iconoclasts, and Civic Patriots: the political culture of the Dutch Revolt* (Ithaca, NY: Cornell University Press, 2008).

— and Rocke, M. (eds), *Power, Gender and Ritual in Europe and the Americas, Essays in Memory of Richard Trexler* (Toronto: University of Toronto Press, 2008).

Autenboer, E. van, 'Een Schutterskonflikt te Antwerpen in 1589: de jonge voetboog contra de oude voetboog', *Taxandria, nieuwe reeks* 37 (1965), 67–111.

—, *Rederijkers en schutters in de branding van de 16e eeuw* (Antwerpen: Provincie Antwerpen, 1978).

—, *De Kaarten van de Schuttersgilden van het Hertogdom Brabant (1300–1800)*, 2 vols (Tilburg: Stichting Zuidelijk historisch contact, 1993).

Autrand, F. (ed.), *Prosopographie et genèse de l'état moderne* (Paris: École normale supérieure de jeunes filles, 1986).

Avonds, P., 'Mechelen en de Brabantse steden (1312–1355). Een bijdrage tot de parlementaire geschiedenis van de Derde Stad', *BTG* 53 (1970), 17–80.

Baillien, H., 'Het oudste Limburgse Gildecharter', *Het Oude Land Van Loon* 16 (1961).

—, 'De Tongerse schutterijen van de 14de tot de 16de eeuw', *Het Oude Land Van Loon* 34 (1979), 5–34.

Baillieul, B., *De vier Gentse hoofdgilden: Sint-Joris, Sint-Sebastiaan, Sint-Antonius en Sint-Michiel: zeven eeuwen traditie van waken, feesten en teren* (Gent: Stadsbestuur, 1994).

Ballard, M., 'An Expedition of English Archers to Liège in 1467 and the Anglo-Burgundian Marriage Alliance', *Nottingham Medieval Studies* 34 (1990), 152–74.

Bamps, C. and Geraet, E., 'Les Anciennes gildes ou compagnies militaires de Hasselt', *Annales de l'académie royale d'archéologique de Belgique*, 4e série 10 (1897), 21–46.

Banker, J. R., *Death in the Community: Memorialization and Confraternities in an Italian Commune in the Late Middle Ages* (Athens; London: University of Georgia Press, 1988).

Barron, C., 'Chivalry, Pageantry and Merchant Culture in Medieval London', in *Heraldry, Pageantry and Social Display in Medieval England*, ed. P. Coss and M. Keen (Woodbridge: Boydell, 2002), 219–42.

—, *London in the Later Middle Ages, Government and People, 1200–1500* (Oxford: Oxford University Press, 2004).

Barthélemy, E. de, *Histoire des archers, arbalétriers et arquebusiers de la ville de Reims* (Reims: P. Giret, 1873).

Beaurepaire, P-Y., 'Les nobles jeux d'arc à la fin de l'Ancien Régime; miroir d'une sociabilité en mutation', in *Société et religion en France et aux Pays-Bas XV ^{e}–XIXe siècles, mélanges a l'honneur d'Alain Lotin*, ed. G. Derengnaucourt (Arras: Artois Presses Université, 2000), 539–51.

—, *Nobles Jeux de l'Arc et loges maçonniques dans la France des lumières* (Cahors: Editions Ivoire-Clair, 2002).

Beer, J. de, *De Schuttersgilden, Overdruk uit het Gedenboek Frans Claes Museum 'De Gulden Spoor' te Antwerpen* (Antwerpen: De Sikkel, 1932).

Benoit, A., 'Le Beauregard de Lille', *RN* 25 (1939), 5–39.

Bergen-Pantens, C. van den, 'Antoine, Grand Bâtard de Bourgogne, bibliophile', in *L'Ordre de la Toison d'Or, de Philippe le Bon à Philippe le Beau (1430–1505). Idéal ou reflet d'une société?*, ed. C. Van den Bergen-Pantens (Turnhout: Brepols 1996), 198–200.

Berger, R., *La Nécrologe de la confrérie des jongleurs et des bourgeoises d'Arras (1194–1361)* (Arras: Commission départementale des monuments historiques du Pas-de-Calais, 1970).

Berghe-Loontjens, E. vanden, *Het Aloude gilde van de Handboogschutters St Sebastiaan te Rousselare* (Rousselare: Ackerman, 1904).

Bernaerts, L., *Chronologie du Grand serment royal et de Saint Georges des arbalétriers de Bruxelles* (Bruxelles: Polycopié, 2007).

Bessmerting, Y. L. and Oexle, O. G., *Das Individuum und die Seinen: Individualität in der okzidentalen und in der russischen Kultur in Mittelalter und früher Neuzeit* (Göttingen: Vandenhoeck und Ruprecht, 2001).

Bijsterveld, A-J. A., 'Looking for Common Ground: From Monastic Fraternitas to Lay Confraternity in the Southern Low Countries in the Tenth to Twelfth Centuries', in *Religious and Laity in Western Europe 1000–1400: Interaction, Negotiation, and Power*, ed. E. Jamroziak and J. Burton (Turnhout: Brepols, 2006), 287–314.

—— (ed.), *Cultuur in het laatmiddeleeuwse Noord-Brabant: literatuur, boekproductie, historiografie* ('s-Hertogenbosch: Stichting Brabantse regionale geschiedbeoefening, 1998).

Black, C., *Italian Confraternities in the Sixteenth Century* (Cambridge: Cambridge University Press, 1989).

—— and Gravestock, P. (ed.), *Early Modern Confraternities in Britain and the Americas* (Aldershot: Ashgate, 2006).

Blieck, G., 'Le Château dit de Courtrai a Lille de 1298 à 1339: une citadelle avant l'heure', *Bulletin Monumental* 3 (1997), 185–206.

—— and Vanderstraeten, L., 'Recherches sur les fortifications de Lille au Moyen Âge', *RN* 70 (1988), 107–22.

Blockmans, F., 'De erfstrijd tussen Vlaanderen en Brabant in 1356', *Bijdragen en Mededeelingen van het Historisch Genootschap* 69 (1955), 11–16.

Blockmans, W., 'Loyaliteitsconflicten in een proces van staatsvorming; Vlaanderen in de 14de en 15de eeuw', *Handelingen van het Vlaams Filologencongres* 31 (1977), 259–2674.

——, 'Stedelijke netwerken in de Nederlanden voor de industrialisatie', *Leidschrift; historisch tijdschrift* 7 (1990–91), 59–68.

——, 'Being Oneself', in *Showing Status: Representations of Social Positions in the Late Middle Ages*, ed. W. Blockmans and A. Jansese (Turnhout: Brepols, 1999), 1–16.

——, *Emperor Charles V, 1500–1558* (London: Arnold, 2002).

—— and Prevenier, W., *The Burgundian Netherlands* (Cambridge: Cambridge University Press, 1986), 42–86.

—— and Prevenier, W., *Le prince et le peuple: images de la société du temps des ducs de Bourgogne 1384–1530* (Anvers: Fonds Mercator, 1998).

—— and Prevenier, W., *The Promised Lands. The Low Countries under Burgundian Rule, 1369–1530* (Philadelphia, PA: University of Pennsylvania Press, 1999).

——, Boone, M. and Hemptinne, T. De (eds), *Secretum scriptorum, liber alumnorum Walter Prevenier* (Leuven: Garant, 1999).

—— et al., *Studiën betreffende de sociaal structuren te Brugge, Kortrijk et Gent in de 14e en 15e eeuw* (Heule: Anciens pays et assemblées d'États, 1971–73).

—— et al., 'Tussen crisis en welvaart; sociaal verhandelingen, 1300–1500', *AGN* 4 (1980).

Boffa, S., *Warfare in Medieval Brabant, 1356–1406* (Woodbridge: Boydell Press, 2004).

Bon, F. Le, *L'Ancien serment des arbalétriers de Nivelles et ses statuts* (Nivelles: Ch. Guignarde, 1886).

Bonnault d'Houet, le Baron de, *Les Francs-Archers de Compiègne, 1448–1524* (Compiègne: Imprimerie Henry Lefebvre, 1897).

Boogaart, T, A., *An Ethnogeography of Late Medieval Bruges; An Evolution of the Corporate Milieu* (Lewiston, NY: Edwin Mellen Press, 2004).

Boone, M., 'Dons et pots-de-vin, aspects de la sociabilité urbaine au bas Moyen Âge. Le cas gantois pendant la période bourguignonne', *RN* 70 (1988), 471–87.

——, *Gent en de Bourgondische hertogen ca. 1384–ca. 1453, een sociaal-politieke studie van een staatsvormingsproces* (Brussel: Koninklijke academie voor wetenschappen, letteren en schone kunsten van België, 1990).

——, 'Réseaux urbaine', in *Le Prince et le peuple, image a la société du temps des ducs de Bourgogne, 1384 – 1530*, ed. W. Prevenier (Anvers: Fonds Mercator, 1998), 232–54.

——, 'Les métiers dans les villes flamandes au bas moyen âge (XIVe–XVIe siècles): images normatives, réalités socio-politiques et économiques', in *Les métiers au moyen âge. Aspects économique et sociaux*, ed. P. Lambrechts et J.-P. Sosson (Louvain-la-Neuve: Fédération internationale des instituts d'études médiévales, 1994), 1–21.

——, 'Une Famille au service de l'état Bourgogne naissant. Roland et Jean d'Uutkerke, nobles Flamand dans l'entourage de Philippe le Bon', *RN* 77 (1995), 233–55.

——, 'Urban Space and Political conflict in Late Medieval Flanders', *JIH* 32 (2002), 621–40.

——, 'La justice en spectacle. La justice urbaine en Flandre et la crise du pouvoir "bourguignon" (1477–88)', *RH* 308 (2003), 43–65.

——, *A La Recherche d'une modernité civique. La Société urbain des anciens Pays-Bas* (Bruxelles: Éditions de l'Université de Bruxelles, 2010).

——, 'The Desired Stranger: Attraction and Expulsion in the Medieval City', in *Living in the City: Urban Institutions in the Low Countries, 1200–2010*, ed. L. Lucassen and W. Willems (New York: Routledge, 2012), 23–45.

—— and Howell, M. (eds), *In But Not of the Market; Movable Goods in the Late Medieval and Early Modern Economy* (Brussel: Koninklijke Vlaamse academie van België voor wetenschappen en kunsten, 2007).

——, 'Entre vision idéale et représentation du vécu, nouveaux aperçus sur la conscience urbaine dans les Pays-Bas à la fin du Moyen Âge', in *Bild und Wahrnehmung der Stadt: Kolloquium des Kuratoriums für vergleichende Städtegeschichte*, ed. P. Johanek (Köln, l'Allemagne Böhlau Verlag 2012), 79–98.

—— and Porfyrion, H., 'Markets, Squares, Streets: Urban Space, a Tool for Cultural Exchange', in *Cultural Exchange in Early Modern Europe*, vol. 2, 227–39.

—— and Prak, M., *Statuts individuels, statuts corporatifs et statuts judicaires dans les villes européennes (moyen âge et temps moderne)* (Leuven: Garant, 1996).

—— and Prevenier, W. (eds), *La Draperie ancienne des Pays-Bas. Débouche et stratégie de survie* (Leuven: Garant, 1993).

—— and Stabel, P. (eds), *Shaping Urban Identity in Late Medieval Europe* (Leuven: Garant, 2000).

—— and Stabel, P., 'New Burghers in the Late Medieval Towns of Flanders and Brabant; Conditions of Entry, Rules and Reality', in *Neubürger im späten Mittelalter: Migration und Austausch in der Städtelandschaft des alten Reiches (1250–1550)*, ed. R. C. Schwinges (Berlin: Duncker und Humblot, 2002), 317–32.

Bos, S., 'A Tradition of Giving and Receiving; Mutual Aid within the Guild System', in *Craft Guilds in the Early Modern Low Countries*, ed. M. Prak, C. Lis, J. Lucassen and H. Soly (Aldershot: Ashgate, 2006), 174–93.

Bossy, J., *Christianity in the West, 1400–1700* (Oxford: Oxford University Press, 1985).

Bouchera, P. and Chiffoleau, J., *Religion et société urbaine au moyen âge, études offertes à Jean-Louis Biget* (Paris: Publications de la Sorbonne, 2000).

Boussemaere, P., 'De Ieperse lakenproductie in de veertiende eeuw opnieuw berekend aan de hand van de lakenloodjes', *JMG* 3 (2000), 131–61.

Bouzy, O., 'Les armes symboles d'un pouvoir politique: l'épée du sacre, la Sainte Lance, l'Oriflamme, aux VIIe–XII siècle', *Forschungen zur westeuropäischen Geschichte* 22 (1995), 45–54.

Braake, S. Ter and Dixhoorn, A. van, 'Engagement en ambitie. De Haagse rederijkerskamer 'Met gdeuchten' en de ontwikkeling van een burgerlijke samenleving in Holland rond 1500', *JMG* 9 (2006), 150–90.

Braekevelt, J., Buylaert, F., Dumolyn, J. and Haemers, J., 'The Politics of Factional Conflict in Late Medieval Flanders', *Historical Research* 85 (2012), 13–31.

Braekevelt, J. and Dumolyn, J., 'Diplomatique et discours politiques. Une analyse lexicographique qualitative et quantitative des ordonnances de Philippe le Bon pour la Flandre (1419–1467)', *RH* 662 (2012), 323–56.

Brand, H., *Over macht en overwicht. Stedelijke elites in Leiden 1420–1510* (Leuven: Garant, 1996).

—— et al. (eds), *Memoria, communitas, civitas: mémoire et conscience urbaines en occident à la fin du Moyen âge* (Ostfildern: Thorbecke, 2003).

Brand, J., 'De geschiedenis van de Hulsterse rederijkers', *Jaarboek Oudheidkundige Kring de vier ambachten* 16 (1960–1), 70–129.

Brassât, B., *La Belle histoire du noble jeu de l'arc en pays de Brie* (Lésée-sur-Seiné: Editions Amatteis, 1991).

Brodman, J. W., *Charity and Religion in Medieval Europe* (Washington, DC: Catholic University of America Press, 2009).

Browers, P-D., 'Les compagnies d'arbalétriers dans l'ancien comte de Namur', *Annales de la société d'archéologie de Namur* 37 (1925), 141–54.

Brown, A., 'Civic Ritual: Bruges and the Count of Flanders in the Later Middle Ages', *EHR* (1997), 277–99.

——, 'Bruges and the "Burgundian Theatre-State": Charles the Bold and Our Lady of the Snow', *History* 84 (1999), 573–89.

——, 'Urban Jousts in the Later Middle Ages: The White Bear of Bruges', *RBPH* 78 (2000), 315–30.

——, 'Ritual and State Building; Ceremonies in Late Medieval Bruges', in *Symbolic Communication in Late Medieval Towns*, ed. J. Van Leewen (Leuven: Leuven University Press, 2006), 1–28.

——, *Civic Ceremony and Religion in Bruges c.1300–1520* (Cambridge: Cambridge University Press, 2011).

Bruaene, A. L. Van, *De Gentse memorieboeken, als Spiegel van stedelijk historisch bewustzijn 14de tot 16 de eeuw* (Gent: Maatschappij voor geschiedenis en oudheidkunde, 1998).

——, 'Sociabilite en competitie. De sociaalinstitutionele ontwikkeling van de rederijkerskamers in de zuidelijke Nederlanden', in *Conformisten en rebellen. Rederijkscultuur in de Nederlanden (1400–1650)*, ed. B. A. M. Ramakers (Amsterdam: Amsterdam University Press, 2003), 45–64.

——, 'The Habsburg Theatre State; Court, City and the Performance of Identity', in *Networks, Regions and Nations, Shaping Identities in the Low Countries, 1300–1650*, ed. R. Stein and J. Pullman (Leiden: Brill, 2010), 131–49.

——, 'Brotherhood and Sisterhood in the Chambers of Rhetoric in the Southern Low Countries', *Sixteenth Century Journal* 36 (2005), 11–35.

——, 'The Chambers of Rhetoric in the (Southern) Low Countries; A Flemish-Dutch Project on Literary Confraternities', *Confraternitas* 16 (2005), 3–14.

——, 'A Wonderfull Tryumfe, for the Wynnyng of a Pryse', *Renaissance Quarterly* 49 (2006).

——, *Om Beters Wille, Rederijkerskamers en de stedelijke cultuur in de Zuidelijke Nederlanden (1400–1650)* (Amsterdam: Amsterdam University Press, 2008), 374–405.

Brulez, W., 'Bruges and Antwerp in the 15th and 16th Centuries, an Antithesis', *Acta Historica Nederlandicae* 6 (1973), 1–26.

Bruyère, P., *Les compagnies sermentées de la cite de Liège aux temps modernes, l'exemple des jeunes arbalétriers (1523–1684)* (Liège: Société des Bibliophiles Liégeois 2004).

Bueren, T. Van, 'Care for the Here and the Hereafter; a Multitude of Possibilities', in *Care for the Here and the Hereafter; Memoria, Art and Ritual in the Middle Ages*, ed. T. van Bueren (Turnhout: Brepols, 2005), 13–34.

Burggraeve, P. de, *Un Landjuweel de la confrérie Gantois de Saint Georges au XVe siècle* (Gand: Siffer, n.d.).

Burgraere, P. de, *Notice historique sur les chefs-confréries gantoises de St.-Sébastien et de St.-Antoine* (Gand: Vander Haeghen, 1913).

Buylaert, F., 'Gevaarlijke tijden, een vergelijking van machtsverwerving en machtsbehoud bij stedelijke elites in laatmiddeleeuws Holland en Vlaanderen', *TVG* 119 (2006), 312–27.

——, 'Baenst, Guy II de, vorstelijk ambtenaar in de Raad van Vlaanderen en de Grote Raad', *Nationaal biografisch woordenboek* (2007), 37–49.

——, 'Sociale mobiliteit bij stedelijke elites in laatmiddeleeuws Vlaanderen. Een gevalstudie over de Vlaamse familie De Baenst', *JMG* 8 (2005), 201–51.

——, 'La noblesse et l'unification des Pays-Bas. Naissance d'une noblesse bourguignonne à la fin du moyen âge?', *RH* 653 (2010), 3–25.

——, *Eeuwen van ambitie, de Adel in laatmiddeleeuws Vlaanderen* (Brussel: Verhandelingen van de Koninklijke Academie voor Wetenschappen, Letteren en Schone Kunsten van België, 2010).

——, 'Memory, Social Mobility and Historiography. Shaping Noble Identity in the Bruges Chronicle of Nicholas Despars (+ 1597)', *Belgisch Tijdschrift voor Filologie en Geschiedenis* 87 (2011), 377–408.

——, 'The Late Medieval "Crisis of the Nobility" Reconsidered: The Case of Flanders', *Social History* 45 (2012), 1117–34.

——, *Repertorium van de Vlaamse adel (ca. 1350–ca. 1500)* (Gent: Academia Press, 2011).

—— and Dumolyn, J., 'Shaping and Reshaping the Concepts of Nobility and Chivalry in Froissart and the Burgundian Chroniclers', *Fifteenth Century* IX (2010), 59–83.

——, De Clerq, W. and Dumolyn, J., 'Sumptuary Legislation, Material Culture and the Semiotics of "vivre noblemen" in the County of Flanders (14th–16th centuries)', *Social History* 36 (2011), 393–417.

Carasso-Kok, M. and Halm, J. Levy-Van, *Schutters in Holland: kracht en zenuwen van de stad* (Zwolle: Waanders, 1988).

Carlier, M., Grevem, A., Prevenier, W. and Stabel, P., *Core and Periphery in Late Medieval Urban Society* (Leuven: Garant, 1997).

Caron, M-T., 'La Noblesse en Représentation dans les années 1430; vêtements de cour, vêtements de joute, livrées', *PCEEB* 37 (1997), 157–72.

Cauchies, J-M., 'La signifiance politique des entrée princières dans les Pays-Bas; Maximilien d'Autriche et Philippe le Beau', *PCEEB* 24 (1994), 19–35.

——, 'Charles le Hardi à Neuss (1474/5); folie militaire ou contrainte politique?', *PCEEB* 36 (1996), 105–16.

——, '"service" du prince "sûreté" des villes. À propos de privileges délivrés aux confréries ou serments d'archers et d'arbalétriers dans les Pays-Bas au XVe Siècle', *RN* 94 (2012), 419–34.

—— and Bousmar, E., *'Faire bans, edictz et statuz: légiférer dans la ville médiévale. Sources, objets et acteurs de l'activité législative communale en Occident, ca. 1220–1550* (Bruxelles: Publications des Facultés universitaires Saint-Louis, 2001).

Cauwenberghe, E. Van, 'Notice historique sur les confréries de Saint Georges', *Messager des sciences historique des arts et de la bibliographie de Belgique* (1853), 269–99.

Chevalier, B., *Les Bonnes Villes, l'État et la société dans la France du XVe siècle* (Orléans: Paradigme, 1985).

Chorley, P., 'The Ypres Cloth Industry 1200–1350: The Pattern of Change in Output and Demand', in *Ypres and the Medieval Cloth Industry in Flanders: Archaeological and Historical Contributions*, ed. M. Dewilde, A. Ervynck and A. Wielemans (Zellik: Instituut voor het archeologisch patrimonium, 1998), 111–24.

Chotin, A.-G., *Histoire de Tournai et du Tournésis, depuis les temps les plus reculés jusqu'à nos jours*, 2 vols (Tournai: Massart et Janssens, 1840).

Classen, A. (ed.), *Urban Space in the Middle Ages and the Early Modern Age* (Berlin and New York: de Gruyter, 2009).

Clauzel, D., *Finances et Politique à Lille Pendant la Période Bourguignonne* (Dunkerque: Beffrois, 1982).

——, 'Le renouvellement de l'échevinage à Lille à la fin du Moyen Age', *RN* 77 (1995), 365–85.

——, 'Les élites urbaines et le pouvoir municipal; le "cas" de la bonne ville de Lille aux XIV et XV siècles', *RN* 78 (1996), 241–67.

Clement, J., 'Antoine de Bourgogne, dit le Grand Bâtard', *PCEEB* 30 (1990), 176–7.

Cock, P. De, *Geschiedenis van het Koninklijk Handbooggild Sint Sebastiaan* (Ninove: Anneessens, 1972).

Coet, E., 'Notice sur les compagnies d'archers et d'arbalétriers de la ville de Roye', *Mémoires de la société des antiquaires de Picardie* 2e série, 10 (1865), 139–220.

Cohn, S. K., 'The Place of the Dead in Flanders and Tuscany: Towards a Comparative History of the Black Death', in *The Place of the Dead: Death and Remembrance in Late Medieval and Early Modern Europe*, ed. B. Gordon and P. Marshall (Cambridge: Cambridge University Press, 2000), 17–43.

——, *Popular Protest in Late Medieval Europe; Italy, France and Flanders* (Manchester: Manchester University Press, 2004).

——, *Lust for Liberty, The Politics of Social Relations in Medieval Europe, 1200–1425* (Cambridge, MA: Harvard University Press, 2006).

——, 'After the Black Death: Labour Legislation and Attitudes towards Labour in Late-Medieval Western Europe', *Economic History Review* 603 (2007), 457–85.

Coigneau, D., '1 februari 1404. De Mechelse voetboogschutters schrijven een wedstrijd uit. Stedelijke toneelwedstrijden in de vijftiende en zestiende eeuw', in *Een theatergeschiedenis der Nederlanden: tien eeuwen drama en theater in Nederland en Vlaandere*, ed. R. L. Erenstein (Amsterdam: Amsterdam University Press, 1996), 30–5.

Coninckx, H., *Eenige aanteekeningen betreffende de handbooggilde te Mechelen* (Mechelen: Koninklijke Kring voor Oudheidkunde, Letteren en Kunst van Mechelen, 1906).
Contamine, P., *Guerre, État et Société à la Fin Du Moyen Âge* (Paris: Mouton, 1972).
———, 'Les Fortifications urbaines au France à la fin du moyen âge. Aspects Financial et économiques', *RH* 260 (1978).
———, *La guerre au Moyen Âge* (Paris: Presses universitaires de France, 1980).
———, *La France au XIVe et XVe siècle, hommes mentalités, guerre et paix (collection d'essaies)* (London: Variorum reprints, 1981).
———, 'The Soldiery in Late Medieval Urban Society', *French History* 8 (1994), 1–13.
———, 'L'armement des populations urbaines à la fin du Moyen Âge: l'exemple de Troyes (1474)', in his (ed.), *La guerre, la violence et les gens au Moyen Âge, II: Guerre et gens* (Paris Ed. du CTHS, 1996), 59–72.
——— (ed.), *Le Moyen âge, le roi, l'église, les grands, le peuple, 481–1541* (Paris: Seuil, 2002).
———, Dutour, T. and Schnerb, B. (eds), *Commerce, finance et société* (Paris: Presses de l'Université de Paris-Sorbonne, 1993).
———, Giry-Deloissen C. and Keen, M. (eds), *Guerre et société en France, en Angleterre et en Bourgogne, XIVe–XVE siècle* (Villeneuve-d'Ascq: Université Charles de Gaulle. Centre d'histoire de la région du Nord et de l'Europe du Nord-Ouest, 1991).
Cools, H., 'In het spoor van "de grote bastaard"', *Het land van Beveren* 33 (1990), 2–7.
———, *Mannen met macht: edellieden en de moderne staat in de Bourgondisch-Habsburgse landen (1475–1530)* (Zutphen: Walburg pers, 2001).
——— and Grummit, D and Gunn, S., *War, State, and Society in England and the Netherlands, 1477–1559* (Oxford: Oxford University Press, 2007).
Copin, J., 'Sceaux d'arbalétriers Belges', *Annales du XXVIe congre de la fédération archéologique et historique de Belge*, 2 vols, vol. 2 (1956).
Cowan, A., 'Nodes, Networks and Hinterlands', in *Cultural Exchange in Early Modern Europe, 1400–1700*, ed. R. Muchembled et al. (Cambridge: Cambridge University Press, 2006), 28–38.
Crombie, L., 'Honour, Community and Hierarchy in the Feasts of the Archery and Crossbow Guilds of Bruges, 1445–1481', *JMH* 37 (2011), 76–96.
———, 'Defense, Honor and Community; the Military and Social Bonds of the Dukes of Burgundy and the Flemish Shooting Guilds', *JMMH* 9 (2011), 102–13.
———, 'The First Ordnances of the Crossbow Confraternity of Douai, 1383–1393', *Journal of Archer Antiquarians* 54 (2011), 92–6.
———, 'Representatives of Civic Pride and Cultural Identities; The Ghent Crossbow Competition of 1498', *Arms and Armour* (2011), 152–64.
———, 'French and Flemish Urban Festive Networks: Archery and Crossbow Competitions Attended and Hosted by Tournai in the Fourteenth and Fifteenth Centuries', *French History* (2013), 157–75.
Croyez, A., *Histoire de Lille*, vol. 1. *La constitution urbaine (des origines à 1800)* (Lille: Raoust, 1935).
Dambruyne, J., *Corporatieve middengroepen. Aspiraties, relaties en transformaties in de 16de-eeuwse Gentse ambachtswereld* (Gent: Academia Press, 2002).
Damen, M., *De staat van dienst: de gewestelijke ambtenaren van Holland en Zeeland in de Bourgondische periode (1425–1482)* (Hilversum: Verloren, 2000).
———, 'Giving by Pouring; the Functions of Gifts of Wine in the City of Leiden, 14th–16th Centuries', in *Symbolic Communication in Late Medieval Towns*, ed. J. Van Leewen (Leuven: Leuven University Press, 2006), 83–100.

Danneel, M., *Weduwen en Wezen in het laat-middeleeuwse Gent* (Leuven: Garant, 1995).
Dantinne, E., 'Notice historique sur les compagnies hutoises des archers, des arbalétriers et des arquebusiers', *Annales du Cercle Hutois de Sciences et Beaux-Arts* 22 (1949), 37–68.
Dauwe, J., *De Kruisboogschutters van St.-Joris te Lebbeke (1377–1796)* (Gent: Koninklijke bond der Oostvlaamse volkskundigen, 1983).
Davis, N. Z., 'Boundaries and the Sense of Self in Sixteenth-Century France', in *Reconstructing Individualism: Autonomy, Individuality, and the Self in Western Thought*, ed. T. C. Heller et al. (Stanford, CA: Stanford University Press), 53–63.
Decavele, J. et al., *Ghent, in Defence of a Rebellious City* (Antwerp: Fonds Mercator, 1989).
Decraene, E., 'Sisters of Early Modern Confraternities in a Small Town in the Southern Low Countries (Aalst)', *UH* 40 (2013), 247–70.
Degrijse, R., 'Brugge en de organisatie van het loodswezen van het Zwin op het einde van de 15de eeuw', *ASEB* 112 (1975), 61–130.
Delaunay, L-A., *Étude sur les anciennes compagnies d'archers, d'arbalétriers et d'arquebusiers* (Paris: Champion, 1879).
Delsalle, P., 'La Confrérie des archers de Cysoing, fondée en 1430 par la Baronne de Cysoing et le Duc de Bourgogne', *Bulletin de la société historique et archéologique de Cysoing et de la Révèle* (1975), 14–19.
Dernier, T., *Notice sur le serment des archers de Saint Sébastien de Quiévrain* (Quiévrain: Lecocq, 1873).
Desmette, P., 'Les archers de Saint Martin à Moustier au XVIe siècle. Visions de l'organisation d'une confrérie militaire un travers d'un document normative', *Revue Belge d'histoire militaire* 30 (1994), 419–39.
Desplat, C. (ed.), *Les villageois face à la guerre (XIVe–XVIIIe siècle)* (Toulouse: Presses universitaires de Mirail, 2002).
Desportes, P., 'Réceptions et inscriptions à la bourgeois de Lille aux XIVème et XVème siècles', *RN* 62 (1980), 541–71.
Devillers, L., 'Notice historique sur les milices communales et les compagnies militaire de Mons', *ACAM* 3 (1862), 5–123.
DeVries, K., 'Hunger, Flemish Participation and the Flight of Philip VI; Contemporary Accounts of the Siege of Calais, 1346–7', *Studies in Medieval and Renaissance History* 12 (1991), 131–81.
——, 'Provisions for the Ostend Militia on the Defense, August 1436', *JMMH* 3 (2005).
—— and Smith, R. D., *The Artillery of the Dukes of Burgundy, 1363 – 1477* (Woodbridge: Boydell Press, 2005).
Dewert, J., *Le Serment des archers de Bass-Wavre* (Nivelles: [n.d.], 1909).
Dixhoorn, A. van, *Lustige geesten, rederijkers in de noordelijke Nederlanden (1480–1650)* (Amsterdam: Amsterdam University Press, 2009).
Doig, J. A., 'A New Source for the Siege of Calais, 1436', *EHR* 110 (1995), 404–16.
Driessens, F., *Het Koninklijk Gild Sint Sebastiaan 1406–2006: tentoonstelling: [Blankenberge, 2006]: catalogus* (Blankenberge: Heemkundig centrum De Benne, 2006).
Duffy, E., *The Stripping of the Altars: Traditional Religion in England, c.1400–c.1580* (New Haven, CN; London: Yale University Press, 2005).
Dumolyn, J., *De Brugse opstand, van 1436–1438* (Heule: UGA, 1997).
——, 'Population et structures professionnelles à Bruges aux XIVe et XV siècles', *RN* 81 (1999), 43–64.

——, 'De Sociografie van laat middeleeuwse gerechtelijke instellingen, het voorbeeld van Jan Wielant (d. 1473), griffier en Raadsheer dij de raad van Vlaandered', *BCRALO* 42 (2001), 7–61.

——, 'Dominante klassen en elites in verandering in het laatmiddeleeuwse Vlaanderen', *JMG* 5 (2002), 69–107.

——, 'Investeren in sociaal kapitaal. Netwerken en sociale transacties van Bourgondische ambtenaren', *TVSG* 28 (2002), 417–38.

——, *Staatsvorming en vorstelijke ambtenaren in het graafschap Vlaanderen (1419–1477)* (Leuven: Garant, 2003).

——, 'Justice, Equity and the Common Good; The State Ideology of the Councillors of the Burgundian Dukes', *The Ideology of Burgundy*, ed. J. D'Arcy, D. Boulton and J. R. Veenstra (Leiden: Brill, 2006), 1–20.

——, 'Les réseaux politiques locaux en Flandre sous la domination bourguignonne; les exemples de Gand et de Lille', *RN* 88 (2006), 309–30.

——, 'Privileges and Novelties; the Political Discourse of the Flemish Cities and Rural Districts in their Negotiations with the Duke of Burgundy (1384–1506)', *UH* 5 (2008), 5–23.

——, 'Une Idéologie urbain "Bricolée" en Flandre médiéval: les *Sept Portes de Bruges* dans le manuscrit Gruuthuse (début du XVe siècle)', *RBP* 88 (2010), 1039–84.

——, '"Our Land is Founded on Trade and Industry." Economic Discourse in Fifteenth-Century Bruges', *JMH* 36 (2010), 374–89.

——, 'Urban Ideology in Later Medieval Flanders. Towards an Analytical Framework', in A. Gamberini, J.-P. Genet and A. Zorzi (eds), *The Languages of Political Society, Western Europe 14th–17th Centuries* (Roma: Viella, 2011), 69–96.

——, 'Economic Development, Social Space and Political Power in Bruges, c.1127–1302', in *Contact and Exchange in Later Medieval Europe, Essays in Honour of Malcolm Vale*, ed. H. Skoda, P. Lantschner and R. L. J. Shaw (Woodbridge: Boydell, 2012), 33–58.

—— and Haemers, J., 'Pattern of Urban in Medieval Flanders', *JMH* 31 (2005), 369–93.

—— and Haemers, J., '"A Bad Chicken Was Brooding." Subversive Speech in Late Medieval Flanders', *PP* 214 (2012), 45–86.

—— and Haemers, J., '"Let each man carry on and remain silent." Middle-Class Ideology in the Urban Literature of the Late Medieval Low Countries', *Cultural and Social History* 10 (2013), 169–89.

Duyse, P. Van, 'Het groot schietspel en de Rederijkersspelen te Gent in Mei tot Juli 1498', *Annales de la Société Royale des Beaux-arts et de Littérature de Gand* 6 (1856), 273–314.

Eckstein, N. A. and Terpstra, N. (eds), *Sociability and its Discontents, Civil Society, social Capital, and Their Alternatives in Late Medieval and Early Modern Europe* (Turnhout: Brepols, 2009).

Ehrich, S. and Obserste, J. *Städtische Kulte im Mittelalter* (Regensburg: Schnell & Steiner, 2010).

Eichberger, D. (ed.), *Women of Distinction, Margaret of York and Margaret of Austria* (Leuven: Davidsfonds, 2005).

Emerson, C., *Olivier de La Marche and the Rhetoric of Fifteenth-Century Historiography* (Woodbridge: Boydell Press, 2004).

Ernstein, R. L. van et al. (ed.), *Een theatergeschiedenis der Nederlanden: tien eeuwen drama en theater in Nederland en Vlaanderen* (Amsterdam: Amsterdam University Press, 1996).

Escher-Apsner, M. (ed.), *Mittelalterliche Bruderschaften in europäischen Städten: Funktionen, Formen, Akteure / Medieval confraternities in European towns: functions, forms, protagonists* (Frankfurt am Main; Oxford: Peter Lang, 2009).

Feller, L., 'La fête faillie: les événements de mai (1284, Lille-Douai)', *RN* 334 (2000), 9–34.

Finot, M., 'Les archers, les arbalétriers et les arquebusiers de Troyes', *Annuaire, Administratif, statistique et commercial du département de l'Aube* 33 (1858), 1–38.

Flynn, M., 'Rituals of Solidarity in Castilian Confraternities', *Renaissance and Reformation* 13 (1989), 53–68.

Folda, J., 'Mounted Warrior Saints in Crusader Icons: Images of the Knighthoods of Christ', in *Knighthoods of Christ: Essays on the History of the Crusades and the Knights Templar, Presented to Malcolm Barber*, ed. N. Housley (Aldershot: Ashgate, 2007), 87–108.

Fons-Melicocq, E. J. de la, 'Bananiers des villes, des corps des métiers et des confréries des archers, des arbalétriers et des arquebusiers dans la nord du France, aux XVe et XVIe siècles', *Annales historiques et littéraire du nord de la France et du midi de la Belgique* 1 (1850), 92–100.

Fouque, V., *Recherches historiques sur les corporations des archers, des arbalétriers et des arquebusiers* (Paris: Dumoulin, 1852).

Fouret, C., 'La Violence en fête: La Course de l'épinette à Lille à la fin du Moyen Age', *RN* 63 (1981), 377–90.

Franke, B. and Welzel, B. (ed.), *Die Kunst der Burgundischen Niederlande: eine Einführung* (Berlin: Reimer, 1997).

Frijhoff, W. T. M., 'De Sprekende stad; stedelijke identiteit en ruimtelijke ordening', in *Sporen en Spiegels, beschouwingen over geschiedenis en identiteit*, ed. J. C. Dekker (Tilburg: Tilburg University Press, 1995), 85–95.

Fris, V., 'Documents gantois concernant la levée du siège de Calais en 1436', in *Mélanges Paul Frédéricq: hommage de la Société pour le progrès des études philologiques et historiques, 10 juillet, 1904* (Bruxelles: H. Lamertin, 1904), 245–58.

Gailliard, J. J., *Recherches sur l'église de Jérusalem à Bruges, suivies de données historiques sur la famille du fondateur* (Bruges: Gailliard, 1843).

——, *Bruges et le Franc, ou leur magistrature et leur noblesse avec des données historiques et généalogique su chaque famille*, 6 vols (Bruges: Gailliard, 1857–64).

Galvin, M., 'Credit and Parochial Charity in fifteenth-century Bruges', *JMH* 28 (2002), 131–54.

Geerts, K., *De spelende mens in de Boergondische Nederlanden* (Brugge: Genootschap voor geschiedenis, 1987).

Geirnaert, N. (ed.), *Militie en vermaak – 675 jaar Sint-Jorisgilde in Brugge: tentoonstelling, Brugge, 18 april–17 mei 199* (Brugge: Koninklijke en Prinselijke hoofgilde Sint-Joris Stalen Boog, 1998).

—— and Vandewalle, A., *Adornes en Jeruzalem: internationaal leven in het 15de- en 16de-eeuwse Brugge* (Brugge: Stad Brugge, 1983).

Genet, J-P. and Lettes, G. (eds), *L'état moderne et les élites XIIIe–XVIIIe siècles: apports et limites de la méthode prosopographique* (Paris: Publications de la Sorbonne, 1996).

Ghysens, J., *Geschiedenis der straten van Aalst* (Aalst: Genootschap voor Aalsterse geschiedenis, 1986).

Ghyslaert, A. and Hosten, E., *De Koninklijk handbooggilde Sint Sebastiaan in Dixmuide* (Dixmude: W. Sackenpré-van Middelem, 1903).

Gilissen, J., 'Les villes en Belgique, histoire des institutions, administration et judicaires des villes belges', *Recueil de la société Jean Bodin* 6 (1954), 531–600.

Gilliodts van Severen, M. L., *Histoire de la magistrature brugeoise* (Bruges: De Plancke, 1888).

——, *Cartulaire de l'ancienne estaple de Bruges: recueil de documents concernant le commerce intérieur et maritime, les relations internationales et l'histoire économique de cette ville*, 4 vols, vol. 1, 862–1451 (Bruges: De Plancke, 1904).

Godar, H., *Histoire de la gilde des archers de Saint Sébastien de la ville de Bruges* (Bruges: Stainforth, 1947).

Gonthier, N., *Cris de Haine et rites d'unité. La violence dans les villes, XIIIe–XVIe siècles* (Turnhout: Brepols, 1992).

Goovaerts, M. A., 'La flotte de Louis de Male devant Anvers en 1356', *BCRH* 13 (1886), 33–58.

Guislin, A. and Guillaume, P. (eds), *De La Charité médiévale à la sécurité sociale* (Paris: Éditions ouvrières, 1992).

Haemers, J., 'A Moody Community? Emotion and Ritual in Late Medieval Urban Revolts', in *Emotions in the Heart of the City (14th–16th Century). Les émotions au cœur de la ville (XIVe–XVIe siècle)*, ed. E. Lecuppre-Desjardin and A.-L. Van Bruaene (Turnhout: Brepols, 2005), 63–81.

——, 'Adellijke onvrede: Adolf van Kleef en Lodewijk van Gruuthuze als beschermheren en uitdagers van het Bourgondisch-Habsburgse hof (1477–1482)', *JMG* 10 (2007), 178–215.

——, 'Le Meurtre de Jean de Dadizeele. L'ordonnance de Cour de Maximilien d'Autriche et les tensions politiques en Flandre (1481)', *PCEEB* 48 (2008), 227–48.

——, *For the Common Good, State Power and Urban Revolts in the Reign of Mary of Burgundy* (Turnhout: Brepols, 2009).

——, 'Social Memory and Rebellion in Fifteenth-Century Ghent', *Social History* 36 (2011), 443–63.

—— and Liddy, C., 'Popular Politics in the Late Medieval City: York and Bruges', *EHR* 128 (2013), 771–805.

—— and Ryckbosch, W., 'A Targeted Public: Public Services in Fifteenth-Century Ghent and Bruges', *UH* 37 (2010), 203–25.

Hanawalt, B. A. (ed.), *Women and Work in Pre-Industrial Europe* (Bloomington: Indiana University Press, 1986).

—— and Reyerson, K. L. (eds), *City and Spectacle in Medieval Europe* (Minneapolis: University of Minnesota Press, 1994).

Haute, C. vanden, *La Corporation des peintres de Bruges* (Bruges: Van Cappel-Missiaen, 1912).

Heyde, R. van de, *Vijf eeuwen verenigingsleven te Leftinge Deel twee, de Schuttersgilden* (Middelkerke: Heemkring Graningate, 1985).

Highfield, J. R. L. and Tests, R., *The Crown and Local Communities in England and France in the Fifteenth Century* (Gloucester: Alan Sutton, 1981).

Hilaire, Y-M. (ed.), *Histoire de Roubaix* (Dunkerque: Éd. des Beffrois, 1984).

Hillebrand, W., 'Chronik der Goslarer Schützengesellschaft', in *Festschrift, 750 Jahre Goslarer Schützen* (Goslar: Schützengesellschaft Goslar, 1970), 21–55.

——, 'Die Ordnungen und Rechnungen der Schützenbruderschaft St. Sebastian zu Goslar 1432–1529', in *Festschrift für Gerhard Cordes, Band 1: Literaturwissenschaft und Textedition*, ed. A. Schwob and E. Streitfeld (Neumünster: Tyska, 1973), 74–90.

Hindley, A. (ed.), *Drama and Community; People and Plays in Medieval Europe* (Turnhout: Brepols, 1999).
Hinte, R. van, 'A Silver Collar from the Wallace Collection, London', *Journal of the Society of Archer-Antiquaries* 14 (1971), 10–15.
Hodevaere, C., 'Le Serment des archers de Saint-Sébastien de la ville de Binche', *ACAM* 25 (1906), 1–8.
Holmes, G., 'The Emergence of an Urban Ideology at Florence c.1250–1450', *Transactions of the Royal Historical Society* 5th series, 23 (1973), 111–34.
Hosten, E., 'Notes et documents, un différend entre archers au 15e siècle', *ASEB* 68 (1925), 77–83.
Houtte, J. A. Van, *Essays on Medieval and Early modern Economy and society* (Leuven: University Press, 1977).
Hoven Genderen, V. van den and Trio, P., 'Old Stories and New Themes; An Overview of the Historiography of Confraternities in the Low Countries from the Thirteenth to the Sixteenth Centuries', in *Religious and Laity in Western Europe, 1000–1400*, ed. E. Jamroziak and J. Burton (Turnhout: Brepols, 2006), 357–84.
Howell, C. M., 'Gifts by Testament in Late Medieval Douai', *PP* 150 (1996), 3–45.
——, *Commerce Before Capitalism in Europe, 1300–1600* (Cambridge; New York: Cambridge University Press, 2010).
Huizinga, J., *Over de grenzen van spel en ernst in de cultuur: rede* (Haarlem: H. D. Tjeenk Willink, 1933).
—— (trans. F. Hopman), *The Waning of the Middle Ages* (London: Penguin, 1990).
Hutchison, E. J., 'Partisan Identity in the French Civil War, 1405–1418: Reconsidering the Evidence on Livery Badges', *JMH* 33 (2007), 250–74.
Hutton, S., 'Women, Men and Markets; the Gendering of Market Space in Late Medieval Ghent', in *Urban Space in the Middle Ages and the Early Modern Age*, ed. A. Classen (Berlin and New York: de Gruyter, 2009), 409–31.
——, *Women and Economic Activities in Late Medieval Ghent* (London; New York: Palgrave Macmillan, 2011).
Hymans, H., *Bruges et Ypres* (Paris: Renouard, 1901).
Ising, A., *Met vliegend vaandel en slaande trom: ontstaan en ontwikkeling van schuttersgilden en schutterijen in Brabant en Limburg* (Hapert: De Kempen, 1986).
Iven, W. et al., *Schuttersgilden in Noord-Brabant: tentoonstelling, Noordbrabants Museum, 's-Hertogenbosch, 21 mei–7 augustus 1983: catalogue* (Helmond: Uitgeverij Helmond, 1983).
Jager, T. De, 'Bergen op Zoom op het Gentse schuttersfeest AD 1497', *Sinte Geertruijds Brinne* 1 (1924), 23–43.
James, M., 'Drama and the Social Body in the Late Medieval English Town', *PP* 98 (1983), 3–29.
Janssens, A., 'Daar komen de Brugse Kruisboogschutters van de oude gilde van Sint-Joris', *BO* 46 (2006), 52–75, 83–113.
Janvier, A., 'Notice sur les anciennes corporations d'archers, d'arbalétriers, de coulveriniers et d'arquebusiers des villes de Picardie', *Mémoires de la société des antiquaires de la Picardie* 14 (1855), 1–248.
Jolles, J. A., *De Schuttersgilden en Schutterijen van Zeeland, Overzicht van hetgeen nog bestaat* (Middelburg: Altorffer, 1934).
——, *De Schuttersgilden en Schutterijen van Limburg: overzicht van hetgeen nog bestaat* 2 volumes (Maastricht: Van Aelst, 1937).

Jones, M. K., 'Les signes du pouvoir. L'ordre de l'Hermine, les devises et les hérauts des ducs de Bretagne au XVe siècle', *Mémoires de la société d'histoire et d'archéologique de Bretagne* 68 (1991), 141–73.

Jones, R., '"What Banner Thine?" The Banner as a Symbol of Identification, Status and Authority on the Battlefield', *Haskins Society Journal: Studies in Medieval History* 15 (2006), 101–9.

Jossen, B. (ed.), *Ordering Medieval Society; Perspectives of Intellectual and Practical Models of Shaping Social Relations* (Philadelphia: University of Pennsylvania Pres, 2001).

Kan, F. J. W. van, 'Around Saint George: Integration and Precedence during the Meetings of the Civic Militia of The Hague', in *Showing Status: Representations of Social Positions in the Late Middle Ages*, ed. W. Blockmans and A. Jansese (Turnhout: Brepols, 1999), 177–95.

——, 'Rondom Sint-Joris. Voorrang tijdens de samenkomsten van de schutters van St. Joris', *Jaarboek die Haghe* (1995), 8–17.

Kanora, H., *De Ridderlijke St Jorisgilde van Eekern* (Brasschaet: Druk. de Bievre, 1929).

Keats-Rohan, K. S. B. (ed.), *Prosopography, Approaches and Applications, a Handbook* (Oxford: Unit for Prosopographical Research, University of Oxford, 2007).

Keesman, W., 'De Bourgondische invloed op de genealogische constructies van Maximiliaan van Oostenrijk', *MTMS* 8 (1994), 162–72.

Kemperdick, S., *Rogier van Weyden, 1399/1400–1464* (Cologne: Konemann Verlagsgesellschaft, 1999).

Knevel, P., *Wakkere burgers de Alkmaarse schutterij; 1400–1795* (Alkmaar: Stedelijk Museum, 1994).

——, *Burgers in het geweer, de schutterijen in Holland, 1550–1700* (Hilversum: Verloren, 1994).

Knight, A. E., 'Processional Theatre in Lille in the Fifteenth Century', *Fifteenth Century Studies* 13 (1988), 99–109.

——, *The Stage as a Mirror, Civic Theatre in Late Medieval Europe* (Cambridge: Brewer, 1997).

——, 'Guild pageants and Urban Stability in Lille', in *Urban Theatre in the Low Countries, 1400–1625*, ed. E. Strietman and P. Happé (Turnhout: Brepols, 2006), 187–208.

—— (ed.), *Les Mystères de la procession de Lille*, vols 1–4 (Genève: Droz, 2001–7).

Koenigsberger, H. G., *Monarchies, States Generals and Parliaments, the Netherlands in the fifteenth and Sixteenth Centuries* (Cambridge: Cambridge University Press, 2001).

Koldeweij, A. M., *Foi et bonne fortune: parure et dévotion en Flandre médiévale; Foi et Bonne Fortune (Exhibition: 2006: Bruges, Belgium)* (Arnhem: Terra, 2006).

Koldeweij, J., 'De Oude koningsvogel van het Sint-Jorisgilde van Bladel Teruggevonden', *Brabants Heem* 42 (1990), 45–8.

Lambrechts, P. and Sosson, J-P. (eds), *Les métiers au Moyen Age: aspects économiques et sociaux* (Louvain-la-Neuve: Fédération internationale des instituts d'études médiévales, 1994).

Laplane, H. de, 'Les Arbalétriers, les arquebusiers et les archers, leur service à Saint Omer et les environs', *Bulletin historique trimestriel de la Société des Antiquaires de la Morinie* 3 (1862/66), 28–41.

Lardin, P. et Roche, J-L. (eds), *La Ville médiévale, en deçà et au-delà de ses murs. Mélanges Jean Pierre Leguoy* (Rouen: Publications de l'Université de Rouen, 2000).

Laurent, H. and Quicke, F., 'La Guerre de la succession du Brabant (1356–7)', *RN* 13 (1927).
LaValley, G., *Les compagnies de Papeguay, particulièrement à Caen. Étude historique sur les Sociétés de Tir avant la Révolution.* (Paris: [s.d]. 1881).
Lecuppre-Desjardin, E., 'Les Lumières de la Ville: recherché sur l'utilisation de la lumière dans les cérémonies bourguignonnes (XIVe–XVe Siècles)', *RH* 301 (1999), 23–43.
——, 'Des pouvoirs inscrits dans la pierre? Essai sur l'édilité urbaine dans les anciens Pays-Bas bourguignons au XVe siècle', *Memini. Travaux et documents* 7 (2003) 7–35.
——, *La Ville des cérémonies, essai sur la communication politique dans les anciens Pays-Bas Bourguignons* (Turnhout: Brepols, 2004).
——, 'Processions et propagande à Valenciennes en 1472. L'intégration des cultes locaux dans la construction de l'image princière', *RN* 86 (2004), 757–70.
——, 'Premier essais d'ethnographie mœurs et coutumes des populations du nord, d'âpres les observations des voyageurs méridionaux au tournant des XVe et XVIe siècles', *RN* 87 (2005), 321–35.
—— and Van Bruaene, A-L. (eds), *Emotions in the Heart of the City, Studies in European History* 5 (Turnhout: Brepols, 2005).
—— and Van Bruaene, A-L. (eds), *De Bono Communi, the Discourse and Practise of the Common Good in the European City, 13th–16th Centuries* (Turnhout: Brepols, 2010).
Leeuwen, J. van (ed.), 'Municipal Oaths, Political Virtues and the Centralised State; the Adaptation of Oaths of Office in fifteenth Century Flanders', *JMH* 31 (2005).
—— (ed.), *Symbolic Communication in Late Medieval Towns* (Leuven: Leuven University Press, 2006), 158–210.
——, 'Rebels, Texts and Triumph; The Use of Written Documents During the Revolt of 1477 in Bruges', in *Strategies of Writing, Studies on Text and Trust in the Middle Ages*, ed. P. Schulte et al. (Turnhout: Brepols, 2008), 301–22.
Lefebvre, J-L., 'Prud'hommes et bonnes gens dans les sources flamands et wallonnes du moyen âge', *Le Moyen Âge* 58 (2002), 457–79.
Lefebvre, L., *Fêtes lilloises du XIVe au XVIe siècle* (Lille: imprimerie Lefebvre-Ducrocq, 1902).
Lemahieu, M., *Het Wezen van de eerste Vlaamse schuttersgilden* (Brugge: Kon Hoofdgilde Sint-Sebastiaan, 2008).
——, *De Koninklijke hoofdgilde Sint-Sebastiaan Brugge, 1379–2005* (Brugge: Kon Hoofdgilde Sint-Sebastiaan, 2005).
Lerberghe, A. van and Louvaert, E., *Esquisse historique de l'ancienne Gilde du Noble Chevalier Saint Georges à Courtrai* (Courtrai: La Sociéte du Noble Chevalier St.-Georges 1973).
Lettenhove, K. de, *Histoire de Flandre*, 6 vols (Bruxelles: vols 1–3, Vandale; vol. 4, Librairie Scientifique et Littéraire; vols 5–6, Delevingne et Callewaert, 1847–55).
Liddy, C., 'The Palmers' Guild Window, St. Lawrence's Church, Ludlow: A Study of the Construction of Guild Identity in Medieval Stained Glass', *Transactions of the Shropshire Archaeological and Natural History Society* 72 (1997), 26–35.
——, 'Urban Politics and Material Culture at the End of the Middle Ages: The Coventry Tapestry in St Mary's Hall', *UH* 39 (2012), 203–44.
Liebrecht, H., *Les Chambres de Rhétorique* (Bruxelles: La Renaissance du Livre, 1948).
Lievois, D., 'Kapellen, huijse, fruit en bloemen bij de westgevel van de Sint-Niklaaskerk in Gent', *HMGOG, Nieuwe Reek* 59 (2005), 71–86.

Lindemans, J., 'De oorlogen tusschen Brabant en Vlaanderen in de XIIIe en de XIVe eeuwe', *Eigen schoon en de Brabant* 4 (1912), 49–53.

——, 'De oude schuttersgilde van Gooik', *Eigen Schoon en De Brabander* (1928), 97–119.

Lis, C. and Soly, H. (eds), *Werken volgens de regels, ambachten in Brabant en Vlaanderen, 1500–1800* (Brussel: VUB Press, 1994).

——, Soly, H. and Damme, D. van, *Op vrije voeten? Sociale politiek in West-Europa (1450–1914)* (Leuven: Kritak, 1985).

Lottin, A. (ed.), *Histoire de Boulogne-sur-Mer* (Lille: Presses universitaires de Lille, 1983).

Lowagie, H., 'Stedelijke communicatie in de late middeleeuwen: aard, motivaties en politieke implicaties', *RBPH* 87 (2009), 273–95.

——, 'Omme messagier ende bode te zine van de vorseide stede. De Brugse stadsboden in de late middeleeuwen', *ASEB* 149 (2012), 3–24.

Luijk, M. van, '"Want ledicheit een vyant der zielen is." Handenarbeid in laatmiddeleeuwse vrouwengemeenschappen', *Madoc: Tijdschrift over de Middeleeuwen* 17 (2003), 114–22.

Lupant, M., 'Drapeaux du Grand Serment Royal et Noble des Arbalétriers de Notre-Dame au Sablon', *Fahnen, Flags, Drapeaux: Proceedings of the 15th International Congress of Vexillology, Zurich, 23–27 August 1993* (Zurich: Swiss Society of Vexillology, 1999), 130–4.

Maesschalck, A. and Viaene, J., 'Het vervoer van de natuursteen op de binnenwateren van het Scheldebekken in het midden van de 15de eeuw, met het oog op de bouw van het Leuvense stadhuis', *BTG* 82 (1999), 187–213.

Malherbe, l'abbé G. de, 'Le Serment des Archers de S. Sébastien à Ronquières', *Annales du Cercle Archéologique du Canton de Soignies* 4 (1907), 12–16.

Marcel, P. and Kerchoven, J. van, *De gilden van Sint-Joris, Sint-Sebastiaan, Sint-Andries, Sint-Pieter, Sint-Adriaan, Sint-Cecilia te Geraardsbergen* (Geraardsbergen: Geschiedenis en Heemkundige Kring Gerardimontium, 2005).

Marechal, J., 'Le Départ de Bruges des marchands étrangers aux XVe et XVIe siècles', *ASEB* 88 (1951), 1–41.

Marnef, G., 'Chambers of Rhetoric and the Transmission of Religious Ideas in the Low Countries', *Cultural Exchange* 1 (2006), 274–96.

Marsh, P., 'Identity; An Ethogenetic Perspective', in *Persons in Groups: Social Behaviour as Identity Formation in Medieval and Renaissance Europe*, ed. P. Trexler (Binghamton, NY: Medieval & Renaissance Texts & Studies, 1985), 17–30.

Martens, M. P. J., *Lodewijk van Gruuthuse. Mecenas en Europees diplomaat ca. 1427–1492* (Brugge: Stichting Kunstboek, 1992).

Matthieu, E., *Histoire de la ville d'Enghien*, 2 vols (Mons: Dequesne-Masquillier, 1876–78).

——, 'Sceaux des serments ou guildes de la ville d'Enghien', *ACAM* 15 (1878), 9–18.

——, 'Concours d'arc à la main à Braine-le-Château en 1433', *Annales de la société archéologique de l'arrondissement de Nivelles* 3 (1892), 100–102.

McRee, M., 'Unity or Division? The Social Meaning of Guild Ceremony in Urban Communities', in *City and Spectacle in Medieval Europe*, ed. B. A. Hanawalt and K. L. Reyerson (Minneapolis: University of Minnesota Press, 1994), 189–97.

Mehl, J-M., 'Une Éducation du corps à la fin du moyen âge et le début de la Renaissance; le tir à l'arc en France et en Angleterre', in *Éducation et hygiène du corps à travers l'histoire: actes du Colloque de l'Association interuniversitaire de l'Est*

(Dijon, 26 et 27 septembre 1989), ed. P. Lévêque (Dijon: Editions universitaires de Dijon, 1991), 109–18.

Melckebeke, G. J. J. van, *Geschiedkundige aanteekeningen rakende de kruis- of voetbooggilde te Mechelen* (Mechelen: Van Moer, 1869).

Melville, G., 'Institutionen als geschichtswissenschaftliches Thema: Eine Einleitung', in *Institutionen und Geschichte: Theoretische Aspekte und mittelalterliche Befunde*, ed. G. Melville (Köln: Böhlau, 1992), 1–24.

Mérindol, C. D., 'Signes de hiérarchie sociale à la fin du moyen âge, d'après les vêtements. Méthodes et recherches', in *Le Vêtement, histoire, archéologie et symbolique vestimentaires au moyen âge*, ed. M. Pastoureau (Paris: Léopard d'or., 1989), 181–223.

Meulemans, A., 'De Kleine Leuvense Schuttersgilden', *Eigen Schoon en de Brabander* 59 (1976), 70–84, 229–46.

Meynies, J., *Archers et arbalétriers au temps de la Guerre de Cent Ans, 1337–1453* (Saint-Égrève: Émotion primitive, 2006).

Million, M., *Les Archers Dunkerquois, histoire de la société des archers réunis de Saint Sébastien, 1322 à 1965* (Dunkerque: Impr. L'Indépendant, 1965).

Monnet, C., *Lille, portrait d'une ville* (Paris: Jacques Marseille, 2003).

Monnet, P. and Oexle, O. G., *Stadt und Recht im mittelalter* (Göttingen: Vandenhoeck & Ruprecht, 2003).

Morgan, D. A. L., 'The Cult of St George c. 1500: National and International Connotations', *PCEEB* 35 (1995), 151–62.

Mosser, N., 'Maria verklaard. Everaert als exegeet in Maria ghecompareirt byde claerheyt (1511)', in *Spel en spektakel: Middeleeuws toneel in de Lage Landen*, ed. H. van Dijk, B A. M. Ramakers et al. (Amsterdam: Prometheus, 2001), 246–62, 369–77.

Moulin-Coppens, J., *De Geschiedenis van het oude Sint Jorisgilde te Gent* (Gent: Hoste Staelens, 1982).

Muchembled, R., 'Die jugend und die Volkskultur in 15. Jahrhundert. Flanderen und Artois', in *Volkskultur des Europäischen Spätmittelalters*, ed. P. Dinzelbacher und H.-D. Mück (Stuttgart: Kröner, 1986), 35–58.

——, *Culture populaire et culture des élites dans la France moderne (XVe–XVIIIe siècles)* (Paris: Flammarion, 1991).

—— et al. (ed.), *Cultural Exchange in Early modern Europe, 1400–1700* 4 vols (Cambridge: Cambridge University Press, 2006–7).

Munro, J. H., 'Industrial Protectionism in Medieval Flanders, Urban or National', in *The Medieval City*, ed. H. A. Miskimin, D. Herlihy and A. L. Udovitch (New Haven; London: Yale University Press, 1977), 229–67.

——, 'Anglo-Flemish Competition in the International Cloth Trade, 1340–1520', *PCEEB* 35 (1995), 37–60.

Murray, J., 'Family, Marriage and Money Changing in Medieval Bruges', *JMH* 14 (1988), 115–25.

——, *Bruges, Cradle of Capitalism, 1280–1390* (Cambridge: Cambridge University Press, 2005).

Naegle, G., *Stadt, Recht und Krone: französische Städte, Königtum und Parlement im späten Mittelater*, 2 volumes (Husum: Matthiesen, 2002).

Nicholas, D., 'Crime and Punishment in Fourteenth-Century Ghent', *RBPH* 48 (1971), 1141–76.

——, *The Domestic Life of a Medieval City; Women, Children and the Family in Fourteenth Century Ghent* (Lincoln: University of Nebraska Press, 1985).

——, *The Metamorphosis of a Medieval City, Ghent in the Age of the Arteveldes, 1302–1390* (Lincoln: University of Nebraska Press, 1987).

——, *Medieval Flanders* (London: Longman, 1992).

Oexle, O. G., '*Conjuratio* et *Ghilde* dans l'antiquité et dans le haut moyen âge', *Francia. Forschungen zur westeuropäischen Geschichte* 10 (1982).

——, 'Les Groups sociaux au moyen âge et les débuts de la sociologie contemporaine', *Annales* 47 (1992), 751–65.

Oman, P., *A History of the Art of War in the Middle Ages*, 2 vols (London: Methuen, 1978, first published 1921).

Oosterman, J. (ed.), 'Oh Flanders Weep! Anthonis de Roovere and Charles the Bold', in *The Growth of Authority in the Medieval West*, ed. M. Gosman, A. Vanderjagt and J. Veenstra (Groningen: E. Forsten, 1999), 257–67.

——, 'De Excellente Chronike van Vlaanderen en Anthonis de Roovere', *Tijdschrift voor Nederlandtse taal en letterkunde* (2002), 22–33.

—— (ed.), *Stad van koopmanschap en vrede: literatuur in Brugge tussen Middeleeuwen en Rederijkerstijd* (Leuven: Peeters, 2005).

Orme, N. and Wensert, M., *The English Hospital, 1070–1570* (New Haven, CT: Yale University Press, 1995).

Ossoba, W., 'Jean de Lannoy', in *Les chevaliers de l'ordre de la Toison d'Or au XVe siècle, notes bio-biographique*, ed. R. deSmedt (Frankfurt am Main; New York: P. Lang, 2000), 109–10.

——, 'Adolphe de Cleves', in *Les chevaliers de l'Ordre*, 120–21.

Ouvry, B., 'Officieel ceremonieel te Oudenaarde, 1450–1600', *Handelingen van de geschieden oudheidkundige kring van Oudenaarde* 22 (1985).

Papin, K., 'De handboogschuttersgilde van Sint-Winnoksbergen in 1469', *Westhoek* 17 (2001).

Paresys, I., 'L'ordre en jeu: les autorités face aux passions Ludiques dans Lille (1400–1668)', *RN* 69 (1987), 535–51.

Parmentier, R. A., *Indices op de Brugsche Poorterboeken*, 2 vols (Brugge: Desclée De Brouwer, 1938).

Pastoureau, M., 'Emblèmes et symbole de la Toison d'Or', in *L'Ordre de la Toison d'Or, de Philippe le Bon à Philippe le Beau (1430–1505). Idéal ou reflet d'une société?*, ed. C. Van den Bergen-Pantens (Turnhout: Brepols 1996), 99–106.

Paterson, W. G., *A Guide to the Crossbow* (London: Society of Archer-Antiquaries, 1990).

Pauw, N. de, *Ypre jeghen Poperinghe angaende den verbonden: gedingstukken der XIVe eeuw nopens het laken* (Gent: Siffer, 1899).

Paviot, J. and Verger, J. (eds), *Guerre, pouvoir et noblesse au moyen âge, mélanges en l'honneur de Philippe Contamine* (Paris: Presses de l'Université de Paris-Sorbonne, 2000).

——, 'Jean de la Clite, seigneur de Comines', *les Chevaliers de l'Ordre*, 111–12.

Paw, G. de, *De Oudenaardse schutterij* (Oudenaarde: Streekmuseum Oudenaarde, 1985), 3–40.

Payne-Gallwey, R., *The Crossbow: Its Military and Sporting History, Construction and Use* (Ludlow: Merlin Unwin, 2007, first published 1903).

Pétillon, C., 'Le Personnel Urbain de Lille (1384–1419)', *RN* 65 (1983), 411–27.

——, 'Les élites politiques de Saint Omer dans la premier moite du XVe siècle, d'âpres l'enquête de 1446', *RN* 81 (1999), 171–7.

Petit-Jean, O., *Historique de l'ancien Grand Serment royal et noble des arbalétriers de Notre-Dame de la Sablon* (Bruxelles: Du Marais, 1963).
Philip, L. B., *The Ghent Altarpiece and the Art of Jan van Eyck* (Princeton: Princeton University Press, 1971).
Piot, C., *Cartulaire de l'abbaye d'Eename* (Brugge: De Zuttere-Van Kersschaver, 1881).
Pirenne, H., *Histoire de Belgique des origines a nos jours*, vols 1–2 of 4 vols (5e edition, Bruxelles: La Renaissance du Livre, 1928).
——, *Les anciennes démocraties des Pays-Bas* (Paris: Flammarion, 1917).
Pleij, H., *Het gilde van de Blauwe Schuit. Literatuur, volksfeest en burgermoraal in de late middeleeuwen* (Amsterdam: Meulenhoff, 1979), 8–23.
——, 'De late triomf van een regionale stadscultuur', in A.-J. A, Bijsterveld (ed.), *Cultuur in het Laatmiddeleeuwse Noord-Brabant. Literatuur, boekproductie, historiografie* ('s-Hertogenbosch: Stichting Brabantse regionale geschiedbeoefening, 1998).
——, 'Restyling "Wisdom", Remodelling the Nobility, and Caricaturing the Peasant; Urban Literature in the Late Medieval Low Countries', *JIH* 32 (2002), 689–704.
Populer, M., 'Le conflit de 1447 à 1453 entre Gand et Philippe le Bon. Propagande et historiographie', *HMGOG* 44 (1990), 99–123.
Potter, F. De, *Jaarboeken der Sint-Jorisgilde van Gent* (Gent: Hage, 1868).
——, *De Rederijkerskamer Maria ter eere, te Gent* (Bruxelles: Hayez, 1872).
——, *Geschiedenis der stad Kortrijk*, 4 vols (Gent: Annoot-Braeckman, 1873–76).
——, *Gent van de Oudsten tijd tot Heden*, 9 vols (Gent: Annoot-Braeckman, 1882–1933, re-print 1975, Brussels).
——, 'Landjuweel van 1497', *Het Belfort* (Gent, no 1894), 185–9.
—— and Borre, P., *Geschiedenis der rederijkerskamer van Veurne, onder kenspreuk: Arm in de beurs en van zinnen jong* (Gent: Annoot-Braeckman, 1870).
—— and Broeckaert, J., *Geschiedenis der stad Aalst voorgegaan van eene historische schets van 't voormalige land van Aalst*, 4 vols (Gent: Annoot-Braeckman, 1873–76).
Powell, A. K., 'The Errant Image: Rogier van der Weyden's Deposition from the Cross and its Copies', *Art History* 29 (2006), 540–52.
——, *Depositions, Scenes from the Late Medieval Church and the Modern Museum* (New York: MIT Press, 2012), 143–57.
Praet, J. Van, *Jaer-boek der keyzerlyke ende koninglyke hoofd-gilde van den edelen ridder Sint-Joris in den Oudenhove binnen de stad Brugge* (Brugge: J. van Praet, 1786).
Praet, J. B. B. van, *Recherches sur Louis de Bruges, seigneur de la Gruthuyse: suivies de la notice des manuscrits qui lui ont appartenu, et dont la plus grande partie se conserve à la Bibliothèque du Roi* (Paris: De Bure, 1831).
Prevenier, W., 'La Démographie des villes du Comté de Flandre aux XIVe et XV siècles. État de la question, essai d'interprétation', *RN* 65 (1983), 255–75.
—— (ed.), *Marriage and Social Mobility in the Late Middle Ages* (Gent: RUG. Seminarie voor geschiedenis, 1989).
—— (ed), *Le Prince et le peuple, image a la société du temps des ducs de Bourgogne, 1384–1530* (Anvers: Fonds Mercator, 1998).
Prud'homme, E., 'Le Serments des archers du saint Sacrement à Masnuy-Saint-Jean', *ACAM* 28 (1898), 177–84.
Putte, F. Vande, *Histoire de Boesinghe et de sa Seigneurie* (Bruges :Vandecasteele-Werbrouck, 1846).
Pycke, J., 'La confrérie de la Transfiguration au Mont-Saint-Aubert puis à la cathédrale de Tournai du 15e au 18e siècle', in *Archives et manuscrits précieux tournaisiens*,

ed. J. Pycke and A. Dupont, vol. 1 (Tournai: Louvain-la-Neuve: Archives de la cathédrale; Université catholique de Louvain, 2007), 123–51.

Quatrebarbes, E. de, *Essai historique sur la chambre ou gilde des archers des Saint-Médard et Sebastien de Hoepertingen* (Liège, Bruxelles: [s.n.], 1978).

Ramakers, B. A. M., *Spelen en figuren, toneelkunst en processiecultuur in Oudenaarde tussen Middeleeuwen en Moderne tijd* (Amsterdam: Amsterdam University Press, 1996).

——, 'Rederijkers en stedelijk feestcultuur in her laatmiddeleeuwse Noord-Brabant',in A.-J. A. Bijsterveld (ed.), *Cultuur in het Laatmiddeleeuwse Noord-Brabant. Literatuur, boekproductie, historiografie* ('s-Hertogenbosch: Stichting Brabantse Regionale Geschiedbeoefening, 1998), 37–54.

Rambourg, P., 'Les repas de confrérie à la fin du Moyen Âge: l'exemple de la confrérie parisienne Saint-Jacques-aux-Pèlerins au travers de sa comptabilité (XIVe siècle)', in *La Cuisine et la table dans la France de la fun du Moyen Âge*, ed. F. Ravoire and A. Dietrich (Caen: Publications du CRAHM, 2000), 51–78.

Régibo, E., *Historique de la Gilde de St. Sébastien de Renaix d'après des documents groupés par Edmond Régibo, Président de la Gilde* (Renaix: [s.d.], 1911).

Reintges, T., *Ursprung und Wesen der spätmittelalterlichen Schützengilden* (Bonn: L. Röhrscheid, 1963).

Renson, R., 'The Flemish Archery Gilds, from Defence Mechanisms to Sports Institutions', in *The History, Evolution and Diffusion of Sports and Games in Different Cultures*, ed. R. Renson and P. P. du Nage (Brussels: HISPA, 1976), 135–59.

Reyntens, O., *Boek met den haire* (Aalst: Oudheidkundige Kring van de Stad en het voormalig Land van Aelst, 1906).

——, 'Het Sint Joris gilde te Aelst', *Annales de la société archéologique d'Alost* 9 (1913), 27–64.

Richert, E., *Die Schlacht bei Guinegate, 7 August 1479* (Berlin: G. Nauck, 1907).

Ridder-Symoens, H. de, 'Prosopographical Research in the Low Countries Concerning the Middle Ages and the Sixteenth Century', *Medieval Prosopography* 14 (1993), 27–120.

Rock, P., *Historiek der Tiense schutterijen* (Tienen: Stedelijk Museum Het Toreke, 1982).

Rombaut, L., *Grand serment royal et de Saint-Georges des arbalétriers de Bruxelles, hier et aujourd'hui* (Bruxelles: Serment royale et de Saint-Georges, 1984).

Rosser, G., *Medieval Westminster, 1200–1540* (Oxford: Clarendon Press, 1989).

——, 'Solidarités et changement social: les fraternités urbaines anglaises à la fin du Moyen Age', *Annales économies, sociétés, civilisations* 48 (1993), 1127–43.

——, 'Workers' Associations in English Medieval Towns', in *Les métiers au moyen âge. Aspects économique et sociaux*, ed. P. Lambrechts et J.-P. Sosson (Louvain-la-Neuve: Fédération internationale des instituts d'études médiévales, 1994), 283–305.

——, 'Going to the Fraternity Feast; Commensality and Social Relations in Late Medieval England', *Journal of British Studies* 33 (1994), 430–46.

——, 'Myth Image and Social Process in the English Medieval Town', *UH* 23 (1996), 5–25.

——, 'Finding Oneself in a Medieval Fraternity: Individual and Collective Identities in the English Guilds', in *Mittelalterliche Bruderschaften in europäischen Städten: Funktionen, Formen, Akteure / Medieval confraternities in European towns: functions, forms, protagonists*, ed. M. Escher-Apsner (Frankfurt am Main; Oxford: Peter Lang, 2009), 29–46.

Rubin, M., *Charity and Community in Medieval Cambridge* (Cambridge: Cambridge University Press, 1987).

——, *Corpus Christi; The Eucharist in Late Medieval Culture* (Cambridge: Cambridge University Press, 1991).

——, 'Fraternity and Lay Piety in the Later Middle Ages', in *Einungen und Bruderschaft in der spätmittelalterlichen Stadt*, ed. P. Johanek (Köln: Böhlau, 1993), 1–14.

Sablon du Corail, A., 'Les étrangers au service de Marie de Bourgogne; de l'armée de Charles le Téméraire à l'armée de Maximilien (1477–1482)', *RN* 84 (2002), 389–412.

Sagher, T. de, 'Origine de la guilde des archers de saint Sébastien à Ypres (1383–1398)', *Annales de la société d'histoire et d'archéologie de Gand* 5 (1903), 116–30.

Samin, F., *De la Groote Gulde à l'ancien grand serment royal et noble des arbalétriers de Notre-Dame au Sablon* (Bruxelles: Bruxelles Ancien Grand Serment Royal et Nobles des Arbalétriers de Notre-Dame au Sablon, 2001).

Schnerb, B., *Les Armagnacs et les Bourguignons: la maudite guerre.* (Paris: Perrin, 1988).

——, *Bulgnéville (1431): l'état bourguignon prend pied en Lorraine* (Paris: Economica, 1993).

——, *l'État Bourguignon, 1363–1477* (Paris: Perrin, 1999).

——, 'Tournai et Azincourt; l'histoire d'un désastre dans Campin', in *Campin in Context. Peinture et société dans la vallée de l'Escaut à l'époque de Robert Campin, 1375–1445*, ed. L. Nys and D. Vanwijnsbergne (Valenciennes: Bruxelles: Tournai: Presses universitaires de Valenciennes; Institut royal du Patrimoine artistique; Association des guides de Tournai, 2007), 51–61.

Schnyder, A., 'Die St. Ursula-Bruderschaft der Kolner Leiendecker', *Jahrbuch des Kolnischen Geschichtsvereins* 52 (1981), 1–192.

Schodt, A. de, 'La Confrère de Notre-Dame de l'Arbre Sec', in *ASEB* 28 (1876–7), 141–87.

Schrijver, M. de and Dothee, C., *Les Concours de tir à l'arbalète des gildes médiévales* (Anvers: Antwerps Museum en Archief Den Crans, 1979).

Sellier, M., *Notice Historique Sur la Compagnie Des Archers Ou Arbalétriers Et Ensuite Des Arquebusiers de la Ville de Châlons-sur-Marne* (Paris, [s.d.] 1857).

Serdon, V., *Armes du diable: arcs et arbalètes au Moyen Age* (Rennes: Presses universitaires de Rennes, 2005).

Shenton, C., 'Edward III and the Symbol of the Leopard', *Heraldry, Pageantry, and Social Display*, 69–82.

Simons, W., 'Islands of Difference. Beguinages in the Medieval Low Countries', in *The Low Countries: Arts and Society in Flanders and the Netherlands. A Yearbook* 12 (2004), 205–14.

——, *Cities of Ladies, Beguine Communities in the Medieval Low Countries, 1200–1565* (Philadelphia: University of Pennsylvania Press, 2001).

Small, G., 'Les origines de la ville de Tournai dans les chroniques légendaires du bas moyen âge', in *Les grands siècles de Tournai (12e–15e siècles): recueil d'études publié à l'occasion du 20e anniversaire des Guides de Tournai* (Tournai: Fabrique de l'Église Cathédrale de Tournai, 1993), 81–113.

——, 'Centre and Periphery in Late Medieval France; Tournai', in *War, Government and Power in Later Medieval France*, ed. C. Allemand (Liverpool: Liverpool University Press, 2000), 124–74.

——, 'Local Elites and 'National Mythologies in the Burgundian Domains in the Fifteenth century', in *Building the Past/ Konstruktion der eigenen Vergangenheit*, ed. R. Suntrup and J. R. Veenstra (Frankfurt am Main: Lang, 2006), 229–45.

—, 'Municipal Registers of Deliberation in the Fourteenth and Fifteenth Centuries: Cross Channel Observations', in *Les idées passent-elles la Manche?: savoirs, représentations, pratiques (France–Angleterre, Xe–XXe siècles)*, ed. J.-P. Genet and F.-J. Ruggiu (Paris: PUPS, 2007), 37–66.

—, *Late Medieval France* (Basingstoke: Palgrave Macmillan, 2009).

Smet, J. J. de, *Mémoire sur les guerres entre le Brabant et la Flandre au quatorzième siècle* (Bruxelles: Hayez, 1855).

Smit, J. G., *Vorst en Onderdaan, studies over Holland en Zeeland in de late middeleeuwen* (Leuven: Peeters, 1995).

Soens, T., Van Onacker, E. and Dombrecht, K., 'Metropolis and Hinterland? A Comment on the Role of Rural Economy and Society in the Urban Heart of the Medieval Low Countries', *BMBGN* 127 (2012), 82–8.

Soisson, J-P., *Charles le Téméraire* (Paris: B. Grasset, 1997).

Sommé, M., 'Étude comparative des measures à vin dans les états Bourguignons au XVe siècle', *RN* 58 (1970), 171–83.

—, 'Les Approvisionnements et vin de la cour de Bourgogne au XV siècle sur Philippe le Bon', *RN* 79 (1997), 949–78.

Sosson, J-P., 'La Structure sociale de la corporation médiévale, l'exemple des tonneliers de Bruges de 1350 a 1500', *RBPH* 44 (1966), 457–78.

—, *Les Travaux publics de la ville de Bruges. 14ᵉ–15ᵉ siècles, les matériaux, les hommes* (Bruxelles: Crédit communal de Belgique, 1977).

Spufford, P., *Money and Its Use in Medieval Europe* (Cambridge: Cambridge University Press, 1988).

Stabel, P., *De kleine stad in Vlaanderen: bevolkingsdynamiek en economische functies van de kleine en secundaire stedelijke centra in het Gentse kwartier (14de–16de eeuw)* (Brussel: Paleis der Academiën, 1995).

—, 'Demography and Hierarchy; The Small Towns and the Urban Networks in Sixteenth-Century Flanders', in *Small Towns in Early Modern Europe*, ed. P. Clark (Cambridge: Cambridge University Press, 1995), 226–208.

—, *Dwarfs Among Giants, the Flemish Urban Network in the Late Middle Ages* (Leuven: Garant, 1997).

—, 'Van schepenen en ontvangers, politieke elite en stadsfinancien in Axele en Hulst', *TVSG* 18 (1992), 1–21.

—, 'The Market Place and Civic Identity in Late Medieval Flanders', in *Shaping Urban Identity in Late Medieval Europe*, ed. M. Boone and P. Stabel (Leuven: Garant, 2000), 43–64.

—, 'Guilds in Medieval Flanders: Myths and Realities of Guild Life in an Export-Oriented Environment', *JMH* 30 (2004), 187–212.

—, 'From Market to Shop, Retail and Urban Space in Late Medieval Bruges', *UH* 9 (2006), 79–109.

—, 'Organisation corporative et production d'œuvres d'art à Bruges à la fin du moyen âge et au début des temps modernes', *Le Moyen Âge: Revue d'histoire et de philologie* 113 (2007), 91–134.

—, 'Composition et recomposition des réseaux urbains des Pays-Bas au Moyen Age', *UH* 12 (2008), 29–63.

—, 'Militaire organisatie, bewapening en wapenbezit in het laatmiddeleeuwse Brugge', *RBPH* 89 (2011), 1049–73.

Stein, H., *Archers d'autrefois; archers d'aujourd'hui* (Paris: Longuet, 1925).

Stein, R. (ed.), *Powerbrokers in the Late Middle Ages* (Turnhout: Brepols, 2001).
—— and Pollmann, J., *Networks, Regions and Nations: Networks, Regions and Nations: Shaping Identities in the Low Countries, 1300–1650* (Leiden: Brill, 2010).
——, 'An urban network in the Low Countries. A cultural approach', in *Networks, Regions and Nations*, 43–72.
Stoop, P. de, 'Particularités sur les corporations et métiers de Bruges', *ASEB* 5 (1843), 3–36.
——, *De St.-Jorisgilde: Blijspel met zang in één bedrijf* (Gent: Annoot-Braeckman, 1845).
Strickland, M. and Hardy, R., *The Great Warbow* (Stroud: Sutton, 2005).
Strietman, E., 'Pawns or Prime Movers? The Rhetoricians in the Struggle for Power in the Low Countries', in *European Medieval Drama, 1997. Papers from the Second International conference on 'Aspects of European Medieval Drama' Camerine, 4–6 July 1997*, ed. S. Higgins (Turnhout: Brepols, 1998), 111–21.
——, 'Perplexed but not in Despair? An Investigation of Doubt and Despair in Rhetoricians Drama', in *Akteure und Aktionen: Figuren und Handlungstypen im Drama der Frühen Neuzeit*, ed. C. Meier, B. A. M. Ramakers, H. Beger (Münster: Rhema, 2008), 63–80.
—— and Happé, P. (eds), *Urban Theatre in the Low Countries, 1400–1625* (Turnhout: Brepols, 2006), 163–80.
Sweetinburgh, S., *The Role of the Hospital in Medieval England, Gift-Giving and the Spiritual Economy* (Dublin, Ireland; Portland, OR: Four Courts Press, 2004).
TeBrake, W. T., *A Plague of Insurrection: Popular Politics and Peasant Revolt in Flanders, 1323–1328* (Philadelphia: University of Pennsylvania Press, 1993).
Terlinden, C., 'The History of the Scheldt', *History* 16 (1920), 185–97.
Terpstra, N. (ed.), *The Politics of Ritual Kinship, Confraternities and Social Order in Early Modern Italy* (Cambridge: Cambridge University Press, 2000).
Thijs, A. K. L., 'Religion and Social Structure; Religious Ritual in Pre-Industrial Trade Associations in the Low Countries', in *Craft Guilds in the Early Modern Low Countries*, ed. M. Prak, C. Lis, J. Lucassen and H. Soly (Aldershot: Ashgate, 2006), 157–73.
Thoen, E., 'Verhuizen naar Brugge in de late Middeleeuwen. De rol van de immigratie van de poorters in de aanpassing van de stad Brugge aan de wijzigende economische omstandigheden (14e–16e eeuw)', in *Beleid en Bestuur in de oude Nederlanden, Liber Amicorum Prof. Dr. M. Baelde*, ed. H. Soly and R. Vermeir (Gent: RUG. Vakgroep Nieuwe geschiedenis, 1993), 337–43.
Tlusty, B. A., *The Martial Ethic in Early Modern Germany, Civic Duty and the Right of Arms* (Basingstoke: Palgrave Macmillan, 2011).
Toorians, J., *Het vendel: Het vendelzwaaien in de historische schuttersgilden* (Berger: Hitgeverij Gesto, 1969).
Trenard, L., *Histoire de Lille, tome 1* (Lille: Faculté des lettres et sciences humaines de Lille, 1970).
Trexler, R. C. (ed.), *Persons in Groups: Social Behavior as Identity Formation in Medieval and Renaissance Europe*. (Binghamton, NY: Medieval & Renaissance Texts & Studies, 1985).
——, *Church and Community, 1200–1600* (Roma: Edizioni di Storia a Letteratura, 1987).
Trio, P., *De Gentse Broederschappen (1182–1580)* (Gent: Maatschappij voor Geschiedenis en Oudheidkunde te Gent, 1990).
——, *Volksreligie als spiegel van een stedelijke samenleving* (Leuven: Universitaire Pers Leuven, 1993).

―, 'Middeleeuwse broederschappen in de Nederlanden. Ean balans en perspectieven voor verder onderzoek', *Tijdschrift voor de Geschiedenis van het Katholiek Leven in de Nederlanden, trajecta* 3 (1994), 97–109.

―, 'Les confréries comme expression de solidarité et de conscience urbaine aux Pays-Bas à la fin du Moyen Age', in *Memoria, Communitas, Civitas- mémoire et conscience urbaine en occident à la fin du moyen âge*, sous la direction de H. Brand (Ostfildern: Thorbecke, 2003), 131–41.

―, 'The Chronicle attributed to "Oliver van Diksmuide"; A Misunderstood Town Chronicle of Ypres from Late Medieval Flanders', in E. Kooper, *The Medieval Chronicle V* (Amsterdam: Rodopi, 2008), 211–31.

Trowbridge, M., 'The *Stadschilder* and the *Serment* Rogier van der Weyden's "Deposition" and the Crossbowmen of Louvain', *Dutch Crossing* 23 (1999), 5–28.

―, 'Processional Plays in Aalst', *Mediaevalia* 29 (2007), 95–117.

Twycross, M. (ed.), *Festive Drama, Papers from the Sixth Triennial Colloquium of the International Society for the Study of Medieval Theatre* (Cambridge: D. S. Brewer, 1996).

―, 'The Archduchess and the Parrot', in *Gender and Fraternal Orders in Europe, 1300–2000*, ed. M. F. Cross (Basingstoke: Palgrave Macmillan, 2010), 63–90.

Uytven, R. van, 'Economie et financement des travaux publics des villes brabançonnes au Moyen Age et au XVIe siècle', in S. Cavaciocchi (ed.), *L'Edilizia prima della Rivoluzione industriale secc. XIII-XVIII* (Florence: Le Monnier 2005), 669–92.

―, 'Stadsgeschiedenis in het Noorden en Zuiden', *AGN* 2 (1983), 188–253, 543–6.

―, 'Stages of Economic Decline; Late Medieval Bruges', in J-M. Duvosquel and E. Thoen (eds), *Peasants and Townsmen in Medieval Europe* (Gent: Snoeck-Ducaju & Zoon, 1995), 259–69.

―, 'Showing off one's Rank in the Middle Ages', in *Showing Status: Representations of Social Positions in the Late Middle Ages*, ed. W. Blockmans and A. Jansese (Turnhout: Brepols, 1999), 19–34.

Vale, M., 'An Anglo-Burgundian Nobleman, and Art Patronage; Louis de Bruges, Lord of la Gruthuyse and Earl of Winchester', in *England and the Low Countries in the Late Middle Ages*, ed. C. Barron and N. Saul (Stroud: Sutton, 1995), 115–31.

―, 'A Burgundian Funeral Ceremony: Olivier de la Marche and the Obsequies of Adolf of Cleves, Lord of Ravenstein', *EHR* 111 (1996), 920–38.

Van den Neste, E., *Tournois, joutes, pas d'armes dans les villes de Flandre à la fin du Moyen Âge (1300–1486)* (Paris: Ecole des chartes, 1996).

Vandermaesen, M., 'Toverij en politiek rond de troon van Lodewijk II van Nevers graaf van Vlaanderen. Een merkwaardige aanklacht (1327–1331)', *HMGOG* 44 (1990), 87–98.

―, Brugse en Ieperse gijzelaars voor koning en graaf, 1328–1329. Een administratief dossier', *ASEB* 130 (1993), 119–44.

―, Ryckaert, M. and Coornaert, M., *De Witte Kaproenen: de Gentse opstand (1379–1385) & de geschiedenis van de Brugse Leie* (Gent: Provinciebestuur Oost-Vlaanderen, 1979).

Vandewalle, A. et al., *Brugse ambachten in documenten, de schoenmakers, timmerlieden en schrijnwerkers (14de–18de eeuw)* (Brugge: Gemeentebestuur, 1985).

―, *Hanzekooplui en medicibankiers, Brugge, wisselmarkt van Europese culturen* (Oostkamp: Stichting kunstboek, 2002).

Vanhoutryre, L. A., *De Brugse Kruisbooggilde van Sint-Joris* (Handzame: Familia et patria, 1968).

Vanloffeld, E., *Van Huyslieden tot schutten Limburgse schutterijen, vroegen en na* (Eisden: Maasmechelen, 1994).

Vannerus, J., 'Trois documents relatifs aux concours de tir à l'arbalète, organisés à Malines en 1458 et en 1495', *BCRH* 97 (1933), 203–54.

Vanvaeck, M., *Faith and Fortune along the Way: Pilgrims' Badges and Profane Insignia. (Geloof & Geluk' ('Faith & Fortune') in the Bruggemuseum–Gruuthuse, Bruges, from 22 September 2006 until 4 February 200)* (Antwerpen: Peter Wouters for OKV, 2006).

Vaughan, R., *Philip the Bold; The Formation of the Burgundian State* (London: Longmans, 1962).

——, *John the Fearless; The Growth of Burgundian Power* (London: Longmans, 1966).

——, *Philip the Good; The Apogee of Burgundy* (London: Longmans, 1970).

——, *Charles the Bold; The Last Valois Duke of Burgundy* (London: Longmans, 1973).

Velde, A. van de, 'De oudste inventaris van het St Sebastiaansgild te Brugge', *ASEB* 57 (1907), 91–134.

Verbruggen, J. F., 'De organisatie van de milite te Brugge in de XIVe eeuw', *ASEB* 87 (1950), 163–70.

——, *Het Gemeenteleger van Brugge van 1338 tot 1340 en de namen van de Weerbare Mannen* (Bruxelles: Palais des Académies, 1962).

——, *De slag bij Guinegate 7 augustus 1479: de verdediging van het graafschap Vlaanderen tegen de koning van Frankrijk, 1477–1480* (Brussel: Koninklijk Legermuseum, 1993).

—— (trans. K. DeVries), 'Flemish Urban Military against the French Cavalry Armies of the Fourteenth and Fifteenth Centuries', *JMMH* 1 (2002), 145–69.

—— (trans K. DeVries), 'Arms and the Art of War: The Ghentenaar and Brugeois Militia in 1477–79', *JMMH* 7 (2009), 135–46.

Vereecke, J. J. J., *Histoire militaire de la ville d'Ypres, jadis place-forte de la Flandre occidentale* (Gand: Van Doosselaere, 1858).

Verhavert, J., *Het ambachtswezen te Leuven* (Leuven: Universiteitsbibliotheek, 1940).

Verhoeven, G., 'Van 'prosen' en prijzen. Een zestiende-eeuwse oplossing voor de financiering van de gezondheidszorg', *Fibula* 29 (1988), 13–19.

Verhulst, A., 'An Aspect of the Question of Continuity between Antiquity and Middle Ages: the Origin of the Flemish Cities between the North Sea and the Scheldt', *JMH*, 3(1977), 175–205.

Vermeersch, V. (ed.), *Bruges and the Sea: From Bryggia to Zeebrugge* (Antwerp: Mercatorfonds, 1982).

Vigne, F. de, *Recherches historiques sur les costumes civils et militaires des gildes et des corporations de métiers, leurs drapeaux, leurs armes, leurs blasons* (Gand: Gyselynck, 1847).

Vincent, C., *Des charités bien ordonnées: les confréries normandes de la fin du XIIIe siècle au début du XVIe siècle* (Paris: École normale supérieure de jeunes filles, 1988).

——, 'Pratiques de l'assistance dans la vie associative professionnelle médiévale: aumônes ou secours mutuels?', in *De la charité médiévale à la sécurité sociale: économie de la protection sociale du Moyen Âge à l'époque contemporaine*, ed. A. Guislin and P. Guillaume (Paris: Ed. ouvrières, 1992), 23–30.

——, *Les confréries médiévales dans le royaume de France, XIIIe–XVe siècle* (Paris: Albin Michel, 1994).

——, 'La Vitalité de la communauté paroissiale au XVe siècle à travers quelques exemples de fondations rouennaises', *RN* 86 (2004), 741–56.

Voitron, P., *Notice sur le local de la confrérie de Saint Georges à Gand (1381 à 1796)* (Ghent: Messager des sciences historiques de Belgique, 1889–90).
Vooren, G. A. C., 'Gildebroeders en gildezusters van het Sint-Sebastiaansgilde te Aardenburg, 1472–1595', *Vlaamse Stam; Maandblad van de Vlaamse veringing voor familiekunde* 4 (1968), 21–33.
Walsh, R. J., *Charles the Bold and Italy (1467–77) Politics and Personnel* (Liverpool: Liverpool University Press, 2005).
Waswo, R., 'Our Ancestors, the Trojans: Inventing Cultural Identity in the Middle Ages', *Exemplaria: A Journal of Theory in Medieval and Renaissance Studies* 7 (1995), 269–90.
Waterschoot, W., 'Het landjuweel te Antwerpen in 1496', *SH* 18 (1983), 49–68.
Wauters, A., *Notice historique sur les anciens serments ou gildes d'arbalétriers, d'archers, d'arquebusiers et d'escrimeurs de Bruxelles* (Bruxelles: Briard, 1848).
Wellens, R., 'La Révolte Brugeois de 1488', *ASEB* 102 (1965), 5–52.
Werveke, H. van, 'Ambachten en erfelijkheid', *Mededeelingen van de Koninklijke Vlaamsche Academie voor wetenschappen, Letteren letteren en schoon kunst van België* 4 (1923).
—— , *De Gentsche stadsfinanciën in de middeleeuwen* 4 (1942).
Willame, G., *Notes sur les serments Nivellois* (Nivelles: Guignardé, 1901).
Win, P. de, 'Simon de Lalaing', in R. De Smedt (ed.), *Les chevaliers de l'ordre*, 75–7.

Unpublished theses

Ducastelle, C. and Cardot, J-M., 'Les Confréries ou serments d'arcs et d'arbalestier au moyen âge du nord de la France, études apogée sur les exemples du Douai et de Lille', Masters dissertation, Université du Lille III (1992).
Van Steen, S., '"Den ouden ende souverainen gilde van den edelen ridder Sente Jooris": het Sint-Jorisgilde te Gent in de 15e eeuw, met prosopografie (1468–1497)', Masters dissertation, University of Ghent (2006).
Zutter, G. de, 'Kunst en kunstambacht in het leven van een schuttersgilde. Het Sint-Sebastiaansgilde te Gent', Masters dissertation, University of Ghent (1975).

Index

Aalst, archery guild of 24–5, 27, 59, 61, 65–6, 104, 145
Aalst, crossbow guild of 17, 24, 27, 54–5, 60, 66, 68, 98, 101–06, 114, 132–4, 141, 157, 167, 185, 203
Aalst, town of 12, 14–15, 213
Adolf of Cleves 139–143
Adornes, Bruges family 53, 73, 87, 91, 96
Adornes, Amselmus 73, 91, 140
Aertricke, Bruges family 53, 73
Amiens 154, 164, 169, 186
Amsterdam 164, 175
Annappe 24, 148–9, 194
Anthony, Great Bastard of Burgundy 74, 97, 155–6, 183–4
Antwerp 44, 164, 182–3, 201, 204, 209
Ardenbourg 92, 160, 203
Armentières 12, 108, 133, 206
Arras, town and guilds of 65, 185, 197–8, 144
Arras, treaty of (1435) 46, 213
Arras, treaty of (1482) 49
Artevelde, Jacob van 11, 151, 208
Artevelde, Philip van 11
Ath 132
Athis-sur-Orge, Treaty of (1305) 8, 150
Augsburg 161
Avesnes 167
Axele 24, 60, 117

Baldwin IV, count of Flanders 28–9
banners 39, 46, 112–13, 183
Bapaume 160

Beguines 124–5
belfries 2, 34–5
bequests 17, 117–19
see also charity
Berchem 185
Bergen op Zoom 186
Bergues see Sint-Winnoksbergen
Béthune 61, 149, 166, 185
Biervelt 144, 149
Boezinghe 24
Bouc van Pieter Polet 18, 154, 163–4, 175–6, 177–8, 218
Bovyins 175
Breydel, Bruges family 95–7, 139
Bruges, archery guild of 24, 34, 42, 44–6, 48, 49, 53, 56, 58, 68–88, 93–6, 102–03, 134, 139–42, 147, 155, 194–5, 198–9, 205, 213, 215, 222
Bruges, crossbow guilds of 1, 2, 17–18, 24, 34, 42, 45–9, 53, 56–8, 60, 65, 69–88, 92–3, 105–07, 134, 140–2, 147, 152, 155, 157, 180, 185–6, 188, 203, 204, 206, 210, 211, 213
Bruges, town of 7, 9, 11–13, 15, 65, 69–88, 140–2, 147, 154, 155, 161, 206–07, 210, 213
Brussels 23, 44, 107, 117, 140, 157, 163, 169, 183, 185, 186, 203, 213, 215, 217–20, 222

Caen 30
Calais, siege of (1436) 45–6, 137, 154, 174, 212, 213
Cambrai 114, 197, 211

candles *see* lights
Caprijk   12, 135
Cassel   149
Chambers of Rhetoric   4, 36–7, 59, 68–9, 86–8, 116–17, 165, 184–5, 195, 197, 201, 217
see also drama
chapels   3, 57, 89, 100–09, 187–8, 221, 223
charity   3, 93, 104, 107, 115, 119–25, 182–3, 221
see also Hospital of Saint George *and* bequests
Charles the Bold, duke of Burgundy   10, 47–8, 66, 87, 95, 108, 138, 140, 144–5, 155, 215
Charles V, duke of Burgundy and Holy Roman Emperor   11, 145, 148–9, 194
Charles V, king of France   30, 173
Charles VI, king of France   45, 211
Charles VII, king of France   45, 47, 213
Chièvres   167
Christine de Pisan   143
Clarout, van, Bruges family   74
cloth *see* livery
Clyte *see* Commines
Cockelare   149
Commines   24, 136–7, 203
Commynes *see* Commines
Compiègne   65
Condé   1, 107, 109–11
confraternities   86–8, 100–03, 135
Corneille, Bastard of Burgundy   26
Courtrai, archery guild of   24–5, 43, 143–4, 197, 204–05, 217–20
Courtrai, Battle of (1302)   8, 22–3, 38, 150
Courtrai, crossbow guild of   117, 184–5, 196, 203, 204–06
Courtrai, town of   143, 204–05
craft guilds   32, 53–4, 55–6, 60–3, 75, 80–6, 93–8, 120, 163, 193
Croix   12, 24–5, 193–4, 195
Croy   186
culveriniers, guilds of   41–2, 47, 56, 62, 90, 197–8
Cysoing   24, 64, 105, 194

Dadizeele   40, 138–9, 149
Dagobert I, Frankish King   30–1
Dagobert II, Frankish King   30–1
Damme   76, 198–9, 204, 210
Dendermonde   24, 44–5, 54, 62, 66, 90, 93, 102, 117, 144, 146, 181, 187, 204, 210, 213
Dendrer, river   199–200
Diest   182
Dixmuide, Olivier van   18, 46, 212
Dixmuide, town and guilds of   1, 213, 217–20
Dordrecht   175
Douai, archery guild of   46, 47, 48, 56, 90, 94, 133, 166, 196, 205
Douai, crossbow guild of   1, 24, 46, 48, 51, 54–6, 62, 63–4, 65, 90, 92, 93, 101, 103, 106–07, 128, 133–4, 147–9, 161, 166, 170, 196, 210
Douai, town of   12, 14, 133, 196–8
drama   1, 101, 165, 179–88, 195, 210, 214
see also Chambers of Rhetoric
Drincham   21, 24, 26
drinking, *see* feasts *and* wine
Dudzele   198–9

Edward III, king of England   9, 11, 208
Edward IV, king of England   74, 140
Eecloo   219
Elverdinge and Vlamertinge   24, 26
Enaeme, Abbey of   18, 153
Engelbert, count of Nassau   49, 139
Enghien   103, 146, 203
Estreés *see* Wattingies and Estreés
Euregnies   162
Excellent Chronicle of Flanders   19, 157, 180–5

feasts   17, 51, 55, 71, 89, 93–9, 155–6, 198–9, 221–2
see also wine
Fleurus   175
Floreffe   33
Franc of Bruges   7, 97
Franciscans   18, 102, 133
Francs-Archers   26

Geraardsbergen   185, 200, 213
Ghent, archery guilds of   24, 33, 45, 56, 105–06, 114–25, 199, 213

Ghent, crossbow guilds of 6, 17, 18, 24, 28–9, 33, 45, 56, 57, 61, 63, 68, 93–4, 99–100, 103, 105–07, 114–25, 128–9, 139–42, 147–8, 152, 154, 155, 157, 159, 160, 161, 163, 164–5, 168, 170, 174–9, 185–6, 203, 206, 208, 211–14, 215–16, 218, 222–3
Ghent, town of 7, 9, 11–12, 15, 45, 114–25, 139–42, 161, 167, 201, 210
Golden Fleece, Order of 49, 53, 92, 102, 137, 139–40
Gouda 164
Gravelines 21, 25
Guelders Duchy of 47
Guild-hall 89, 93, 116, 187–8, 211
guild-sisters 57, 66–9, 100, 108, 117–25, 223
Guinegate, Battle of (1479) 48
guns see culveriniers
Guy of Dampierre, count of Flanders 8, 33

Haarlem 164
Ham 45, 92
Henry III, duke of Brabant 23
Henry V, king of England 45–6
Henry VIII, king of England 41
Hoods see Kaproenen
Hospital of Saint George 119–25, 147–8
Houthem 24, 148
Hue de Lannoy 63
Hulst 12, 56, 170, 176–7, 181, 203, 215, 217

Ingelmunster 24, 101
Isabella Eugenia, sovereign of the Spanish Netherlands 91, 223

Jan of Dadizeele 138–9, 141–2
Jan van Gruuthuse 139
Jean II, king of France 10, 169
Jean Villiers, lord of l'Isle-Adam 154
Jehan de Lannoy 137
John II, king of France 9
John III, duke of Brabant 9
John the Fearless, duke of Burgundy 10, 21, 45–6, 136, 144–6, 148, 152–4, 193–4

Jousts 147, 155, 159, 165, 168, 185–6, 217
  Epinette, Jousters of 36, 129, 135–6, 179, 206–07
  White Bear, Jousters, 31, 36, 73, 74, 86–8, 95, 135–6, 140, 206–07

Kaproenen 22, 37–8
Koekelare 24

La Bassée 24
Langhemark 93
Lannoy, town 24, 136–7
Lannoys, noble family 63, 136–7, 193
Laon 1, 164
Lenneke 200
Lens 167, 196, 213
Lessines 200
Leuven 104–05, 163
Liedekerke 217–20
Liège 19, 59, 164, 175
Lier 203, 214
lights 105–06, 132–4
Lille, archery guild of 21–2, 24, 27, 41–3, 48, 49, 54, 56, 57, 59, 65, 90–1, 98–9, 101–02, 129–30, 132–5, 144–5, 156, 166–7, 193–200, 205
Lille, crossbow guild of 1, 24–5, 41–3, 45, 47, 49, 54, 55, 56–8, 59, 61–3, 65, 89–91, 93, 94, 98–9, 105, 114, 126–7, 129–30, 131–5, 140, 146, 155–6, 160, 166–7, 170, 181, 183–4, 186, 193–200, 206, 213, 222
Lille, town of 8, 12, 14, 16, 25, 39, 41–3, 62, 64, 129–30, 132, 134–5, 145–6, 161, 166, 192–200, 206–07
Linkebeeke 155
livery 3, 17, 21, 26–7, 55, 89, 130–2, 135, 137, 141, 148–50, 152–3, 163–4, 181–8, 212
Lo 24
Lodewijk van Gruuthuse 53, 74, 87, 139–42, 203
lotteries 147–8
Lys, river 204–05
Louis of Male, count of Flanders 9, 43–4, 151–2, 210, 221
Louis of Nevers, count of Flanders 9, 43–4, 151

Louis XI, king of France 10, 48–9, 141–2, 145, 156

Maastricht 204
Margaret of Bavaria, duchess of Burgundy 69
Margaret of York, duchess of Burgundy 42, 66, 95, 108, 118, 177
market place 2, 116, 132–3, 168, 207
Mary, Duchess of Burgundy 10, 48, 105, 138–41, 156, 176–7, 215
Maubeuge 203
Maximillian Habsburg, archduke of Austria/ Holy Roman Emperor 10, 29, 48–9, 105, 118, 121, 139, 147, 156–7, 176, 221
Mechelen, archery guild of 22, 24, 195
Mechelen, crossbow guild of 24, 48, 147, 155, 164–5, 186, 187, 204, 206, 211, 214
Mechelen, town of 9, 44, 164
Menin 24, 149, 182, 200, 219
Merovingian(s) *see* Dagobert I *and* Dagobert II
Metteneyes, Bruges family 73, 77, 79, 87, 95
militia 22, 37–9, 44–9, 116
Mons 107, 138, 167, 170–2, 180, 210

Namur 211
Neuss, siege of (1474) 47–8, 155
Nieuwpoort 24–5, 149, 194–5, 206
Ninove 12, 45–6, 135, 199–200
Nivelles 54, 107

Orchies 8, 76
Oostende 181
Oudenaarde, archery guild of 130–1, 185, 205, 218
Oudenaarde, crossbow guild of 14, 18, 24, 27, 44, 46, 56, 62, 69, 92, 100, 128–9, 130–1, 141, 151, 153, 160, 162–3, 165, 169, 170, 173–4, 183–5, 186, 187, 196, 199, 202–05, 212–14, 215–16, 218
Oudenaarde, town of 12, 14–15, 130–1, 162–3, 183, 201, 202–05, 210, 213

papegay 34, 51, 54, 71, 73, 89–93, 101, 129, 132, 155, 197–9, 223

Paris 1, 152–3, 164, 180
Pecquencourt 24, 62, 90, 103
Philip IV, king of France 8
Philip of Burgundy (son of Anthony the Great Bastard) 141–2
Philip of Cleves 139
Philip the Bold, duke of Burgundy 9, 10, 42, 51, 144–6, 148, 152
Philip the Fair, duke of Burgundy 11, 29, 42, 147, 156–7, 176, 178, 183, 215–16
Philip the Good, duke of Burgundy 10, 14, 21, 45–7, 60, 74, 75, 98, 140, 143, 145, 148, 149, 154–5, 162–3, 169, 176, 193–4, 214
Philippe de Croy 138
Pieter Polet *see* Bouc van Pieter Polet
plays *see* drama
Poperinghe 200, 205
prizes 1, 3, 57, 117, 136, 147, 153, 159–60, 166, 168, 179–88, 210
processions 34, 107, 113, 132–5, 147, 159, 170, 184, 199
  Procession of the Holy Blood, Bruges 35–6, 134–5, 206–07
  Procession of Notre Dame de la Trielle, Lille 34, 93, 130, 134–5, 206–07
  Procession of Oudenaarde 14, 185, 202
  Procession, Tournai 151, 209

Quiévrain 23

Rade, Willem and Barbera de 124
Richard II, king of England 211
Reims 164
Robert III, count of Flanders 9, 150–1
Roeland of Uutkerke 74
Rotterdam 175
Roubaix 62, 90, 92, 166, 196, 204
Rouen 30, 153

Saint-Omer 21, 167
Scheldt, river 8, 14, 44, 171, 182, 201–02, 204
seals 35, 108–12, 147, 164
's-Hertogenbosch 164, 182

INDEX

Simon de Lalaing 23, 46, 138
Sint-Winnoksbergen 24–5, 62, 64, 98, 144, 149
Sluis 1, 24, 74, 109–10, 188
Slypen 76

Themseke, Bruges family 73, 77
Thérouanne 48–9
Tielt 24, 64, 149
Tournai, archery guild of 27, 166, 205
Tournai, crossbow guild of 1, 19, 27, 30–1, 55, 109–11, 130, 156, 161–2, 163, 164, 165, 168, 170, 172–3, 180, 183–4, 185, 187–8, 191–2, 203, 204, 209, 211, 213–15, 216
Tournai, town of 7, 76, 156, 162, 196, 197–8, 201, 208, 211
town Accounts 15–16, 31–4, 128–35, 160, 166–7
town hall 2, 34
Town walls 34–5, 41–2, 57, 64, 128, 146–7
Tsolles, Jan 78, 95–7

Urban V, Pope 10
Utrecht 204, 216

Valenciennes 29, 107, 197–8, 201
Verdun 197
Veurne 109–10, 197, 206
Vlamertinge *see* Elverdinge and Vlamertinge

Wattingies and Estreés 24, 64, 98, 136, 194
Wauvrin 148, 196
Wervick 185, 199
Weyden, Rogier van der 104–05, 112
wine 3, 20, 33–4, 51, 55, 59, 65–6, 79, 89–90, 129–30, 132, 160, 166–7, 170, 175, 185–6, 195–7, 202–03, 205–06
women *see* guild-sisters

youth 2, 57–9, 66, 99–100, 107, 114–18, 129–30, 206
Ypres, archery guild of 24, 57, 149, 167, 170, 197–8, 205
Ypres, crossbow guild of 1, 22–3, 46, 57, 92, 147, 152, 157, 160, 181, 186, 197–8, 200, 203, 210, 212
Ypres, town of 7, 12–14, 197, 205–06, 210

Zuienkerke 24, 145, 149